I Call Myself an Artist

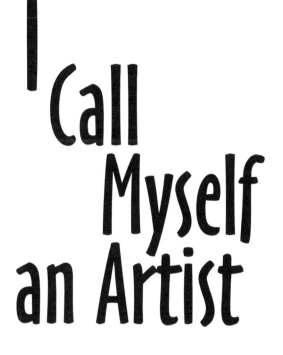

I Call Myself an Artist

Writings by and about Charles Johnson

edited by Rudolph P. Byrd

INDIANA UNIVERSITY PRESS
Bloomington & Indianapolis

This book is a publication of
Indiana University Press
601 North Morton Street
Bloomington, Indiana 47404-3797 USA

www.indiana.edu/~iupress

Telephone orders 800-842-6796
Fax orders 812-855-7931
Orders by e-mail iuporder@indiana.edu

The paper used in this publication meets the minimum requirements of American National Standard for Information Sciences—Permanence of Paper for Printed Library Materials, ANSI Z39.48-1984.

Manufactured in the United States of America

Cataloging information for this book is
available from the Library of Congress

ISBN 0–253–33541–8 (cloth)

1 2 3 4 5   04 03 02 01 00 99

To Walter L. Miller
Philosopher and Mathematician

Contents

IV. Reviews and Cultural Criticism

V. Charlie's Pad

VI. Interviews and Conversations

VII. Reading Charles Johnson

Preface

It is the morning of November 13, 1997. The occasion is the unveiling of twelve postage stamps, which will serve the dual purpose of honoring twelve African American writers and promoting world literacy. The writers whose images will appear on stamps that will be sold in Ghana and Uganda are Maya Angelou, Rita Dove, Mari Evans, Henry Louis Gates, Jr., June Jordan, Toni Cade Bambara, Sterling A. Brown, Alex Haley, Stephen Henderson, Zora Neale Hurston, Richard Wright, and Charles Johnson.

The imagination and force behind this occasion are born of the determination of E. Ethelbert Miller, member of the Department of Afro-American Studies at Howard University. Miller originally conceived of this project and persuaded the Inter-Governmental Philatelic Corporation to authorize the creation and production of these stamps for sale in Africa.

The setting for this historic occasion is the Marion and Gustave Ring Auditorium of the Hirshorn Museum on the Mall in Washington, D.C. The expectant guests assembled in the auditorium are chiefly friends, colleagues, and family members of the honorees. As this event is unfolding in the political center of the nation, also present are elected officials. Very fortunately for the participants and for posterity, the photographer documenting this event is Roland Freeman.

Hidden beneath black velvet with gold lettering that proclaims the sponsorship of the Inter-Governmental Philatelic Corporation, the oversized replicas of the twelve stamps dominate the stage. Resting on easels, these replicas were created from photographs by Gary Aagaard, a white painter based in the Southeast.

At 10:00 A.M. the master of ceremonies assumes his place at the lectern. A generous Miller has persuaded Clifford Alexander, the civil rights lawyer and father of the poet Elizabeth Alexander, to assume this charge. The very embodiment of elegance and authority, Alexander, in a strong and resonant voice, invites the honorees to assume their seats on the stage. Who wouldn't do his bidding? With the exception of Henry Louis Gates, Jr., who is on a research assignment in Africa, all the living honorees are present. Under the sound of Alexander's voice, the honorees assume their seats on an elevated stage.

For a moment, silence reigns in the auditorium. I have traveled to Washington from Emory University in Atlanta at the invitation of Charles Johnson. Along with many others, I have traveled to the Ring Auditorium on a cool, overcast morning in November to witness the public bestowal of a fully earned honor upon one of our most important living writers.

Dressed in a dark blue suit, tie, and cowboy boots, Johnson is seated between Rita Dove and Maya Angelou. Johnson's grizzled hair contrasts sharply with his otherwise youthful face and body. Occasionally he exchanges pleasantries with a radiant Dove as Alexander gracefully executes his duties as master of ceremonies. Many bring greetings, including H. Patrick Swygert, president of Howard University. The retiring and natty Miller also addresses the audience. Transformed at the lectern, his medley of images and phrases, effectively conveying the force of the corpus of the honorees, earns him cheers from many members of the audience. And from some of the honorees.

Finally the moment has come. Each honoree or designated representative is invited to assume his or her place before each oversized stamp. The filmmaker Louis Massaih will unveil the stamp for Toni Cade Bambara. A friend of many years, Jack Dennis, will unveil the stamp honoring Sterling A. Brown. Julia Wright has traveled from Paris to perform this honor for her father, Richard Wright. Alongside an ebullient June Jordan, Johnson stands expectantly before his own oversized stamp and image. After a signal from Alexander, each unveils his or her stamp.

At every stage of the unveiling, which is accompanied by some laughter and the expected flourish from those honorees who have given themselves over completely to this event's drama, Freeman is the phlegmatic and omnipresent figure with a camera who is joined now by other photographers and members of the press. The bright flash of the cameras intensifies the light of the stage. Beneath the applause and other spontaneous expressions of approval there is the sound of the shutter and advancing film. Click. Slide. Click.

The collective unveiling successfully accomplished, Alexander invites the honorees, in pairs and in alphabetical order, to the lectern to deliver remarks which, in every instance, are brief but filled with the joy and formality of the occasion. That the stamps are an honor for the individual writer and the clan is the theme forcefully and sincerely sounded by each speaker.

Johnson approaches the lectern accompanied by George Haley, the brother of the late Alex Haley. Unexpectedly, Johnson is the first to speak, and he generously recalls an aphorism by Alex Haley: "Find something you love and praise it." Full of regard for Johnson but intent upon accuracy, George Haley gently offers a correction: "Find the good and praise it." Their remarks delivered in a timely fashion, Johnson and Haley return to their seats. Deeply moved, Johnson ruminates and remains, until Alexander masterfully brings this well-paced ceremony to a close, a silent figure, both inside and outside of the event.

ΰ ΰ ΰ

How is a writer like a stamp? Is there a way in which the two are analogous? Are they linked, somehow, by a common purpose? I thought a great deal about these questions at each stage of the unveiling of these stamps, which, over time, will assume, I hope, a certain significance, a certain reality beyond the enlarging kingdom (or republic) of black letters.

In her remarks, Rita Dove briefly addressed the relationship between a writer and a stamp, between imagination and postage, and thereby provided me with a suggestive framework for contemplating the questions very much on my mind. Practicing on this occasion the economy of language that is one of the hallmarks of her poetry, Dove asserted that "stamps are messages."

By extension, then, the writer is a messenger or a vehicle, like a stamp, for conveying messages. Further, as the vehicle for the communication of messages, the writer is also, like a stamp, both a symbol and an agent of the *process* of communication. To be sure, depending upon the messages and our collective state of mind at the point of their transmission, the messages a writer feels called to deliver will either divide or unite us, inspire admiration or antipathy for the messenger— the writer. Grounded in our collective past as well as in the shifting patterns of present realities, the writer delivers these messages out of need and sometimes a sense of urgency that is often in conflict with our bottomless desire for praise, blandishments, and other species of opiates. When the writer is committed to our collective health and identifies fully with such a vision of renewal and power, then the messages, delivered with a deep sense of empathy, love, and hope, contain the stern wisdom of the ages: evolve or die.

Charles Johnson is such a writer, such a messenger. And in the broadest terms, evolve or die is the message, the challenge, that vibrates at the core of each work of fiction. "I call myself an artist," Johnson asserts.[1] Confidently delivered, this assertion provides us with a useful framework for contemplating the several strengths which collectively constitute Johnson's artistry.

In the interviews, fiction, and nonfiction collected here for the first time, we have a greater sense of how Johnson defines himself as a symbol and agent of the process of communication. As editor of this volume, I have sought to represent in a balanced fashion Johnson's conception of his own place in the African American literary tradition, his regard for such literary ancestors and mentors as Richard Wright and John Gardner, his journey from cartoonist to philosopher to fiction writer, his interest in film, and his commitment to create what he terms philosophical black fiction.

A range of selections that span the past twenty-five years, Johnson's own writings are balanced by reviews and literary criticism which place his ever-enlarging corpus in a meaningful intellectual framework. Thus we have a greater sense of how others have interpreted his acts of communication as an artist, as well as the many directions in which his expansive imagination has taken him.

Above all, as editor of this volume I have selected materials which I hope will anticipate and address many of the needs and interests of Johnson's expanding readership, as well as generate new scholarship on a remarkably productive and remarkably young writer.

As a symbol and agent of the process of communication, of *communion*, Johnson is a writer of our age whose messages will deliver him, whole and engaging, to readers whose interests are as varied and whose questions are as urgent as his own: to readers of this century—and the next millennium.

Rudolph P. Byrd

Note

1. Quoted in Rebecca Carrol, *Swing Low: Black Men Writing* (New York: Crown Traders Books, 1995), p. 115.

Acknowledgments

Permission to reprint the following selections
is gratefully acknowledged:

"*Oxherding Tale and Siddhartha*: Philosophy, Fiction and the Emergence of a Hidden Tradition," by Rudolph P. Byrd from *African American Review* (Vol. 30, No. 4)

"Charles Johnson: Free at Last," by Stanley Crouch from *Notes of a Hanging Judge* (Oxford University Press, 1990)

"Johnson Revises Johnson: *Oxherding Tale* and *The Autobiography of an Ex-Colored Man*" by Vera Kutzinski from *Pacific Coast Philology* (Vol. 23, No. 1–2)

"The Phenomenology of the Allmuseri: Charles Johnson and the Subject of the Narrative of Slavery" by Ashraf A. Rushdy from *African American Review* (Vol. 26, No. 2)

The following works by Charles Johnson are reprinted here with his permission from the sources listed:

Excerpt from *Oxherding Tale* by Charles Johnson from *Literary Outtakes* (Fawcett Columbine, 1990) edited by Larry Dark

"Kwoon" by Charles Johnson from *Prize Stories 1993: The O. Henry Awards* (Doubleday, 1993) edited by William Abrahams

"Philosophy and Black Fiction" by Charles Johnson from *Obsidian: Black Literature in Review* (Vol. 6, No. 1&2)

"The Writer's Notebook" by Charles Johnson from *First Words* (Chapel Hill: Algonquin Press, 1993) edited by Paul Mandelbaum

"Where Fiction and Philosophy Meet" by Charles Johnson from *American Visions* (June 1988)

"Whole Sight: Notes on New Black Fiction" by Charles Johnson from *Callaloo* (Vol. 7, No. 3)

"Novelists of Memory" by Charles Johnson from *Dialogue* (USIA, January 1989)

"Phenomenology of the Black Body" by Charles Johnson from *Michigan Quarterly Review* (Fall 1993)

"On Writers and Writing" by Charles Johnson from *On Writers and Writing: John Gardner* (Addison-Wesley Publishing Company, 1994) edited by Stewart O'Nan

"Absence of Black Middle-Class Images Has Global Impact" ["Black Images and Their Global Impact"] by Charles Johnson from *National Minority Politics* (Vol. 5, No. 11, November 1993)

"What Is Man" by Charles Johnson from *What Is Man? The Oxford Mark Twain* (Oxford University Press, 1996) edited by Shelley Fisher Fishkin

"Journal Entries on the Death of John Gardner" by Charles Johnson from *New Myths: The Literary Legacy of John Gardner*

"One Meaning of *Mo' Better Blues*" by Charles Johnson from *The Films of Spike Lee: Five for Five* (Stewart, Tabori & Chang, 1991)

"Black Fiction's Father Figure" [Review by *Richard Wright: Works*] by Charles Johnson from *The Chicago Tribune* (November 19, 1991)

"Spike Lee Does the Right Thing" by Charles Johnson from *Seattle Weekly* (November 18, 1992)

"Inventing Africa" [Review of Kwame Anthony Appiah's *In My Father's House*] by Charles Johnson from *New York Times Book Review* (June 21, 1992)

"Widening the Racial Divide" [Review of Dinesh D'Souza's *The End of Racism*] by Charles Johnson

"The King We Left Behind" by Charles Johnson from *Common Quest* (Fall 1996)

"A Capsule History of Black Comics" by Charles Johnson from *Still I Rise: A Cartoon History of African Americans* (W. W. Norton, 1997)

"Critic, Not Cynic: Charles Johnson and Stanley Crouch" from *Seattle Weekly* (November 22, 1995)

Autobiographical Acts

I Call Myself an Artist

Sometime in the 1920s my great-uncle, William Johnson, left the home of his family in South Carolina to live in Evanston, a northern suburb of Chicago. He was a young man then, dark-skinned, tall, good-natured, pious, industrious and, I suspect, a product of Booker T. Washington's "boot-strap" philosophy of racial uplift. Once North, he married, and started his own milk company, which served the black neighborhoods in my hometown. The Great Depression brought his company to an end, but by the 1940s Will Johnson had started another business—the Johnson Construction Company—that would be profitable for decades and result in the creation of numerous churches, apartment buildings, and residences not only in Evanston but across other suburbs of Chicago. His success made him the patriarch of my family. And, most important of all, it allowed him to offer jobs to his relatives still living in South Carolina.

One man who accepted his invitation for work in the North was Benny Lee Johnson, my father, who was the "middle" child in a family of twelve children. Six boys. Six girls. My father was, in fact, sandwiched by birth between two girls, and thus was a bit to one side, a bit adrift from his siblings on my grandfather Richard's farm outside Abbeville. He was always, I believe, a proud man, responsible but shy, a person who valued regularity, enjoyed churchgoing, and measured himself by the quality and quantity of his labor. In all the years I've known him he has never uttered an oath stronger than the word "Shoot!" when he was angry. If Benny Lee identified with anyone, it was *his* father, who in addition to being a farmer was also the local blacksmith and a carpenter. There can be no question that my father loved life down South— hunting in winter, the rhythm of life close to the land, a tightly knit family that worked together—and, as a boy, he had fresh ideas for how to help Richard get crops in early, and for expanding his sideline as a blacksmith. If you have seen the character Hoke, played by Morgan Freeman in the film *Driving Miss Daisy*, then you have seen my father. He could have stayed in South Carolina forever, he tells me, but when life became economically harder on the black family farm in the 1940s, my father had to find work elsewhere. My aunts, his sisters, say he cried the morning he left them to join his Uncle Will in Illinois. He was twenty-five years old that day, and his plan was to make a little money and return as soon as he could.

Doubtlessly, my father would have gone back to that life he often described to me as idyllic (if you ignored racism, which his family generally did because they seldom had to interact with white people). But once he reached Evanston he met a woman five years his senior, Ruby Elizabeth Jackson, the only child of an only child (a maternal grandmother I always knew as Nana) who had lived in Evanston since age twelve and was *glad* her parents—Charles and Beatrice Jackson—left Georgia. This woman, my mother, was most suited for cities. Not that she was a woman familiar with nightclubs or a fast life. On the contrary, she was a church-girl, a virgin and proud of it (my father would have been attracted to no one else) but one with a wide interest in everything novel, which the Chicago area offered in abundance. I know she loved her father, a dark, handsome man who worked as a mechanic and was dead at age fifty from a heart attack before I was born; and she and her mother, whom she called "Bee," were more like mutually dependent sisters than mother and daughter. Both had an artist's eye for the beautiful, the unusual, the eccentric, and loved gardening. And in my mother's five-feet-four-inch frame there dwelled just a bit of the soul of an actress—a playful knack for saying or doing things simply for the effects they might create on others. Her hope had been to be a schoolteacher, a dream she never realized because she had a severe case of asthma that dated back to her childhood.

In many ways my father and mother seemed as different as two people could be: he was a quiet, deeply conservative, pro-black man with a fifth-grade education, who until the 1960s voted Republican ("I can always find work when they're in office," he said); yet she was emotional, moody, a high school graduate who believed in integration, belonged to three book clubs, and always voted for Democrats ("They do more for our people," she said). But in fact they actually complemented and completed each other. He *listened* to her; she relied, physically and emotionally, on *him*. And both were, like so many in that first wave of black southern immigrants to Evanston, children of the black church. Given her health and age, my mother would only have one child, who arrived a year or so after she met Benny, which meant he had now a family of his own in the North and would never live on the farm again.

And so I was born on April 23 (Shakespeare's birthday), 1948, at Community Hospital, an all-black facility. That place, and the remarkable person behind it, Dr. Elizabeth Hill, deserve a mention in this memoir because prior to its creation, Dr. Hill—one of the area's first black physicians—was barred by segregation from taking her patients to all-white Evanston Hospital. Instead, she was forced to take them to a hospital on the south side of Chicago, and quite a few of her patients died in the ambulance on the way. Almost single-handedly (so I was told as a child), Dr. Hill organized black Evanston (and some sympathetic whites) to create a black hospital. My Uncle Will would go nowhere else for treatment, even after Evanston Hospital was integrated. My father's sister and other black Evanstonians found life long work there before its closure in the late 1970s. And every black baby born to my generation in Evanston came into the world there—my classmates and I all had in common the fact that we had been delivered by Elizabeth Hill, who never married and considered all of us to be her "children." Even when I was in my teens she knew me on sight and would ask what I'd been up to since last I saw her.

₩ ₩ ₩

Predictably, then, I grew up in a black community in the 1950s that had the feel of one big extended family. Ebenezer A.M.E. Church, where I was baptized (and later my son) and married, was a central part of our collective lives. Naturally, Uncle Will was a big church donor and one of its elders. (By the time I knew him he was a bald, bullet-headed, pot-bellied man who wore suspenders, studied the evening news on television as if it were an oracle, and smiled down at me from his great height with all the affection he gave the children of his nephews and nieces. Because no one in our family had yet gone to college, he'd tell me, "Get an education, that's the most important thing you can do," and I'd say, "Yes, *sir*, Uncle Will. I *will* get an education.") But my parents and relatives—all quietly pious since we were all Methodists, remember, so "shouting" and "getting happy" were frowned upon—and neighbors also had significant roles at Ebenezer: my mother sometimes taught Sunday school, my cousins sang in the choir, I was an usher. In an atmosphere such as this, where my Uncle Will had built the very structures black Evanston people lived and worshipped their god in, where everyone *knew* their neighbors and saw them in church on Sunday, it was natural for grown-ups to keep an eye on the welfare of their neighbors' children—I'm referring to my earliest playmates—and to help each other in innumerable ways. In short, Evanston in the 1950s was a place where, beyond all doubt, I knew I was loved and belonged.

There were never any days when my family missed a meal. This was due to my father's occasionally working three jobs (a day job doing construction, an evening job as a night watchman, and helping an elderly white couple with their chores for a few hours on the weekend). So no, we weren't as poor as some of my friends who had no father at home. But neither were we wealthy or middle-class. Ever so often my mother took a job to help make ends meet. One of these was as a cleaning woman for Gamma Phi Beta sorority at Northwestern University, where my Nana was already working as a cook. And she brought me along with her since she couldn't afford a baby-sitter. I remember her telling me that the sorority's chapter said no blacks would ever be admitted into its ivied halls. There are two great ironies in this story. The first is that my mother brought home books thrown out by the sorority girls when classes ended, and in those boxes I found my first copies of Shakespeare's tragedies. The other irony is that decades later in 1990 Northwestern's English department actively (and generously) pursued me for employment by offering me a chair in the humanities, which I declined.

Along with those books from Northwestern University, my mother filled first the aged apartment we lived in before 1960, then my parents' first home with books that reflected her eclectic tastes in yoga, dieting, Christian mysticism, Victorian poetry, interior decorating, costume design, and flower arrangement. On boiling hot midwestern afternoons in late July when I was tired of drawing (my dream was to be a cartoonist, which I shall discuss in a moment), I would pause before one of her many bookcases and pull down a volume on religion, the Studs Lonigan trilogy, poetry by Rilke, *The Swiss Family Robinson*, Richard Wright's *Black Boy*, an 1897 edition of classic Christian paintings (now in my library), or Daniel Blum's *Pictorial History of the American Theatre 1900– 1956*, which fascinated me for hours.

As an only child, books became my replacement for siblings. This early exposure to so many realms of the imagination can only be the reason why I came up with the idea of making myself read at least one book a week after I started at Evanston Township High School, from which, by the way, my mother had graduated in the late thirties. I must confess that before high school I was an avid science fiction and comic book reader, my collection of the latter reaching to about 2,000 comics. My self-imposed schedule of reading one book per week saw me start with all the James Bond novels and end with Plutarch's *Lives of the Noble Grecians*. I spent hours each week at a newsstand selecting "that" book I'd spend seven days of my life with. And, as might be expected, it happened that one week I finished early—on a Tuesday, I recall—and I thought, "God, what do I *do* now with the rest of the week?" So I read a second book and discovered, "Gee, I read *two* this week and my head didn't explode or anything." Then it became easy to make it three a week, and I *did* think—but only once—that someday it might be nice to have my name on the spine of a volume I'd written.

Mother's slim volume on yoga also helped me make the first, tentative steps on a path that would later prove invaluable for my life and literary interests. It contained a short chapter on "Meditation." Although the book's hatha yoga postures struck me as being excruciatingly hard, I decided to try out the author's instructions for clearing the mind. After half an hour of this—the most tranquil thirty minutes I'd ever known, one that radically slowed down my sense of time and divested me of desire—I felt both deeply rewarded and a little scared, as if I'd been playing with a loaded pistol. As much as I'd enjoyed this first pass at *dhyana*, I suspected (and rightly) that if I kept it up, I'd become too dispassionate, too peaceful, and would lack the fire—the internal agitation—to venture out into the world and explore all the things, high and low, that I, as a teenager, was burning to see, know, taste, and experience. Quietly, and without telling anyone what I'd done, I put her book back on the shelf and promised myself that someday—someday!—I would investigate this marvelous thing more deeply after I'd sated myself on the world that called me so powerfully.

And so, again, ours was a house of not just provocative books but also inexpensive art objects that Mother found at flea markets and rummage sales. When she couldn't find them, she *built* them—for example, bookcases made from old cigar boxes, which I helped her resurface and paint. We'd read the same books together sometimes, Mother and me, and discuss them (I think she relied on me for this, even raised me to do it, since my father had little time for books), and when I was twelve she placed the most unusual book of all in front of me. A blank book. A diary. "Some people write down what happens to them every day in books like these," she said. "You might enjoy this." Enjoy it? Oh, she knew me well! Like any kid, I enjoyed receiving gifts at Christmas and on my birthdays, but from my earlier years of being praised for my drawing ability in elementary school (art class was the one place where I excelled), the things I wanted *most* invariably turned out to be the things I had to make myself. Once I started writing on those pages about my feelings, about my friends and relatives, and once I saw how I was free to say *any*thing that came into my head about them, I was addicted. But remember what I said—Mother was a shrewd woman. I realized why she'd given me that first diary when we all sat one evening at the dinner table. She looked up from her plate, and in the most casual of voices asked, "Why don't you like your Uncle George?" I stopped chewing. I couldn't swallow. For maybe five seconds I thought she was psychic, a mind-reader. Then I remembered the diary. She'd been *reading* my entries. But what could I do? I didn't want to stop spilling my thoughts out, or give up the pleasure that came from seeing them externalized and in some strange way thereby made more manageable.

No, my only choice was to hide it, which I did—behind my dresser, under my mattress, wherever I thought she wouldn't look. Since that day I've filled up probably a hundred diaries, journals, and writer's notebooks. Crates worth of them containing poetry, essays to myself, whatever was in my head at that time—most of them are gathering dust in my father's garage because after filling up one I seldom look back, though if I wish to, I can reach behind me twenty years to this very day and read you an entry. (If nothing else, a journal or diary teaches us how silly we were, in retrospect, to be so upset about things that occupied us two decades ago.)

ひ ひ ひ

Like so many things I owe to my mother, I am indebted to her for seducing me with the beauty of blank pages. But this was by no means a new infatuation. As with books, it was into drawing that I regularly retreated as a child. There was something magical to me about bringing forth images that hitherto existed only in my head where no one could see them. I remember spending whole afternoons blissfully seated before a three-legged blackboard my parents got me for Christmas, drawing and erasing until my knees and the kitchen floor beneath me were covered with layers of chalk and the piece in my hand was reduced to a wafer-thin sliver.

Inevitably, the passion for drawing led me to consider a career as a professional artist. From the Evanston Public Library I lugged home every book on drawing, cartooning, and collections of early comic art (Cruikshank, Thomas Rolandson, Daumier, Thomas Nast) and pored over them, considering what a wonderful thing it would be—as an artist—to externalize *every*thing I felt and thought in images. Some Saturday mornings I sat on the street downtown with my sketchbook, trying to capture the likeness of buildings and pedestrians, who were probably amused to see a black kid studying them out of the corner of his eye, then scribbling furiously. And I made weekly trips to Good's Art Supplies to buy illustration board with my allowance and money earned from my paper route (and later from a Christmas job working on the assembly line at a Rand McNally book factory in Skokie, and from still another tedious after-school job cleaning up a silks-and-woolens store where well-heeled white ladies did their shopping). Good's was a tiny little store packed to the ceiling with the equipment I longed to buy. The proprietor, a fat, friendly man, tolerated my endless and naive questions about what it was like to be an artist and what materials were best for what projects; he showed me a book he'd self-published on his own theory of perspective (I never bought it), and after he'd recommended to me the best paper for my pen-and-ink ambitions, I strapped my purchase onto the front of my bicycle and pedaled home. (For a Christmas present my folks finally did buy me one of Good's drawing tables; I moved back furniture in my bedroom and set it up like a shrine. When I went away to college, it went with me, like an old friend.)

But if drawing brought me my deepest pleasure and my first sense of my own talents, it also led to my life's first real crisis. By my early teens I was determined to be nothing *but* a commercial artist. I told my father so. Without thinking this through, and without ever having known any black artists, he told me with the gravest concern for my economic future that, "They don't let black people do that. You should think about something else." I pleaded with him that I didn't *want* to do anything else. But Dad would not budge. For days after this conversation I was gloomy, crushed, and directed many an evil thought his way. A future without art? I would rather have died than not pursue drawing and self-expression as far as it could take me.

By some stroke of luck I was at that time a reader of *Writer's Digest*, mainly for their profiles of famous cartoonists who were my idols. One issue featured an advertisement for a correspondence course in cartooning taught by Lawrence Lariar, a man who'd published over one hundred books—both as a mystery writer and cartoonist—was cartoon editor for *Parade* magazine, a former Disney studio "story man," and each year served as editor for *The Best Cartoons of the Year*. My anger at my father's lack of faith in my future as an artist prompted me to write to Lariar, saying, "My dad tells me I won't be able to have a future as a cartoonist because I'm black, and I just want to know what you think." Lariar, a true liberal—a Jewish man (he changed his name decades earlier) who once took gleeful pleasure in his neighbor's anger when he invited a group of black artists to his Long Island home to give them instruction—fired back a letter to me within a week: "Your father is wrong," he said. "You can do whatever you want with your life. All you need is a good drawing teacher." I read this letter to my father. He hated to *ever* admit he was wrong, but he shrugged his big, tired shoulders and gave me a headshake that definitely meant, "Okay, what do *I* know about this?" I wrote Lariar back, asking, "Will you be my teacher?" His reply was all right, but I'd have to pay for his two-year course. No free lunches here. After a long talk with Dad he agreed to make the monthly payments for me.

ᘰ ᘰ ᘰ

I was by this time a high school student *hungering* to publish *any*where as a cartoonist. For two years I dutifully performed the cartooning exercises Lariar mailed me, sent them back, then studied his remarks and revisions. Since my family has relatives everywhere, I made a summer trip by Greyhound to Brooklyn, where our relatives put me up on a roll-away bed. In New York I made the journey out to Long Island to visit Lariar, shop talk about drawing (he loaded me down, dear man, with original art from syndicated strips of his own), then I carried my "swatch" (a cartoonist's portfolio of samples) all over Manhattan, pounding the pavement as I went by the company that published Archie Comics ("We'd hire you but all our illustrators live in New York") and every cartoon editor's office that would let me inside the door. No sales, then. Still, I was encouraged enough by the time I completed Lariar's lessons—I was then seventeen—to approach the editor of my high school paper, the *Evanstonian*, with an offer to illustrate their articles. Reluctantly, he agreed. He let me try a cartoon about a rock-and-roll group that looked like the Beatles. And I guess he was satisfied with my effort because he kept giving me assignments. Around this time I heard from a white classmate who also drew, Tom Reitze, about a Chicago company that manufactured magic tricks and was looking for illustrators (Read: cheap labor) for their catalog. I was at their door the next day. They gave me six tricks to draw. They paid two dollars per illustration. But I *was* paid for the first time and, so not to forget the day I became a "professional," I framed one of those dollars. It hangs right now on my office wall.

Something you must understand about Evanston in 1965 is that, unlike many places, the public schools were integrated. From the time I started kindergarten I was thrown together with kids of all colors, and so I found it natural to have friends both black and white. As kids, we thought bigotry was atavistic and—even worse—just not cool. Evanston Township High School, we constantly heard, was rated in the mid-1960s as the second-best public high school in the nation, right behind our competitor, New Trier. It was a big school, almost like a small college—my graduating class had 1,000 students; black students made up 11 percent of the population. In its progressive curriculum we found a first-rate education provided, clearly, by the wealthy white Evanston parents who sent their children there. My friend Reitze went on to Harvard; the much-celebrated Los Angeles installation artist, Franklin "Buzz" Spector, was my classmate (he wanted to be a poet then) at ETHS, and later at Southern Illinois University. True enough, white Evanstonians may have funded all those art and photography classes for their kids—but I took advantage of them too, and ran myself ragged playing soccer one year, and dreamed up with Reitze a comic strip for the school paper. Loosely based on the then-popular character "Wonder Warthog," ours was called "Wonder Wildkit" (the wildkit was the symbol for our football team). Reitze wrote, I drew. It ran the year we were seniors and, to my surprise, won a journalism award in national competition (along with a single-panel cartoon I'd published) for high school cartoonists. Truth is, until that moment I was unaware that such an award even existed.

And to its credit, ETHS offered a yearly creative writing class taught by short-story writer Marie-Claire Davis. At the time she was publishing in the *Saturday Evening Post*. As a cartoonist, I thought writing stories was fun and I came alive in my literature classes, where we read Orwell,

Shakespeare, Melville, and Robert Penn Warren, but writing wasn't the kick for me that drawing was. Regardless, I let a buddy talk me into enrolling in Marie's class with him. We talked to each other the whole time and barely listened to poor Marie. (But she put Joyce Cary's lovely book *Art and Reality* in front of us, without discussing it in class, and with the hopes that we might read it on our own, which I did, and something in me so enjoyed his essays on art that I thought, yeah, someday I'd like to do a book like this too.) When I turned in my first story, "Man Beneath Rags" (about homeless people), Marie took it to the *Evanstonian* and published it. Then she did another, "50 Cards 50" (about racially directed Christmas cards), and a third, "Rendezvous" (a science-fiction satire). All this pleased me to no end, but my only obsession, as always, was with comic art.

So my "swatch" had grown. I was prepared senior year to attend an art school just outside Chicago (my father had driven me to the interviewer's motel because I missed him at school and, though fatigued-looking, he seemed pleased with my samples). Providence, however, had something else in mind. During the waning days of May I sat talking with my art and photography teacher, a gentle but gloomy man who said to me in all candor, "Chuck, an artist has a tough life. If you're going to be a cartoonist, it'll be even harder. I think you should go to a university, not art school, and get a professional degree." Looking back, I *know* he was saying the artist's life had been hard on *him*. Nevertheless, his words bothered me—I couldn't afford to blow my one shot at college when my whole family was counting on me. I tramped upstairs to my advisor's office, told her what he'd told me, and said, "It's so late in the year. Are there *any* schools still accepting applications?" She looked through her big book and came up with Southern Illinois University in Carbondale. "You could major in journalism," she said. This was not my first choice, I can assure you; it had the reputation of being a "party school." My advisor shrugged when I said this. "You can always transfer after the first year, if you like, and finish at the University of Illinois."

꙳ ꙳ ꙳

Thus, I went to SIU in the fall of 1966 with the plan of transferring later. I was among a wave of Illinois black kids who enrolled that year, most of them pouring into "Little Egypt" from the Chicago area. I cannot speak for how those other students felt, but I know I arrived as eager for education and naive as any young man could be. "College" was a nearly mythic place, I thought, where one was supposed to pursue and achieve "wisdom." After arriving in Carbondale I soon learned that few (if any) students and faculty were there for that lofty, transcendent reason. Most of the students I met said, bluntly, that they "just wanted that piece of paper" so they could get a good-paying job and leave school as soon as they could. I listened. I understood their feelings, but that wasn't how I felt. My overriding concern in those days was with acquiring new skills. As many skills as I could in as many disciplines as possible. Nor was I alone in this desire, for another journalism major I met—a Ghanaian student named Fortunata Massa—remarked to me, "The thing I like most about America is that no matter what you want to learn, there is someone here who can teach it to you."

In effect, we were both skill-junkies, technique-junkies in 1966. My belief was that if you gave me a good teacher I could put what *he* knew together with what *I* knew and the product of this fusion would be greater than its two original parts.

Within a few days of unpacking in my dormitory room I found my way to the campus newspaper, the *Daily Egyptian*, and showed them my "swatch." They hired me that day (and for pay). It probably helped my case that I was a journalism major because the *Egyptian* was a product of the School of Journalism, founded by a seasoned newsman named Howard Long, who during my undergraduate years enjoyed my draftsmanship and kindly took me under his wing. For the *Egyptian* I drew everything—illustrations, panel cartoons, and two comic strips I coauthored with a dormitory friend and English major, Charles Gilpin, who was devoted to being a novelist and told me enthusiastically about his classes with a young professor named John Gardner. Sometime later that year I wheedled my way onto the town paper, the *Southern Illinoisan*, as a political cartoonist. And I sent copies of every published drawing to my parents and Lariar, with whom I kept up a spirited correspondence. College, as it turned out, fed my creativity. New ideas in an open, intellectual environment became raw material for my pen.

All journalism majors were required to take a class in philosophy. I chose a huge lecture course taught by a brilliant professor, John Howie, on the pre-Socratics. Somehow (I don't know how), and with some gift he had (I don't know what), Howie was able to *sing* the ethical problems Empedocles and Parmenides wrestled with in such a way that I—sitting there in my seat among a sea of students—felt in my depths that these were *my* problems today, matters I had to come to some conclusion about. My imagination had not been so stimulated, I felt, since the day I first discovered drawing; my mind had never been engaged so thoroughly in the process of questioning the world around me. Right then and there, I knew I had to do *more* of this; I decided quietly, with certainty, that I had to live close to philosophy for the rest of my life—for the very sake of my intellectual life. Yes, I kept taking journalism classes, but I took just as many in philosophy and was but five credits short of having that as my undergraduate major.

Something else I learned at SIU that first year was the meaning of loneliness. For the first time in my life I was separated from the extended family of blood relations and neighborhood friends I knew in Evanston. And this *was* a party school. But I'd never been a party person. Friday and Saturday nights, therefore, were times when I felt most alone at college that first year. The usually raucous dormitory was empty as a tomb—everyone, it seemed, was out dating or partying on Greek Row. (They'd fall in by daybreak, leaving puddles of vomit down the stairwell; and I recall writing freshman composition papers, ten dollars each, for some of the guys so they could have the night off to get loose. I would also do for free handwriting analysis for them because for some reason I'd gotten interested in the pseudo-science of grapho-analysis; and writing those papers for pay wasn't so much a task as it was fun since writing came easily to me.) In those days Morris library was open all night. Adrift in my loneliness, I saw its lights as you might a beacon. I went there after I finished my homework and whatever drawing assignments I'd nailed down for the week. As might be expected, the library was nearly as empty as my dorm. Only clusters of Asian students sat studying together, a fact that deeply impressed me then as it does now when I think of my Chinese and Vietnamese students and how difficult it must be for them to pull straight A's in a foreign country and when English is their second language.

Most of the night I drifted among the stacks, pulling down whatever titles caught my eye: obscure poetry, works of Western and Eastern metaphysics I hadn't yet read, every oversized book on art the library had, and novels by Sartre, London (*Martin Eden*), all the "philosophical" fiction writers. With about thirty books in front of me, I'd sit down and start flipping through them, sampling each. After a few more hours I'd have six or seven I wanted to live with for the week, and at 3:00 A.M. I'd check them out and return to the dorm to spend the rest of the week reading between classes.

Those were solitary but productive days, and unexpectedly rewarding on a personal level. I made several lifelong friends, among them Scott Kramer, another philosophy major from Chicago. When not in philosophy classes together, we'd play chess, or exchange literary works we'd discovered (it was Kramer who put Herman Hesse's *Damien* in my hand, which led me to read *Siddhartha*, a work I felt I had to respond to one day, and did in *Oxherding Tale*, my second novel); or we'd go to an off-campus movie with a beautiful, deeply spiritual girl we knew—a religion major named Jill Walter (she is now Chaplain Jill Walter-Penn and recently had the honor of being invited to NASA to deliver the official prayer for the astronauts who went up in the resurrected Challenger space shuttle); or Kramer and I would coauthor dreadfully didactic metaphysical plays—one is called "The Transcendental Descent," and Kramer, who now teaches philosophy at Spokane Community College, threatens to someday publish this drek we dashed off on a night we were bored. Or we'd sit together, smoking and drinking beer, through each and every episode of "Star Trek's" first season on the dorm's TV—we were, I should add, fans from the start. We were also, I guess, pretty typical of alienated, dreamy intellectual and artistic wannabees, the sort of "serious," brooding young men who quoted Plato, argued about existentialism, and ever so slightly began to ease into the dress and life-styles appropriate for hippies by 1967. The other kids in the dorm (business and agriculture majors) doubtlessly had good reason to think we were strange, particularly after our corner of the dorm and circle of associates began to attract other nonconformist personalities—would-be musicians who idolized Jimi Hendrix and the Rolling Stones, and fledgling writers devoted to Richard Brautigan and Kurt Vonnegut.

ʊʊ ʊʊ ʊʊ

That next summer of 1967 a surprise awaited me in Evanston. On the evening of my first night back home, my father announced that, "You have to get up early tomorrow. I got you a job for the summer with the city. You're going to be a garbageman." He'd volunteered me for the last job in the world I would have chosen. But I knew, as he knew, that I couldn't just sit idle for the summer, so I set my clock early and rode with him down to the city yard—he was employed as a night watchman those days—at 6:00 A.M.

As it turned out, the older men I worked with on the trucks that summer knew and respected my father, and they gladly extended their friendship to "Benny's boy." Naturally, the work was hard. In those days garbagemen walked from house to house with a huge, plastic tub, which they filled to the brim with waste, then swung on their backs as they tramped down alleys in ninety-degree heat. After a few weeks of getting used to maggots at the bottom of cans, my clothes soaked by sewage, and stumbling on the occasional dead rat, I began to enjoy this job. I was outside doing physical work—not cooped up in an office—and I certainly didn't mind getting off work in the early afternoon. If we finished too early, we'd buy some brew, park the truck in the shade, then cool off and shoot the breeze until quitting time.

It was on one of those afternoons that another SIU student working on the garbage trucks told me about his friend who'd enrolled in a martial arts school in Chicago. He told me that at this place, Chi Tao Chuan of the Monastery, the teaching was so wickedly effective that when his friend was attacked on the street after only two weeks of studying at the "kwoon" (training hall) he responded with moves that killed his assailant on the spot. I opened another beer and listened carefully to everything he said. I'd long wanted to systematically study a fighting art, partly because what I'd seen of Japanese karate impressed me (one high school friend started before we graduated), and partly because the Chicago area in the late 1960s was a pretty dangerous place for blacks and "longhairs" like my friend Kramer, who was once briefly hospitalized by a group of blue-collar toughs who just didn't like his looks.

Later that week I called the kwoon and asked for an interview. The voice on the other end, that of the school's junior-level instructor, warned me, "You should be prepared for the unexpected. The person you think is the master here may not be; the one who looks like a beginner might be ahead of everyone else." Two of my best buddies from high school, Luther and Napolean, agreed to visit the school with me. It was, if I remember rightly, something of a trek from Evanston— first a bus ride into Chicago, then an "El" trip over to the west side, and finally a bus ride into a neighborhood that looked so run-down and rough I figured you needed to be a martial artist of something just to make it to the school's door.

We knocked and a young instructor peered through the shade over the window and invited us inside a darkly lit, below street-level room. No other students had yet arrived. He asked us to wait for the school's master. As we sat quietly on the floor, just inside the door, my eyes tracked the room, moving from the training equipment—heavy bags and a wooden dummy—to the small, elegant Buddhist shrine where all who entered were asked to say a prayer, and on to the array of traditional Asian weapons mounted on one wall: flexible instruments such as staffs and spears, broadswords and farm implements the Chinese had found a way to use as weapons. The *feel* of this place, so meditative with its faint traces of incense in the air, so simple in its stark furnishings, struck me as exactly right for what I needed at this juncture in my life: a discipline of the body that also required an ongoing testing of the spirit.

After a few moments the school's master arrived. He was a Westerner. A middle-aged, unshaven white man dressed in a worn, black trench-coat. He carried a wrinkled shopping bag close to his body. You might have mistaken him on the street for a homeless person. You might have thought the bag contained a bottle of Thunderbird. His student told him we'd come for an interview. He nodded, then sat down beside us. Right then I noticed that the fingers on his left hand did not bend— they'd been broken so often, he told us, that hand was useless now except as a weapon. From his bag he withdrew a long knife—I'd never seen so huge a blade before—and kept it in full view as he explained how beginners in this school *started* with black sashes to show his con-tempt for karate systems, where black belts symbolized achievement. After their first promotion, each of his students specialized in the fighting techniques of one of the traditional Chinese animals—tiger if you were a big guy, black panther if you were smaller but had the tiger's spirit (this was to be my style), crane if you were tall and angular, and snake if you were small, cowardly, and needed to understand how to inflict pain on others by first absorbing large doses of it yourself. The school also offered firearms and knife training taught by one of his instructors just returned from a tour in Vietnam. Something else he said, half-jokingly, was that, "You don't have to be a Buddhist to get good at this system, but it *helps*." Napolean sat as attentively and absorbed by all this as I did. But Luther, our group's six-feet-four funny man, displayed a bit too much lip and sass that day ("I'm a lover, not a fighter" was his favorite saying), and the master interrupted his lecture without warning, and barked, "You can't train here. Get out!" Shocked as thoroughly as if he'd been slapped, Luther looked at us, then scrambled to his feet and was out the door in the time it takes to read this sentence. "You two are fine," the master said. "You can start on Tuesday." After the interview we stepped back outside into the noise and stink of the street, and found Luther waiting for us. He was visibly sad and angry—he wisecracked all the way home about the school's master, but he was pleased Napolean and I would try this out together. Unfortunately, on Tuesday when the instructor led us through muscle-banging calisthenics and introduced us to a "horse-riding" stance that sent waves of pain through muscles in our bodies where we didn't even know we *had* muscles, Napolean decided kung-fu (the word means "hard work") was not for him and dropped out. Thus, I was alone. I decided, however, that since I'd started I'd see this through.

That summer saw me hauling garbage every morning until my back begged for mercy. Nights, I'd make the trek to the kwoon. In every respect, it was an early martial arts studio, one that predated the rules of safety found now in most schools; it was devoted less to learning elegant forms and tournament competition than to animal-like fighting that involved its practitioners forcing themselves into a nearly trance-like state. I remember learning stances, the proper ways to strike and kick, and an exercise that required us to throw 45 punches to the front, side, and back in the space of 10 seconds. The master lectured often on principles of fighting and, just as often, on what he thought genuine manhood was all about. No one sparred with safety equipment. We were told that if an intruder came into the school and wouldn't leave we should kill him—we were within our legal rights to do so since he would be trespassing. There, in that studio, the students had the seriousness of monks (some of them planned to start a monastery for the school in South America), and the master expected total commitment of one's life to the school. Often I wondered if I'd exit the studio alive. For example, I stuck around one evening after class to watch a promotion test. The students up for promotion fought their instructors at sparring time. I watched one beginner after another struck down—and one knocked unconscious—when they got a little too eager to score against those superior to them in rank. And I knew, with growing anxiety, that my own promotion test was only two months away in the fall. I was dead certain I'd be injured. Returning to SIU in September, I swore to do everything I could to prepare myself for that night.

I barely remember the start of my second year in college. What I *do* recall is leaving my fourth-floor dormitory room late each evening, slipping down into the basement with a towel, and clearing away furniture to work out in a musty storage room. Every night I religiously went through my routine—offensive and defensive techniques—until I was drenched with sweat. I systematically worked on that exercise of throwing 45 punches in 10 seconds by checking myself against a stopwatch, and brought down my initial speed from 15 seconds to 2 and at last 3 seconds *below* what was required a week or two before the promotion test was scheduled. I felt ready when I returned to Evanston. I slept at my parents' home the night before, then lugged my suitcase down to the kwoon, intending to catch the last train to Carbondale by 10:00 P.M. after the test was over—that is, if I was in any condition to catch a train.

By some great, good fortune the school's master had rethought these tests after the injuries that occurred two months earlier. This time beginners fought beginners. My memory may be tricking me, but it seems we fought *all* evening long for the master's pleasure; he wanted everyone to try out everyone else. We sparred two against one; we kept going until nearly every student was too tired to stand. Apparently, he liked the way I moved—"Pa Kua!" he shouted, winking at his instructors (he was referring to another fighting system I knew nothing of at the time)— and when at last we sat in a circle, dripping sweat, working to steady our breathing, he awarded me and another SIU student the only "double" promotions to blue sash given that evening.

I'm at a loss to explain how I felt, at nineteen, as we received our membership cards and congratulations. The room was aglow. Though tired in every cell, my body felt transparent; my mind, clear as spring water. I couldn't have cared less if I missed my train and spent all night roaming downtown Chicago—I just *wanted* someone to jump me— before the next train at 8:00 A.M. I count this as one of the best nights of my life, a rare kind of rite-of-passage that showed me, as a young man, something about my capacity for discipline, enduring pain, and pushing myself beyond my expectations.

During holidays I returned to Chi Tao Chuan of the Monastery for lessons. The master started me on a 1,000-move set, one I could work on when I was away at college. But the 300-mile commute made training there difficult. Slowly, I eased into working out with a karate club on campus, won promotions easily, and decided to change styles because this one was nearby. As with the previous year, drawing and philosophy absorbed virtually all my free time when I was not in class.

꩜ ꩜ ꩜

My second summer home found me again working the garbage trucks in early June. A few days after being back in Evanston, as I was reading Nietzsche's *Beyond Good and Evil*, Luther and Napolean dropped by to razz me for not having a date. But I knew something else was on their minds—they were grinning and acting goofier, it seemed to me, than usual, as if waiting for the other one to spring a secret on me. After several evasive looks and elbowing each other, Napolean said, "Have you met Joan?" I shook my head, no. "Who the hell is Joan?" They traded off telling me the story of the latest "fox" they'd found. Joan New was a student at National College of Education in Evanston and was staying over the summer with Luther's two cousins, Josephine and Martha, girls I'd gone to high school with and loved like family; they rented the apartment above Luther's family. Naturally, Luther had made his suavest play for Miss New. She iced him instantly. *That*, I thought, spoke volumes about her character. I put Nietzsche aside, and decided okay—okay, since they were pulling me toward the door, I'd meet Joan for their sake and so they'd leave me alone. Really, all I wanted that evening was to say hello to Luther's cousins.

We traveled the few blocks to Luther's house. I walked in behind my two oldest friends. His cousins squealed when they saw me, "Chuckie!" We did our round of hugs. Just off to our left, sitting on the sofa, was a woman whose smile was brighter than a sun going nova. Oh yes, I tried to stay calm. I tried to act casual. But something way back in my brain said, *This is it. You don't have to look anymore.* Before the evening was over I'd asked her out. However, as luck would have it, my first car—a Corvair convertible my father bought secondhand for me—was in the shop. I cancelled that first date and made another. Somehow *that* fell through, too, and I was certain this girl was going to give up on me as being hopelessly disorganized. By the third attempt we were, thank heaven, in each other's company. In fact, we spent nearly every night that summer going to movies and art museums in the Loop, gospel concerts (her idea, not mine), picnics, and parking on the beach near Northwestern University.

I've always felt there was more than coincidence to our meeting in the summer of 1968. We were both twenty. Furthermore, we were born exactly seven days apart (I'm older by a week). For all I know, we were conceived at exactly the same moment only forty minutes from each other, though Joan's south Chicago—Bigger Thomas country—was far different from my sleepy, suburban Evanston. She and her two brothers and three sisters lived in Altgeld Gardens, a housing project where murder and theft were, she told me, too ordinary to get overly excited about. Her mother died when she was six, thus Joan never knew her. Instead, her grandmother, a devoutly Christian woman who lived in a walk-up apartment with no water, raised Joan and her sisters into young women who were all the more stunning and mature to me because they, as a family, had remained strong and loving in an environment that can only be described as an urban battlefield. She didn't drink or smoke, curse or screw around. When we met she'd almost given up on black men and was settling into the thought of being single for the rest of her life. She was educated, extremely independent and, though kind toward everyone, had one of Hemingway's "built-in shit detectors." More than anything else that summer—and I didn't know if we had a future beyond one summer—I wanted to make her happy, to see as often as I could her disarmingly gentle smile, and hear her easy laughter (her sense of irony was comparable to my own). My parents took to her immediately, especially my father, who seemed to see in Joan something of himself—frugality, a lack of pretense and, yes, unshakable morality.

I missed Joan sorely after I returned to school. In her absence, I wrote poetry for her (which Kramer put to music for me), managed to sneak her image or name into the cartoons I published that year, and for her birthday I did her portrait in oil. "It looks like a big, color cartoon," my friends observed. And they were right.

That same year I attended a public reading at SIU by Amiri Baraka (né Leroi Jones), the poet and principal theoretician for the Black Arts Movement. He appeared onstage in a dashiki, flanked by two scowling attendants who watched the crowd as closely as if they were members of the Secret Service. For nearly an hour Baraka read poetry and lectured. He took no questions from whites in the audience, and he repeated a message that hit me as forcefully as John Howie's lectures had two years earlier. He said, "Take your talent back to the black community." At that moment I thought he was talking to *me*. I had been publishing as a cartoonist/illustrator for three years, but in late 1968 I was starting to feel that my work was growing stale; the excitement and thrill of discovery was missing—I was only doing "assignments" for others, selling one-page scripts to a company called Charlton Comics (they bought my high school story "Rendezvous" and had their own artist illustrate it), and teaching a cartooning class at SIU's "Free School." I wondered: What if I directed my drawing and everything I knew about comic art to exploring the history and culture of black America? In 1968 we had only a handful of black cartoonists at work—Ollie Harrington, who was then living in east Berlin; Morrie Turner, who did "Wee Pals"; and Walt Carr, a staff artist at Johnson Publishing Company in Chicago. But no one was generating books about black cultural nationalism, slavery, or African-American history.

I walked home from Baraka's lecture in a daze. I sat down before my drawing board, my inkwell, my pens. I started to sketch. I worked for a solid week, cutting my classes. The more I drew and took notes for gag-lines, the faster the ideas came. After seven days I had a book, *Black Humor*. My only problem was I didn't know where to send it. In the spring of 1969 I showed it to the editors at the *Daily Egyptian*, but they were as baffled as I was about who might want this work. On the other hand, they did have something to offer me that year—an internship as a reporter on the *Chicago Tribune* for the summer.

And before the end of the school year something else came along that broke my spell of "dryness." During spring term on a day when I was bored, I wrote a letter to the local PBS station, WSIU-TV, asking if they'd be interested in my hosting a "how-to-draw" series for them. I never expected them to reply. Yet, they did, and asked me in to talk about this project. WSIU, a small station, was looking for an inexpensive series it could feed to other PBS stations around the country. This idea, they said, looked like a possibility. All they needed was two cameras, a drawing table, and me behind it. Scott Kane, the director, came up with a title for the show, "Charlie's Pad," which I wasn't exactly crazy about, but I thought, what the hell, it's cute.

Regardless, I *was* nervous about appearing before a camera for the first time. Kramer, who'd moved out of the dorm and had his own apartment, agreed to let me use it—and his expensive tape equipment—one weekend when he was out of town. I holed up at his place from Friday night until Sunday afternoon, living on egg sandwiches and coffee, and reading a text I'd written over and over into his tape machine; I replayed it, studied my mistakes, then kept going over it for thirty hours until I felt I sounded smooth enough to pass the audition WSIU-TV wanted me to do. Although that test was choppy, they felt I'd be communicative enough to pull off fifty-two fifteen-minute installments on every aspect of cartooning from composition to perspective. My "bible" for the series was Lariar's old lessons from my high school days. "We'll start shooting next fall," Kane told me, "when you come back from summer break."

At the *Chicago Tribune* I worked on that newspaper's "Action Express" public service column under editor James Coates. The column had a big, white van that we drove around Chicago, stopping in places like the south side, where I (being only one of two blacks on the *Trib*), would ask neighborhood people, like members of the Black Stone Rangers, what problems they had and how the paper might address them. Oftentimes, though, we invented our own questions for the column when readers didn't provide the kinds of queries that interested us. For example, I dreamed up a few about black history ("What can you tell me about Marcus Garvey's back-to-Africa movement?"). All in all, this was a great summer: evenings with Joan as we flew around the city in my Corvair, and days on the newspaper (instead of hauling garbage), where I had an eventful discussion with their book editor, Bob Cromie.

His office groaned with stacks of books sent to him for review. How I wound up there, I can't say, but I found myself standing beside him with the manuscript for *Black Humor*, asking his advice about where to send it. He suggested John H. Johnson down the street at *Ebony*. With his recommendation, I dropped off the book, and before the summer was over they'd accepted it for publication in 1970. What do I recall from that trip to his company? Only fragments come to me—Mr. Johnson, a trim, polished man, treating me kindly in his office overlooking Michigan Avenue, and laughing out loud at some of the cartoons. Oh, and this: the odd feeling that five years after dreaming about seeing my name on the spine of a book it was actually about to happen.

ꙮ ꙮ ꙮ

All my drawing between 1966 and 1969, and the moving back and forth between two departments—philosophy and journalism—made it inevitable that I would need a fifth year to graduate. However, Joan was ready to finish in June 1970. I nervously proposed, a sort of proposal-in-reverse. We'd both be twenty-two years old and penniless, I said. But I wanted to get married. Yet, and yet: "I'm determined to be an artist," I said, "and that means I'm probably going to have it rough, and I don't want to take you through that. Maybe we should wait until I'm more secure." And her reply?

"But if we wait until you're successful, we may *never* get married."

I had to admit that she had a point. We decided to plan for a June 14 wedding, two days after her graduation.

Back in Carbondale, I resumed classes and started the work of shooting three installments (once a week) for "Charlie's Pad." More publications followed, plus I was invited by a friend in philosophy, a black master's degree student named Tom Slaughter, to serve as a discussion-group leader for a black history survey course offered by the newly formed Black Studies department.

And then came the U.S. action in Cambodia.

Demonstrations were everywhere on campus that year. My political cartoons for the *Egyptian* had grown so archly political in their call for revolution that my editor cancelled a series of panels and told me to "concentrate on everyday things." By spring war protesters took to the streets, their special target on campus being the Vietnam Studies Center, which some people believed was doing research for the government. A curfew was established, one I broke with three friends, and for my trouble I received a lungful of tear gas thrown by the Carbondale police. A few days later SIU's vice president cancelled classes before the violence led to fatalities.

With the school shut down, I caught a train to Chicago and filed a story about the demonstrations at the *Tribune* (they'd made me a correspondent after I returned to school). Then I went to my parents' house to make preparations for marriage.

We had, of course, nothing in those days. Joan borrowed a wedding dress. We jerry-rigged the entire ceremony at Ebenezer A. M. E. Church. Luther was my best man; Jim Coates took pictures for us. And lots of family and friends covered the gift table four feet deep with everything they thought we would need. After the ceremony we caught a train back to Carbondale. There was no honeymoon; we both started work the next day.

Joan commenced teaching elementary school in DuQuoin, Illinois. I went to work part-time on the *Illinoisan*, where I did *every*thing to earn fifty dollars a week—news stories, interviews, wedding and obituary announcements, farm news, the police report, a column, political cartoons, and on Saturday night I proofread the Sunday morning edition.

And it was at this time that I began to seriously devote myself to writing fiction.

With my emotional life focused on marriage, one published book behind me, another, *Half-Past Nation-Time*, accepted for publication, and the "Charlie's Pad" series starting its broadcast life (it would run for ten years, even in Canada), I decided to venture into another field— the novel. Over the last year a novel idea had been intruding upon my thoughts, a story about a young black man who enrolls in a martial arts school like the one I attended in Chicago, but in this story I intended to bring forth all the Eastern philosophy embodied in that experience. Because the idea would not leave me alone, I wrote the book that summer. My rate of production was ten pages a day. It was the first of what I call my "apprentice novels." And it was not good. On the other hand, I'd never organized 250 pages of anything before in my life, so I said, "Alright, I know I can always produce 250 pages. Let's try another book and in this one improve character, then plot, description, and the fusion of ideas and events."

In two years I went through six books this way. SIU was at that time on a quarter system. A quarter lasts ten weeks. For years I'd been comfortable with organizing my life in ten-week blocks. You start a class in January; you're done by mid-March. I really saw no reason why one couldn't write a novel—three drafts in all—in that time. The second novel was about the "middle passage," but in that version, which I researched while taking a course in African-American history, the white captain tells the tale in his ship's log (therefore, I was never able to get him close enough to the Africans on board to understand them). The second book was about a young black militant's conflict with his family's conservative (to him) values. And the last three novels comprised a trilogy that traced the life of a black musician from childhood until middle age; I'd intended for it to be 1,000 pages, but when I reached 949, Joan—who was having difficulty adjusting to the long hours I put in at the typewriter on our kitchen table—said, "We have to go out today and *do* something!" I agreed with her. I killed off my character on page 950, then we went out to one of Carbondale's better restaurants and had a nice meal.

By the end of the sixth book I was still working part-time on the *Illinoisan*, and preparing in the fall of 1972 for my written examinations for the master's degree in philosophy (I memorized the positions of eighty philosophers from Thales to Sartre). I was also planning a seventh novel, which I knew I wanted to be different from the first six, which were in the style of naturalistic black authors I admired: Richard Wright, James Baldwin, and John A. Williams, and also influenced by black cultural nationalism. From the start, the "philosophical novel" interested me more than any other literary tradition. My personal taste ran toward Sartre, Malraux, Herman Hesse, Thomas Mann, Ralph Ellison, Voltaire, and Herman Melville—the world-class authors who understood instinctively that fiction and philosophy were sister disciplines. Yes, there were the existential stories of Wright, the Freudian adventure of Ellison, and the beautifully transcendental fiction and poetry of Jean Toomer, but beyond these three I found little I was willing to call genuine philosophical black literature. Filling that void was what I decided to devote myself to as a writer; I had no interest in just "publishing books" because as a cartoonist with so much work in print I'd exhausted my interest in just seeing my name on things.

Ⅶ Ⅶ Ⅶ

Nevertheless, I knew that for this new book I needed a good teacher. I'd read John Gardner's perennially magical *Grendel,* so one afternoon when I was skimming the *Illinoisan* and noticed an ad for his course "Professional Writing," I didn't hesitate to phone him and squeeze myself into his class. I attended that class only once. The other writers, I noticed, were all beginners, and I walked into Gardner's home, where the class met, with six book-length manuscripts under my arm. We agreed that I would simply meet him in his office when I had new chapters to show.

To shorten a long story I've told many times in other publications, John was the mentor in fiction I was looking for. He sometimes referred to himself as my "literary father" because for the first few years of our ten-year friendship I accepted his word on literature as law. And why not? No literary novelist I've known has demonstrated Gardner's dedication to the theory and practice of great fiction. He was steeped in Greek, medieval, and contemporary philosophy (unfortunately, his knowledge of the East was slight, and on the subject of Buddhism we argued hotly); a man who knew twelve languages, wrote in seventy-two-hour stretches without sleep and, given the fact that he'd been ignored as a writer for fifteen years, devoted himself to encouraging young writers everywhere. Art for him was—as it was for me—a matter of life and death; beauty was a queen we both longed to serve. With Gardner looking over my shoulder and scolding me whenever I started to go wrong, and after reading eighty books on magic and folklore, I wrote *Faith and the Good Thing* in nine months, which I thought was an incredibly long incubation period for a book. It was Gardner who slowed me down, helped me understand that 90 percent of writing is revision, and that, "Any sentence that can come out *should* come out."

I continued marketing cartoons, selling what would be my last professional drawing to *Players* magazine in 1973. I completed my master's degree with a fifty-page thesis written in a week, entitled, "Wilhelm Reich and the Creation of a Marxist Psychology." Marxism was my passion and political orientation throughout graduate school. It provided a pathway to the style of philosophy I would concentrate on for three years at the State University of New York at Stony Brook: phenomenology. As Joan and I were packing to travel to Long Island, the Gardners were leaving southern Illinois for Vermont. We would see them at different times around the country, and I would write him long, essayist letters on the nature of art until his death in a motorcycle accident in 1982, but we would never again work as closely as in those early SIU days.

By the time *Faith* was published in 1974 I was immersed in studying literary theory, and German and French phenomenology at Stony Brook, teaching a class called "Radical Thought" (everything from Marx's "1844 Manuscripts" through Mao Tse-tung), then courses in "Third World Literature" and "The Black Aesthetic" (the worst course I ever taught). I studied with professors Don Ihde, Homer Goldberg, and Jan Kott, and at night—over a period of four months—went through each word in Webster's 2,129-page *New Twentieth Century Dictionary* to build my own personal lexicon for writing. I trained at an Issinryu karate school, and began wrestling with early drafts of *Oxherding Tale*, the book I sometimes refer to as my "platform novel." The reference is to the Platform Sutra of the Sixth Patriarch, a foundational work of Buddhism. For me, *Oxherding Tale* was to be similarly foundational in that I hoped to lay the groundwork for my future fiction. After teaching, I speed-read every book in Stony Brook's graduate library on slavery, for this was to be a neo-slave narrative for the second half of the twentieth century, a fiction that would explore bondage and freedom not merely in physical and legal terms but also in ways psychological, phenomenological, sexual, and spiritual. I wanted it to be a reply to Hesse's *Siddhartha*, which I loved, and to realize my plans to thematize Eastern thought vis-à-vis the black experience, which I had not successfully done in my first "apprentice" novel.

It was the most ambitious book I had ever undertaken. On Long Island I began generating the first of 2,400 pages I would throw away to realize the 250 pages of the final manuscript. Added to which, and most important of all that year in 1975, Joan gave birth to our son, Malik. His birth was a blessing; fatherhood was a role I'd long wanted to enter into. But we were living on my $4,000 teaching assistantship! I needed a job, badly. And in philosophy during the mid-1970s jobs were becoming scarce. So when the English department at the University of Washington called to ask if I'd apply for an assistant professor position in creative writing (they'd read *Faith*), I said, yes. Before leaving Stony Brook in 1976 I passed my exams and had my dissertation topic approved—a book of phenomenological aesthetics applied to black American literature.

From the moment we arrived in Seattle I felt I'd found the region, the landscape, and the lifestyle I'd been looking for since I left Evanston. I fell to teaching those first few years with a passion for the profession I'm certain I acquired from Gardner; I split my short-story writing classes in half if too many students signed up, and taught the second class for free. Because UW's first classes for me were on the art of the short story, I found myself writing short fiction in the evenings after work—*Oxherding Tale* was still giving me trouble—as well as aesthetic essays on black fiction, articles on Gardner, and book reviews.

Then in the winter of 1977 I wrote my first docudrama for PBS, "Charlie Smith and the Fritter Tree," broadcast as the first program in the last season of the *Visions* series in 1978. The call to script this came from Fred Barzyk at WGBH's New Television Workshop in Boston. After doing a documentary on the life of the oldest living American, Charlie Smith (he died in 1979 at age 137), he needed a black writer capable of comedy set in the slavery era and the Old West, where Smith had been a black cowboy. I wrote the teleplay during the summer of 1977 and by December, we were shooting on location in New Orleans (Smith was sold there at age twelve to a Texas rancher) and little cow-towns in Texas, with actors Glynn Turman and the late Richard Ward playing Smith. This would be the first of many PBS historically based dramas I'd be called on to write in the late seventies and early eighties, among them "Booker," the first show in the *Wonderworks* series—it received both a 1985 Writers Guild Award for best script in the children's show category and an international Prix Jeunesse award. Barzyk and I would continue to do PBS projects over the years. Our most recent effort was "Fathers and Sons," a ten-minute monologue on the plight of young black males performed by John Amos as a segment for *Listen Up!*, broadcast in March 1992.

Back at Washington after the Smith show, the English department gave me early tenure in 1979. I hunkered down to work again on *Oxherding Tale* and finished it in the summer of 1980. Although I had realized all I'd hoped for in this book, New York publishers simply could not understand it. The notion of what a "black" novel was in the early 1980s was very limited indeed. Protest fiction, the overtly "political novel," or all too familiar "up from the ghetto," naturalistic fiction was in vogue and defined a narrow range of acceptable—and commercial—black fiction. My agents, Anne and Georges Borchardt, sent it to over twenty-five publishing houses before John Gallman at Indiana University Press accepted it; to this day, Anne says that selling this difficult book—it appeared in 1982—was one of the triumphs of her career.

Once finished, though, I put that book out of mind. I took my first sabbatical, using the year away from teaching to work as one of two writer-producers for *Up and Coming*, a dramatic series about a black family produced at KQED in San Francisco by Avon Kirkland. (His most recent work is "Simple Justice," broadcast January 18, 1993, on PBS). On that production, which lasted six months, I made one of the best friends of my life, screenwriter Art Washington, who came on as the other writer-producer. (His latest picture is a black boxing drama, "Percy and Thunder," for TNT's prestigious *Writers Cinema* series.)

ඊ ඊ ඊ

And it was in San Francisco that I began to train religiously again in kung-fu. I enrolled in grand master Doc Fai Wong's choy li fut studio, working out after my KQED workday was over; I began lifting weights then too, having lots of free time since Joan and Malik remained in Seattle while I holed up in an efficiency at John Muir Apartments. After more than a decade of avoiding the practice of meditation and making only a scholarly commitment to Buddhism, I fully surrendered to both in San Francisco. That decision came none too soon. While I worked on *Up and Coming*, my mother, who'd gone into Evanston Hospital for an operation, died. On top of that, Joan announced to me long-distance that we were going to have a second child.

Through that period meditation was a rock and refuge. I wrote and read a tribute to my mother at the funeral, explaining to a church packed with her friends and family how she had pointed me on the path to art. This was the only time I have seen my father cry. He is now seventy. He has never remarried. Her absence is something we have felt palpably since 1981, and it has made us closer as father and son.

I returned from the funeral to complete my time at KQED. For two weeks I was simply too gloomy and grief-stricken to do much except meditate, train at Master Wong's studio, and brood. Washington talked me through those days right up through the show's wrap-party in December. I returned to Seattle just three days before Joan gave birth to our daughter, Elizabeth, who is named after my mother.

I shifted my choy li fut training to the recently opened Seattle branch of Master Wong's school, which kept its doors open for four years. When *Oxherding Tale* was published the English department gave me another early promotion, this one to full professor. The next summer, 1983, I began work on *Middle Passage*, reaching back to my second "apprentice" novel with the intention of doing it right this time. Over the years I'd accumulated all the research I needed on slavery. What was missing was knowledge of the sea and its literature. As I wrote the first draft over the next nine months I read everything I could find related to the subject—Homer, *The Voyage of Argo*, the Sinbad stories, all of Melville and Conrad, ships' logs from the nineteenth century, slave narratives composed by Africans who'd come to the New World on those boats, nautical dictionaries, and even one study of Cockney slang in order to individuate the voices of the sailors on board ship.

But the first draft needed more work, according to Anne Borchardt (who is always right). I suggested to her and Georges that while I re-drafted the book they might offer the stories I'd been publishing since 1977 as a collection. They sold the collection, *The Sorcerer's Apprentice*, to Atheneum in 1985. As it went into production, I left Seattle for one semester to accept a visiting distinguished professorship at the University of Delaware and, since I would again be living alone for a few months, commenced work on a new book, a philosophical study, that publisher Gallman was urging me to write.

After the publication of *Oxherding Tale* I gave a reading at Indiana University. Gallman had a dinner for me, one that included some old friends, like writers Scott Sanders and John McCluskey, Jr. During dinner Gallman said that what he *really* wanted to publish was a critical book on black writing since 1970. Would *I* do this? he asked. The thought of such a book made me nervous. I toyed with the food on my plate. An unspoken rule of the book world, I knew, was that a writer shouldn't say what he honestly feels about his contemporaries, as John Gardner discovered when he published *On Moral Fiction* and angered dozens of writers with his judgments of them. But, then again, I had read the bulk of black fiction since the late 1960s. "Tell you what," I said. "If you'll let me write a theoretical opening, a phenomenological overview that I started when I was at work on my dissertation, I'll do the second part as a survey of black writing. I'll provide analysis, titles, and authors for anyone who mightn't have read these works and would be interested in reading black authors other than the two or three black women being promoted right now to the exclusion of everyone else."

Thus was conceived *Being and Race: Black Writing since 1970.* Gallman provided me with the opportunity to resurrect the two drafts I'd written after leaving Stony Brook *and* create something unusual in African-American letters: a phenomenological literary manifesto. I must confess, too, that I used the occasion of this book, which took a year and a half to write (it appeared in 1988), to provide a theoretical extension for the aesthetic position represented by *Oxherding Tale.*

If I had not been completely inundated with work before, after returning to Seattle from Delaware I found myself constantly buried. The French publisher Flammarion flew me to Paris for a week of book promotion when their edition of *Oxherding Tale* appeared in February of 1986. *The Sorcerer's Apprentice* was published that same year and became a runner-up for the 1987 Pen/Faulkner Award (the prize went to my good friend Richard Wiley for *Soldiers in Hiding*). Added to all this, grand master Wong gave me and a longtime friend in the martial arts, Gray Cassidy, permission to resume choy li fut classes in Seattle after the demise of our original school. He named our studio "Twin Tigers." We started classes in my backyard, my carport (in winter), then secured a space at a neighborhood center, where we remain today (we have since renamed the studio "Blue Phoenix Kung-fu").

In 1987 I accepted a three-year appointment as director of the creative writing program at UW. Plus the job of serving as one of the fiction judges for the 1988 National Book Award (our choice was Pete Dexter for *Paris Trout*). It was a hectic period, these last few years of the 1980s. I worked on finishing *Middle Passage*, did interviews after the publication of *Being and Race* (and an essay based on it for *Dialogue*, a publication of the U.S. Information Agency), kept on practicing kung-fu, and made a lecture sweep for the government's Arts America program through Eastern Europe, lecturing on my work and multiculturalism. I was also one of ten writers producing a monthly book review for the *Los Angeles Times*, and now and then for the *New York Times Book Review* and the *Washington Post*.

ᛃᛃ ᛃᛃ ᛃᛃ

Come summertime of 1989 *Middle Passage* was finally completed. While in Evanston visiting my father, I made a trip to my mother's grave and placed fresh flowers there. I remembered how in 1969 I'd visited a fortune-teller in Carbondale at the urging of my roommate, who swore by her—an elderly, white-haired woman named Ella Tweedy. In her home, sitting at her table on which rested a crystal ball, she'd read my palm, and said, "You have a mission. You're protected—and everyone associated with you—until it's done. It involves writing. You'll have two children, be well known for what you do, and have lots of money." At the time she said this I'd laughed. Writing? I was a cartoonist—it was all I ever thought about. But twenty years later, there at Sunset Cemetery where many of my relations were buried, I decided to commune with them for a little while: my Uncle Will, who died at age ninety-seven, my mother, and her parents. I asked their blessing for this third, difficult, philosophical novel I'd produced.

I genuinely believe my ancestors heard this prayer. The following year, as I was winding up my time as director of the creative writing program, Northwestern University courted me heavily with a job offer. My own department counteroffered with an endowed professorship, the first in the history of writing at UW. Since Johnsons have a tendency to be doggedly loyal to whoever has supported them, my family and I decided to remain in Seattle.

Two months later *Middle Passage* was nominated for the National Book Award. Contrary to what some might believe, its appearance on the "short list" did not surprise me, since I had been a judge in 1988 and had some idea of how the nominating process worked for this prize; I felt, in short, that it *had* to be nominated after the reviews the book received. Another factor was this: I felt, as many critics did, that the reading public and academic establishment was again becoming interested in that long-forgotten species, black male writers. During the late 1970s and early 1980s we had been systematically ignored. It was time, I believe many people felt, for black male novelists to be awarded a degree of recognition.

So I came to the award ceremony prepared to win. In my (rented) tuxedo pocket was a tribute to Ralph Ellison, which I told his wife Fanny I intended to read if I won. At our table, sitting with me, was my publisher and friend Lee Goerner; my agents of sixteen years, Georges and

Anne; and critic Stanley Crouch. This was my way of saying thanks for
the insightful *Village Voice* review he'd written for *Oxherding Tale* in
1983, a two-page analysis that led directly to the book's purchase by
Grove Press for a paperback edition. In New York, on that evening
of November 27 in the Plaza Hotel—the fortieth anniversary of the
NBA—the air was full of excitement in a room packed with people
I'd long admired: my first editor, Alan Williams, Russell Banks, Gloria
Naylor, Saul Bellow, fiction judges Catherine Stimpson, William Gass,
and Paul West (who caused an unnecessary stir when he complained
to the newspapers about too much ethnic diversity in the books nomi-
nated), and Terry McMillan; and the other fiction nominees: Joyce
Carol Oates, Jessica Hagedorn, and Elena Castedo.

Strange to say, there was only the slightest suspense for me that
evening. It seemed the ceremony had barely started, and all the nominees had walked to the stage to receive their plaques, when Stimpson
announced, "The winner is *Middle Passage.*" Lee Goerner threw his
napkin straight toward the ceiling. I heard Terry McMillan shout from
across the room. Two chairs away from me, Crouch said, "Charles!" and
gave me one of his winks. But by then I was moving toward the stage,
shaking hands, pulling the tribute from my tuxedo. I asked Stimpson,
"Can I have five minutes?" She had no idea what I was planning to do,
but said, "All right."

For an instant I was tearful and choked up while reciting the names
of people I knew I had to acknowledge—my agents, my publisher, and
John Gardner. Then I settled back into my teacher's mode and read the
Ellison tribute. Later I learned he was pleasurably shocked by this. But
there was no way I could stand before the world after receiving a prize
like the National Book Award, and as only the second black man in
thirty-seven years to be so honored, and simply talk about *myself.* That
would have been a clear violation of Buddhist ethics. The tribute to
Ellison, as I saw it then (and now), was a once-in-a-lifetime opportunity
to celebrate one of the greatest authors of this century, and to remind
the audience that his aesthetic vision in *Invisible Man*, so rich, so original, and inventive, is the standard by which black fiction in the future
must be judged. Like the day of my marriage, the days my children were
born, and that night of my first martial-art promotion, I count the experience of reading that tribute to seventy-six-year-old Ralph Ellison as
one of the finest moments of my life.

It is now three years since that ceremony. For a long time I was busier
than any human being has a right to be—on the road doing book promotion and lectures in America and Asia for fourteen months, sitting
for over one hundred interviews, fielding more requests for writing assignments than I should have been able to handle, turning out television
and motion-picture scripts, and teaching, teaching, teaching. So many
people have asked me, "Has your life changed?" When I reply, "Not

really," they're usually disappointed, though that is the truth. Quantitatively life changed, for my workload increased about tenfold. Qualitatively, though, it is the same life and labor—that of devoting myself to a genuinely philosophical black American fiction—it was two decades before.

Fiction

First Words
Excerpts from the Early Fiction

Man beneath Rags
(1965, age 17)

Evening was growing colder as the white-collar workers scurried home to warm fires and after-dinner pipes. A large pair of eyes, half closed by cataracts, watched them with uncomprehending envy. Calloused hands rubbed vigorously together to fight the chilling night air, as a bent back leaned against a locked doorway. A doorway that is always locked.

Another human shuck in tattered cloth joined him on his doorstep throne. Exchanging names was unnecessary. Two pair of eyes, tired and bored, watched humanity passing. Exhausted minds recalled better days, happier moments, dead ambitions. Thick tongues licked long, drooping lips as a half-empty flask sprang from the remains of a once-proud jacket, and into a hand that welcomed the friendship which the decanter offered. The bottle was passed without a word. They were silent strangers, and in some way also brothers, united in defeat and misery.

A dark figure with a dangling nightstick rounded the corner, and trod silently towards them. Automatically they rose and separated, leaving behind a thousand silent companions. They didn't run. They were still men.

50 Cards 50
(1966, age 17)

Richard stared in awe at the glistening Christmas tree before him. Little silver angels and stars gleamed from each branch as the huge pine illuminated the entire room. There were no presents under the tree, but Richard was, nevertheless, the happiest boy in Harlem.

As he sat arranging a nativity scene, the apartment doorbell chimed, and his mother admitted a portly mulatto woman bearing ribboned packages. Richard ignored them; like most eight-year-old boys, his thoughts were on Santa Claus, the rotund deity who would deliver gifts to children throughout the world. Richard was wondering how Santa would enter their apartment since it lacked a chimney. They certainly couldn't leave the door open—not in *their* neighborhood.

The cheerful "goodbye" and "Merry Christmas" of the mulatto woman aroused Richard from his fantasies. He noticed a tempting package on the sofa across the room. His mother must have bought it from the woman who had just left. After reassuring himself that his mother had returned to her kitchen chores, Richard stole across the room, and gave vent to childish curiosity by unwrapping the box. His nervous fingers lifted the lid and a chocolate Santa Claus grinned foolishly at him, as his sleigh drew him across the narrow width of cardboard. There were fifty such cards in the box, and Richard stared dumbly at them for long minutes.

These were not the jolly men with rosy cheeks and button noses that he had seen on street corners, jangling bells and seeking charity. They were not like the red-suited Santas he had seen inside the shiny pages of the magazines his mother brought home. For some reason, the ebony Santa was meant for him, alone. For some peculiar reason which he could not grasp, he was not supposed to visualize a Santa Clause with bright cheeks and a merry, red nose. Richard suddenly realized that the room was strangely dark, and he no longer cared how Santa entered their apartment.

Rendezvous
(1966, age 18)

Dense smoke curled slowly above the still cylinders of exploding gasses, each a dull, ashen gray, pock-marked with meteors. Both had crashed violently mere yards from one another and hurled their frail occupants, swathed in space-age shrouds, to safety on the yielding, white pumice of the soundless world, the mute moon.

Commander Jarius Langford Dillin, USAF pulls himself slowly, agonizingly toward the remnants of the USSR's finest and most elaborate instrument for piercing the bleak cosmos. He stops at the still figure spread-eagled before him, helplessly drowning in its cumbersome flight helmet and pressure-resistance suit—a woman. The woman, her Ukranian features beaming in undisguised joy, clutches the Commander to her as the two clumsily embrace through their bulky flight uniforms. Their two smashed vehicles finally explode in two silent, blinding blazes of white flame and then vanish moments later from the absence of oxygen.

The two figures, mocking human anatomy in their monstrous uniforms, cast their eyes earthward to await the rescue ships they know will eventually come. The Commander, his eyes now on the woman, quietly whispers into the radio-communicator lodged in his gleaming helmet, "Natasha, I love you, but we simply can't go on meeting like this."

Even though he thought his son's ambition to become a cartoonist impractical, Johnson's father funded two years of correspondence art classes. Johnson went on to publish more than a thousand drawings, including these samples of a high-school comic strip.

Individuality, not collectivity, is vehicle for attaining equality
(1968, age 20)

To the *Daily Egyptian:*

Much ado about race is made with justification these days, and virtually everyone agrees that the desirable end of all civil rights endeavors should be universal equality. The means for attaining this goal is undoubtedly where our conflict arises. Sprouting up everywhere are a myriad of self-appointed groups, black and white, who assume their union of forces will somehow alleviate the current race crisis.

If equality and eventual brotherhood are the goals in sight, the vehicle for attaining this goal must lie within the individual, not in collective forces. The individual must undergo the grueling chore of recognizing himself as a unique entity and define his own goals, strengths and weaknesses.

Having done so, he will be in a position to appreciate and respect others who have done the same, and perhaps be eager to help those who still struggle with their existence.

The progress of race relations must take place in the enlightenment of the individuals that compose our society, not in the groups who sacrifice the individual for a collective intelligence.

More from *Oxherding Tale*

After digging through an old box of drafts for my second novel, Oxherding
Tale *(Indiana University Press, 1982), I came up with a scene I dropped
from the end of Chapter 3.* —C. J.

From Chapter Three

And when at last the hour of Flo Hatfield's party came, I descended
the uncarpeted stairs slowly, like Daniel tipping into the lion's den,
wearing a pair of striped duck pantaloons and a black jacket, stepping
into a haze of tobacco patchouli incense and opium so thick I could
taste as well as smell these powerful odors as I paused outside the parlor,
my knees banging together, carrying the book of philosophy (Aurelius)
I'd been reading earlier to steady myself—I was always thinking meta-
physically at the moment Reality reared back to swat me into stranger
waters. All Flo Hatfield's guests were actors or musicians who brought
their instruments, or poets who had to be seen to be believed. One
swanlike gentleman, a book reviewer who resembled woodcuts I'd seen
of the Devil, with a tightly drawn mouth and conical nose between his
spectacles—this dry fellow nodded sideways at one of Flo's still lifes and
told his neighbor, "It's beautiful, all that balance and clarity, but it's obviously an illusion, a *lie*, because we find nowhere in Nature anything
that unambiguous," then he slipped into schoolroom French, rolling his
*r*s softly, for the benefit of a few brittle scholars. Two playwrights at a

tulipwood table drained off Boilermakers in a gin duel. By a window, a group of actresses—they called themselves actresses, at least, and all drank Bloody Marys—were composing verses for a poem, very pornographic, each contributing a line. And Flo?

She entered the room provocatively, sashaying a little, the fingers of her left hand on her hip. Yet what baffled me most that evening were the elegant gentlemen, the powdered women who worshiped beauty and achieved only the grotesque, who were witty because they could not be candid, who in the parlor's glimmering green-gold lamplights—in this claustrophobic gourd of old dry smoke—favored mechanical dolls pieced together from paste and bailing wire, puppets turned loose, as in an E. T. A. Hoffmann tale, where the marionettes murder their creator. *Dead*, Reb's voice whispered through my memory, *All dead, Freshmeat.*

A Pink Lady took two sandwiches from my salver, and said to a Cup of Bitters, "You know, the last time Arthur and I made love, he wouldn't give me back my *clothes*, not a stitch. He made me chase him into town, into a saloon before he gave them back to me," and Cup of Bitters, one hand on her throat, confessed, "Well, Richard, the ass, used to *wear* my underthings. You don't blame me for leaving him, do you?" Sweat began to stream inside my clothes. My throat tightened. Flo Hatfield's necklace. Too snug. But I didn't dare remove it, for as my employer she had me by the short hairs. All that evening her eyes ranged over me. She lifted her head and laughed like a young, young girl. I felt a kind of torpor, a languor or marshiness like sleepiness in my limbs; I was aware of her eyes grabbing at me, an object in the midst of other objects, her look a beacon or ray that realized something corrosive in me, as if it was not I who made a meaning for myself—as I swore to do that night in Jonathan's house—but rather the meaning was already there, preceding me, waiting like a murderer at a boardwalk's end. As if, to speak plainly, all my possibilities had shifted to the skin's seen surface. The thickness of the world's texture thinned. The room was, in a single stroke, epidermalized. In this state, transfigured, my fingers were so stiff and fumblesome, without feeling, that I spilled my tray on a Tom Collins, who swore like a blacksmith and started to strike me. Apologizing, I began mopping up the mess, and cursed Master Polkinghorne for sending me here.

A few men, wearing the black silk cravats then fashionable (they all spent, I suspected, a small fortune on clothing) argued politics, and with their wives and mistresses, who seemed so comfortable in the World Cave, nibbled at the eggbread and grilled fowl Zilphey brought from the kitchen. "You find," remarked one Lemon Cooler, an art patron in barbaric jewelry, to a very confused Hot Buttered Rum with a lump of food stuck to the seat of his trousers, "so few people who truly know *how* to eat. Most are pigs. They dump anything down their esophagus. Like," she lowered her voice, "this guacamole. Now, in Nice, they prepare food lovingly, as if Christ Himself were coming to dinner." Help-lessly, Hot Buttered Rum asked, "Who? The *pigs?*"

Two feet away, Cup of Bitters told Pink Lady, "The *only* punishment equal to the crime of rape is prefrontal lobotomy. I've researched the subject of rape thoroughly. Would you care to hear my conclusions?" Pink Lady said she was dying to hear this but preferred to wait until Cup of Bitters sold it as an exclusive interview to the *Abbeyville Register.* I placed my empty tray on a long table of wine and sweetmeats, gulping for air, my back to Flo Hatfield and a pale, wounded-looking Whiskey Neat—a frail, teacup-passing fellow—whose head was tipped toward Flo as she sat before the fireplace, feeding it letters from her husbands to help it burn. "Boy," he said to me in a voice just short of demand, "Please freshen this glass for me." For an instant I was distracted by a Brandy Alexander who told Two Fingers of Rye, "These colored bruise so easily! It so chanced that yesterday a boy asked me if I knew where City Hall was, and—" Whiskey Neat pushed his glass into my hand. "Can you hear?" I did hear him, but could not speak because this little pismire regarded me with such disdain, and because, for all my self-control, my body reacted to this slight. Whiskey Neat waited for me to speak. He waited, in fact, for me to stammer, slur my words, brutalize the language as a signal of my Negroness, a sign that we in our bodies were not the same. My motions seemed to be slowing down. "Can this boy speak?" he asked Flo, and I whispered a *Yes* lost in the blitz of laugh-ter, chatter, and the big, hectoring voice of a Rum Grog whose argument for the necessity of Negro slavery drew from the most recent scientific studies, the Old Testament, from history, and the subordination of one creature by another in the natural world. Beneath his voice, one of the Bloody Marys whined, "Every theater director I've met already knows someone who looks *exactly* like me, it's like *everyone* is so anonymous these days." Dizzily, I made my way toward the door, frowning and fight-ing to stay polite, over the Boilermakers, both heaped on the floor after consuming forty-eight ounces of straight gin in fifteen minutes. But now I could not perform the simplest act, such as pouring water, without causing catastrophe all around me.

"So," roared Brandy Alexander, "this colored boy looking for City Hall nearly fainted, and I couldn't figure out why. All I said was, 'You're a block past it,' and *he* thought I said, 'You're a black bastid.' Why," he asked me, "are Negroes so sensitive?" I closed my eyes, counting twenty. "To speak frankly, sit, I have no idea. I don't know many of them."

The entrance was blocked by a Rum Grog, a fat man wiping con-densation off his glass with his handkerchief, puffing at a Tequila Sun-set. Rags of smoke hung in air hot and rubbery. Wind outside changed pressure inside the room. Suddenly, I could not breathe. Rum Grog would not let me pass. "This country, in my view, runs on economic fact," he was saying, "not goodwill. We brought these people here as one essential ingredient in an agrarian society. Their purpose as a group, and every group has its teleology, or sense, is tied in the Negro's case to a specific form of production. . . . " Rum Grog inflated his lungs. "*If* the Abolitionists have their way, and if the North, then South, move to manufacture and no longer *need* the Negro, what then? Of course, we shall always need him poetically, but they will be, as a people, without a national purpose, if you follow me. It will be centuries before the nation discovers what to *do* with them. Can we ship them all back to Africa, eh? Answer me that. Be careful now." Before his neighbor could answer, he hemmed, "Not on your life. For I put it to you, is it reasonable to suppose that they are any more suited for a life in Africa than they are for full participation in an America that no longer needs slave labor? They are *here*, but not truly here. Do you see the dilemma?" His neighbor did not, so he turned toward me, and asked, "Do *you* see the problem?"

Pulling free, I stumbled, tipping over a table of pastries, then struck out from this morgue, the party roaring on behind me when I came crashing through Zilphey's kitchen, then lumbered, full of rage, my thoughts tangled like twine, onto a back porch that bellied out, low, into the yard. . . .

Kwoon

David Lewis' martial-arts *kwoon* was in a South Side Chicago neighborhood so rough he nearly had to fight to reach the door. Previously, it had been a dry cleaner's, then a small Thai restaurant, and although he Lysol-scrubbed the buckled linoleum floors and burned jade incense for the Buddha before each class, the studio was a blend of pungent odors, the smell of starched shirts and the tang of cinnamon pastries riding alongside the sharp smell of male sweat from nightly workouts. For five months, David had bivouacked on the back-room floor after his students left, not minding the clank of presses from the print shop next door, the noisy garage across the street or even the two-grand bank loan needed to renovate three rooms with low ceilings and leaky pipes overhead. This was his place, earned after ten years of training in San Francisco and his promotion to the hard-won title of *sifu*.

As his customers grunted through Tuesday-night warm-up exercises, then drills with Elizabeth, his senior student (she'd been a dancer and still had the elasticity of Gumby), David stood off to one side to watch, feeling the force of their *kiais* vibrate in the cavity of his chest, interrupting them only to correct a student's stance. On the whole, his students were a hopeless bunch, a Franciscan test of his patience. Some came to class on drugs; one, Wendell Miller, a retired cook trying to recapture his youth, was the obligatory senior citizen; a few were high school dropouts, orange-haired punks who played in rock bands with names like Plastic Anus. But David did not despair. He believed he was duty bound to lead them, like the Pied Piper, from Sylvester Stallone movies to a real understanding of the martial arts as a way that prepared the young, through discipline and large doses of humility, to be of use to themselves and others. Accordingly, his sheet of rules said no high school student could be promoted unless he kept a B average, and no dropouts were allowed through the door until they signed up for their G.E.D. exam; if they got straight A's, he took them to dinner. Anyone caught fighting outside his school was suspended. David had been something of a punk himself a decade earlier, pushing nose candy in Palo Alto, living on barbiturates and beer before his own teacher helped him see, to David's surprise, that in his spirit he had resources greater than anything in the world outside. The master's picture was just inside the door, so all could bow to him when they entered David's school. Spreading the style was his rationale for moving to the Midwest, but the hidden agenda, David believed, was an inward training that would make the need for conflict fall away like a chrysalis. If nothing else, he could make their workouts so tiring none of his students would have any energy left for getting into trouble.

Except, he thought, for Ed Morgan.

He was an older man, maybe 40, with a bald spot and razor burns that ran from just below his ears to his throat. This was his second night at the studio, but David realized Morgan knew the calisthenics routine and basic punching drills cold. He'd been in other schools. Any fool could see that, which meant the new student had lied on his application about having no formal training. Unlike David's regular students, who wore the traditional white Chinese T-shirt and black trousers, Morgan had changed into a butternut running suit with black stripes on the sleeves and pants legs. David had told him to buy a uniform the week before, during his brief interview. Morgan refused. And David dropped the matter, noticing that Morgan had pecs and forearms like Popeye. His triceps could have been lifted right off Marvin Hagler. He was thick as a tree, even top-heavy, in David's opinion, and he stood half a head taller than the other students. He didn't *have* a suit to fit Morgan. And Morgan moved so fluidly David caught himself frowning, a little frightened, for it was as though the properties of water and rock had come together in one creature. Then he snapped himself back, laughed at his silliness, looked at the clock—only half an hour of class remained—then clapped his hands loudly. He popped his fingers on his left hand, then his right, as his students, eager for his advice, turned to face him.

"We should do a little sparring now. Pair up with somebody your size. Elizabeth, you work with the new students."

"*Sifu?*"

It was Ed Morgan.

David paused, both lips pressed together.

"If you don't mind, I'd like to spar with you."

One of David's younger students, Toughie, a Filipino boy with a falcon emblazoned on his arm, elbowed his partner, who wore his hair in a stiff Mohawk, and both said, "Uh-oh." David felt his body flush hot, sweat suddenly on his palms like a sprinkling of salt water, though there was no whiff of a challenge, no disrespect in Morgan's voice. His speech, in fact, was as soft and gently syllabled as a singer's. David tried to laugh:

"You sure you want to try me?"

"Please." Morgan bowed his head, which might have seemed self-effacing had he not been so tall and still looking down at David's crown. "It would be a privilege."

Rather than spar, his students scrambled back, nearly falling over themselves to form a circle, as if to ring two gun fighters from opposite ends of town. David kept the slightest of smiles on his lips, even when his mouth tired, to give the impression of masterful indifference—he was, after all, *sifu* here, wasn't he? A little sparring would do him good. Wouldn't it? Especially with a man the size of Morgan. Loosen him up, so to speak.

He flipped his red sash behind him and stepped lower into a cat stance, his weight on his rear leg, his lead foot light and lifted slightly, ready to whip forward when Morgan moved into range.

Morgan was not so obliging. He circled left, away from David's lead leg, then did a half step of broken rhythm to confuse David's sense of distance, and then, before he could change stances, flicked a jab at David's jaw. If his students were surprised, David didn't know, for the room fell away instantly, dissolving as his adrenaline rose and his concentration closed out everything but Morgan—he always needed to get hit once before he got serious—and only he and the other existed, both in motion but pulled out of time, the moment flickerish, fibrous and strangely two-dimensional, yet all too familiar to fighters, perhaps to men falling from heights, to motorists microseconds before a head-on collision, these minutes a spinning mosaic of crescent kicks, back fists and flurry punches that, on David's side, failed. All his techniques fell short of Morgan, who, like a shadow—or Mephistopheles—simply dematerialized before they arrived.

The older man shifted from boxing to *wu*-style *ta'i chi Chuan*. From this he flowed into *pa kua*, then Korean karate: style after style, a blending of a dozen cultures and histories in one blink of an eye after another. With one move, he tore away David's sash. Then he called out each move in Mandarin as he dropped it on David, bomb after bomb, as if this were only an exhibition exercise.

On David's face, blossoms of blood opened like orchids. He knew he was being hurt; two ribs felt broken, but he wasn't sure. He thanked God for endorphins—a body's natural pain-killer. He'd not touched Morgan once. Outclassed as he was, all he could do was ward him off, stay out of his way—then not even that when a fist the size of a cantaloupe crashed straight down, driving David to the floor, his ears ringing then, and legs outstretched like a doll's. He wanted to stay down forever but sprang to his feet, sweat stinging his eyes, to salvage one scrap of dignity. He found himself facing the wrong way. Morgan was behind him, his hands on his hips, his head thrown back. Two of David's students laughed.

It was Elizabeth who pressed her sweat-moistened towel under David's bloody nose. Morgan's feet came together. He wasn't even winded. "Thank you, *Sifu*." Mockery, David thought, but his head banged too badly to be sure. The room was still behind heat waves, though sounds were coming back, and now he could distinguish one student from another. His sense of clock time returned. He said, "You're a good fighter, Ed."

Toughie whispered, "No shit, *bwana*."

The room suddenly leaned vertiginously to David's left; he bent his knees a little to steady his balance. "But you're still a beginner in this system." Weakly, he lifted his hand, then let it fall. "Go on with class. Elizabeth, give everybody a new lesson."

"David, I think class is over now."

Over? He thought he knew what that meant. "I guess so. Bow to the master."

His students bowed to the portrait of the school's founder.

"Now to each other."

Again, they bowed, but this time to Morgan.

"Class dismissed."

Some of his students were whooping, slapping Morgan on his back as they made their way to the hallway in back to change. Elizabeth, the only female, stayed behind to let them shower and dress. Both she and the youngest student, Mark, a middle school boy with skin as smooth and pale as a girl's, looked bewildered, uncertain what this drubbing meant.

David limped back to his office, which also was his bedroom, separated from the main room only by a curtain. There, he kept equipment: free weights, a heavy bag on which he'd taped a snapshot of himself—for who else did he need to conquer?—and the rowing machine Elizabeth avoided, calling it Instant Abortion. He sat down for a few seconds at his unvarnished kneehole desk bought cheap at a Salvation Army outlet, then rolled onto the floor, wondering what he'd done wrong. Would another *sifu*, more seasoned, simply have refused to spar with a self-styled beginner?

After a few minutes, he heard them leaving, a couple of students begging Morgan to teach them, and really, this was too much to bear. David, holding his side, his head pulled in, limped back out. "Ed," he coughed, then recovered. "Can I talk to you?"

Morgan checked his watch, a diamond-studded thing that doubled as a stop watch and a thermometer, and probably even monitored his pulse. Half its cost would pay the studio's rent for a year. He dressed well, David saw. Like a retired champion, everything tailored, nothing off the rack. "I've got an appointment, *Sifu*. Maybe later, OK?"

A little dazed, David, swallowing the rest of what he wanted to say, gave a headshake. "OK."

Just before the door slammed, he heard another boy say, "Lewis ain't no fighter, man. He's a dancer." He lay down again in his office, too sore to shower, every muscle tender, strung tight as catgut, searching with the tip of his tongue for broken teeth.

As he was stuffing toilet paper into his right nostril to stop the bleeding, Elizabeth, dressed now in high boots and a baggy coat and slacks, stepped behind the curtain. She'd replaced her contacts with owl-frame glasses that made her look spinsterish. "I'm sorry—he was wrong to do that."

"You mean win?"

"It wasn't supposed to be a real fight! He tricked you. Anyone can score, like he did, if they throw out all the rules."

"Tell him that." Wincing, he rubbed his shoulder. "Do you think anybody will come back on Thursday?" She did not answer. "Do you think I should close the school?" David laughed, bleakly. "Or just leave town?"

"David, you're a good teacher. A *sifu* doesn't always have to win, does he? It's not about winning, is it?"

No sooner had she said this than the answer rose between them. Could you be a doctor whose every patient died? A credible mathematician who couldn't count? By the way the world and, more important, his students reckoned things, he was a fraud. Elizabeth hitched the strap on her workout bag, which was big enough for both of them to climb into, higher on her shoulder. "Do you want me to stick around?"

"No."

"You going to put something on that eye?"

Through the eye Morgan hadn't closed, she looked flattened, like a coin, her skin flushed and her hair faintly damp after a workout, so lovely David wanted to fall against her, blend with her—disappear. Only, it would hurt now to touch or be touched. And, unlike some teachers he knew, his policy was to take whatever he felt for a student—the erotic electricity that sometimes arose—and transform it into harder teaching, more time spent on giving them their money's worth. Besides, he was always broke; his street clothes were old enough to be in elementary school: a 30-year-old man no better educated than Toughie or Mark, who'd concentrated on shop in high school. Elizabeth was another story: a working mother, a secretary on the staff at the University of Illinois at Chicago, surrounded all day by professors who looked young enough to be graduate students. A job sweet as this, from David's level, seemed high-toned and secure. What could he offer Elizabeth? Anyway, this might be the last night he saw her, if she left with the others, and who could blame her? He studied her hair, how it fell onyx-

black and abundant, like some kind of blessing over and under her col-
lar, which forced Elizabeth into the unconscious habit of tilting her
head just so and flicking it back with her fingers, a gesture of such
natural grace it made his chest ache. She was so much lovelier than
she knew. To his surprise, a line from *Psalms* came to him, "I will praise
thee, for I am fearfully and wonderfully made." Whoever wrote that, he
thought, meant it for her.

He looked away. "Go on home."

"We're having class on Thursday?"

"You paid until the end of the month, didn't you?"

"I paid for six months, remember?"

He did—she was literally the one who kept the light bill paid. "Then
we'll have class."

All that night and half the next day David stayed horizontal, hating
Morgan. Hating himself more. It took him hours to stop shaking. That
night it rained. He fended off sleep, listening to the patter with his full
attention, hoping its music might have something to tell him. Twice he
belched up blood, then a paste of phlegm and hamburger pulp. Jesus,
he thought, distantly, I'm sick. By nightfall, he was able to sit awhile
and take a little soup, but he could not stand. Both his legs ballooned
so tightly in his trousers he had to cut the cloth with scissors and peel
it off like strips of bacon. Parts of his body were burning, refusing to
obey him. He reached into his desk drawer for Morgan's application
and saw straightaway that Ed Morgan couldn't spell. David smiled rue-
fully, looking for more faults. Morgan listed his address in Skokie, his
occupation as a merchant marine, and provided no next of kin to call
in case of emergencies.

That was all, and David for the life of him could not see that night,
or the following morning, how he could face anyone in the studio again.
Painfully, he remembered his promotion a year earlier. His teacher had
held a ceremonial Buddhist candle, the only light in his darkened living
room in a house near the Mission District barely bigger than a shed.
David, kneeling, held a candle, too. "The light that was given to me,"
said his teacher, repeating an invocation two centuries old, "I now give
to you." He touched his flame to the wick of David's candle, passing the
light, and David's eyes burned with tears. For the first time in his life,
he felt connected to cultures and people he'd never seen—to traditions
larger than himself.

His high school instructors had dismissed him as unteachable. Were
they right? David wondered. Was he made of wood too flimsy ever to
amount to anything? Suddenly, he hated those teachers, as well as the
ones at Elizabeth's school, but only for a time, hatred being so sharp
an emotion, like the business end of a bali-song knife, he could never
hang on to it for long—perhaps that was why he failed as a fighter—
and soon he felt nothing, only numbness. As from a great distance, he
watched himself sponge-bathe in the sink, dress himself slowly and

prepare for Thursday's class, the actions previously fueled by desire, by concern over consequences, by fear of outcome, replaced now by something he could not properly name, as if a costly operation once powered by coal had reverted overnight to the water wheel.

When six o'clock came and only Mark, Wendell and Elizabeth showed, David telephoned a few students, learning from parents, roommates and live-in lovers that none were home. With Morgan, he suspected. So that's who he called next.

"Sure," said Morgan. "A couple are here. They just wanted to talk."

"They're missing class."

"I didn't ask them to come."

Quietly, David drew breath deeply just to see if he could. It hurt, so he stopped, letting his wind stay shallow, swirling at the top of his lungs. He pulled a piece of dead skin off his hand. "Are you coming back?"

"I don't see much point in that, do you?"

In the background he could hear voices, a television and beer cans being opened. "You've fought professionally, haven't you?"

"That was a long time ago—overseas. Won two, lost two, then I quit," said Morgan. "It doesn't count for much."

"Did you teach?"

"Here and there. Listen," he said, "why did you call?"

"Why did you en*roll?*"

"I've been out of training. I wanted to see how much I remembered. What do you want me to say? I won't come back, all right? What do you want from me, Lewis?"

He did not know. He felt the stillness of his studio, a similar stillness in himself, and sat quiet so long he could have been posing for a portrait. Then:

"You paid for a week in advance. I owe you another lesson."

Morgan snorted. "In what—Chinese ballet?"

"Fighting," said David. "A private lesson in *budo*. I'll keep the studio open until you get here." And then he hung up.

ﾂ ﾂ ﾂ

Morgan circled the block four times before finding a parking space across from Lewis' school. Why hurry? Ten, maybe 15 minutes he waited, watching the open door, wondering what the boy (and he was a boy to Morgan's eye) wanted. He'd known too many kids like this one. They took a few classes, promoted themselves to seventh *dan*, then opened a storefront *dojo* that was no better than a private stage, a theater for the ego, a place where they could play out fantasies of success denied them on the street, in school, in dead-end jobs. They were phony, Morgan thought, like almost everything in the modern world, which was a subject he could spend hours deriding, though he seldom did, his complaints now being tiresome even to his own ears. *Losers,* he thought, who strutted around in fancy Oriental costumes, refusing to spar or show their skill. "Too advanced for beginners," they claimed, or, "My *sensei* made me promise not to show that to anyone." Hogwash. He could see through that shit. All over America he'd seen them, and India, too, where they weren't called fakirs for nothing. And they'd made him suffer. They made him pay for the "privilege" of their teachings. In 20 years as a merchant marine, he'd been in as many schools in Europe, Japan, Korea and Hong Kong, submitting himself to the lunacy of illiterate fak(e)irs—men who claimed they could slay an opponent with their breath or *ch'i*—and simply because his hunger to learn was insatiable. So he had no rank anywhere. He could tolerate no "master's" posturing long enough to ingratiate himself into the inner circles of any school—though 80 percent of these fly-by-night *dojos* bottomed out inside a year. And, hell, he was a bilge rat, never in any port long enough to move up in rank. Still, he had killed men. It was depressingly easy. Killed them in back alleys in Tokyo with blows so crude no master would include such inelegant means among "traditional" techniques.

More hogwash, thought Morgan. He'd probably done the boy good by exposing him. His own collarbones had been broken twice, each leg three times, all but two fingers smashed, and his nose reshaped so often he couldn't remember its original contours. On wet nights, he had trouble breathing. But why complain? You couldn't make an omelet without breaking a few eggs.

And yet, Morgan thought, squinting at the door of the school, there was a side to Lewis he'd liked. At first, he had felt comfortable, as if he had at last found the *kwoon* he'd been looking for. True, Lewis had come on way too cocky when asked to spar, but what could you expect when he was hardly older than the high school kids he was teaching? And maybe teaching them well, if he was really going by that list of rules he handed out to beginners. And it wasn't so much that Lewis was a bad fighter, only that he, Morgan, was about five times better because whatever he lacked now in middle age—flexibility and youth's fast reflexes—he more than made up for in size and experience, which was a polite word for dirty tricks. Give Lewis a few more years, a little more coaching in the combat strategies Morgan could show him, and he might become a champion.

But who did he think he was fooling? Things never worked out that way. There was always too much ego in it. Something every *sifu* figured he had to protect, or save face about. A lesson in *budo?* Christ, he'd nearly killed this kid, and there he was, barking on the telephone like Saddam Hussein before the bombing started, even begging for the ground war to begin. And that was just all right, if a showdown—a duel—was what he wanted. Morgan set his jaw and stepped onto the pavement of the parking lot. However things went down, he decided, the consequences would be on Lewis—it would be *his* call.

Locking his car, then double-checking each door (this was a rough neighborhood, even by Morgan's standards), he crossed the street, carrying his workout bag under his arm, the last threads of smog-filtered twilight fading into darkness, making the door of the *kwoon* a bright portal chiseled from blocks of glass and cement. A few feet from the entrance, he heard voices. Three students had shown. Most of the class had not. The two who had visited him weren't there. He'd lectured them on his experience of strangling an assailant in Kyoto, and Toughie had gone quiet, looked edgy (fighting didn't seem like fun then) and uneasy. Finally, they left, which was fine with Morgan. He didn't want followers. Sycophants made him sick. All he wanted was a teacher he could respect.

Inside the school's foyer, he stopped, his eyes tracking the room. He never entered closed spaces too quickly or walked near corners or doorways on the street. Toward the rear, by a rack filled with halberds and single-edged broadswords, a girl about five, with piles of ebony hair and blue eyes like splinters of the sky, was reading a dog-eared copy of *The Cat in the Hat*. This would be the child of the class leader, he thought, bowing quickly at the portrait of the school's founder. But why bring her here? It cemented his contempt for this place, more a daycare center than a *kwoon*. Still, he bowed a second time to the founder. Him he respected. Where were such grand old stylists when you needed them? He did not see Lewis, or any other student until, passing the curtained office, Morgan whiffed food cooking on a hot plate and, parting the curtain slightly, he saw Wendell, who would never in this life learn to fight, stirring and seasoning a pot of couscous. He looked like that children's toy, Mr. Potato Head. Morgan wondered, Why did David Lewis encourage the man? Just to take his money? He passed on, feeling his tread shake the floor, into the narrow hall where a few hooks hung for clothing, and found Elizabeth with her left foot on a low bench, lacing the wrestling shoes she wore for working out.

"Excuse me," he said. "I'll wait until you're finished."

Their eyes caught for a moment.

"I'm done now." She kicked her bag under the bench, squeezed past Morgan by flattening herself to the wall, as if he had a disease, then spun round at the entrance and looked squarely at him. "You know something?"

"What?"

"You're wrong. Just *wrong*."

"I don't know what you're talking about."

"The hell you don't! David may not be the fighter, the killer, you are, but he *is* one of the best teachers in this system."

Morgan smirked. "Those who can't do, teach, eh?"

She burned a look of such hatred at Morgan he turned his eyes away. When he looked back, she was gone. He sighed. He'd seen that look on so many faces, yellow, black and white, after he'd punched them in. It hardly mattered anymore. Quietly, he suited up, stretched his arms wide and padded barefoot back onto the main floor, prepared to finish this, if that was what Lewis wanted, for why else would he call?

But at first he could not catch sight of the boy. The others were standing around him in a circle, chatting, oddly like chess pieces shielding an endangered king. His movements were jerky and Chaplinesque, one arm around Elizabeth, the other braced on Wendell's shoulder. Without them, he could not walk until his bruised ankles healed. He was temporarily blind in one blackened, beefed-over eye. And since he could not tie his own sash, Mark was doing it for him. None of them noticed Morgan, but in the school's weak light, he could see blue welts he'd raised like crops on Lewis' cheeks and chest. That, and something else. The hands of the others rested on Lewis' shoulder, his back, as if he belonged to them, no matter what he did or didn't do. Weak as Lewis looked now, even the old cook Wendell could blow him over, and somehow it didn't matter if he was beaten every round, or missed class, or died. The others were the *kwoon*. It wasn't his school. It was theirs. Maybe brought together by the boy, Morgan thought, but now a separate thing living beyond him. To prove the system, the teaching here, false, he would have to strike down every one of them. And still he would have touched nothing.

"Ed," Lewis said, looking over Mark's shoulder. "When we were sparring, I saw mistakes in your form, things someone better than me might take advantage of. I'd like to correct them, if you're ready."

"What things?" His head snapped back. "What mistakes?"

"I can't match your reach," said Lewis, "but someone who could, getting inside your guard, would go for your groin or knee. It's the way you stand, probably a blend of a couple of styles you learned somewhere. But they don't work together. If you do this," he added, torquing his leg slightly so that his thigh guarded his groin, "the problem is solved."

"Is that why you called me?"

"No, there's another reason."

Morgan tensed; he should have known. "You do some warm-up exercises we've never seen. I like them. I want you to lead class tonight, if that's OK, so the others can learn them, too." Then he laughed. "I think I should warm the bench tonight."

Before he could reply, Lewis limped off, leaning on Mark, who led him back to his office. The two others waited for direction from Morgan. For a moment, he shifted his weight uncertainly from his right foot to his left, pausing until his tensed shoulders relaxed and the tight fingers on his right hand, coiled into a fist, opened. Then he pivoted toward the portrait of the founder. "Bow to the master." They bowed. "Now to our teacher." They did so, bowing toward the curtained room, with Morgan, a big man, bending deepest of all.

The Writer's Notebook

A Note on Working Methods

I started keeping a diary when I was about 12; my mother suggested the idea. In college the diary transformed into a journal in which I wrote poetry, brief essays to myself, and (as with a diary) tried to make sense of daily events. When I started writing fiction, the journal moved more in the direction of being a writing tool. I use cheap, spiral notebooks. Into them go notes on everything I experience; I jot down images, phrases used by my friends, fragments of thoughts . . . (I now keep an entirely separate journal for recording personal matters.) These writing notebooks sit on my desk 15-inches deep, along with notebooks I kept from college classes (I save everything, it's shameless) . . .

When I write, I sit down and let a first draft flow out for as long as inspiration stays with me. I let that first draft be chaotic, if need be: a rush of everything I can feel, imagine, or dredge up. Then I go over it and weed out the junk. Somewhere around the third draft, I begin going through my notebooks hunting for thoughts, images I've had, or ideas about characters (usually observations I make of people around me). Although it takes at least six hours to go back through all these notebooks, I can count on finding some sentence, phrase, or idea I had, say, 20 years ago that is currently useful. I don't carry any of the journals with me—I can't afford to lose them. Instead, I jot notes on whatever is available—hotel stationery, the margins of an old newspaper—and slip it into the notebooks when I get back home.

Characters

Crew of Republic

Rutherford Calhoun
Capt. Ebenezer Falcon +
Peter Cringle, Mate
Josiah Squibb, Cook
Tommy., cabin-boy
Rev. Meadows
Matthew McIntosh, boatswain. +
Lighthands (boys) +
Ngonyama

~~Extras~~
Squibb's parrot
Unga-golahit

New Orleans

Isadora Bailey
Madame Toulouse
Papa Zeringue
Santos

Makanda, Ill.

Jackson Calhoun
Peleg Chandler

Bangalang

Owen Bogha
Ahman-de-bellah

Aquarius

El
The King

Number of locations = 5
Total characters (named) = 19
Number of major characters = 10
   + = died during mutiny.

<u>Chapter Outline</u>

Chap. One ——— The bargain.

Chap. Two ——— Calhan meets Capt. Falcon and learns that Zernihsk has financed this voyage. He learns life at sea, the hardware and hardship, and the crew. He tells story of his brother.

Chap. Three ——— All musera slave are taken on board. The revolt. Calhan is captain by default.

Chap. Four ——— The wandering. He learns of Allmusera culture. Supplies sd low. Slaves die of disease. The ghost ship is following them. They sight land.

Chap. Five ——— Journey to the Dystopia. } A world without black.

Chap. Six ——— Escape from the Dystopia. }

Chap. Seven ——— Back at sea, wandering sh space and time.

Chap. Eight ——— Journey to Dystopia } A world without whites. A few of the Allmusera stay here.

Chap. Nine ——— At sea again, storms and violent weather, etc.

Chap. Ten ——— Rutherford boards the Ghost ship. Sees Capt Falcon and the dead crew and himself. The magical ship returns him to New Orleans.

Character Note :

Tommy is a Dickensian type orphan. His father died of drink when he was a year old, his mother went insane when he was eight. To avoid the orphanage in New Orleans, he went to sea. Rutherford (and Isadora) will take the ship's boy in —— Rutherford is thinking of returning to Makanda, farming, with his new family.

Chapter #8
As R. lies sick, thinking of his decision to marry Isadora (chap #7), he now has the motivation to ask Meadows why he killed his family. R. is afraid of the responsibility. He wonders if he's up to the requisites Meadows paints for a householder.

Character Note: Tommy is a Dickensian type orphan. His father died of drink when he was a year old, his mother went insane when he was eight. To avoid the orphanage in New Orleans, he went to sea. Rutherford (and Isadora) will take the ship's boy in—Rutherford is thinking of returning to Makanda, farming, with his new family.

Chapter #8 As R. lies sick, thinking of his decision to marry Isadora (Chap #7), he now has the motivation to ask Meadows why he killed his family. R. is afraid of the responsibility. He wonders if he's up to the requisites Meadows paints for a householder.

Note for Sea Story, Chap. One
Isadora explains her virtues to Rutherford, as the old woman in the Chaucer tale does—a
monologue on beauty. Once done, she asks him, "Well, what do you have to say?"
I was scared to death.

Sheraton-Palace Hotel

Falcon—

Eating for him was a
Task. He fell to it with a
silent, single-minded
determination, seldom
looking up from the table,
shoveling it down with
efficient, steady fork lifts
that favored a man bailing-hay.
In fifteen minutes he was done
and sprang up from the table,
Throwing down his wadded up

(over)

SAN FRANCISCO, CALIFORNIA
415/392-8600

Napkin, and was off to
see to some shipboard
chore.

Falcon—

Eating for him was a task. He fell to it with a silent, single-minded determination, seldom
looking up from the table, shoveling it down with efficient, steady fork lifts that favored a man
bailing hay. In fifteen minutes he was done and sprang up from the table, throwing down his
wadded up (over)
[on reverse] napkin, and was off to see to some shipboard chore.

The Allmuseri are Nominalists,
Radical empiricist — each object is
unique for them. They have no universals,
no generic terms. Their language is
impossible to learn. They have, therefore,
no "science." The novel's thematic
tension is between

universals —— vs. —— nominalism
(Zen seeing)

Rutherford's encounter with them
leads to his truly seeing Isadora (and
each person) as a distinct individual
who can be subsumed under no
general categories whatsoever.

The Allmuseri are nominalists, radical empiricists—each object is unique for them. They have no universals, no generic terms. Their language is impossible to learn. They have, therefore, no "science." The novel's thematic tension is between universals—vs.—nominalism (Zen seeing) Rutherford's encounter with them leads to his truly seeing Isadora (and each person) as a distinct individual who can be subsumed under no general categories whatsoever.

Is Ngonyama an outlaw
or criminal among the Allmuseri.
He's been captured with them; he
is responsible for their capture & is
treated badly by them. He knows
English because he is the only one
among them to have contact with whites.

Rutherford learns that Falcon
hates life — he goes to sea precisely
because it is dangerous and he hopes
shipping out will destroy him; he cares
not at all if it destroys his crew,
as well.

Is Ngonyama an outlaw or criminal among the Allmuseri. He's been captured with them;
he is responsible for their capture and is treated badly by them. He knows English because he
is the only one among them to have contact with whites.
  Rutherford learns that Falcon hates life—he goes to sea precisely because it is dangerous
and he hopes shipping out will destroy him; he cares not at all if it destroys his crew, as well.

Chapter 6

1. Rutherford is captain. All the duties of the station fall to him; he is responsible for the well-being of 28 other people. Ergo, he experiences a reversal in his life = he goes from being social parasite to _service to others_.
2. Cringle tells his story (biography).
3. Squibb falls sick.
4. Rutherford's remembrances of Isadora.

NOTE

There must be in Cringle's biography a connection foreshadowed for how he turns the Aquarians around.

Chapter 6 1. Rutherford is captain. All the duties of the station fall to him; he is responsible for the well-being of 28 other people. Ergo, he experiences a reversal in his life—he goes from being social parasite to service to others. 2. Cringle tells his story (biography). 3. Squibb falls sick. 4. Rutherford's remembrances of Isadora. Note: There must be in Cringle's biography a connection foreshadowed for how he turns the Aquarians around.

Chapter 6 = Pacing

① Cringle and R. discuss being lost. He steps outside Falcon's cabin to look at the stars. Seque into... (2 pages or 3)

② Insert by Cringle on perception. (½ page)
   Background on Cringle (1–2 pages)
   — whitespace break —

③ Sighting the ghost ship. Rumours among crew of what it means. (2–3 pages)

④ Diseases spread. Squibb dies. (extend over 5 pages)

⑤ Looking up from Squibb's body, as Tommy hands him the spy-glass, they see land. (1 page maybe: long paragraph)

Chapter 6 — Pacing
1. *Cringle and R. discuss being lost. He steps outside Falcon's cabin to look at the stars.*
   Seque into . . . 2 pages or 3)
2. *Insert by Cringle on perception. (1/2 page) Background on Cringle (1–2 Pages)*
   —whitespace break—
3. *Sighting the ghost ship. Rumours among crew of what it means. (2–3 pages)*
4. *Diseases spread. Squibb dies. (extend over 5 pages)*
5. *Looking up from Squibb's body, as Tommy hands him the spy-glass, they see land. (1 page*
   maybe: long paragraph)

Falcon & C. talk.

Intro Allmuseri in general (Don't mention Ngonyama).

C. talks with Meadows. Learns Falcon had a stroke. Also that McIntosh will be Mate, and is training ship's dogs to be killers of slaves.

C. reflects on McIntosh's racism.

Cringle refuses to brand blacks and is demoted.

Ship sets sail.

Squibb seeks his Beloved. What is discover(ed), drawing nearer to her, is that, "I am she."
His quest for the Others turns back upon himself, liberating him. Where duality was now
there is unity.

Falcon makes Rutherford promise that he will get him safely back to New Orleans.

Falcon makes Rutherford promise that he will get him safely back to New Orleans.

Jackson Calhoun is spiritual, like the Allmuseri—he carries that African spiritualism over into a racist system.

For the Allmuseri, every single human action, situation, and deed is the opportunity to practice sacrifice to their God, <u>was</u>, in fact, their God in action, each tribesman being but a transparency for his unfoldment; each deed to them, therefore, was shot full of spirituality, whether it be signing a treaty with a neighboring tribe or taking a shit. No place was profane. No object divorced from divinity. No person or thing for these Allmuseri could dwell outside the order of the Whole.

his mind like a tongue of flame in a windless place, motionless and steady.

Isadora takes Calhoun to church, where the minister's sermon is a version of the "duties of the householder," which terrify Rutherford.

his mind like a tongue of flame in a windless place, motionless and steady.
Isadora takes Calhoun to church, where the minister's sermon is a version of the "duties of the householder," which terrify Rutherford.

Tommy = "Is That her, Cap'n ?"

R.   "Aye, That's her."

Tommy = "Who's That gennelmum with her ?"

R. "His name is Jackson." I said. "He's my brother."

Tommy: "Is that her, Cap'n?"
R. "Aye, that's her."
Tommy: "Who's that gennelmum with her?"
R. "His name is Jackson," I said. "He's my brother."

So it was done; I was the new captain of The Republic. It figured, in a way, that a Negro wouldn't gain control of the steering-wheel until the ship was leaking like a basket, damaged damned near beyond repair, and everyone ready to bail out. The Allmuseri behead Falcon. Later, when R. sees him on the Phantom ship, his head keeps falling off. Allmuseri have no fingerprints (identity). Allmuseri practice—once a week it is their custom to give up a new (or old) desire.

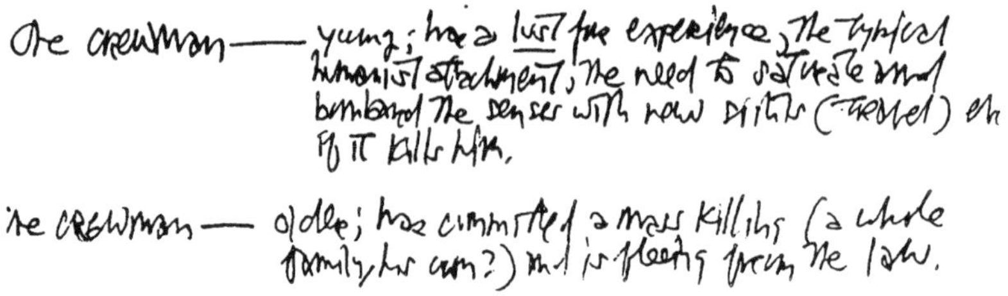

[handwritten draft notes]

One crewman—young; has a lust for experience, the typical humanist attachment, the need to saturate and bombard the senses with new sights (travel) even if it kills him.

One crewman—older; has committed a mass killing (a whole family, his own?) and is fleeing from the law.

He knew a whole encyclopedia of facts but nary a single truth.

More importantly, Falcon was <u>*rude*</u>*. And there was—who can doubt it?—magic in this. His solution to a dangerous world was to make himself dangerous.*

Tommy—innocent to irony

Cringle—During his childhood. Thought struck Cringle thunderously, left him frozen, physically immobilized for long minutes and staring into space, his eyes fixed on an idea, a vision so concrete it seemed superimposed upon the spot where he stood. It was a dangerous thing, these visions. In school, friends covered for him; at home, it frightened his parents, who feared Peter would hurt himself during these instants of

He had visions to this day, though not so frequently as before

Falcon—Never having been loved, he settled on being feared.

The Work of the World

We knew all along this was coming:

The collapse of civilization, the massive nervous breakdown of a social world smothering in its own contradictions and endless conflicts,
the inevitable and long-promised destruction of everything we hold
dear—all of it gone, vanished, buried like Pompeii under shards of dusty
rubble and mounds of brown sod. How did that Chinese saying go? "A
thousand years a city, a thousand years a forest."

For weeks I wandered, dazed and shaken, through this surreal waste-
land—the planet's scorched, quiet capitals, along the unpopulated
shores by her polluted seas, beneath petroleum-stained skies—and
found myself at this colony, a black man barefoot and shirtless, among
other survivors of the world's end, the cyclical Cataclysm, the recurrent
collapse of each and every fragile, created thing. We work in an hour
suspended outside time (for like all concepts, that of historical time lies
buried in ruin too)—just a heartbeat after dancing Shiva has once again
destroyed the world, all names and forms (*maya*), in order to balance
things out, and just a heartbeat before he strikes the drum to signal it
is necessary to begin the laborious process of building anew: the reinvention of languages, manipulation of Nature, and conjuring of ephem-
eral products from the earth, and for no purpose other than to encourage
beauty's efflorescence and the eruption of forms in which the divine
spirit may dwell and take delight.

And of course everyone gathered here, regardless of race or gender or religion, is crucial to that process. Is the rhythm of rising and falling away. I do not know their real names. Nor do they know mine. We have forgotten them. We change names as we change chores—or workclothes. Today my brown friend with his head down is simply called Shoveler. The woman in the red dress near me says her name is Digger. I am called Mover. The differences—the false dualisms—that divided us so badly before and led to the world's wreckage have disappeared. Like a dream, they can hardly be remembered. Nothing concerns us now except the question of who is willing to work. To create. To put his tired shoulder to the wheel, her parched hands on the wheelbarrow, our jobs and lives being interchangeable now—all have two good hands, two good arms, and a common goal: this thousand-year task of pulling a world phoenix-like from the ashes, reclaiming it from the forest.

But we wonder: What was the Old World about? Why the anger, wars, hatreds, petty bickering and insignificant battles over things we should have known we could never keep for long, including life itself? In the aftermath of smash-up, in this debris where no telephone rings, no television's pale light flickers through the front windows of homes in the evening, and no newspaper's glaring headlines manufacture history—here nothing matters save stoking the fire that converts into plumes of white smoke the last vestiges of the Old World; cutting and carrying stone slabs; raising a haven for humanity's future in the distance; and reinforcing the earthen dais on which rests the shattered, scarred yet persisting rock that symbolizes the hope our offspring will sojourn on through time after we are gone.

After hours of hauling stones to the scaffold I am sticky with sweat and I ache in my joints. I decide to rest, joining my thirteen brothers and sisters in a circle at the base of the rock. Here will be the new city's center, one our children or grandchildren may see in its glory, though most likely none of us will live that long. It goes without saying that we are a colony by accident—but a community, *satsang*, just the same. The man who a moment before struggled behind a green wheelbarrow now hands each of us a wedge of cheese and crusty chump of bread from a sack. We share the last bottle of Coca-Cola in the world, handing it to the person at our right after the most parsimonious of sips. Below us the forest darkens and fills with the sound of insects as light drains from the sky, leaving just the dancing, strange brilliance of the fire at twilight. No one speaks. In the wake of world's end words echo loudly against the backdrop of the Void's silence; each is energy unleashed—sacred—and so we use words sparingly. If I require a tool I need only say, "Hammer"; if my sister needs aid clearing albumen-white bones off the rock, all she need say is, "Help." And so it is best now to be silent as we rest and eat, to listen to the new world that we, like midwives, are easing from wreckage's womb.

A few of us watch the flames, fascinated by the rise of each brilliant, fugitive spark, so heartbreakingly brilliant and individual, but only for a second, for suddenly the blazing particles are gone, folded back into darkness—just as impermanent, we know, as the scaffold into which we pour every iota of our lives, labor, and love. Looking into the fire-lit faces across the circle, we wonder: Is one flickerflash instant of beauty worth our lives? Although unspoken, the answer is clear.

An instant might as well be centuries.

This story, a fictional response to Peter Blume's famous painting "The Rock" (1948) at the Art Institute of Chicago, was originally published with an image of the painting in *Transforming Vision: Writers on Art*, selected and introduced by Edward Hirsch (Chicago: Art Institute of Chicago / Boston: Little, Brown, 1994).

Essays & Addresses

Philosophy and Black Fiction

Concluding his 1953 study *The Negro Novelist*, Carl Milton Hughes complained that, "The philosophical novel in which some system of thought as it affects the life of the Negro has yet to appear."[1] If ideas alone—doctrines and theories—are the basic stuff of philosophical novels, then recent Black fiction has clearly put Hughes' complaint to rest: James Baldwin probed storefront Christianity in *Go Tell it on the Mountain*; in *The Outsider* and "The Man Who Lived Underground," Richard Wright explored aspects of European existentialism, as did Cyrus Colter, brooding upon determinism in a distinctly Sartrean novel called *The Hippodrome*; Ralph Ellison treated, among other things, problems of perceptual experience and meaning in *Invisible Man*; and Ishmael Reed, still scathing after all these years, continues to rummage through Egyptian and voduon mythology for a humanism that might speak significantly to us in *The Last Days of Louisiana Red* and *Flight to Canada*.

But there is a deeper issue at the heart of black philosophical fiction, a problem that we should air frequently, because, for all our talk of "Telling it like it is," and for all our fidelity to black life, we often betray our experience by blinking too quickly the analytic dimension native to literary art. Especially now, during the rather heated debate on novelist John Gardner's angry yet important essay called *On Moral Fiction*—a manifesto that claims, and rightly so, that "Fiction is a form of philosophical method, the writer's equivalent to the scientific process," but which mentions only five black writers[2]—it is important to clarify the area where fiction and philosophy overlap, and develop a feeling for how race (Better to say *raciality*, thereby clarifying race as a structure of all perception, like sexuality, spaciality, temporality) figures into how we give form, in literature and life, to our experience.

Clearly, the menagerie of Black caricatures and clichéd situations so popular today in Hollywood, so frequent in trashy fiction—the motor-mouthed dandy, two-faced preacher, hopheads, the spiritual African, ball-busting women, meek Christians, blind Caucasians, fiery Black social activists, all those frustrated, butchered lives—fail, fail utterly to express authentic ways of seeing (And let us assume there *are*, can be, authentic Black ways of seeing). We wonder, What Lord, are Black artists *doing?* Our *interpretation* of our experience, as Ishmael Reed has written in numerous articles, has become rigid, forced into formulaes; it does not permit, as all philosophically (and aesthetically) genuine fiction must, an efflorescence of meaning or a clarification of perception. We have so stylized our sense of the Black world that gifted white writers can conjure the world and speech of Black maids, athletes, and revolutionaries with apparent fidelity: Black life, in fine, has become a frozen gesture, a one-dimensional style of being. How can we, then salvage Black fiction from calcification? The answer is deceptively simple, yet often difficult to achieve, and serves therefore as an ideal against which we can measure ourselves. Realizing that my arguments are likely to anger and annoy, I will first proceed methodologically, at the risk of appearing obtuse, and leave my cranky opinions for last.

Philosophical Black fiction—art that interrogates experience—is, first and foremost, a mode of thought. It is the process of *interpretation*, or hermeneutics in the higher sense. One need not write *about* ideas, putting clothes on concepts as Wright did in *The Outsider*, or as Cyrus Colter did in *The Hippodrome* for a literary work to have philosophical integrity; in fact, that approach often poisons, if one is not careful, the slow process of discovery, which is the first goal of fiction. We have been at theoretical war too long over the problem of reconciling universality with the particulars of Black life (even claiming, madly, that there are no universals worth talking about) when a procedure exists for reconciling universality, or the dominant sense of experience, with Black life. I mean what the philosopher does when he applies the *epoché*, or so-called "phenomenological reduction" to experience. A full description of phenomenological techniques and strategies is not possible here, but I would like to sketch the aspects of the *epoché* that speak most significantly to the process of philosophically serious fiction.[3]

A *fresh* encounter with Black life requires: (1) All presuppositions, whatever we think we know about Black life, all our cherished beliefs in what *is* and how it appears must be suspended, shelved, "bracketed." Aspects of the Black world become, after the *epoché*, only the occasion for universal reflection. (2) With this "bracketing" accomplished, Black experience becomes a pure field of appearances with but two important poles: consciousness and the objects, others, to which it is related intentionally. We describe *how* these appear, and note that Black subjectivity (memory, desire, anticipation, will) stain them with a particular sense. (Here, the poetic act, perhaps even neologism—bending language like soft plastic—is necessary for describing without prejudice what has not been seen, or seen so deeply, before.) (3) Finally, we ask if this look at Black life—stripped in the first stage of all Black particulars, purified or irrealized such that it now stands before us as an instance of *all* experience (Storefront Christianity, say, as the occasion for reflection on the universal theme of religion) of its type—exhibits traits that illuminate our theme. Surely, it must. Buried in the particulars of storefront Christianity—the *way* we approach the supernatural—the theme of religion shows a new face. How, then, does its specific occurance in Black life *vary* our conception of religion?

Because all conception—philosophy—is grounded in perception, there is no reason, in principle, that we cannot work through the particulars of Black life from *within* and discover there not only phenomenon worthy of philosophical treatment in fiction, but also—and here I'll make my wildest claim today—significant new perceptions. Universals are not static (as Robert Bone believes in *The Negro Novel in America*, nor empty as Stephen Henderson argues) but changing, historical, *evolving* and enriched by particularization; the lived Black world has always promised a fresh slant on structures and themes centuries old.

"The world in which we live," writes Ellison of B. P. Rinehart in *Invisible Man*, "was without boundaries. A fast seething, hot world of fluidity . . . "[4] From the fibrous particulars of Black life a perception anchored *in* racial experience is bodied forth, and we come to understand somewhat how new seeing—revitalized vision—occurs in Black fiction. First, Ellison, through a *saying* that is *showing* (A new disclosure of the Real that brings it from concealedness, which phenomenologist Max Scheler has called *alethia*: a revealing based upon the writer's Black situation in the world) is "in-formed" by Black life and simultaneously *gives form* to it. Furthermore, his perception is *a* truth. This is so because art expresses the meaning of the Real *through* a (Black) subjectivity rooted in the specifics of race and class. These contingencies, these very particulars of Black life which seemed so at odds with universality make the universal utterance possible. But, as Blyden Jackson argues in "The Negro's Image of the Universe as Reflected in His Fiction," many Black fictional worlds are dominated by stasis, not fluidity. These expressions are also a truth, but not *the* truth, and at any given time, by a slight modulation of your perception (the subject-pole of our previous discussion), you can see Black life as *either* fluid *or* static (but not both at the same time because the world outruns our perceptual grasp). There is no single true image of the Black world; but neither is each image merely subjective. We can liken the Black world to a tree branching forth innumerable appendages in an endless explosion of meaning. The Black world *appears* in countless guises. For Richard Wright in *Lawd Today* and *American Hunger* southside Chicago in the 1930s is a cesspool, but for Ronald Fair in "We Who Came After," his prologue to *We Can't Breathe,* Chicago is an almost pastoral setting for Black childhood. The point, which has been made elsewhere and more eloquently, is that our experience as Black men and women completely outstrips our perception—Black life is ambiguous, and a kaleidescope of meanings rich, multi-sided, and what the authentic Black writer does is despoil meanings to pin down the freshest interpretation given to him. This is genuine fiction. It is also hermeneutic philosophy, in the sense that the writer is an archaeologist probing the Real for veiled sense. Surely a man should cease writing and shut up when he can no longer peer into Black life and give birth to a new universal. But you are still thinking of universality as a static mold that violates Black life; this is a very dull notion.

What is dangerous, maybe even disastrous, for Black fiction as we approach the 1980s is a self-satisfied acceptance of what we've already seen, codified and institutionalized in the 1960s and 1970s. Fresh perception easily sours into formulae, into typicality, which is the end of thought. We've reached a point where to *be* Black (And, yes, we are talking about Black literature and Being here) is to exist within the easy categories of racial existence outlined by Stephen Henderson's *Understanding the New Black Poetry*, Eugene Redmond's *Drumvoices*, or the visceral but truncated vision of *Roots*; the sum and substance of our lives, to hear our writers tell it, is Black music, Creole dishes, dancing, sass, and certain African survivalisms. Accepting this interpretation (which, like all true perceptions, is partial, one-sided, and badly in need of completion) kills as surely as a knife thrust the evolution—expansion and efflorescence—of Black life.

In their probings, our younger Black novelists have turned in strangely similar Black worlds: cloned worlds. These writers differ in certain respects that are doubtlessly important to them, as they explain in their interviews, but seen from a philosophical distance they show a marked similarity in their ways of seeing. In *Corregidora* and *Eva's Man*, Gayl Jones finds, like Cyrus Colter in "Mary's Covert," Richard Wright, and Ernest Gaines in "Three Men," a Black world without freedom, grimy with sexual humiliation, shame, where human contact is a variation on Hegelian Master-Slave bondage, and escape is possible only through death and deeper levels of self-betrayal. Hal Bennett's books like *Lord of Dark Places,* as well as John A. Williams' *Mothersill and the Foxes,* offer us a sideshow of Black sexual gymnastics, as if Black being was predominantly venereal. Vern E. Smith's highly commercial *The Jones Men* gives us Lennie Jack, who sums up the sense of the contemporary Black world with the observation, "It's cold out there, brother." Perhaps only Ishmael Reed, Al Young in such gentle fictions as *Sitting*

Pretty, and Toni Morrison in *Song of Solomon* are exceptions today. Reacting against the Black world-qua-sewer, they unearth worlds with a pre-established harmony, a range of humor, the fantastic, everyday experience, and grace. If there are dominant philosophical traits in Black fiction, however, they are the particular pain of the Black self in search of an *amonea deverticula*, its agonizings over the paradox of change in the Black world: stasis and flux. Like the Milesians, we seem baffled by motion and identity, and end, curiously like Parmenides, denying changes of state or knowledge for our characters. The sense of *Weltanschauung* in these Black worlds, as Washington poet Colleen McElroy once remarked, "Is that everything fails."

Despite modulations in the lived worlds of these writers, and more I haven't mentioned, there is dangerously little variety of vision, interpretation, or thought. Neither is there completeness, or a full exhibition of multiple interpretations. Intellectual life, for example, is seldom portrayed, and Hughes' conclusion still seems sadly correct (Our only exceptions to this unhappy judgment are Toomer, Wright, and Ellison, whose fictions are the fruit of a process where feeling and thought commingle to *change*, deepen our perception of the Lifeworld in general, and the Black world in particular).

To a degree, I get panicky, peer round, and wait for a kick in the pants when speaking of Black fiction and philosophy in the same breath. As a down-to-earth people, we are, like most Americans, suspicious of philosophy. We value, or so we say, feelings, emotions, actions. You know. Concrete things. Axe-handles. Tea cups. Objects. But even this flimsy dodge does not excuse us from developing serious philosophical fictions—interpretive art that deepens perceptual experience. Feelings are, after all, shamelessly analytic. We aim perceptually at something and, through the emotions of anger or love, cause it to *appear* before us as it could not otherwise. The emotions (and all subjective operations) doorway onto the world, end in knowledge, and therefore are instrumental as a mode for analyzing the appearance (being) of phenomenon in Black life. Secondly, a fictional world is a coherent deformation of Black life (in itself silent as to its meaning) so it makes sense. The writer's shaping process—plotting, characterization, description, dialogue, what he includes *and* excludes—illuminates the Black world. "It seems to me," wrote Blyden, "that few, if any literary universes are as impoverished as the universe of Black fiction. (Of greatest interest) . . . are the things that cannot be found there."[5] Isn't the Black world *also* a field where men interrogate morality? Don't we wonder about religion, political philosophy, the existence of others, the Good, meaning, duty, or thought itself? (Samuel R. Delany, it must be said, struggles with thought and language in such sci-fi fabulations as *Babel-17* and, although his ambition is delightful, it is the world of *Star Wars* aliens, not Black people, where the probing occurs.) No one much cares these days about the particulars of Black life only (this always borders on the exotic, voyeuristic, the sociological). We read the fictions of the racial Other because they disclose the world—a common world, finally—as it might appear if we could be over there in that body, behind those eyes that see a slant on things denied us by the accidents of birth.

I have argued that philosophical hermeneutics and the exploration of meaning are native to all literary production; that universality is embodied in the particulars of the Black world; and that the final concern of serious fiction is the liberation of perception. And I have also argued—without malice, for all our writers are dear to me and struggle against stupendous odds in a white-dominated marketplace—that we abdicate our responsibility as Black creators by embracing all too easy interpretations of our being-in-the-world. We "control" our images too rigidly and, consequently, stifle our fictions with worlds so ossified, so stamped with *sameness* they seem to be the product of a committee, not an individual consciousness grappling with meaning. Personally, I have nothing against *The Jeffersons*, Papa LaBas, Ricard Pryor records, or Kunte Kinte; but the cold facts are that we have frozen our vision in figures that caricature, at best, the complexity of our lives and leave the real artistic chore of interpretation unfinished.

Notes

1. Carl Milton Hughes, *The Negro Novelist* (New York: The Citadel Press, 1953), p. 251.

2. John Gardner, *On Moral Fiction* (New York: Basic Books, 1978). The writers mentioned, very briefly, are Ralph Ellison, Amiri Baraka, Ed Bullins, Toni Morrison, and myself, which indicates that the community of black literary artists should add its voice to this theoretical debate, if only for the sake of completeness.

3. Phenomenology is, or so its founder Edmund Husserl claimed, more than a "Philosophy"—it is a method for examining experience without presuppositions. Important works for a complete discussion of this method are Husserl's *Cartesian Meditations* (Paris: Martinus Nijhoff, 1973); Ronald Bruzina's *Logo and Eidos* (Paris: Mouton, 1970); and Mikel Dufrenne's monumental work, *The Phenomenology of Aesthetic Experience*, trans., Edward S. Casey (Evanston: Northwestern University Press, 1973).

4. Ralph Ellison, *Invisible Man* (New York: Random House, Vintage Books, 1972), p. 487.

5. Blyden Jackson, "The Negro's Image of the Universe as Reflected in His Fiction," *Black Voices*, ed., Abraham Chapman (New York: New American Library, 1968), p. 631.

Whole Sight
Notes on New Black Fiction

When editor Charles Rowell invited me to guest-edit this issue of *Callaloo*, I was both delighted and worried—delighted because through his efforts this consistently handsome, unfailingly diversified publication has almost single-handedly kept alive a forum for black fiction, poetry, and criticism since the demise of older publications such as *Black World* and *Yardbird Reader*; and worried because I knew I'd have to write frankly about black fiction, which is always a dangerous thing to do, tempers being hair-trigger on this subject, and I don't much care to have anyone firing at me.

Before discussing a few of the contributors to this issue, it's necessary to first speak in a spirit of joyful celebration for the progress that has been made in black fiction. Works by women writers, like Toni Morrison and Alice Walker, have been well-received, as they should be, and national attention has been directed, and rightly so, to talented black authors like John Wideman, Paula Marshal, James Alan McPherson, and David Bradley (But many still deserve greater readership—Leon Forrest, for example, Al Young, and John McCluskey Jr., and Nathaniel Mackey to name only a few). Black writing has moved forward, you might say, on two fronts, the commercial, and in respect to content, by which I mean this: a wider audience has opened for a few black writers, and the seldom-discussed experience of black women has, like the experience of women in general, been thematized in literature, thereby bringing to light a level of social discrimination the nation needs to deal with. Only a dumbbell would deny the political and sociological value of these advances, and a reader thinks, "Thank God these problems are out in the open," but my feeling is that these works represent a stage in black literature if the *telos*—or final goal—of art is, as John Fowles wrote in *Daniel Martin,* "whole sight." This phrase is of course difficult to describe, but we know it when we see it in the expansive works of such American high-wire performers as Ralph Ellison, Jean Toomer, and (at times) Richard Wright, to say nothing of the levels of imagination, invention, and interpretation achieved by Melville, Hawthorne, and Poe. We must celebrate the hard-won advances of black fiction in the last decade, for they are crucial steps in the evolution of our literature and consciousness, but the danger in being too easily satisfied, as Donald Hall points out in his magnificent essay, "Poetry and Ambition" (*Kenyon Review,* Fall 1983), is that great models of literature become forgotten, anything goes after a time, and the high-wire of performance may be lowered more than we like.

True and lasting "world-class" literature is, has always been, and shall ever be a sumptuous act of *interpretation* or, as phenomenologist Mikel Dufrenne often says, "a coherent deformation of Reality." In short, the writer shapes a four-dimensional, fictional world such that it clarifies our experience for us and satisfies our hunger for *complete* understanding, his (or her) medium for this being the well-made story. One of my theatre friends puts it this way: Good fiction sharpens our perception; great fiction *changes* it. In one sense, we can perhaps view the evolution of literature the same way we view the progress of science. At any given moment, physicists here and abroad are laboring to answer *objective* scientific questions handed down by Einstein, Bohr, and others—tracking down hypothetical entities like hadrons, for example, or patching up cracks in Unified Field theory; it's a competitive race of sorts, as Watson points out in *The Double Helix.* Similarly, the history of literary practice creates objective aesthetic possibilities, artistic works demanded historically by the foul-ups and partial breakthroughs in past literary art, novels and stories and poems that fill in the blanks and potholes created by the oversights and omissions of those writers (white and black) who preceded us. (No, I'm not talking about your average novel here, only great books that *advance* the form of the novel or story.) The emergence of a "woman's perspective" is, therefore, a revolutionary, objective step forward in culture and consciousness, one that sensitizes us to the relativity of truth; the fiction of, say, Gayle Jones and Ntozake Shange, is *demanded* by the suppression of black women in American literature (and life), if only to make our dialogue on Being more democratic.

I've said that the new black fictions, male and female, are crucial perspectives on Being demanded (almost in a Hegelian sense) to round out our understanding of the Real, but there can be a problem if our emphasis remains too much upon exploring the splintered "perspective" rather than on the goal of achieving *whole sight* in novels and stories exciting *as* novels and stories—thrilling, in other words, as works of imagination and invention. Clayton Riley expressed this eloquently at the 1978 Howard University Black Writer's Conference:

> It is my belief that the artist's first allegiance is to the imagination, as opposed to any prevailing dogma. . . . Artists seek to find out, to explore, taking on in the process the risky business of knowing what is not easy to know—the danger of discovery. In this, writers most especially, have an entire world—not just the fractured world of American racism and psychic social disorder—to employ in structuring systems and methodologies to make up new planets, new societies, new ways of being eminently more human.

Riley places his finger squarely on the problem I only suggested earlier: How do we *conceive* racial being? What is race? What is man? How are we to live? These are the questions lasting, great fiction seeks to answer. The issue of achieving *whole sight* involves, I think, both the promotion of a "black" or "female" perspective in fiction and a *broadening* of our expressions and vision of these perspectives. What is at stake is the fundamental question of how we see life in general and black life in particular, and it returns us to the yet unresolved aesthetic dilemmas raised almost a quarter century ago by Blyden Jackson in his classic essay, "The Negro's Image of the Universe as Reflected in His Fiction." Jackson wrote, "It seems to me that few, if any, literary universes are as impoverished as the universe of black fiction. (Of greatest interest) . . . are the things that cannot be found there." True enough, every writer should "write about what he knows," as the saying goes, but Riley's footnote to this is: Knowing is as limitless as the intellect and the imagination. Furthermore, all perception is, at the instant it arises, also interpretation and shaping, so that, one really begs the question by arguing, "I just want to write it the way it happened," because language and literary art deliver not the event itself—no, never that—but instead a *vision* of that event. Even such microscopic linguistic choices as rendering an event in short, simple sentences as opposed to compound-complex ones, or favoring short vowels and long consonants (instead of the reverse) *alters* the reader's experience of the event.

We know, of course, more than oppression and discrimination. And, as phenomenologist Alfred Schutz tells us in his classic 1932 study, *The Phenomenology of the Social World*, popular political talk very often happens on a high level of abstraction; the language of politics can easily go unexamined, and remain sedimented with theoretical presuppositions about experience. Its concepts are often in violation of direct intuition. For example, it wouldn't be unthinkable to scrap the notion of "race" in a country as genetically mongrelized as America. Any geneticist worth the name can show you that if you go back fifty generations in the life of *any* person, he (or she) shares a common ancestor with every other person on this planet. None of us can be less closely related than fiftieth cousins. "Race" dissolves when we trace the gene back to A.D. 700. Our ancestors necessarily include some Chinese, Arabs, whites, Eskimos, and *all* of us are descendents of Caesar, Lao tzu, Empedocles and Shakespeare.

But let us probe deeper into Blyden Jackson's remarks. Because our conception of race is sometimes limited, and because black fiction has largely confined its explorations to the "fractured universe" of bigotry, we seldom, if ever, find black writers tracing the impact of modern science and technology on our lives (We *do* have a long list of black inventors, you know), or deeply investigating the phenomenon of identity, though we talk endlessly about this, or addressing the primary experiential problem of the 20th century—language and consciousness— or wondering as David Bradley does in *The Chaneysville Incident* (one of the most intellectually interesting novels to come along in years) over the meaning of history as a shamelessly hermeneutic art-form, by which I mean the very *idea* of "history" a a way of making sense of temporal existence (Can the African past ever be recovered when so many tribes were anchored in a specific Lifeworld, and what *were* those Lifeworlds like?), or even for that matter acknowledging that black American culture is not all of a piece but instead a tissue of history interwoven with all the diverse, global contributions that make the Republic a web of European, African, Eastern, and classical influences. (As naturalist Guy Murchie would say, even this issue of *Callaloo*, written by an American, is made of paper invented by the Chinese and printed with ink evolved out of India and from type developed by Germans using Roman symbols modified from the Greeks who got their letter concepts from Phoenicians who had adapted them partly from Egyptian hieroglyphs.)

And for anyone at all acquainted with the philosophy of literary form, the vehicles of fictional expression are themselves shot through with meaning and embody a cultural vision and specific values—the "world" of the classic parable is, for example, experientially different from that of the tale. Some daring writers like Ishmael Reed, a pioneer in literary experimentation, cast their works in popular forms, which they've modified (Detective, or Western, and John A. Williams did the War Story), but it would be a pleasure, I think, to see black writers experimenting with the 19th century architechtonic novel, pre-realistic forms of the 17th century as Russell Banks did in *The Relation of My Imprisonment* (We were in America then, too), the fabliau, classic sea story, pastoral, fable or totem-story, and a galaxy of other forms that are our inheritance as writers, forms that are potentially fertile ground for artistic discovery, and what novelist John Gardner has called, "genre-crossing" in his splendid handbook, *The Art of Fiction*. In a word, black fiction—all art and evolution—can benefit from the revitalizing influence of cross-cultural fertilization (already present in our lives, indeed as the very stuff of our lives) to move closer to the objective of *whole sight*.

Two things should be clear by now:

First, my opinions are cranky, and for that I apologize; and, secondly, the writers I've selected to appear in this issue are pathfinders who have met, in my opinion, some part of this drive for *whole sight*, if not entirely in these stories (Even Homer slept sometime, as they say), then in the past, thereby pushing at the frontier of black fiction and extending its possibilities.

The heart of memorable, enduring fiction is imaginative storytelling reinforced by massive technique. That seems almost too obvious a thing to say, but it's important, I think, to repeat the obvious. And for a long time now some have claimed that the last stronghold of imaginative American literature is science fiction, its proponents pointing to such masters as Ursula LeGuin and the Pole Stanislaw Lem, and tracing its origins back to Plato's *Republic*. Whether this is so, I leave to you to decide, but one thing that no one can deny is that Samuel Delany has made a lasting contribution to the "New Wave" fringe of science fiction (though he doesn't call it that) as a novelist and literary critic, and among black writers he stands alone, except for a few talented newcomers, as the first author to systematically explore the possibilities of a tradition created in the modern era by Mary Shelley and Jules Verne, then nailed down with definition by H. G. Wells. One thinks, of course, of George Schuyler's playful *Black No More* as an early sci-fi novel by a black author and, though its premise is wonderful, it is Delany, a multiple-winner of the Nebula Award, who published his first novel at age 21, who "goes the distance," addressing dilemmas specific to the 20th century, as for example in *Babel-17*, a work which takes on the relationship between language, identity, and our experience of reality. There is no one quite like this man. He is rare. And in "The Mummer's Tale," excerpted from his forthcoming novel, *Flight from Nevèryon* (Bantam, Spring 1985), Delany continues to create imaginative worlds to which, as Melville once said, "we feel the tie."

Rare, too, among contemporary black writers is John McCluskey Jr., who has shown in his novels *Look What They Done to My Song* and *Mr. America's Last Season Blues*, as well as in his short fiction, which has appeared in *Best American Short Stories*, that he loves black people with a positive, lyrical spirit free of the self-hatred, hatred of whites, of self, and the unrelieved gloom and despair that often occur in black fiction. For this reason McCluskey is refreshing. Formerly editor of *Ju-Ju: Research Papers in Afro-American Studies*, McCluskey is presently at work on two novels: one about the phenomenon of black cults, the other a recreation of the life of Frederick Douglass based on his *Pushcart Prize*-cited story (1984), "Chicago Jubilee Rag."

As for Colleen McElroy, well this: her fiction and poetry are as glamorous as she is. McElroy is Professor of English at the University of Washington, formerly editor of the Northwest quarterly, *Dark Waters*, an actress, and a winner of the Callaloo Creative Writing Award. She is the author of numerous volumes of poetry, and her life and work are profiled in the PBS documentary "Spirit of Place" by film-maker Jean Walkinshaw. McElroy is clearly a feminist writer, meaning simply that as a black woman she writes from a center so strong, so self-confident, so sure of her place in the world that polemicism is replaced by wisdom, love, and a remarkably powerful poetic and prose line. Furthermore, her range spans several genres—science fiction, represented here by "The Simple Language of Drones," naturalistic stories, a screenplay for a recent PBS series for young adults, and plays. Only the stingiest critic would doubt that McElroy is one of the best, most balanced black woman poets working today.

Clarence Major hardly needs an introduction. Reams have been written on this man. More can be expected. For twenty years Major, and his colleagues on the Fiction Collective—Ronald Sukenick, Raymond Federman—have been on the cutting edge of experimental fiction in America. While I do not always agree with this non-narrative approach, I appreciate and am somewhat awed by Major's steady effort to interpret for black writing the tradition of experimentation that begins with Sterne's *Tristram Shandy*, then threads through Joyce, Stein, and various European writers. In such original novels as *Reflex and Bone Structure*, and the multi-media *Emergency Exit*, which is a study in ways to structure a narrative once plot has been judged *passé*, he pursues an aesthetically necessary option for black writing. No writer, to my knowledge, has pushed this wing of modernism to the structural limits achieved by Major, and what most of us seek—a place in the literature of the Age—Major earned long ago.

So, having said all that, I will conclude by saying this:

If there is any thematic thread to the body of black fiction from the first Negro novel, *Our Nig* to *Praise Song for the Widow*, if this corpus of literature has any *eidos*—or essence—at all, it is the quest for identity and liberty. You might argue that these themes are at the heart of American literature as such. (Go ahead, I don't mind.) If this hypothesis is workable, then it follows that recent black fiction is on the right track, but also that the conception of freedom and identity in future black writing will be broader, more expansive. The themes, and the techniques to mount them dramatically, will, I'm guessing, grow in depth, expand in breadth, and black literature will be universally recognized as perhaps the truest form of Yankee fiction, the body of stories that, once broadened by *whole sight*, profiles the concerns of the Republic in the most vivid and memorable manner.

Where Philosophy and Fiction Meet

In 1486, the Italian humanist Giovanni Pico della Mirandola delivered a brief discourse called "The Dignity of Man." This pivotal document for the transition from the Middle Ages to the Renaissance has stayed in my thoughts since I first came across it, 20 years ago.

Pico's notion is simple. He says that in the fifteenth-century culture

> *the whole of philosophy (such is the unhappy plight of our time) is occasion for contempt and contumely, rather than honor and glory. The deadly and monstrous persuasion has invaded practically all minds, that philosophy ought not to be studied at all or by very few people; as though it were a thing of little worth to have before our eyes and at our fingertips.*

Well might he be speaking of American attitudes today and of the feelings many blacks have toward philosophy.

Fifteen or so years ago, a young black woman asked me about my college major. When I told her it was philosophy, her cool reply was "Oh, you BS a lot, don't you." Believe me, this isn't so.

But in America, a black philosopher lives with the possibility of being badly misunderstood by blacks and whites both. Like Cross Damon in Richard Wright's *The Outsider* or the nerdish fireman in last year's film *Roxanne*, the philosopher might even hide from friends and co-workers the fact that he's been poring over Kant and Heidegger in the privacy of his room and, stranger yet, has found something in German philosophy that speaks to him. He fears not being seen as a "regular guy," which counts for so much in this country.

Like most Americans, black people pride themselves on being oh so practical. In the popular imagination, philosophy is a profession of zero market value. General Motors, for example, has yet to hire a resident metaphysician; and clearly the president's advisors include no logicians.

Most ludicrous of all is the depressing fact that America has given but one philosophy to the world: pragmatism. This home-grown doctrine—often caricatured by its critics as saying, "If it works, it must be true."—fits nicely into our belief in Yankee know-how and business savvy. "Thus," said Pico five centuries ago, "we have reached a point, it is painful to recognize, where the only persons accounted wise are those who can reduce the pursuit of wisdom to a profitable traffic."

His definition of philosophy is classical: the love of wisdom (Gr. *philein*, to love; *sophia* wisdom). It is this time-honored, dominant goal of philosophy that led me to see that philosophy has always been a sister discipline to art, an activity that seduced me when I was very young.

But what I did *not* see was participation by blacks to any great extent in the philosophical enterprise. According to one of my professors, only 25 blacks had been granted Ph.D.'s in this field before 1970 (although a Ph.D. does not a philosopher make), and it's easy to understand why.

The members of my own family threw a fit when I telephoned them one evening to say that I was changing my major from journalism (a cash-value degree) to philosophy. "To what?!" said my grandmother. "What're you going to *do* with that?" And who can blame them for panic? I was the first person in my family to go to college. Six generations of Johnsons since slavery were counting on me to make good—that is, to make a good living.

I wanted badly to read them Pico's beautiful declaration that "I have never philosophized save for the sake of philosophy, nor have I ever desired or hoped to secure from my studies and my laborious researches any profit or fruit save cultivation of the mind and knowledge of truth." I decided that might further damage my case and convince them I was unemployable.

Fortunately, I found support for my need (and such it was) for philosophy, and a counterargument for my family and friends, in the finest work of Afro-American literature—in its small but significant metaphysical wing. I urged skeptics to remember that a few Harlem Renaissance writers had backgrounds in philosophy, and that one of W. E. B. Du Bois's great hopes was to develop a philosophical method for the interpretation of race relations.

Moreover, it struck me as a philosophy student, then later as a writer, that in the domain of fiction blacks had a tradition of broaching fundamental questions of being and race, culture and consciousness. In fact, you might argue (and I did) that as far as world literature is concerned, the vitality of philosophical discourse has passed in the latter half of this century from the small province of academic seminars to the pages of our finest stories. The "novelist of ideas" reaches a wider audience than his counterpart does in stuffy journals. And who, asked my friends, might these black writers be?

Well, I said, we can start with Jean Toomer, whose lovely and language-rich *Cane* ushered in the Harlem Renaissance and advanced the American short story as a form. Besides being technically accomplished, his work in such poems as "Blue Meridian" does something more. There, he prophesies that the new man of tomorrow's American will be a "blue man." Toomer's choice of imagery seems strange until we recall that throughout Indian pictorial art, Krishna is often portrayed in human form, but his skin is as blue and borderless as the sky itself, to suggest infinity and the transcendence of dualism.

Toomer's "new [blue] man" is, therefore, emblematic of a being as enlightened as any *bodhissatva*. A cross-cultural being. A breaker of polarities. So that, when he writes, "It is a new America / To be spiritualized by each new American," we have in Toomer an imaginative continuation of Emersonian transcendentalism by a black poet who provides the foundation for a dialogue between the black experience and the profound reflections of selfhood long a part of Vedic literature.

Next, I reminded them that although Richard Wright is generally read, and rightly, as a writer of racial protest, his finest works, including *Native Son* and his Dostoyevskian parable, "The Man Who Lived Underground," are compatible with the most interesting ideas in continental philosophy during the thirties and forties. In fact, Wright made an effort to learn Husserlian phenomenology from one of its most important practitioners, Jean-Paul Sartre, according to Sorbonne critic Micéal Faber.

And what shall we say about the final works of his life? Wright's last years saw him experimenting with, of all things, Japanese haiku—a form saturated with the Chan Buddhist vision of nature. Wright's twilight interests tell us that formal virtuosity as a way of unearthing new meaning in literature and life is as important as the chore of opposing racism, for the greatest culture crime of bigotry is its oversimplification of the vast richness of human experience.

And it is Wright who prepares the way for Ralph Ellison's magnificent feast of fictional styles in *Invisible Man*, a highly symbolic, Freudian tale that declares itself to be, at bottom, about the ambiguities of perception and interpretation in the racial world. Ironically, though, militant friends of mine in 1968 decided that Ellison was "not a black writer." I suspect they were echoing John Oliver Killens, who wrote in his review of *Invisible Man* that Ellison betrayed black World War II veterans by portraying them as madmen.

Despite the beachheads established in American literature by these black authors of "philosophical" fiction and despite the eventual concession of my family that metaphysical study had importance, I discovered that in the early seventies our finest authors had inspired fewer imitators than did the politically "engaged" work of writers in the black arts movement of the 1960s.

It is that very same cultural nationalism—a serious roadblock for genuine black fiction and philosophy—that makes me uncomfortable, precisely because I was once one of its converts. Indeed, my first publication would never have come about if it had not been for the black arts movement.

This story begins winter term at Southern Illinois University. I was a bored 20-year-old, at a stalemate with my creative work as a cartoonist. So I went, out of curiosity, to a public reading on campus by Amiri Baraka. Flanked by stern-faced guards, he read poetry and counseled the young artists in the audience to bring their talents back to the black community.

Now, I can't speak for everyone there that night, but I was convinced this charismatic, brilliant black man was talking to *me*. I dragged home in the rain, dazed, seeing nothing on either side of me because my brain reeled with a hundred images for moving American comic art toward expressing the culture of people of color.

For a week straight I stayed in my room drawing, eating little and sleeping less, the gag-lines and compositions coming faster than I could keep up with them. When I finally emerged, after days of ditching my classes, exhausted and profoundly grateful to this man who triggered new directions of thought in my work, I had a book, *Black Humor*, that would see publication within a year. Before drifting fully into fiction, I would finish six collections of this kind, see more than 1,000 drawings published in *The Chicago Tribune, Black World* and scores of other periodicals and produce and co-host one how-to-draw public television series, "Charlie's Pad."

Unfortunately—or perhaps fortunately—this conversion could not last. As many critics today recognize, the built-in danger of this cultural nationalism is the very tendency toward the provincialism, separatism and essentialist modes of thought that characterize the Anglophilia it opposes. My brief flirtation with this inescapable style of thought soon became frustration after I'd written six novels in two years (one each school quarter) under its spell. When, under the supervision of the late John Gardner, I wrote my next novel, I began to ease toward Pico's philosophy. I simply had no other choice. I was never good at group-think.

The endless questions I wanted to explore—our experience of technology, the nature of personal identity, even the relationship between the Indian religions that inspired Gandhi's nonviolent civil disobedience and the methods of Martin Luther King—were either dismissed by nationalist thinkers as irrelevant to black life or systematically excluded by the narrowly political and often naive approach of black cultural ideology.

Therefore, I revisited Toomer, Wright and Ellison. I resigned myself to being a bit out of step, if need be, with the literary and political trends of the seventies and even to going unpublished if the sort of philosophical fiction I envisaged was unacceptable. My agent can verify that I did incur the cost: My second novel of this period, *Oxherding Tale*, which I think is my best, went through 25 publishers before Indiana University Press took the great risk of releasing it.

Throughout those difficult years I tried to maintain that most insecure of positions demanded by philosophy: namely, a perpetual openness to thoughts and feelings wherever I found them. And a tremendous source of help for this was my 11-year association with John Gardner.

Although he never claimed to be an original philosopher, the outstanding model he provided to thousands of young artists was invaluable. Here was a man who, at 48, already knew 12 languages but taught himself Greek in order to provide his students at Breadloaf with his own translation of Homer's *Iliad*, a work he thought of the highest excellence. Here was an author who experienced rejection for 15 years, then published 32 books and more than 100 stories in numerous forms and genres. Here was a man who wrote for 72-hour stretches without sleep, often rising from bed (so his fiancée tells me) mumbling sleepily, "Time to do God's work."

Gardner was a classical scholar and critic of contemporary fiction, librettist, translator and musician (his instrument was the French horn) who spear-headed the national debate on "moral fiction" (and suffered severe criticism for doing so). He supported good writing by anyone, regardless of race—here, in Africa and Japan. For Gardner, as his students can testify, the beauty and basic soundness of good craftsmanship (*technē*) was a form of truth, and fiction itself he called "concrete philosophy." Shoddiness of any sort and slipshod work in art *and* thought, or things done in haste or indifference were, for this poet-philosopher, the very denial of the good, the true and the beautiful. Or, as he once put it, if our furniture were as poorly made as our fiction, we would always be falling onto the floor.

In the lives of these writers I've mentioned, all of whom left a large, lasting impression on American literature (and me), we see that they are "philosophical." But it is more important to say that Pico's restless spirit of inquiry and dedication to excellence at all costs lives within them, as it must in anyone who wishes to remain artistically vital and to grow. The philosophical writer is simply the man or woman who, all concerns for profit aside, wishes only to be open to the world of culture and consciousness in all the fascinating, constantly changing forms it takes. They leave us gifts of beauty that enrich the world for those who follow. And this, for the philosopher, has always been reward enough.

Novelists of Memory

During the last two decades remarkable and still uncharted transformations have taken place in the literature of black America. Once dismissed as "provincial" by white critics of another era, and plagued by poor sales and little publicity, the fiction of the finest Afro-American authors in the 1980s frequently appears on that perennial barometer of popularity, the best-sellers' list, receives critical acclaim and extensive classroom use, and is regarded by many as being the most exciting—as well as controversial—writing published today. Perhaps most significant of all, many of the preeminent leaders of this pioneering new fiction are black women who, as a group, were long the "invisible" authors in a literary tradition almost as old as the nation itself.

But even though black fiction has changed and, by virtue of this, is transforming the American novel and short story, it nevertheless brings to its present the artistic promise and problems, both political and esthetic, of its past. In fact, the Harlem Renaissance of the 1920s and slave narratives of the 19th century are as much at the heart of this 1980s renaissance in black letters as the explosion of new thematic and technical directions taken by contemporary authors. In order to fully appreciate these changes, and how the past prefigured the present, we must look back to the first large-scale outpouring of Afro-American creativity, during the period between two world wars.

The word *renaissance* when applied to the 1920s is something of a misnomer. What came to pass, in point of fact, was the first genuine flowering of black fiction brought about by a unique ensemble of social changes. The most significant of these occurred when rural blacks, fleeing lynching and segregation in the South, migrated to urban centers like New York City's Harlem and found themselves side-by-side with Africans, northern blacks free since the Revolutionary War and liberal whites fascinated, during the jazz-and-gin-baby era, with black folkways. In other words, all the ingredients were present for the creation of a progressive, international black consciousness and culture. It was also the heyday of that great West Indian political showman, Marcus Garvey. Garvey's United Negro Improvement Association inspired Harlemites with a "Back to Africa" movement which, by the 1950s, would be succeeded by the separatist philosophy of the early Nation of Islam.

Recording these massive changes in his essay "The New Negro" (1925), scholar Alain Locke reported that "the day of 'aunties,' 'uncles' and 'mammies' is equally gone. Uncle Tom and Sambo have passed on. . . . In the very process of being transported the Negro is being transformed." A key element for "the new Negro's" emergence, he noted, was the frequent return of writers like poets Langston Hughes and Claude McKay and satirist Wallace Thurman to black folk sources for inspiration. Two of these authors are critical for shaping the fiction of the 1980s. The first is Jean Toomer, whose only published book, *Cane* (1923), a hypnotic montage of poetry and short fiction, delivered a portrait of southern black life as so mythic and shot through with elemental mysteries that it clearly belongs in the tradition of American transcendentalism stretching back to Emerson and Thoreau. This is doubly so for his visionary poem, "Blue Meridian" (1936), a Whitmanesque work where Toomer envisions the American of the future as a spiritualized being destined to break all forms of false duality between blacks and whites, men and women. The other seminal author is Zora Neale Hurston, noted both for her ground-breaking anthropological work in *Mules and Men* (1935) and her beautiful use of southern folk material in such stories as "The Gilded Six-Bits" (1933) and her most famous novel, *Their Eyes Were Watching God* (1939). Here, as in her other works, Hurston reveals herself to be a prophetic writer, fully 50 years ahead of her time in exploring the complex relationship between black men and women, and in using the most crucial Renaissance idea—the importance of the common folk—to portray the "new Negro" female on subtler levels than did her contemporaries.

Yet despite the astonishing fertility of the Harlem Renaissance, several forces brought it to an end—or perhaps to a 40-year interruption, if we consider the 1980s to be its continuation, as I shall argue here. One force was external—the Great Depression. The other was internal—a fickleness by the movement's white patrons, such as arts promoter Carl Van Vechten, who encouraged the Renaissance writers because they considered the Negro to be a creature free of white men's cares during the Roaring Twenties. These years were characterized by America's moral fatigue after World War I, the popularity of Freud's idea that civilization was based on the repression of eros, and the notion that people of color were less inhibited and closer to natural rhythms—even to the subconscious—than their white brothers. As poet Sterling Brown noted in "A Century of Negro Portraiture" (1966), the stereotypical image of "the Exotic Primitive" reinforced during the '20s became as misleading about black life as the earlier racist myths of the contented slave and violent, bestial black created by Plantation School writers of the Old South like Joel Chandler Harris and Thomas Dixon. Another decade would have to pass—one that saw the creation of the Federal Writers Project, which sponsored such talents as Richard Wright, Willard Motley, Ralph Ellison and Frank Yerby—before an even newer image of black America entered our literature. It came in 1940 as an overnight best-seller called *Native Son*.

Richard Wright's brutal thriller about a black chauffeur who accidentally murders his employer's daughter wasn't merely the first best-seller by a black writer. It was also the birth of the black proletarian protest novel and the achievement of a new level of intellectual complexity in Afro-American storytelling. Many blacks, as it turned out, recoiled at the relentless wretchedness of the protagonist Bigger Thomas's life in southside Chicago, and argued that Wright had ignored positive features of black culture. For all these complaints, *Native Son* remains after almost 50 years our most phenomenologically successful portrait of inner-city poverty and dehumanization, and is responsible for inspiring a full generation of authors: Chester Himes; James Baldwin, who first criticized, then continued Wright's tradition of protest fiction from the decade of the 1950s until his death in 1987; John A. Williams; and Ralph Ellison, whose many-splendored *Invisible Man* (1952) stands at the summit of imaginative black writing in the 20th century. Correction: *Invisible Man* has repeatedly been selected, and rightly, as one of the 10 finest novels by *any* American, black or white, since World War II.

Clearly, *Invisible Man* is indebted to *Native Son* for certain themes, such as the social "invisibility" of black Americans and the "blindness" of whites to their individuality, and also for a few paradigmatic situations—for example, the relationship of blacks to modern mass social movements like Ellison's fictional Brotherhood; Ellison, however, conceives his picaresque masterpiece in an exuberant Hegelian spirit that blends several literary genres, from Mark Twain to William Faulkner, from the slave narrative to the surrealistic Kafkaesque parable, as he traces in chapters that rise and crest like separate short stories the progress of a nameless black student from one intellectual "posture" of 20th-century life to another. And, as if this were not enough, Ellison gives our age a new metaphor for social alienation. It is a tour de force of writing technique. *Invisible Man* spills over with stylish set pieces: the opening chapters that satirize black colleges based on the accommodationist teachings of Booker T. Washington; the Harlem eviction scene in which every object reveals black history; Ras's monologue to Todd Clifton, which captures the essential thought of Black Nationalism in the style of Garvey; allusions to James Joyce and Sigmund Freud; and concerns spanning the Harlem Renaissance and years following it.

Individual Vision

Almost everything one could want in a novel or artistic vision is here: humor, suspense, black history from which Ellison's vivid imagination teases forth truth beneath mere facts, and a rogues' gallery of grotesques. It is also here, as well as in his many essays and interviews from 1952 through 1988, that Ellison reiterates a point he feels we must never forget: "The thing that Americans have to learn over and over again is that they are *individuals* and they have the responsibility of individual vision."

If Ellison's protagonist could forget this as he "boomeranged" from one racial abuse to another, how much easier it was to forget the priority of "individual vision" in the tumultuous years following *Invisible Man's* publication. By the late 1960s, in a decade marked by political assassinations, an unpopular war and a growing new militancy represented by the rise of the Nation of Islam and its charismatic spokesman Malcolm X, the trend in black arts and letters shifted from individualism to the call for a communal art outlined by proponents of the Black Arts Movement, an outgrowth of the Black Power Movement. These changes, one sees in hindsight, were inevitable. The dominant themes in black literature were paranoia and genocide. The "evidence" for a black American holocaust seemed to many Afro-Americans irrefutable as new histories documented three centuries' worth of racial oppression. Children were dynamited in a black church, and Martin Luther King Jr. was assassinated at a motel in Memphis, Tennessee. It was a period when novelist John A. Williams could write powerfully, in *The Man Who Cried I Am* (1967), of the secret, international "King Alfred" plan to squash African countries just breaking free of colonialism and to suppress inner-city riots in America. Sam Greenlee's *The Spook Who Sat by the Door* (1969) became the most unexpected best-seller of the early 1970s because, as one militant friend told me, young blacks read it to gain recipes for insurrection.

If blacks were to survive, according to the reasoning of the day, and if black culture was to be preserved, the artist must pull together with all people of the African Diaspora. Furthermore, many advocates of the Black Arts Movement proposed, in addition to the celebration of culture by people of color, the need to retreat from the deep, structural causes of racism: namely, individualism seen as selfishness, crude materialism and Anglophilia in all its diverse forms. It was, all in all, a call for a new American humanism—a new spirituality—very much in line with other varieties of "countercultural" thought in the air by 1968. Among the frontline fighters for this brave, new black art were the late John Oliver Killens, whose *The Cotillion* (1972) is a no-holds-barred comedy of racial manners cast in the black-nationalist mode; poetic talents like Haki Madhubuti (Don L. Lee), the early Nikki Giovanni and a politically converted Gwendolyn Brooks; and, in theater, where the "communal" emphasis works better perhaps than in the novel, Ed Bullins and his mentor, the polymathic theoretician and playwright, Amiri Baraka (LeRoi Jones).

More than any writer, Baraka is responsible for defining the style and syntax of cultural-nationalist poetics in the decade of the 1960s. He counseled young artists to bring back their talents to their communities, as he himself had done when he moved from a life as LeRoi Jones, the celebrated 1950s Beat Generation poet, to become an *imamu* (teacher), a prime mover in Newark politics and an indefatigable lecturer. His ever-evolving oeuvre includes numerous plays and collections of essays and poetry; a significant work on black music, *Blues People* (1963); a novel, *The System of Dante's Hell* (1965); political tracts; and ethical works like "A Black Value System" (1970). With poet Larry Neal he coauthored the controversial 1968 anthology *Black Fire* (recalling the Harlem Renaissance magazine *Fire*, which was intended to "burn up" old-fashioned ideas about blacks), and more will doubtlessly have been added to his unique and singularly important literary career by the time you read this.

But this astonishing phase of Afro-American literary history would develop its own limitations, the first and foremost of these being a tendency toward separatism that ran counter to the push for integration by the majority of blacks. Secondly, it teetered often toward "essentialism," or the belief in an inherent racial nature. Sadly, many subjects worthy of artistic treatment were bypassed if they did not seem immediately relevant to the political problems of the moment. In addition, the emphasis on promoting a distinct "black identity" often led in the work of many authors to one-dimensional portraits of whites as well as a highly selective reading of the African and American past that oversimplified the complexity of historical phenomena.

Fortunately, as interest in the Black Arts Movement came under criticism, something new was percolating in black fiction, a movement that would diversify and deepen the subject matter and style of Afro-American literature, indicating a return to Ellison's individual vision. For example, in his essay, "A Black Criterion" (1967), Clarence Major wrote that the black poet "must chop away at white criterion and destroy its hold on his black mind because seeing the world through white eyes from a black soul causes death. . . . With the poem we must erect a spiritual nation we all can be proud of." No question that Major in the 1960s agreed with Baraka, whom he acknowledges in this esthetic statement. But soon thereafter Major's fiction underwent an extraordinary change, one fostered perhaps by his affiliation with the Fiction Collective, a cooperative publishing venture started in the early 1970s by a handful of "experimental" writers.

Easing back from black nationalism, Major began the steady, single-handed enterprise of interpreting for black American literature modernist techniques pioneered by James Joyce, Gertrude Stein and Samuel Beckett, Major's particular contribution being the esthetic interface between painting and prose expressions. For this he is especially well suited; he is himself a painter, ethnolexicographer and poet, and in his principal experimental work, *Emergency Exit* (1979), all these strands are orchestrated. Yet no one can easily categorize Major; his recent work, *Such Was the Season* (1987), returns to a more conventional narrative to tell a story of Atlanta politics through the voice of an elderly black woman, which proves, if nothing else, that since the 1960s Major considers all forms of fiction—and all subjects—to be proper fields for black artistic expression.

Satire and Sentiment

Equally innovative in the way they *interpret* black life are Ishmael Reed and Al Young, two California-based novelists and coeditors of the literary journal *Quilt*. As early as 1967, Reed published his first novel, *The Free-Lance Pallbearers*, which a *Village Voice* reviewer praised for "opening up a new area of satire. He has the nerve to extend his range to the black world itself." Reed's free-wheeling style of social comedy, the first to appear since Wallace Thurman's barbed satire, *The Blacker the Berry* (1929), crackles throughout all his fiction, especially his best-known novel, *Mumbo Jumbo* (1972), a detective story set during the Harlem Renaissance, which is metaphorically treated as an epidemic of black creativity called "Jes Grew." As might be expected, Reed has championed innovative writers of all colors during his 21-year career, and has waged a one-man war against what he sees as the oversights of the East Coast publishing world—for example, the dismissal of black folk-art forms and popular fiction (detective stories, even soap operas), all forms Reed himself has worked with. Lately, he has also challenged what he sees as an antimale tendency in black feminist writers, debating supporters of Alice Walker's *The Color Purple* (1982) and publishing a novel satirizing them, *Reckless Eyeballing* (1986). Whatever his detractors may say of him, all must admit that Reed is a writer of acute originality and courage.

Al Young is also a comic writer, but in a gentler fashion. A veteran poet, free-lance journalist, musician and screenwriter currently at work on a film biography of Charlie Parker, Young is far more concerned with vivid character portrayals and positive emotions than social protest. In fact, in a 1972 interview called "Statement on Aesthetics, Poetics, Kinetics," he explained that "I've always believed the individual human heart to be more revolutionary than any political party or platform." And so he demonstrates in novels like *Snakes* (1970), which chronicles the life of a young musician, and in his forthcoming *Seduction by Light*, a drama about blacks in Hollywood. He urges readers to remember those aspects of black life that balance the brutality of racism and the pain of dislocation. And it is no surprise that at a 1987 writers' conference where Young read from his autobiographical essay, "Unripened Light," the music he selected to accompany his work was that old favorite, "Accentuate the Positive."

This concern of Young's with the "individual human heart" is also found in two story collections by James Alan McPherson, a protégé of Ralph Ellison, whose Pulitzer Prize-winning *Hue and Cry* (1970) contributed to the revival of the American short story. In this first collection, in his second, *Elbow Room* (1977), and in such remarkable autobiographical writings as "Going Up to Atlanta" (1987), McPherson creates a vivid collection of white and black characters who, in their anguish and frustration, strike a universal chord of human suffering and redemption. Although not a prolific writer, nor a prose stylist, McPherson focuses his energies on brutally honest stories about white, black and interracial couples who betray one another, as in his story "Hue and Cry"; or upon militants who bully less politically committed blacks with guilt and self-loathing, in "Of Cabbages and Kings." In his most anthologized story, "A Solo Song: For Doc," he creates a moving tale of the black Pullman porters who provided a special form of service that helped make the railroads prosper before their employers, out of fear of these men, forced them to leave.

Despite the highly individual vision of these authors, something of the communal approach of the 1960s remains, but with an unusual genealogical slant inspired by the popularity of Alex Haley's *Roots* (1976). This account of Haley's ancestors, it should be noted, didn't simply make finding one's history a fad—no, it gave to the 1970s an interpretative metaphor (and a positive one) as compelling as that provided by Ellison's *Invisible Man* two decades before. Both Haley's generation-spanning saga of the American descendants of African Kunte Kinte and Ernest Gaines's story of an old slave woman's triumph over oppression in *The Autobiography of Miss Jane Pittman* laid the foundations for a new wing in black American fiction, what one might call the "novel of memory." This is not Proustian remembrance by any means. For many black authors memory is a moral obligation, an effort to honor their elders and enshrine the meaning of their lives—biographies of quiet heroism and courage left out of white versions of history—in the theater of the novel, poem or play. Also significant is how these retellings of history extend the time-honored tradition of black autobiography, a form originating with the slave narrative and represented by such modern classics as *The Autobiography of Malcolm X*, which Haley helped the influential Muslim leader compose.

Bear in mind that these praise songs for one's predecessors do not question the accuracy of memory, nor do they take as a theme the philosophical problem of history as an interpretative chore. For this we must turn to David Bradley's ambitious *The Chaneysville Incident* (1981), a stunning historical novel about the historical imagination itself. Among the new crop of "novels of memory," *Chaneysville* is vividly distinguished by bringing readers the excitement and downright mystery of uncovering the past. Its protagonist, John Washington, a black historian, is driven by his father's death and his white girlfriend's slave-owning predecessors to uncover a slave catastrophe that happened a hundred years ago in Pennsylvania, one hushed up by the locals and implicating men now come into prominence. Ploughing through a dense forest of documents, musty relics and "cold facts" that refuse to offer up their meaning, John discovers the hermeneutic or interpretative dimension of "History," a shape-shifting phenomenon capable of changing before his eyes as he chases it. In other words, for the first time in black American fiction, history is viewed not as a *donnée* but as a human project that must be continually achieved, and then only provisionally, and not until all the black historian's imagination and passions are brought to bear on the task of creating a theory (fiction) linking all the fragments into a coherent pattern. In this sense, Bradley's novel, filled with fully detailed characters and research into Pennsylvania history, broadens the intellectual field prepared by *Roots* and becomes a remembrance novel for an entire region of America.

John Edgar Wideman, Bradley's onetime teacher and a former Rhodes scholar, has also devoted himself to this quasi-biographical project. In "The Return of Albert Wilkes," one of a triptych of narratives in *Sent for You Yesterday* (1983), his character Carl thinks, "If I don't wake up Homewood [the neighborhood in Pittsburgh where the author grew up] will be gone. If I run far away, the Homewood streets will disappear." The theme of "returning home" is highlighted again and again in Wideman's five novels, his stories and *Brothers and Keepers* (1984), a biting meditation on the imprisonment of his brother for robbery (while he the novelist went on to success in the white world) and on the destinies that simultaneously divide and bond brothers. Even his brilliant essays on language counsel other writers that the black speech learned in childhood must not be lost when they are overtaken by worldly success and its official tongue, standard English. Not always an easy writer to read, given his frequent reliance on stream-of-consciousness techniques, Wideman writes fiction that is nevertheless a treasury—and transmission—of the American past for future generations.

On the larger literary landscape of the 1980s that transmission includes the recovery of black authors either overlooked or misunderstood during their own time. Thus, critic Henry Louis Gates Jr. has endeavored to make available, in the valuable 30-volume Shomburg Collection published by Oxford University Press, 19th-century narratives and popular novels written by black women authors. Gates's feat of excavation and reconstruction demonstrates that considerably more Afro-American literature was written a century ago than was imagined, and that black women were pivotal, not peripheral, to this work. Most important among the later re-discoveries is the fiction and folkloric research of Zora Neale Hurston, who after her brilliant career spent her last days in anonymity, her contributions to anthropology and literature ignored until vigorously championed by one of America's best-selling authors, Alice Walker.

Walker's third novel, *The Color Purple* (1982) looks back, as one might expect, to Hurston, then forward to black feminism in the post-civil-rights period signaled in 1970 by the appearance of an important anthology, *The Black Woman*. At this time, and for 18 years to follow, a shift occurs in the character of fiction by black women. It emerges as a literature indebted to Hurston and dedicated to disclosing a social perspective long slighted in American letters yet linked in two ways to the earlier Black Arts Movement. On the one hand, it generally celebrates the community of women rather than individualism; and, on the other, it often presents a positive, spiritual image of the Afro-American female as a Conjure Woman—a modern-day black wizard and *griot* or tribal storyteller—open to magical, non-Western ways of thought and feeling.

Three Sisters

These elements do not account, however, for the public excitement and controversy triggered by *The Color Purple*, especially by its film version directed by Steven Spielberg. Like a surgeon's probe, Walker's simple story about a southern girl abused by whites and black men, then lifted from oppression after learning her own strength (and after a lesbian encounter), became the focal point for problems festering in the black family. According to government statistics, half the black children born in the United States today are born to single parents, and half of these are teenagers, like Walker's heroine Celie at the beginning of the novel. Little wonder that Walker's protagonist could become emblematic of the concerns of black women in a period when drug abuse, AIDS and black male unemployment have so badly pressured the family, the fundamental social unit in the black world. It is for these sociological reasons, more so than for artistic ones, that Walker's novel stands at the pinnacle of women's writing in the 1980s. Her use of an epistolary form here is, for example, esthetically interesting, but she is not quite as convincing in delivering the attraction of single-gender affairs as, say, James Baldwin in *Another Country* (1960), or the darker, political side of sexuality, which Gayl Jones uncovers so well in her novels *Corregidora* (1975) and *Eva's Man* (1976).

However, the most gifted storyteller among the new women writers is, beyond all doubt, Gloria Naylor. Naylor's *The Women of Brewster*

Place (1982), a collection of interlocking stories first published in *Essence* magazine, presents the lives of several black women abandoned or betrayed by their husbands, lovers or sons. Their experiential world is identical to those of Walker and Jones, and to the universe of seven scarred and scared black women in Ntozake Shange's 1975 play *for colored girls who have considered suicide/when the rainbow is enuf*, where her characters describe how "bein alive & bein a woman & bein colored is a metaphysical dilemma." But Naylor knows her women better as individuals; she slides easily from examining a welfare mother's triumph over despair after she sees a black production of *A Midsummer Night's Dream* to portraying a bottomed-out 1960s civil-rights worker who achieves sisterhood with her more conservative, often annoying mother. Her latest book, *Mama Day* (1988), praised as a positive love story set on an all-black island (and using a Conjure Woman motif), shows Naylor's ever-increasing tonal range and imagination.

These writerly virtues can also be found in the consummate prose mastery and lyrical narratives of America's most honored black writer, Toni Morrison. Her best book, *Beloved*, recipient of the 1988 Pulitzer Prize for fiction, was also, as it turned out, a lightning rod for literary controversy, first because it did not receive the National Book Award, then because 40 black writers and critics published an "open letter" in *The New York Times Book Review*, lamenting Morrison's being passed over for the Pulitzer Prize in previous years.

Like many of the "novelists of memory," Morrison interprets the slave past in *Beloved* in ways thoroughly consistent with the Black Arts period, thus sidestepping the social complexities and ambiguities found in Bradley's novel. Yet no one has offered, sentence-by-sentence, a more painfully compelling and microscopically detailed account of the daily humiliation of 19th-century bondage than Morrison achieves in her story about a Medea-like woman who murders her daughter to save her from a slavemaster. Most interesting of all, Morrison renders this spell-inducing tale not in the naturalistic style of previous Afro-American novels about the Peculiar Institution of slavery but with the "magical realism" we have come to associate with Gabriel García Márquez, filling her protagonist's world with slavery's restless ghosts and luscious imagery that suggests enchantment hidden even in the most ordinary of things.

The writers of the new Afro-American renaissance reveal themselves to be as diverse and individual as their predecessors in the 1920s, though all are clearly united in the common task of examining the social and political forces that have shaped American culture—this, in vivid contrast to many of their white counterparts who in the 1980s retreated into "minimalism," or recording hermetically private lives with little connection to the nation's multicultural past or common future. Many oversights and oversimplifications inherited from the 1960s have, in books by the best of these writers, been replaced by broadening of the black cultural vision to include themes and literary traditions not previously associated with the "black" experience. For in their work it is precisely the nature—the imaginative boundaries—of racial life that is being tested in each new story, novel and play. If this is, on the whole, potentially the most exciting experiment in contemporary fiction, it is because here the cutting-edge questions of personal identity, our relationship to our forebears and the meaning of freedom are dramatically thrown into relief. As such, black literature has become, after a century of neglect, a literature central to the ongoing effort to define the American experience and the adventure of democracy in the modern age.

A Phenomenology of the Black Body

A bawdy old black folktale celebrates the physical superiority of black men:

> Two white farmers sat before the stove in a general store in Alabama, arguing over who had the longest tool as an old Negro named Willis swept the front porch. They agreed to compare lengths. The man with the longest would get $25 for each additional inch. The first unzipped his fly. Six inches. The second did the same. Seven. The first turned to Willis, and said, "Let's see yours, Willis." The janitor trembled and shook his head. "Nassuh, Ah doan think Ah'd better do that, sar." The white man became angry. "I said for you to get in on this heah bet, Willis!" Afraid to say no, the janitor uncoiled his tool on the table—it took a while, friend: Willis just kept throwing it out like a fishing line. Twelve inches. Someone said, "God damn!" The two men gave Willis $125, and he raced home to show the money to his wife Maybelle. Staring skeptically at her husband, Maybelle asked. "You got alla that just for being big?" Willis whooped and went into hysterics. "Honey, that was the easiest money Ah ever made! Them white folks just better thank the Lord Ah wasn't on hard."

Laughing at the good fortune of Willis, we may lose sight of the fact that his triumph is based on cultural assumptions that lock him into the body and, to echo W. E. B. DuBois, create in his life a "double-consciousness" in need of resolution. This essay seeks to define the ambiguity of his situation and describe the harrowing constraints upon both Willis and his white competitors.

Our past experience as a people can often be understood through its expression in language, myths, stereotypes, symbols, and folktales like this one. As multi-layered complexes, they present collectively shared and communicated meanings. But before we can talk intelligently about the "black experience" of the body, in this or any other narrative, we must first get clear on what is essential to all experience—the correlate of consciousness and its content, *noesis-noema*, or subject and object. A rule for phenomenology is that there is never an object without a corresponding subject, and that "Consciousness is always conscious-ness *of* something," to quote Edmund Husserl. Given the universality of these structures for consciousness, it is reasonable to say that there is neither an impenetrable "white" or "black" experience, which are mutually exclusive, but rather that there are diverse human variations upon experience, which can always be communicated imaginatively or vicariously across racial, political, and cultural lines through language in its two analytic forms: philosophy and literature. Perhaps this point is disagreeable to proponents of cultural pluralism, but it is a presup-position of the philosophy of experience—phenomenology—that is here assumed as a working methodology. The symbol of the black body, for example, if interrogated, should disclose a racial experience wrought mythically. Our folk literature simultaneously conceals and reveals our primordial racial situation, and must be carefully unpacked if we wish to wrench self-understanding from it.

Black writers, particularly novelists and poets in search of fresh ways of seeing things familiar, frequently feel the power of folk myths and stereotypes and, so moved, wrestle with uncovering their meaning. Weaving in and out of Frantz Fanon's works are thematizations of black consciousness from the vantage point of existential phenomenol-ogy, but without a turn to the body as the radix for interpreting racial experience. In his controversial essay, "The Primevil Mitosis," Eldridge Cleaver brooks the stereotype of Black American physicality by now checking his own feelings (as an experiencing subject) against the myth, now rendering its terms rigidly abstract, now pursuing its more painful political implications. His conclusion: "The gulf between the Mind and Body will be seen to coincide with the gulf between the two races."[1] But *is* there such a gulf between the Mind and Body?

Cleaver assumes a basic division between the bodily and mental experiences of blacks and whites. Racism is the given, historically con-stituted and lying in wait for black consciousness, concealing the ethical dualism which has—over long centuries of Western cultural develop-ment—made white "good" and black "evil." Cleaver, focusing on one aspect of the phenomenon, the psycho-physical, finds that blacks are stripped of a mental life, which leaves them only a bodily existence (albeit a superior one like that of our janitor Willis), and he assigns them the name, "The Supermasculine Menial." He writes: "The body is tropical, warm, hot; Fire! It is soft, pleasing to the touch, luscious to the kiss. The blood is hot. Muscles are strength."[2] Alienated from this sensuous profile of the body, whites are characterized by Cleaver as "The Omnipotent Administrator." Weakness, frailty, cowardice, effeminacy, decay, and impotence are profiles associated with the white man's situation of abstraction from the body. Here, Cleaver's concerns in *Soul on Ice* are basically political, sexual, and polemical, not philosophical. But his attempt to explain our experience of embodiment may yield more philosophically than the author knows. His division recalls Paul Ricoeur's belief that, "It is possible for man to take two divergent and non-reconcilable perspectives upon himself because within man there is a non-coincidence which is that of the *finite* and the *infinite*,"[3] or of the physical and mental, consciousness and the body. It is even more illuminating when compared to Fanon's statement that, "There are times when the black man is locked into his body."[4]

Sexuality is not truly at issue in *Soul on Ice*. That is merely the manifestation of a larger problem of consciousness and the body in the black experience. The issue at stake is how blacks experience their own bodies within a world of racial restriction. By speaking descriptively, by casting the problem in absolute and often simple terms, Cleaver offers us the occasion for a broader consideration of experience, the body, and black consciousness.

Modern philosophy in the West since Descartes has entertained the idea that man is not identical with his physical being. In a crude formulation, man is presented mythologically and often philosophically as a mixture of mind and matter, spirit and flesh, consciousness and body, carnal shell and *Ka*, and remains to himself something of a mystery. The dialectic of matter and mind, subject and object, is a thread running the length of Western intellectual history, beginning with Plato's world of flux and world of forms. The later sundering of man and the world into mental and physical substances by Descartes in *The Meditations* throws light on the issue Cleaver is trying to bring to clarity— consciousness is experienced as being identical with, yet curiously distinct from, the body. One could almost categorize Western philosophy along the lines of whether a particular approach is primarily concerned with the subject of experience, consciousness, idealism, or the soul; if it emphasizes the object, matter, materialism, the body; or if it seeks a reconciliation between the two. Maurice Merleau-Ponty offers a simple but concise formulation to correct this false dualism that underlies the division between "The Omnipotent Administrator" and "The Supermasculine Menial": "I am my body."[5] It is that which reeves the subject to a world, anchors him in history, thus individualizing him, and makes possible perception and "meaning." It is my point of reference on the universe. I, as subject, am often at "one" with it, yet my relation as a human self to my body is also that of *radical otherness*. I *am* my body while I am also *not* my body (or I experience myself as not simply reducible to my body as the empirical object of physics, chemistry, neurology). Experience without "embodied consciousness" is as unthinkable as experience without the *noesis-noema* correlate: it is the irreducible way we are in the world. I am conscious of the world through the medium of my body.

To say that the body is our anchorage in the world is to bring this discussion to a consideration of "intentionality," the structure which gives meaning to experience. Intentions are at the heart of consciousness, or the *noesis*-pole, to the extent that they determine the manner in which we perceive the world. At this instant, let us say that I am a white administrator on campus. A strapping black student with a full natural, dashiki, coal-black complexion, and dark sunglasses comes into my office with a "dip-down," rolling gait. If my hobby is painting, perhaps I look toward the colorfulness of his clothing, and see him as a future subject for my canvas. Suppose I have just read Claude McKay's *Home to Harlem*, a novel which emphasizes the natural spontaneity of blacks; in this case I see the rhythms of his walk, the musicality of his movements in contrast to my own. Or, finally, suppose I am concerned that my daughter is being bused across town to a black school—Will she encounter people like this? In each instance the same student presents these multiple profiles of himself; they *are* his appearances, and each discloses a different "meaning." We have yet to speak of *his* experience upon entering the room and what my intentionality causes to arise in his consciousness. To "intend" an object or content of consciousness is to be "in-formed" by it as well as to *give form* to it. The mind is in no way passive; it is a participant in each act of knowing—self and object being inseparable poles of experience. It is also possible *not* to see other "meanings" or profiles presented by the object if the perceiver is locked within the "Natural Attitude," as Husserl calls it, and has been conditioned culturally or racially to fix himself upon certain "meanings." Rollo May, for example, reports of a patient who could not see an object placed before him on a table—it remained invisible on the basis of his inability to bring it forth intentionally as a content of consciousness.[6]

But consciousness is "embodied." Our desires, too, are "embodied," and it is clearly the case that every act of intending involves, to some extent, "interest." By this I mean that acting, willing, and intending are closely related. I see the student in a certain way because I fear for my daughter while she is across town. To *perceive* a content is to *conceive* that content. "The theory of the body image is, implicitly, a theory of perception."[7]

My body for me is not an assemblage of organs juxtaposed in space; my possession of it is undivided, and I know where my limbs are through a *body image*, know, when I sit at my desk, how my crossed feet appear, though I cannot see them. In all perception within a figure-ground relationship, where I either bring an object forth for attention or let it remain undifferentiated in the "ground," my body is the third term: it points me to the left or right, determines up and down, allows me to know space because as "embodied consciousness" I am in space, and know time because embodiment has temporality as one of its structures.

Right and left, established by the body, are sources of the lawful and forbidden; the body is emblematic; if I am "downcast," the body gestures accordingly with a drooping posture. "The body is our general medium for having a world."[8] The blind man's stick is no longer alien to him, not a mere object, but his bodily extension; the woman with a feather in her hat keeps a safe distance between it and things that might snap it off, but without looking: she *feels* these distances. All this is understood by the term *body image*, or in the work of Fanon, *body schema*. We see that motility is basic to intentionality.

Our first phenomenological act in a thematization of the black body involves a suspension or bracketing of all sociological and scientific theories concerning race. We wish to purify a field in which the body becomes the primary focus of racial consciousness. Whether black or white, the body is still experienced as having an ambiguity, a non-coincidence of mind and matter. I *am* my body, but clearly there is magic in the fact that when I say "Spread your fingers" the digits on my hand do so. I see my hand on my desk and sometimes it is alien; perhaps I do not even recognize it as *mine* when I see it in a photograph. Stranger still, I know that I cannot see myself as others see me, white and black, as if the secret of my body and the objectivity of its "outside" belongs, not to me, but to everyone else. Furthermore, I am black. I do not see what the white other sees in my skin, but I am aware of his intentionality, and—yes—aware that I often disclose something discomfiting to him. My body gives me the world, but, as that world is given, it is one in which I can be unseen. I walk down the hallway at the university and pass a professor I know well. He glances up quickly, yet does not acknowledge that he knows me. He has seen a black, a body, that remains for him always in the background, seldom figured forth save as maid, taxi driver, or janitor. Passing, he sees me as he sees the fire extinguisher to my left, that chair outside the door. I have been seen, yet not seen, acknowledged as present to him, but in a peculiar way. I call down the hallway, "Professor Peterson!" Recognizing me, he says, "Ah, Charles," and figures me forth. He offers me his hand and, shaking it, I see perhaps what he has seen: the darkness of the black body suggests "stain" primordially. For him, and at odd moments for me, this stain of my skin gives in a sudden stroke of intentionality "darkness," "guilt," "evil," an entire galaxy of meanings. Yet, it is *I* who perceive myself as "stained," as though I were an object for myself and no longer a subject. In fact, the stain of the black body seems figuratively to darken consciousness itself, to overshadow my existence as a subject. Is it this way for him? Cleaver writes:

> The chip on the Supermasculine Menial's shoulders is the fact that he has been robbed of his mind. In an uncannily effective manner, the society in which he lives assumed in its very structure that he, minus a mind, is the embodiment of Brute Power. The bias and reflexes of the society are against the cultivation of even the functioning of his mind, and it is borne in upon him from all sides that the society is deaf, dumb, and blind to his mind.[9]

That is, incapable of the intentionality that would allow the Supermasculine Menial to disclose an interiority. We shall call this situation the "black-as-body." Quoting Fanon: "In the white world the man of color encounters difficulties in the development of his bodily schema. Consciousness of the body is solely a negating activity . . . the body is surrounded by an atmosphere of uncertainty."[10] I am aware of each of my limbs through my *body image*; similarly, I am aware of my skin surface, my epidermal encasement through my *body image*, and particularly when I am "seen." "Saying that I have a body is thus a way of saying that I can be seen as an object and that I try to be seen as a subject, that another can be my master, so that shame and shamelessness express the dialectic of the plurality of consciousness, and have a metaphysical significance."[11] Fanon warns that "though Sartre's speculations on the existence of the Other may be correct . . . their application to a black consciousness proves fallacious. That is because the white man is not only the Other, but also the master, whether real or imaginary." And again: "Jean-Paul Sartre has forgotten that the Negro suffers in his body quite differently from the white man."[12]

The experience of the black-as-body becomes, not merely a Self-Other conflict, nor simply Hegel's torturous Master-Slave dialectic, but a variation on both these conditions, intensified by the particularity of the body's appearance as black, as "stained," lacking interiority and, as Fanon writes, as being "overdetermined from without." The body as opaque and consciousness as invisible is developed in Cleaver's brief essay. And if that consciousness is not experienced by the Other as invisible, it is the repository for the offscum of racial relations—to black subjectivity is attributed the contents that white consciousness itself fears to contain or confront: bestial sexuality, uncleanliness, criminality, all the purported "dark things." In R. W. Shufeldt's *The Negro, A Menace to Civilization* (1907) and Thomas Dixon Jr.'s. *The Leopard's Spots*, the idea is extended to include black blood, which carries the germ of the underworld and the traits of lower orders of animals; one drop of black blood, for example, will cause a white family to revert to Negroid characteristics even after a full century; the mulatto, though possessing white blood, is depicted as dangerous because his surface "outside," not being stained, betrays the criminality and animality of his interior.[13]

The stereotype with which we began discloses the black-as-body but, as a pure literary presentation, it conceals the original situation of "embodied consciousness" made a problem for itself by "stain." Consider the concern our grandparents had with body complexion, "brightening the race" through careful marriage, the terrible importance of fair skin, curly hair, and "yellah women." They were not fools, these old folks; they knew what they experienced. And understood skin-bleaching creams and straightening combs as important because these changed their stained "outsides" upon which, in this social system, the depth of their "insides" would be gauged by others. (Indeed, critic Robert Bone has called Christianity in James Baldwin's *Go Tell it on the Mountain* a "spiritual bleaching cream.") Stain recalls defilement, guilt, sin, corpses that contaminate, menstruating women; and with them come the theological meanings of punishment, ostracism, and the need to be "cleansed." It was never so much that, "If you're light, you're alright," meant that whiteness was rightness on the basis of the lack of pigmentation alone; rather, it meant that, "Washing a Moor white over three generations," degree by painful degree, led to his social recognition by the Other as human subject, as—in some cases—his possessing a soul, an "inside."

I am walking down Broadway in Manhattan, platform shoes clicking on the hot pavement, thinking as I stroll of, say, Boolean expansions. I turn, thirsty, into a bar. The dimly-lit room, obscured by shadows, is occupied by whites. Goodbye, Boolean expansions. I am *seen*. But, as a black, seen as stained body, as physicality, basically opaque to others—a possibility that, of course, whites themselves have in a room of blacks. Their look, an intending beam focusing my way, suddenly realizes something larval in me. My world is epidermalized, collapsed like a house of cards into the stained casement of my skin."[14] My subjectivity is turned inside out like a shirtcuff. "And so it is not I who make a meaning for myself, but it is the meaning that was already there, pre-existing, waiting for me,"[15] much like a mugger at a boardwalk's end. All I am, can be to them, is as nakedly presented as the genitals of a plant since they cannot see my other profiles. Epidermalization spreads throughout the body like an odor, like an echoing sound. This feeling differs little from that of sexuality: a sudden dizziness and disorientation, an acute awareness of my outside, of its being for others, a tight swell at my temples. But it is not the pathological feeling of "inferiority" alone that Fanon speaks of when my being is stolen—it is Cleaver's perception of the black-as-body. Yet, Fanon is correct. "For not only must the black man be black; he must be black in relation to the white man."[16] Because it is from whites that the intention, the "meaning" of the black body comes. I sit at the bar, ignoring the Others; but the body is acutely aware of them, knows immediately when someone outside my peripheral vision has stood up. It is intense, as though consciousness has shifted to the skin's seen surfaces.

Our body responds totally to this abrupt epidermalization; consciousness for the subject is violently emptied of content: one, in fact, draws a "blank," though clearly for the white Other my interiority is, if not invisible, a space filled with sensuality, crime, or childlike simplicity. There are physiological reactions: the pulse and adrenalin increase, the seen skin becomes moist, as if the body is in open conspiracy with the white Other to confirm the sudden eclipse of my consciousness entirely by corporeality. I feel its sleepy awkwardness, and know myself not as subject but as slumberous, torpid matter. The Other awaits my slurring my words; my mouth, dry as ash, seems ready to realize his expectation. He awaits a signal of my "Negroness"—perhaps my brutalizing the language when I order a beer: some signal that we in our bodies are not the same. If I am the sort of "Negro" brought up to be a "credit to the race," I must forever be on guard against my body betraying me in public; I must suppress the profile that their frozen intentionality brings forth—I police my actions, and take precautions against myself so the myth of stain, evil, and physicality, like a Platonic form, does not appear in me.

Or, let us say, I sit sipping espresso with a white friend in the Village, discussing Borges, Barthelme, Baraka, basketball, the incredible Pele. I've smoked myself into a sore throat; I sip the scum-surfaced coffee merely to wet my lips, to ease my throat. Our conversation turns circuitously and comes to Walt Frazier. The Other slaps my knee soundly. He says, "Man, that cat is the most beautiful animal I've ever seen on a basketball court. I mean, he moves like—like a cheetah, or a big jungle cat." Make no mistake: this comes from him as the highest compliment. He is "hip," you see, liberal, a Left Bank intellectual—it is merely a *faux pas*. He has not reduced us to a "nothingness." The reduction is to "muscles are strength." Paradoxically, we are reduced to the body as the subject of physics—Brute Power. Yet, as with the rush of sexuality, a torpor glazes over my consciousness, a languor arises like a sleepiness in my limbs. The thickness of the world's texture is thinned. The body commonly extends itself in vehicles, buildings, machines, clothing. "Consciousness is being toward the thing through the intermediary of the body—to move one's body is to aim at things through it; it is to allow oneself to respond to their call."[17] But the black-as-body must see such a call as dubious, even though the "White Only" signs have been torn down, because there remain strict territorial boundaries, real or imagined, when we experience the searing Sartrean "look" of the hate-stare, when the world is epidermalized. Our body in these cases comes awake, translates itself as total physicality—it, oddly enough, feels as if it is listening with its limbs to the Other as my interiority shrivels like something burned, falls into confusion, feels threatened and, if it does not make me constitute myself as hatred (unable to change the world, I emotionally change myself), it momentarily, like a misty field, hazes over.

But we have not completely answered the question raised by Cleaver. There are black modes of flight from the black-as-body situation to consider. So far we have said that in a situation structured by a color-caste system, a black's consciousness and his lived-world (*Lebenswelt*) are frequently epidermalized and thrown into confusion when others intend him as the black-as-body. Once I am so one-sidely seen, I have several options open to me on the level of consciousness. These are also stages in recent black history:

(A) I accept this being seen only from the outside, accept my human possibility of being matter *sans* mind for the Others. I craftily use this invisibility of my interior to deceive, and thus to win survival, as the folk-hero Trickster John frequently does in the "Old Marster and John" cycle. My stain is like the heavy make-up of a clown; it conceals me completely. The motto of this useful opacity is the rhyme: "Got one mind for whitefolks to see / Got another one that's really me." That is, not being acknowledged as a subject is my strength, my chance for cunning and masquerade, for guerrilla warfare: I am a spy in the Big House. I cynically play with their frozen intentions, presuppositions, and stereotypes; I shuffle and appear lazy to avoid work, or—if I am a modern—I manipulate their basic fear of me as Darkness and Brute Power to win concessions. It is what Ralph Ellison calls "Rinehartism" in his novel *Invisible Man*. In Richard Wright's "novel-of-ideas," *The Outsider*, the protagonist is Cross Damon, a black existential hero with an extensive background in Heidegger, Husserl, and French phenomenology, who is freed from his former life by a freak subway wreck in Chicago. He assumes a new identity, but needs a false birth certificate. He thinks: "He would have to present to the officials a Negro so scared and ignorant that no white man would ever dream that he was up to anything deceptive." By shuffling, head-scratching, eye-blinking, and butchering the language, Cross pulls off the grotesque deception, and the author explains:

> And as he stood there manipulating their responses, Cross knew exactly what kind of man he would pretend to be to kill suspicion if he ever got into trouble. In his role as an ignorant, frightened Negro, each white man—except those few who were free from the race bias of their group—would leap to supply him with a background and an identity; each white man would project out on him his own conception of the Negro and he could safely hide behind it. . . . He knew that deep in their hearts those two white clerks knew that no human being on earth was as dense as he made himself out to be, but they wanted, needed to believe it of Negroes and it helped them to feel racially superior. They were pretending, just as he had been pretending.[18]

(B) Perhaps I vindicate my eloquence, culture, and my charm to demonstrate to the Other that I, despite my stained skin, do indeed have an inside. "Y'know, I was just thinking about Boolean expansions," I tell the barkeeper. I self-consciously sprinkle my speech with French (my interiority is Continental, you see). Perhaps I pretend that I am not Afro-American at all, but part Indian, Jamaican, or an African—a flight from the historical experience of American antebellum slavery in which epidermalization reaches its acme.

(C) Or I am radical, and seize the situation at its root by reversing the negative meaning of the body and, therefore, the black-as-body: "It is beautiful," I say, "I am a child of the Sun." The situation of the black-as-body possessing non-cognitive traits is not rejected in this most recent variation of cultural nationalism, but rather stood upon its head: the meaning still issues from the white Other. I applaud my athletic, amorous, and dancing ability, my street-wisdom and savoir-faire, my "soul," the food my body eats ("Yeah," I scream at my white friend in the Village, "we're naturally superior to you at sports. Uh huhn, and we satisfy our women better *too!*"); I speak of the communal ("single-body") social life of my African ancestors before the fifteenth-century slave trade, their bodily closeness to the earth. I am Antaeus in this persuasion of the alienated black self's phenomenological pilgrimage to itself, and the whites—flesh-starved invaders, freebooters, buccaneers, seamen who bring syphilis to ancient Africa—are alienated physically from the earth. They see their lost humanity in me. They steal me to take it home. If I am a member of the early Nation of Islam and believe in its mythology of Yacub, the black scientist who created a "white beast" from the black community, I intend the whites as quasi-men "grafted" from the original black-as-body until, by degrees, the Caucasian appears as a pale and pitiful abstraction from myself, ontologically removed several stages from the basic reality which I represent.

Curiously, this persuasion in which stain and the black-as-body are inverted is ahistorical; it must involve a complete reconstitution of cultural meanings with the black body as its foundation: two thousand years of color and symbolism must be recast. Hence, we see the black-as-body in this profile generating new cultural forms: African dress (body extensions), Swahili (what my body speaks), the Nation of Islam and Black Church of Christ (my interiority is black, you see), but behind such a cultural revolution, which I create, is the enigma of the black-as-body in a state of stain. I portray my body to myself as "luscious to the kiss," beautiful, "tropical," soulful, sensuous—as "Fire!" My knowledge is natural, from "Nature" (another vast body) and is called "mother-wit," a form of knowing antithetical to the lifeless thoughts in the upper recesses of the Omnipotent Administrator's brain. I intend the white body as pitifully unstained, stiff, decadent, rigid, unnatural, cerebral, and pasty like something left under my kitchen sink, away from the skin-darkening sun, for too long a time. No attempt to bridge the false dualism of the Supermasculine Menial and the Omnipotent Administrator, between the body and consciousness, is made in these variations.

It should be clear that what is described in Cleaver's "The Primevil Mitosis" is a general human possibility based upon the ability of "embodied consciousness" to be made a problem for itself within a racial caste system. As we have seen, the problem is not diminished by the customary strategies for escaping it. The black body remains an ambiguous object in our society, still susceptible to whatever meanings the white gaze assigns to it.

Postscript, 1993

This essay, which originally appeared in the Winter 1976 issue of *Ju-Ju: Research Papers in Afro-American Studies*, was written in 1975 as my "style paper" for the Ph.D. program in philosophy at SUNY-Stony Brook. Back then all doctoral candidates were required to submit for the faculty's approval an essay using the methods of one of the three principal schools of twentieth-century philosophy—analytic or British, American philosophy (pragmatism), or phenomenology—and since aesthetics was my field of concentration, I chose the latter. If memory serves, this was easily one of the hardest years of my life. As a graduate student living on a teaching assistantship, I was broke, but that June saw the birth of our son Malik, and the feverish writing of the first draft for *Oxherding Tale*, a novel I would publish seven years later. I remember monkishly retreating into one of the foulest apartment buildings in Port Jefferson, New York (it was all we could afford that summer) and, when I wasn't working on the novel, reading Sartre's *Being and Nothingness*, Heidegger's *Being and Time*, and Merleau-Ponty's *The Phenomenology of Perception* back-to-back in about the space of a month. Out of that context of unemployment and impoverishment and general concerns for my son, and fresh from my immersion in these seminal works of the German and French phenomenological movements, this essay was conjured.

Looking back across eighteen years at this descriptive analysis, I realize that my hope was to examine the black male body as a cultural object and to inquire into how it has been interpreted, manipulated, and given to us, particularly in popular culture. In general, too little has changed in the social world since the essay was first published. Indeed, for a few years things got worse. In the Bush campaign's exploitation of Willie Horton to frighten voters in 1988, in the racial slur about "Gorillas in the Mist" from the policeman who beat Rodney King as he would a dangerous animal, in the television footage of black male destructiveness during the Los Angeles riot, in the rise of the white supremacy movement in the last decade, in Pat Buchanan's attack on NEA for funding a film about gay black men (and ex-Klansman David Duke's startling though brief political success), in the decimation of black communities by AIDS, in the sexual harassment charges against Clarence Thomas, who according to Anita Hill described himself as "Long Dong Silver," in the sexist "gangster" lyrics offered by Ice T and other rap artists, in the gang-banging legions of Crips and Bloods, in the relentless barrage of statistics about murder among young black men and their failure to support their families, and even in the popular novels of several black women authors during the decade of the 1980s, we find that the black male as "Negro beast"—violent, sex-obsessed, irresponsible, and stupid—still has great currency and acceptance in our culture.

However, it's important to point out that none of these cultural meanings cluster around the black *female* body. In an amazing and revolutionary feat of cultural reconstruction, contemporary black women have made dominant the profile of the female body as, first and foremost, *spiritual*: a communal-body of politically progressive, long-suffering women who are responsible, hard-working and compassionate, who support each other in all ways, protect and nurture their children and live meaningful lives without black male assistance. The black female body is, in fact, frequently offered to us as the *original* body of a humankind descended from a black Eve of Africa. Clearly, this profile owes much to both black cultural nationalism of the late 1960s (variation "C" in the essay) and to the embracing of feminism by many black women in the 1980s. Nevertheless, like the Negro Beast stereotype, the Ur-mother profile is a mythology that obscures and one-dimensionalizes our possibilities for experiencing each black person as individual, historical, and so unique that—as in the case of my son or daughter, for example—it must be said that no one like them has ever lived before or will ever live again.

Recently one of my colleagues in African-American Studies said to me that black women have succeeded in culturally "defining" themselves in their own terms and not those of the racial (or gender) Other. If he's right, then we have no choice but to conclude that black males have *not* done this quite as well as their female counterparts. As my friend, a gentle and scholarly man, put it: "People don't know who we are. Even *we* aren't sure who we are."

But isn't that precisely the perennial human dilemma? That we are, after all, beings who must fashion moment by moment what meaning our lives will have, beings in *process* who are subject in a single lifetime to change, transformation, self-contradiction, and constant evolution? In phenomenological terms, one can only achieve adequateness in describing the black male body by employing what some philosophers have called "genetic phenomenology," *i.e.*, by examining an individual as he (or she) exhibits over time a series of profiles or disclosures of being. For a life is process, not product (or pre-given meaning). It more resembles the verb, not the noun.

This, just maybe, explains the current interest of young people in the unusual life of Malcolm X. There is much for critics of culture and philosophers to discuss in Spike Lee's monumental film tribute to this slain leader. Begin with the opening scene when Malcolm Little—a drug-dealer, pimp, and thief—visits a barber shop and has lye combed into his hair, which straightens it so thin another customer says, "It looks white." Go next to Malcolm in solitary confinement at Charles-town State Prison, where he is made to live like a caged animal. Then contrast both of these scenes to Malcolm X on his knees in a temple in Mecca, his hands raised to Allah, an ancient, haunting Muslim prayer sliding from his black throat like song. Here, the black male body is the instrument of the Most High. It is a global body connected to America, Africa, and the Middle East. It is capable of surrender and strength. It is cleansed of drugs, tobacco, and alcohol. It is the temple, the re-pository, of two millennia of Islamic scholarship, the living vessel for a culture that achieved a remarkably high level of sophistication when Europe was struggling through its Dark Ages—indeed, the culture that preserved Aristotle and transmitted him back to the West. For the first time in motion-picture history, and perhaps in pop culture, the black male body is experienced as the embodiment of intellectual, political, and spiritual ideals.

And yet all these profiles are of *one* life. If Malcolm X had not been slain in 1965, we doubtlessly would have witnessed more, an unfolding of idea and image that, for the phenomenologist, can only suggest the open-ended character of being. If there has been some slim progress since I first published "A Phenomenology of the Black Body," it is of this sort. A gradual accumulation of profiles that expand and qualify our experience of black men: General Colin Powell coolly professional at the center of the Persian Gulf conflict, athlete Arthur Ashe, widely admired for his courage and humanitarianism, astronaut Ron McNair honored for his contributions to the nation and NASA, Seattle mayor Norm Rice laboring, day in day out, to serve an American city that still works. Any accounts we have of black males in the future must, I believe, take these men—and the meanings their lives embody—into con-sideration.

Notes

1. Eldridge Cleaver, *Soul on Ice* (New York: Dell, 1968), p. 174.
2. *Ibid.*, p. 169.
3. Cited in Don Ihde, *Hermeneutic Phenomenology: The Philosophy of Paul Ricoeur* (Northwestern University Press, 1971), p. 56.
4. Franz Fanon, *Black Skin, White Masks* (New York: Grove Press, 1967), p. 225.
5. Maurice Merleau-Ponty, *The Phenomenology of Perception*, trans. Colin Smith (New York: The Humanities Press, 1970). The discussion of the body is developed in Part One.
6. Rollo May, *Love and Will* (New York: Dell, 1969), p. 229.

7. Merleau-Ponty, *op. cit.*, p. 206.

8. *Ibid.*, p. 146.

9. Cleaver, *op. cit.*, p. 171.

10. Fanon, *op. cit.*, p. 110.

11. Merleau-Ponty, *op. cit.*, p. 167.

12. Fanon, *op. cit.*, p. 138.

13. George Kent, *Blackness and the Adventure of Western Civilization* (Chicago: Third World Press, 1972), p. 173.

14. The term "epidermalization" was first used in a phenomenological sense by Professor Thomas Slaughter, of the Afro-American Studies Department at Rutgers, in his unpublished paper, "Epidermalizing the World."

15. Fanon, *op. cit.*, p. 134.

16. *Ibid.*, p. 110.

17. Merleau-Ponty, *op. cit.*, p. 138.

18. Richard Wright, *The Outsider* (New York: Harper & Row, 1953), p. 159.

Introduction to John Gardner's
On Writers and Writing

O n the day of his fatal motorcycle accident on September 14, 1982, on a lonely though not particularly dangerous curving stretch of road in Susquehanna County, Pennsylvania, John Gardner, the embattled advocate for higher artistic and moral standards in our fiction, was snatched at age forty-nine from the stage of contemporary American literature before we could properly measure either his contribution to literary culture or the man himself. In the wake of his staggeringly prolific, driven, and very public life as a popular novelist, critic, teacher, and classics scholar, he left behind a workroom loaded with intriguing projects: some recently completed, like his widely used handbook on craft *The Art of Fiction*; some unfinished, like his proposed opus *Shadows*; and some works, such as the novel *Stillness*, written for the purpose of "self-therapy" during his stormy first marriage, that he might not have published in the form given to us posthumously. There were, of course, rumors flying that his death was suicide, that he willingly rode the machine that became one of his symbols, a '79 Harley-Davidson *hog*, into oblivion. But as always the truth is otherwise, more banal than rumor, and far more illustrative of the mission that made him one of the most inventive novelists and outstanding writing teachers of our time: he died en route to yet another meeting with one of his students at the State University of New York (SUNY)–Binghamton, with yet another stack of manuscripts strapped to the back of his black, monstrous bike.

As one foot soldier in that coast-to-coast army of young artists he inspired and influenced forever, perhaps his only black former apprentice now publishing (for reasons I don't know, he also claimed Toni Morrison), my filing cabinet, indeed my entire home, groans with material by and about Gardner, for it was his peculiar trait, like D. H. Lawrence, to externalize on the page everything he felt, thought, and experienced as a way of taking control of his life. One library wall in my house holds a still life he painted in 1980, a present to me and my wife when we bought our first home in Seattle (a city he disliked, though he never told me why); it is balanced on either side by his lovely Lord John Press broadside "On Books" (a paean to their physical beauty) and his eulogistic poem to his dearest friend, sculptor Nicholas Vergette, who died of cancer in 1974. Thirty of his books, criticism, translations, poetry, and adult and children's fiction stretching from *The Forms of Fiction* (1962) to *Stillness and Shadows* (1986) fill one bookshelf in my study, along with copies of his literary journal *MSS* (in its earliest incarnation he published early works by Joyce Carol Oates and William Gass), and no less than ten critical volumes on his work that range from studies of his major novels to his short fiction to collected interviews (he gave more than 140). On the shelf below sits his photograph: he peers out from the frame, tired, shorthaired in 1982, wearing his black fisherman's sweater, Dunhill tobacco smoke streaming from the pipe in his mouth. Somewhere in one of my desk drawers is one of his big churchwarden pipes he gave me two decades ago in an effort to wean me off cigarettes.

In disorganized envelopes I have stacks of his letters (some of our correspondence is in a special collection devoted to him at the University of Delaware, and has been edited by a black graduate student); the copy for produced radio and theater plays ("The Temptation Game," "Helen at Home") and unproduced ones ("Death and the Maiden") for opera librettos and musical comedies; videotapes of the low-budget film based on his best-selling novel *Nickel Mountain* and the animated version of *Grendel* (which I know disappointed him, being the Walt Disney fan he was), plus a tape of his freewheeling public-television "Writer's Workshop" interview with James Dickey and William Price Fox before an audience of baffled yet enchanted University of South Carolina students (to whom he—relaxed, longhaired, and handsome in his black leather jacket and maybe a little drunk—said, "What happens when you have a really fine character is that you get not only a sense of that kind of person in that kind of town but yourself and everybody around you. Finally you get a kind of control over the universe, a kind of fearlessness from having understood other people"); handwritten essays on the nature of moral art he gave me when he guided me through the composition of my novel *Faith and the Good Thing*; his lecture notes (faded dittos now) from classes on the epic and black literature he taught at Southern Illinois University in the early 1970s; yellowed book reviews (happily, most are now collected in this extremely valuable addition to Gardner scholarship), prefaces, introductions, letters to the editor, and statements he wrote for popular magazines, obscure journals, now-defunct publications, and to endorse novels long forgotten; and his early interviews, one of which he granted as a favor to me on January 21, 1973, when I was a young reporter and philosophy master's-degree student at Southern Illinois University. There he confessed his affection for the works of R. G. Collingwood and Alfred North Whitehead, his belief in the "connectedness" of all life, his disdain for most famous writers at the time, then, in a way both grim and optimistic, concluded:

> I think a certain kind of America is doomed, though something greater may be coming. The novelist and only the novelist thrives on breakdown, because that's the moment when he can analyze the beauty of the values that are falling and rising. . . . The end of a great civilization is always a great moment for fiction. When the old England at the end of the nineteenth century fell, along came Dickens; when Russia fell apart, along came Tolstoy. . . . One looks forward to the fall of great civilizations because it gives us great art.

Over two decades I've returned again and again to this profusion of archival documents, remembering minutiae about the man, his work, and always I come to the same conclusion, that no American fiction writer in our generation will be able to match the incredible ambition, the unusual aesthetic project—two parts Dickensean and one part Sartrean—that this farm boy from upstate New York brought to Yankee literature in the postwar years.

I was twenty-four years old when I drifted into his orbit, and perhaps he saw me as an oddity among his other Carbondale students, not simply because I was black but in terms of the creative baggage I brought along behind me: two published books of comic art; more than a thousand individual political drawings, some of which he'd encountered on the editorial pages of the town newspaper, the *Southern Illinoisan*; and an early how-to-draw PBS series I'd hosted, which most likely he'd seen when flipping channels (he wouldn't have missed the first season of "Kung Fu"). I say oddity because, as the only professional cartoonist among his Southern Illinois writers, my imagination and creative skills at the time were directed toward a stylized, broad-stroke form of expression—caricature, boiling things down to their essential visual traits—that Gardner himself favored in his favorite writers (for such influence on his work see his lively essay "Cartoons," in this volume). Included in my baggage were six novels I'd written in the two years before I met Gardner, all heavily influenced by the Black Arts movement and authors I then admired (Richard Wright, James Baldwin, John A. Williams). Naturally, I knew of him before we met in the fall of 1972 in his workshop "Professional Writing," which convened in the evening at his farmhouse on Boskeydell Road. Like R. Buckminster Fuller, he was a local celebrity, particularly after he published *Grendel,* which cemented his reputation among critics. Friends of mine took his English classes, and spoke with excitement about him; they also said he was the bitterest man they'd ever known—this because for fifteen years he wrote in virtual obscurity as an underpublished author whose closet spilled open with brilliant, original fiction. Enrolling in his course, I wasn't sure what to expect.

What I *did* know after pounding out six novels, and reading as widely as I could in literature and philosophy as well as every handbook on craft and theory I could find, was that after writing a million words of fiction I needed a good teacher, a genuine mentor, a senior craftsman with greater experience than mine whom I could apprentice myself to, adding what he'd learned to what I'd already discovered. That circumstances should have brought me, six book-length manuscripts under my arm, to the Gardners' home on a rainy September night is one of those formative, fork-in-the-road events in my life that I have never fully been able to unkey. A few editors who'd rejected my fiction remarked that I could stand improvement on such matters as "voice" and "prose rhythm." Gardner's reply was, "Oh, I can help you with *that.*" And it was true: he prided himself, as a trailblazer of the New Fiction that arose in the early 1970s, on his prodigious understanding of technique, his gift for voice and narrative ventriloquism, his magisterial, musical prose, which, for example, in the opening paragraph of his story "John Napper Sailing Through the Universe," achieved nearly perfect pitch in fully cadenced, poetic lines that seamlessly fused image and idea. He was, I learned soon enough, so immersed in modern, medieval, and classical philosophies that on any occasion in his office, in his car, as we walked across campus, or at a party, he could answer my graduate-student questions about the history of ideas and offer, always to my shock, his own thought-provoking opinion on the strengths and weaknesses of any Western metaphysical system—as well as opinions, always fresh, about any aspect of theater, painting, sculpture, music, or popular culture.

True enough, there were in the early 1970s a few good authors teaching creative writing (which, incidentally, Gardner once told me was "a joke" in terms of how it was then approached, a touchy-feely affair with little foundation in skill acquisition), and any one of them could have added to my repertoire of technique. John Barth, say, with whom Gardner felt a certain competitiveness, most likely because our national magazines heralded him as *the* high priest of literary invention. Or his friend William Gass, whose symphonically orchestrated books he often praised. But for *this* Illinois colored boy raised happily in the African Methodist Episcopal church in a Chicago suburb by a conservative, hardworking father and a mother with the soul of an actress, it was Gardner's personality, not just his knowledge of *techne,* that made him both an artist and a human being I could deeply respect. Unlike his equally skillful postmodern contemporaries, experimentalists and poly-technical innovators who rolled their eyes or looked confounded when the touchy subject of religion or spirituality came up, Gardner—the son of a sermonizer—was as frank and forthcoming as Flannery O'Connor about the significance of morality and the life of the spirit in literature. He praised my characters in *Faith* for their "dignity," a characteristic he complained was missing in so many stories, all by acclaimed authors, who (he felt) wallowed in fashionable despair, entropy, defeatism, cheap fireworks, and a cynical vision of humankind. (By the way, for the an-cient Greeks, the word *cynic* meant "doglike.") Gardner, and perhaps *only* Gardner, had the courage to say, as he does in "A Writer's View of Contemporary American Fiction," that "at a conservative estimate, 90 percent of the so-called new fiction is soporific." Read: boring, despite its dazzling originality.

Added to that, and most important of all, I saw in Gardner's bound-less self-confidence and passion for writing in the early '70s exactly the same do-or-die love I had since my teens for drawing. For Gardner, writing was not a "career." It was not so pedestrian an enterprise as to be ranked among the various professions from which we might freely choose—doctor, lawyer, soldier, or stockbroker. On the contrary, it was more like a calling. ("Fiction is the only religion I have," he told a *New York Times Sunday Magazine* reviewer.) It was one way for men and women to make their stab at immortality, heal the conflicted human heart, transcend the idiocies of daily life (yet help us at the same time see how heroism can reside in ordinary living), and celebrate the Good. Sometimes it seemed as if Gardner was interested in nothing short of fiction worthy of winning a writer lasting fame (glory) based on—and here is the trick—hard-won achievement. When pushed to the wall about his preferences, it seemed he *approved* of nothing less, and in our conferences and conversations he pushed me gently, then some-times roughly, to imagine harder and with greater precision of detail, write with fairness for every character in my book, and hold in contempt any sentence I composed that fell below the level of the best sentence I'd ever written. He was a teacher who could fill you to overflowing with confidence. He was also capable of wounding you in the most painful way by pulling the covers off your conceits and holding them up—like a puppy by its ears (his image)—before you.

In "A Writer's View of Contemporary American Fiction," which nicely categorizes fictional visions in terms of their relationship to religion, Gardner identifies himself as a "troubled Christian orthodox writer." Can anyone who knew him doubt that he saw something akin to salvation in art? Late one spring afternoon I drove to his farmhouse to pick up one of my chapters. He sat alone in the house that day at the long, mead hall–size table in his dining room, drinking whiskey from a Mason jar and editing a home movie, a western, his family and friends had written and performed. On the table nearby were recent reviews of *Jason and Medeia*. Many of them were negative. One reviewer had called Gardner a "clever student." I knew these notices angered and disappointed him. Timidly, I nodded toward the reviews, asked him what he thought, and he replied quietly, hardly looking up from his editing machine, "They just try to keep you from getting to heaven."

All this was heady stuff for me; it was precisely the kick-in-the-fanny, challenging wake-up call that I'd been hungering for a teacher to give me. Unbeknownst to him, I took notes on even his casual remarks about fiction. I read his three-decker, architectonic novel *The Sunlight Dialogues* with a pencil in my fist, flagging every linguistic device, strategy, and technique I did not know. I ordered all his earlier works of criticism. And since the melodic substructure of his best prose fascinated me, I copied out in longhand the first chapter of *The Wreckage of Agathon*, a work he felt disappointed with, but by transcribing each of his sentences onto a notepad I discovered that, as I turned from one page to another, I could *feel* how his next sentence had to flow, what metrical beats it needed to have, even if I had no idea what its content might be. Slowly, I began to see. Gradually, a picture of man and method began to emerge. By degrees, the musical *logos* of his fiction became something I was able to intuit and feel from within, as well as the greater artistic game plan behind his challenging himself from book to book, story to story, by selecting different classical or contemporary literary forms (or several combined) to serve as the ground, the general shape or mold for his stories—a mold he could reconfigure as he wrote, and at the same time use to stay in touch with other writers, living and dead, who'd also used that form.

At dinner one evening I heard his wife, Joan, joke about the archaic language Gardner displayed in *Jason and Medeia*; she said it was there because she'd chided him about not having any "big words" in his novels. So Gardner took his magnifying glass and walked through every word in *The Compact Edition of the Oxford English Dictionary* before revising his update of the classic story. We laughed, but her anecdote haunted me for days. I thought if Gardner had gone to such trouble (a task I now believe every writer needs to perform), then perhaps I should do the same with a Christmas present my parents had given me, the 2,129-page *Webster's New Twentieth-Century Dictionary*. It took me five months to plough through it, night after night, during my first year in the philosophy Ph.D. program at SUNY–Stony Brook, and the exercise proved invaluable.

So yes, I painstakingly studied Gardner, testing my regimen and secular, post-Christian "religious" faith in the discipline of fiction against his own (and always I fell short). If he recommended a book, I bought then pored over it, regardless of the century or culture that produced it. I'm convinced no one else could have gotten me—a philosophy student then oriented toward Marxism and, in fiction, toward protest literature—interested in *Morte d'Arthur*, Geoffrey Chaucer, Longinus, the

Wakefield pageant cycle, Fulgentius, *Beowulf*, or Caedmonic poetry. But he did, because he, like his fellow post-sixties "experimental" writers, had found a way to make the practice of fiction interesting again after decades of naturalism. Not that they couldn't write in the great tradition of American naturalism—they did, now and then, just to show they could, to show that naturalism was but *one* of the innumerable ways a story could be told and the universe imagined and interpreted. "I believe that the art of the thirties, forties, and fifties was fundamentally a mistake," Gardner told Joe David Bellamy in a 1973 interview, "that it made assumptions that were untrue about art, basically wrong assumptions that went wrong in the Middle Ages, too. . . . It seems to me that we are a play out of the seventeenth century. Seventeenth-century civilization is us. . . . In the fifteenth and sixteenth centuries all the genres break down. It becomes impossible to write a straight romance, or a straight anything. And everybody who is anybody starts form-jumping."

He credited himself and other New Fictionists rightly for developing fresh strategies for solving the problem of viewpoint, opening our fiction to exciting new (and sometimes old) ontologies, and for unsealing a door to "fabulation" closed since the mid-nineteenth century. Inside that room of fictional possibilities was a tale- and yarn-telling tradition still close to the roots of oral storytelling, where one could find philosophical insight in fairy tales, folktales, and myths: stories about fantastic creatures—golems and grendels—we are not likely to bump into at the corner supermarket, but in the New Fiction we could. For in the universe of the mind (and the college-based experimentalists were interested in nothing if not mind, perception, epistemology), Frankenstein's monster and J.F.K., quarks and Pegasus, Rip Van Winkle and Chairman Mao all existed side by side as phenomenal objects for consciousness, none more "real" than another in our dreams or between the covers of a book. In what Gardner called "the vivid and continuous dream" that is art, each could be a meaning dramatized, allowed to live, and lead us to laughter and tears and learning as powerfully as did the ghost and flesh in the Middle English poem "The Debate of Body and Soul."

Here, in short, was a post-1960s "school" of writers who found a way of freeing the imagination, but in Gardner's case it involved a return to ancestral traditions and forms. Perhaps now we take for granted this "turn" in American storytelling from sod-busting "realism," what with television offering us a series about a family of dinosaurs, Hollywood dishing up films about coneheads and characters based on video games, and literary writers like Valerie Martin retelling the Jekyll and Hyde story from the viewpoint of Jekyll's housekeeper in her superb psychological thriller *Mary Reilly*. But thirty years ago, at the moment Gardner was fusing realism and fantasy in his midwestern farmhouse, Joanna Russ in the East was just then looking at medieval literature in terms of its lessons for the "New Wave" of speculative fiction that emerged in the early '70s, and replacing sci-fi's earlier reliance on the "hard" sciences of physics and chemistry with an interest in the latest research from such fields as biology and anthropology (her friend Samuel R. Delany was looking at theories of language games and much, much more); and in the West, Ishmael Reed was studying Egyptian myths and taking Saturday-morning cartoons as a model for editing his novels. As in the politics of the '60s, the *moment* called for innovation, throwing out nets in every direction—pop culture, high culture, Third World culture, science—in the hope that as writers they could haul to the surface something to propel fiction's evolution.

However, Gardner differs in many important respects from these other innovators. "Newness" for its own sake did not appeal to him. And in contrast, for example, to Russ (whose essays include a defense of man-hating) and Reed (who once called Western cultural forms "diseased"), he was dissatisfied with pyrotechnics and novelty if their purpose turned out to be nothing more than political or religious propaganda; if character—which is at the core of his aesthetics—suffered; if cartoon strategies, for all their fun, completely abandoned fidelity to mimesis, and lost the authorial generosity that comes only from minutely rendered details of setting and social gesture; if, in the end, he felt the novelty of the New Fiction replaced convincing models of moral behavior with events and emotions that slyly and subversively promoted something unhealthy for humankind. "A healthy life is a life of faith," he told Bellamy, "an unhealthy, sick, and dangerous life is a life of unfaith." Nevertheless, a writer could not preach his faith in a story. It had to be concretized, the idea incarnated—made flesh—in specific people, places, and things delivered with *haeceittias* (thisness). Real art was not, he said, in the sermon we hear in church on Sunday morning, but instead in "the arches and the light."

Looking back over the collected pieces in *On Writers and Writing*, we see that during his spectacular career much of Gardner's energy was invested in defining, evaluating, and trying to correct—in his criticism and stories—the products of the New Fiction school, of which he was a leading figure. At times he was guilty (as he admits) of its self-conscious excesses that distract us from the "fictional dream," but he was always struggling to use the positive contributions of this period to create a lasting work worthy of the best in Dickens, Melville, and Tolstoy. It is also true that as he scrapped with his brothers and sisters in the movement for the New, he was revising and refining his theory that the process of fiction itself is moral and life-affirmative. But just a moment. Is this really a "theory"? And is it really "morality" that Gardner means? It's clear from his criticism that he was firmly opposed to "moralizing." Apparently, he was not intractably Christian, insofar as he said a finely done work could make him believe in the value of a Buddhist vision. I think, just maybe, we are better off seeing his interconnecting essays in this book as presenting a credible *description* of what happens when writers write well. And rather than using the inflammatory word "moral," we might be more accurate if we say that what Gardner wanted was a *responsible* fiction, one that did not insult the intelligence of readers as thoughtful and educated as himself.

"All my life," he wrote his fiancée Susan Thornton, whom he was to marry on September 18, four days after his fatal accident, "I've lived flat-out. As a motorcycle racer, chemist, writer . . . I was never cautious." This was hardly something Gardner needed to tell us. We could see it in everything he did. While he helped those of us fortunate enough to study with him believe we could distinguish ourselves as artists, provided we were willing to sweat enough, be unsatisfied enough, rewrite enough, none of us believed we could match *his* breakneck schedule. I cannot speak for his New Fiction contemporaries, but I know for a fact that Gardner could write for seventy-two-hour stretches without sleep; compose an introduction to one of his collections of poetry and portions of *The Art of Fiction* while recuperating in a hospital bed from an operation for colon cancer. Some critics believe Gardner's incredible drive, his "fire in the belly," dated back to his teens and the accidental death of his younger brother, a tragedy he blamed himself for and dramatized in his story "Redemption." As to the truth of this childhood "wound," I cannot say. But I do know he was a writer who boasted he could read in twenty-seven ancient and medieval languages by the time he earned his Ph.D. at age twenty-five, and that in his late forties he polished up his Greek in order to provide his students at the Breadloaf Writers Conference with his own translations of Homer. He traveled to Japan in the '70s to lecture and returned with sixteen stories by Kikuo Itaya—an eighty-five-year-old writer hardly known in his homeland, which Gardner translated with Nobuko Tsukui, introduced with a memorable essay called "Meditational Fiction," and published under the title *Tengu Child* with Southern Illinois University Press.

Week after week on the pages of the Sunday *New York Times Book Review*, and in other national forums for literary discourse, he attempted to separate novelistic wheat from the chaff, genuine fiction from fakery. However, Gardner was not given to writing puff pieces, reviews I would call no better than extensions of the blurbs and promotional copy in press releases. Always his intention was to understand, to imagine the various alternatives an author had at his or her disposal for solving problems on the level of the sentence or for a book's overall structural design, to *analyze* what constructions in the stories of writers he admired— Saul Bellow, Vladimir Nabokov, Marguerite Young, John Cheever, Larry Woiwode—worked, and which ones did not. Only in his reviews do we find a consummate teacher and technician examining the works of his peers as he would an assignment turned in by one of his students in a college writing class. Often the effect is shocking—he said *that* about John Updike?—but it is a testament to Gardner's professionalism that publicity and public acclaim never blinded him to the basic question

every reviewer and critic must ask: What exactly *do* we have here? (As
an analogue, consider the equally courageous reviews of black fiction
by MacArthur fellow Stanley Crouch.) In principle, it seems, very little
contemporary fiction worked perfectly for Gardner; like an elder craftsman disappointed by his finest achievements, he regarded even the
most lauded literature by others as being in need of some repair.

He lectured, read, and taught across America and abroad for twenty
years. His students included the famous (Raymond Carver took his first
class at Chico State) and scores of aspiring writers who mailed him
manuscripts—perfect strangers whose work he corrected with the same
meticulous, line-by-line editing he brought to his own fiction. What
could prompt a busy man to behave this way? An incident he enjoyed
relating reveals something about the demons that drove him. After one
of his readings, a woman approached him and said, "You know, I think
I like your stories, but I'm not sure I like *you*." He did not hesitate before
he replied, "That's all right, I'm a better person when I write," meaning
that no matter how pigheaded, stupid, or imperfect a writer might be
in his personal life (and certainly the stories of how badly many outstanding writers have lived are legion), what he did on the page offered
an opportunity—perhaps the *only* chance for some—to speak with clarity and precision, work in a spirit of love and compassion, and revise
his thoughts and feelings to the point where they could be most helpful
and do no harm. In an unpublished 1976 preface to the writing exercises
that now appear in *The Art of Fiction*, he wrote that a sane, moral writer

> never forgets that his audience is, at least ideally, as noble and generous
> and tolerant as himself, so that to turn characters into cartoons, to treat
> his characters as innately inferior to himself, to forget their reasons for
> being as they are, to treat them as brutes, is disgraceful. . . . If you write,
> even through the mouth of a sympathetically observed character, some-
> thing Tolstoy, Socrates, or Jesus would not write—think twice. You live
> in a world in which it's possible to buy flavored, edible panties (straw-
> berry, lemon-lime—), a world where the word "asshole" passes for ele-
> vated diction. Think about it.

Seventeen years later we are demanding that record companies place
rating labels on "gangsta" rap music filled with obscenities, the abuse
of women, and calls for killing police officers; and television and motion pictures must now contend with a groundswell of public backlash
against the gratuitous, make-believe violence that some feel is related
to the streets of urban America turning into combat zones. If Gardner
had lived, the current hand-wringing over depictions of violence and
cruelty, and the sense that moral demands apply even to make-believe,
might have prompted him to say, "I told you so," and repeat his oft-stated
belief that "even bad art is powerful."

To put this simply, Gardner's energy, his self-punishing schedules,
his devotion to all good fiction wherever he found it, *shamed* those of

us who watched him work, and still had the audacity to call ourselves writers. Just the same, he labored with self-doubts. In a 1977 *Atlantic* interview, he said, "I'm one of the really great writers; I haven't proved that yet, but I feel that it's coming." Did it come? More specifically, did any of the New Fiction novelists create works that have become part of the language, the culture? As I grow older and find myself less ensorcelled by pyrotechnics and more appreciative of spirited storytelling and old-fashioned page-turners, I wonder how various characters and tales have down through the centuries become common coin in our culture. Melville, of course, languished for years before being rediscovered, as did Zora Neale Hurston; and surely there is often more than a little media hype, literary and academic fashion, politics, and the impact of Hollywood involved when an author's efforts become a household word.

Be that as it may, the rare event does occur when a serious writer creates something that becomes emblematic for some sector of our experience. In "More Smog from the Dark Satanic Mills," Gardner praises Pär Lagerkvist's *The Holy Land* for compressing the complexity and difficulty of modern life "into a few stark and massive symbols in which all our experience and all human history are locked." To my eye, this event arises when a writer—traditional or experimental, literary or pulp—stumbles consciously or unconsciously, by genius or dumb luck, upon an archetypal character (Raskolnikov, Lolita, Candide, Huck Finn) or an imaginative situation (as in Fowles's *The Collector*, Dickey's *Deliverance*) or a flexible concept that organizes a welter of complex feelings and ideas (Ellison's *Invisible Man*, Heller's *Catch-22*, Haley's *Roots*). In some cases this naming, this dramatizing, crystallizes an experience we all know but until the creation occurs have not found a way to utter. Or it may be a fictional situation or premise so fertile (Malory's *Morte d'Arthur*, Goethe's *Faust*, Defoe's *Robinson Crusoe*) and intriguing that other writers feel compelled to keep retelling it, updating it for their age, going it one better, as Gardner himself did with the Beowulf legend. Did the New Fiction of the early '70s body forth its "King Lear," its *Oliver Twist*, its great white whale? Eleven years after Gardner's death the jury is still out, as perhaps it must be, though I think it safe to say that the intense interest in Gardner's work in the decade after his death, the effort finally to take measure of the man, suggests happily that his devotion to good writing will result in longevity for his books on writing craft, for *Grendel* as an example of the New Fiction's principles at their best, and, one hopes, for his short and long fiction as well.

Gardner would have been sixty this year. Readers born too late to remember the post-1960s debates and battles over fiction's purpose might find it difficult to feel the passion or the reason for fierce position-taking that crackles along the surface of Gardner's book reviews. These are *more* than reviews. They are brief position papers, extensions of his ongoing thoughts about art's meaning; but a few readers might ask, why all the fuss? After all, by the mid-1980s—when the concept of "moral" fiction was no longer tied so tightly to Gardner himself—few, if any, major American novelists questioned in their interviews and public statements the significance of a moral vision for fiction, even if they had distanced themselves from Gardner when he was alive, which many did after he published *On Moral Fiction*. For most authors today moral responsibility in their products is a *given*, though as always the definition of what defines "moral" varies from writer to writer, as it should. But it was Gardner who served as our point man, our "trip wire" in the task of clearing away land mines planted by less faithful novelists and critics along the path where traditional ethical concerns and artistic creation meet.

Furthermore, if three decades ago during the heyday of the New Fiction, writers were arguing about technique, today the battlefield of aesthetic debate has shifted to "multiculturalism," to denunciations of English departments for marginalizing women and writers of color, and to a dismissal of the very canon of "dead white male writers" Gardner's scholarship was based upon. Oh yes, he died too soon by ten years, long before we had finished with him. We needed his intimate knowledge of the classics, his great love of fine storytelling regardless of the culture or race that produced it, and his compelling arguments against easy art and proselytizing in these years that have seen English departments politicized and torn apart from within at so many major American universities.

Moreover, we needed the author of "Amber (Get) Waves (Your) of (Plastic) Grain (Uncle Sam)," who was one of Jimmy Carter's favorite writers, when the Grand Old Party of his parents caved in to the religious right and Pat Buchanan during the 1992 presidential campaign, retreating from politics proper to cultural warfare in the form of appeals to "family values" and the priority of "character." Aren't these matters— values and cultural vision—that reside at the heart of what one might call "Gardner country"? We wonder: Where might he have positioned himself in respect to Allan Bloom, Roger Kimball, Dinesh D'Souza, and Rush Limbaugh (who could easily be a Gardner concoction, one of his "earnest babbling . . . short-legged, overweight, twitching cartoon creations")? How might he have responded to our present controversy over abortion (there is one answer in *Mickelsson's Ghosts*), homosexuality (he tries to understand how one man can love another in *Freddy's Book*), or Hillary Clinton's "politics of meaning" speech (our First Lady might do well to read *October Light*)? Because Gardner was that species of poet-philosopher on whom nothing in the social world was lost, we can find hints in his huge *oeuvre* for these questions and use them to construct responses to present dangers, guesses that are consistent with his position at the time of his death—but, sadly, that is the very best we will be able to do.

As his former student and friend, I thankfully add *On Writers and Writing* to my burgeoning shelf of books by and about John Gardner. I have no idea what words appear on his headstone in upstate New York, no idea if the man's fierce spirit lives on, but for years I've entertained the thought that these lines by Italian poet Jacopone da Todi might be fitting for how most of us would like to remember his furious and illuminating passage among us.

> *La guerra è terminata:*
> *de la virtù battaglia,*
> *de la mente travaglia*
> *cosa nulla contende.*

> *The war is over.*
> *In the battle of virtue,*
> *the struggle of spirit,*
> *all is peace.*

Black Images and Their Global Impact

Two years ago I was lecturing in Japan on black American literature and culture. After a presentation in Tokyo, my wife and I were taken to dinner by three Japanese educators, one of them being a young teacher who told me of her enthusiasm for American motion pictures.

And then, because we were getting along so well, she blurted out, "I just *have* to say this: you don't seem at all like Eddie Murphy! You're more like—like a black Yuppie."

There was silence all around the table. I cleared my throat and wondered what was the best way to handle this. At last, after taking a deep breath, I said, "I hate to tell you this, but all black people in America don't act like Eddie Murphy does in his movies."

"Oh!" Now she'd realized her blunder. Even worse, this was Japan, where her dishonoring a guest was a very serious mistake indeed. "I never meant to be insulting—"

Although I assured her I was not insulted, she kept on apologizing right up until my wife and I returned to our hotel.

Since that evening I have felt miserable for my Japanese colleague, but I've felt even worse for middle-class black professionals—that generally ignored, hard-working, educated, law-abiding, often religious and sometimes "square" class of Americans who, since the 1960s, have been the subject of belittlement by members of the black underclass, the white liberal media, self-appointed radical spokespersons, by some novelists, by academics black and white and now, it seems, by foreigners too.

In their judgment the black middle-class is not "black" enough. It doesn't take four years of college to see that there is a whopping amount of racism involved when someone insists upon identifying black American life with the social pathologies of the ghetto, with the scatological, sex-obsessed language of Eddie Murphy in his "Raw" performance, the offensive comedians on HBO's "Def Comedy Jam," or with the nihilistic lyrics on rap recordings by Ice T and 2 Live Crew.

My friend in Tokyo, I suspect, would have been horrified if I'd identified the essence of *her* culture with the Yakuza or Japanese mafia; my Italian associates in the States would gag if I complained that none of them seem enough like Marlon Brando's "godfather"; and my Jewish friends would have a conniption-fit if I asked them why they fall so short of the model given to us by Woody Allen.

But the badass-Stagolee-street culture image is, I fear, how too many media-indoctrinated Americans have preferred to see black life for the last 30 years, despite the fact that during the last three decades incredible persons of color, like Colin Powell, astronaut Ron McNair, and Seattle mayor Norm Rice—to name only a few—have passed through our lives.

However, we cannot blame others for our devastatingly poor public relations. We can only blame ourselves. One more anecdote may point clearly to where I believe the problem lies. One of my friends, a black professor, recently gave a lecture, very eloquent and erudite. Afterwards a young black student told him, "I like the way you speak, but *I* don't want to talk like that because then I wouldn't be black anymore."

We can no longer afford, as a people, to allow personal and professional excellence to be defined as "white." Or to allow our achievers to be dismissed as Uncle Toms, oreos or "buppies."

We all know how hard it can be for our young people—or any youngsters—to excel academically, on their jobs, and as parents. Consider how much *harder* this is when built into black culture since at least the 1960s is an attitude that sneers at hard work, good citizenship, and traditional morality! Our crisis, if we presently have one—and I believe we do—is fundamentally one of (ethical) values and (social) vision.

Put another way: we must invest as much energy in cultural housecleaning as we do in political activism.

What so many people, and too many of them left-leaning college teachers, denounce as "middle-class values" are precisely now—and have been since Reconstruction and Booker T. Washington's "philosophy of the toothbrush"—the cure for salvaging our ravaged, inner-city communities, for rebuilding our families and achieving economic parity with whites, Asians, Hispanics, and anyone else with whom we must compete in the domestic and international marketplace.

What are those "middle-class" values?

First of all, these values no longer belong to any class or race. They are *human* values. Call them conservative, if you like, but once we dispense with labels they will be seen simply as the formula for successful living at any time. They are: a strong work ethic, self-reliance, delayed gratification, discipline, an appreciation of the individual, a commitment to education, dedication to one's family, marital fidelity, a respect for all life, the capacity for self-sacrifice and religious piety.

This is the formula our most quoted leader, Dr. Martin Luther King, Jr., had in mind when he said, "We must work on two fronts. On the one hand, we must continually resist the system of segregation—the system which is the basic cause of our lagging standards; on the other hand, we must work constructively to improve the lagging standards which are the effects of segregation. There must be a rhythm of alternation between attacking the cause and healing the effects."

He also said, more pointedly:

"We are often too loud and boisterous, and spend too much on alcoholic beverages. These are some of the shortcomings we can improve here and now . . . Even the most poverty stricken among us can be clean, even the most uneducated among us can have high morals. By improving these standards, we will go a long way in breaking down some of the arguments of the segregationists."

No more needs to be said.

Northwestern Commencement
Address, 1994

The first thing I want to say is how grateful I am to receive this honorary degree from Northwestern University. This school and this town mean more to me than you can imagine. I was born and raised here. In fact, I came into the world at Community Hospital. I went to Noyes elementary school, and I graduated from Evanston Township High. I was baptized right down the street at Ebenezer A.M.E. Church. My great uncle William Johnson, who came to Evanston in the 1920s, started a milk company before the Great Depression, and when that failed he started a construction company. That company built Springfield Baptist Church on Emerson Street, and he also built residences and apartment buildings all over these northern suburbs of Chicago.

My father came to Evanston from South Carolina to work for my Uncle Will. This is how he met my mother, who had always wanted to be a schoolteacher, but never realized her goal. However, she did fill our house on Dodge Avenue with books from the three book clubs she belonged to. Yet some of her books did not come to our house from book clubs. Quite a few arrived at our house as orphans from Northwestern University.

I'll tell you how this happened. In the early 1960s my grandmother worked as a cook at Gamma Phi Beta sorority house when I was in middle school, and sometimes my mother worked there, too, over the holidays as a cleaning woman in order to make a little extra money.

Along with the clothing the sorority girls threw away after their classes ended, they also tossed out their books. My mother, bless her, brought them home—boxes and boxes of them. Some nights I'd flip them open, lying half on my bed and half off, my toes barely touching the floor. In those boxes I first encountered Shakespeare's *Romeo and Juliet* and *Hamlet*, Mary Shelley's *Frankenstein*, and other college-syllabus classics that I devoured with the pleasure, the delight, the wicked knowledge that the girls of Gamma Phi Beta would never be able to say they knew something their cleaning woman's son didn't know. I would like to accept this honorary doctor of arts degree for both my late mother and my late grandmother.

And there are two thoughts I'd like to share with those of you graduating today. Neither is profound or new, but I have found both to be valuable in helping me, as an American writer, to define myself both as an individual and as part of the larger human community.

The first is simply this: Don't repeat the most serious error of my generation in the 1960s by believing that the mistakes, political and moral, of your predecesors (white and black) disqualify them as significant voices in our ongoing effort to make sense of the world. The eighteenth-century philosopher David Hume may have been dead wrong about the intelligence of Africans, but he must be heard when he discourses on epistemology and the nature of the self; a D. H. Lawrence invites our hatred when, in his essay "On Being a Man," he writes, "I am not a nigger and so I can't know a nigger, and I can never fully 'understand' him." But what aspiring writer cannot learn something about the metaphoric and poetic possibilities of language by pouring over *Sons and Lovers*? The first black poet in America, Phillis Wheatley, makes us very uncomfortable when she describes Africa as a "land of error and Egyptian gloom." But Phillis Wheatley—along with Thomas Paine and Thomas Jefferson—*must* be read if we want to understand the American past and the possibilities of the American future. We cannot blame Hume for not having the racial and social savvy of a modern scholar nor Lawrence or Wheatley for lacking the insight of contemporary intellectuals. Without them, we would have no insight at all.

If we know anything (and what we know is always "vanishingly small," according to philosopher Bertrand Russell), it is because we have built hesitantly, painstakingly upon the past, ever revising and re-envisioning the sense or meanings made by our forebears. Therefore the generation of the twenty-first century cannot afford to be ahistorical. Serious artists especially must devote themselves to a lifelong study of the theory and practice of great literature, and to all the historical forms that life and life's expression have taken down through the ages. Like archaeologists, you must constantly recover where we have been—with all our blunders—in order to take even the most tentative steps forward.

No one has expressed this better, I think, than author Ralph Ellison. We are all diminished by his death on April 16th this year. Yet Ellison, whose masterpiece, *Invisible Man*, has rightly been called the greatest

American novel in the second half of the twentieth century, has left us with much to build upon, if we will only heed his words.

For forty years, Ellison told us in his interviews and essays that "the thing that Americans have to learn over and over again is that they are *individuals* and they have the responsibility of individual vision." In his novel, he expands upon this wisdom when he writes, "The conscience of a race is the gift of its individuals who see, evaluate, record. . . . We create the race by creating ourselves and then to our great astonishment we will have created something far more important: We will have created a culture."

But how is this done? What is there in the American experience that makes this possible? Ellison gives us the answer to that question in what I consider to be one of his most important statements. He said, "By a trick of fate (and our racial problems notwithstanding), *the human imagination is integrative—and the same is true of the centrifugal force that inspirits the democratic process.*"

The second point I would like to make is that my generation leaves you unfinished *ethical* business. In his recent book on the Civil Rights Movement, *Black in Selma*, attorney J. L. Chestnut, Jr., makes clear a moral consequence that came from the noble work of ending Jim Crow, America's unique version of apartheid. Chestnut says: "The young people in Selma were ready to act. They didn't have jobs, houses, mortgages, or ties to the white power structure. They didn't necessarily want to go to school anyway. The movement gave them a chance to rebel against parents and teachers and rewarded them for knocking authority—the natural bent of teenagers. We are paying a price for that now." He feels that "a generation has grown up with their concept and appreciation of authority undermined—the family's, the law's, society's. But we had no choice. For us to progress, some generation was going to have to break with authority."

I think authority must always be questioned. But when I look back on the legacy that my generation leaves for you, I have to come to the conclusion that the automatic rejection of the wisdom of our elders cannot be separated from the breakdown of the family in the last twenty years, from the rise of the druglords, from the present crisis in education, from gang warfare, from the cynicism of the Me Generation, from the Yuppie attitude of "He who dies with the most toys wins," from the indifference to the homeless, or from the increasing racial (and sexual) hostilities that are now so much part of the texture of our daily lives. We have reached a point where it is almost possible to speak of the cultural Balkanization of America into separate regions of interpretation now called the Black experience, now the Hispanic experience, now the Women's experience, yet seldom if ever does anyone speak of the *human* experience that grounds all our viewpoints and makes them intelligible. And, tragically, little is said these days about that one-time centerpiece concept of humanism: the brotherhood (and sisterhood) of humankind.

While every serious writer, thinker, and citizen must nurture his or her independence of thought, we dare not forget our interdependence. It is not enough to say we need others. On the contrary, we *are* the Others, for consciousness itself is, in the final analysis, a social phenomenon.

And so the fundamental challenge that my generation leaves you is a *moral* challenge. Each individual will be called upon to come to terms (as we must over and over again throughout history) with civilized life's most important imperatives: tolerance, the desire for truth at all cost, service, and the experience most lacking in the twentieth-century's final decade—*love*.

As you move into the next millennium, take Marx and the French critic Derrida along if you wish, but take Gandhi, Martin Luther King, and Mother Teresa as well. Take her favorite prayer from Saint Francis, a version of which Mother Teresa had members of the United Nations General Assembly read together on the fortieth anniversary of that organization. The words are six hundred years old, three times as old as this republic, and doubtlessly will endure when all we are as Americans—all our trials and struggles—is but the briefest of footnotes in a future historian's doctoral dissertation:

> *Lord, make me an instrument of thy peace.*
> *Where there is hatred, let me sow love;*
> *Where there is injury, pardon;*
> *Where there is doubt, faith;*
> *Where there is despair, hope;*
> *Where there is darkness, light;*
> *Where there is sadness, joy.*
> *O divine Master, grant that I may not so much seek*
> *To be consoled as to console,*
> *To be understood as to understand,*
> *To be loved as to love;*
> *For it is in giving that we receive;*
> *It is in pardoning that we are pardoned;*
> *It is in dying (to self) that we are born to eternal life.*

Introduction to
Mark Twain's *What Is Man?*

In the first book of his five-volume study of Western philosophy, *The Classical Mind*, W. T. Jones observed that "the central problem of culture is to reconcile the mechanistic, nonteleological view of nature, which Atomism first formulated and which modern science has largely adopted, with an ethical, religious, and humanistic conception of man. . . . The whole history of philosophy since the seventeenth century is in fact hardly more than a series of variations on this central theme."

At the heart of these perspectives on our experience—determinism vs. free will, essence vs. existence—is our realization that as human subjects our relationship to our bodies is often that of radical otherness. We know ourselves to be physical creatures, our bodies as *objects* that occur in a world of *things*, and that the flesh can be approached quantitatively, measured and analyzed in strictly material terms. How often have we heard that on the market are bodies are worth (in the decade before the dollar's devaluation below the yen and mark) no more than ninety cents in chemicals, reducible to five pounds of minerals, one pound of carbohydrates, one quarter ounce of vitamins, and a few pounds of protein? As material beings, our bodies and brains both obey the laws of physics, the caprice of Nature, accident, and chance, and for this modern, materialist orientation we are to a very large degree indebted to the bifurcation of man into mind-substance (*res cogitantes*) and body-substance (*res extensae*) by René Descartes, who regarded animals to be no more than machines, their behavior based almost entirely on external stimuli, and their learning (if it can be called that) so directly determined by past experience that we can all but predict how they will conduct themselves in the present and future. Philosopher Don Ihde points out in *Existential Technics* that, "From Descartes on, the 'world' has frequently been characterized as a 'mechanism' which at one time was sometimes tinkered with by the Maker—but which today runs without tinkering. Even our bodies and those of animals were, and continue to be, interpreted along *technological* lines. We are contrivances of pumps (hearts), levers (arms), and electrical systems (nerves)."

But even when we admit, "I am my body," and that the creations of our own hand—the machine and computer—can be seen as its analog, we nevertheless feel that we are *not* merely matter blindly subservient to natural forces beyond our will; we feel the self (or soul) cannot be reduced to the empirical objects of physics, chemistry, or neurology, and this persistent belief in the primacy of consciousness over a purely naturalistic interpretation of being finds its finest expression in the world's great religions as well as in the better texts of modern humanism.

Neither view is wrong. These are age-old antinomies, and depending upon the evidence selected either orientation can be compellingly (yet only provisionally) argued. Phenomenologist Paul Ricoeur defines the problem succinctly in *Fallible Man* when he says, "It is possible for man to take two divergent and non-reconcilable perspectives upon himself because within man there is a non-coincidence which is that of the *finite* and the *infinite*," or of the physical and the mental.

It is not surprising that these two perspectives, often at war within a single consciousness, are the interlocutors that Mark Twain sets to debating one another in *What Is Man?* How could he, one of America's greatest storytellers, ignore a theme central to Western culture since the seventeenth century, or fail to wonder about its implications for good and evil? In the book's preface, Twain states his belief that "millions upon millions of men" have struggled with this problem, reached their conclusions, and remained silent "because they dreaded (*and could not bear*) the disapproval of the people around them." Nor is it surprising that Twain selected the Socratic dialogue to present his views, for it is a dramatic strategy particularly useful for dealing with antinomies by giving an author the advantage of splitting himself into two selves, as it were: an Old Man, a Young Man. With this device Twain could explore these "non-reconcilable perspectives" by in effect arguing with himself, taking now the romantic side of the naive young idealist, now that of the elder apparently advocating a mechanistic vision of the world in a funny, frequently hilarious conversation sprung from the cranky thesis that "the human being is merely a machine, and nothing more." However, what does surprise us and pique our curiosity is our discovery that Twain put off publishing this book for twenty-five years, and then only released it in a limited edition of 250 copies for his friends.

H. L. Mencken, believing he understood the reason for Twain's hesitancy and long delay, wrote in a 1919 essay, "His own speculations always half-appalled him. . . . He was not only afraid to utter what he believed; he was even a bit timorous about *believing* what he believed." For this critic, Twain's fear of making public his 140-page rumination on human nature ("a book representing him more accurately than any other, both as artist and as man," says Mencken) is understandable to the degree that "Mark knew his countrymen; he knew their intense suspicion of ideas" that so openly challenged American religious and social prejudices.

On at least one point Mencken is right. These are hardly ideas that at first blush will win instant converts, though Twain's ultimate goal, I believe, was not to produce in *What Is Man?* a work that might satisfy the philosophers (it won't, and perhaps his reluctance to publishing was based on knowing this), but rather to make the strongest possible statement about human vanity, which, far from being at odds with Christian piety, is by the book's conclusion overwhelmingly supportive of it. In her afterword to this edition, critic Linda Wagner-Martin reminds us that "the dialogue was not meant to be fun. Or funny. Or a mere pastime. It was intended to be what it was, a fairly rigorous philosophical exercise."

So let us examine its rigor, one proposition at a time.

Twain's Old Man bases his argument on a tenuous analogy between men and metal (as well as stone) steam engines, establishing no more than a whimsical, metaphoric connection between the two. He and the Young Man are unaware that his comparison comes dangerously close to the Fallacy of Division (assuming the parts of anything are the same as the whole), and after this confusing choice of metaphor, the Old Man hurries to the first principle in his "infernal philosophy": "Whatsoever a man is, is due to his *make*, and to the *influences* brought to bear upon it by his heredity, his habitat, his associations. He is moved, directed, COMMANDED, by *exterior* influences—solely. He *originates* nothing, not even a thought." Against the Young Man's feeble objections, Twain's country metaphysician counters that "personally you cannot claim even the slender merit of *putting borrowed materials* together. That was done *automatically*—by your mental machinery, in strict accordance with the laws of that machinery's construction. And you not only did not make that machinery yourself, but you have *not even any command over it*."

Like the Young Man, we listen attentively, leaning forward in our chair, wetting our throats perhaps with whiskey, chewing on these statements, and remembering that, yes, Kant's *Critique of Pure Reason* makes credible the claim that in its operations the mind imposes form upon our experience as a means for making spatial and temporal experience itself possible. And psychology, we recall, suggests discernible patterns in thought processes, patterns over which we have no control, at least in the Freudian tradition, and which are based on external influences, environment, perhaps even sensations far below our level of conscious awareness.

Yet something here feels very wrong. "No man ever originates anything," the Old Man insists. "All his thoughts, all his impulses, come
from the outside." This claim in a single sentence eliminates Kantian *a
priori* judgments, necessary and universal, that come to us independent
of external influences, for example, our knowing the interior angles of
a triangle must equal two right angles. The Old Man, expanding on his
description of the machine-like operation of the mind in Chapter V, in
a section called "The Thinking-Process," says, "Men observe and combine, that is all. So does a rat." He leaves no room whatsoever in *What
Is Man?* for abstract thinking—observing many trees, for example, then
forming a thesis about trees as such, which is the very exercise in reason
that has made the Old Man's general theorizing about "man" possible,
and which the rat with its less complex mental "machinery" is, as far
as we know, incapable of doing. And regarding the Old Man's insistence
that "a man's brain is . . . merely a machine; and it works automatically,
not by will power. *It has no command over itself, its owner has no command over it*," we eagerly wait for the Young Man to raise his hand in
objection and to reply that far from the scene of their conversation, in
India, there is a tradition of yoga as old as Patanjali and a practice called
meditation (*dhyana*) based on rigorous exercises in concentrated control
of the senses (*dharana*) intended to achieve precisely the mastery over
thought, control of emotional response, and de-conditioning from un-
desirable past influences that the Old Man has so emphatically and
dogmatically denied.

Unfortunately, Twain's Young Man knows nothing of cultural traditions that swept through the East and have no Western parallel. For the
philosophically trained, late twentieth-century reader, he caves in far
too soon when he should be offering alternative metaphors and demanding that the other define foundational and soon to become troublesome terms such as a man's "make." Instead, he offers no resistance as
the Old Man reduces Shakespeare to "a Gobelin loom," qualifies his
theme of determinism a bit by allowing for the virtue of "training in
the right direction," and proceeds on to outline a phenomenologically
stronger yet no less provocative law for man's psychological life: the
ego-deflating "Gospel of Self-Approval."

In a word, Twain's "gospel," the centerpiece concept in his theory of
human nature, is an argument for self-interest based on the simple
observation that men pursue pleasure and avoid pain at all cost. "From
his cradle to his grave a man never does a single thing which has any
FIRST AND FOREMOST object but one—to secure peace of mind,
spiritual comfort, for HIMSELF." His "make"—loosely defined as character and conscience—determines the specific form of this "Master
Impulse" within each and every human mind, ensuring that "he always
looks out for Number One—*first*." On the surface, says the Old Man,
and before proper reflection, a deed may seem, as the Young Man puts
it, "noble . . . beautiful . . . its grace . . . marred by no fleck or blemish

or suggestion of self-interest," but behind the virtues we have for centuries called love, selflessness, charity, magnanimity, and forgiveness lurks the fact, the "iron law," that these are nothing more than forms of self-gratification. A man gives a beggar his last coin not because he is compassionate or generous but rather because the suffering he would experience, inflicted by his conscience (or childhood upbringing or public disapproval) would be greater than if he turned away. "Thinking of *his* pain . . . he must buy relief from that," says the Old Man, "a man cannot be comfortable without *his own* approval."

This "iron law," according to Twain's philosopher, covers all cases of human behavior: the mother goes naked to clothe her child for her sake, not the child's; a white slave master, he would be forced say, frees his Negro bondsman for *his* sake—so *he* can sleep peacefully at night—rather than, first and foremost, for any idealistic principles such as justice or Christian mercy. And because "a man performs but one duty—the duty of contenting his spirit, the duty of making himself agreeable to himself," some people will even gladly choose death over life to appease the "Master Impulse" of feeling good about themselves. In the Old Man's metaphysic, "None but gods have ever had a thought which did not come from the outside," which casts men as slaves shaped by their social conditioning (i.e., the ideas of other men and women), specifically by a superego (to use a Freudian term Twain did not know) that deprives them of peace when they betray this impulse. In this case, even "Self-Sacrifice . . . describes a thing which does not exist."

Does the Old Man's determinism and giving primacy to the pleasure principle seem familiar? It should, for its origin is in the so-called enlightened hedonism of the Greek Atomist Epicurus, who wrote:

> For it is to obtain this end that we always act, namely, to avoid pain and fear. . . . And for this cause we call pleasure the beginning and end of the blessed life. For we recognize pleasure as the first good innate in us, and from pleasure we begin every act of choice and avoidance, and to pleasure we return again, using the feeling as the standard by which we judge every good.
>
> And since pleasure is the first good and natural to us, for this very reason we do not choose every pleasure, but sometimes we pass over many pleasures, when greater discomfort accrues to us as the result of them: and similarly we think many pains better than pleasures, since a greater pleasure comes to us when we have endured pains for a long time. Every pleasure then because of its natural kinship to us is good, yet not every pleasure is to be chosen: even as every pain also is an evil, yet not all are always of a nature to be avoided. Yet by a scale of comparison and by the consideration of advantages and disadvantages we must form our judgment on all these matters. . . .

Completeness in any analysis of the hoary pain-pleasure hypothesis as the universal and primary human motivation requires us to raise one further objection: what of the pathological mind? Does pleasure or "peace of mind" always follow, for example, the deeds of a murderer, a serial killer? Why, then, do many express contrition at their trials? Narratives provided by such men, many of whom state that their actions have *only* brought pain, point to a conclusion contrary to the Old Man's and Epicurus's.

Our Young Man knows well enough that if he can find but *one* counterexample to the "Gospel of Self-Approval," he will be able to free himself from the tyranny of the Old Man's *idée fixe*. But, sadly, he can think of none, for the explanation based on self-interest does, in fact, seem to account for some portion of human behavior. Yet and still, the Old Man's ideas are far from systematic, coherent, consistent, or complete. In Chapter IV, "Training," he portrays men as lacking an inherent sense of good and evil and the mind as something like John Locke's *tabula rasa*, insisting that "he gets *all* his ideas, all his impressions, from the outside." However, later in that same chapter, he adds to training another major influence, "*temperament*—that is, the disposition you were born with. *You can't eradicate your disposition nor any rag of it. . . .* You have a warm temper? . . . You will never get rid of it." Both men disguise from themselves the difficulty this inclusion of nature adds to his earlier argument based on nurture.

For example, in Chapter III, the Old Man insists that through training, associations, and environment we arrive at "a soldier's pride, a soldier's self-respect, a soldier's ideals," in other words, a soldier's superego, which compels soldiers in one of Twain's examples to go down with their ship, the *Berkeley Castle*, so that women and children can be saved in the lifeboats. But, having admitted the potency of temperament, don't we undermine the extent to which training can shape the socializing influences of the "Interior Monarch"? It would seem so, for in the book's final chapter the Old Man grumps, "Beliefs? Mere beliefs? Mere convictions? They are powerless. They strive in vain against inborn temperament." He goes on to add, "Beliefs are *acquirements*, temperaments are *born*; beliefs are subject to change, nothing whatever can change temperament." Little wonder the Young Man is confused.

More damaging to his argument, at least to twentieth-century eyes, is Chapter VI, where instinct and thought are discussed, initially in an outrageous and, I believe, intentionally funny way when the Old Man refuses to morally put men on the same level as rats because "that would not be fair to the rat. The rat is well above him there." But problems soon arise when with his machine-model for the mind the Old Man observes, "I think that the rat's mind and the man's mind are the same machine, but of unequal capacities—like yours and Edison's; like the African pigmy's and Homer's; like the Bushman's and Bismarck's." Here racial essentialism rears its ugly nineteenth-century head in Twain's understanding of a man's "make." Not much later he adds, "As a thinker and planner the ant is the equal of any savage race of men; as a self-educated specialist in several arts she is the superior of any savage race of men."

The author of *What Is Man?* could not, I fear, escape the pitfall that awaits anyone who attempts to be a thoroughgoing empiricist or strictly scientific when addressing human nature; at best what one achieves is a pseudo-science or, in our own time, an essentialism based on genetics or the dubious findings relating race to test scores in the controversial study *The Bell-Curve* by Herrnstein and Murray.

Equally thorny is the section called "A Difficult Question" in which the Young Man says, "Now when *I* speak of a man, he is *the whole thing in one*, and easy to hold and contemplate." By this he means precisely what we all experience when we contemplate our embodiment—that we never experience ourselves as, say, a chemical process, or in the terms we apply to machines. Much like David Hume in *A Treatise of Human Nature*, where a radically empirical approach is used to deny the existence of the self and question even causation, the Old Man replies, "We all use the 'I' in this indeterminate fashion, there is no help for it. We imagine a Master and King over what you call The Whole Thing, and we speak of him as 'I,' but when we try to define him we find we cannot do it." Neither an *I* nor the Soul can be apprehended through direct perception. The self or soul is not *given* as an object during the moment of sensation. The Old Man shares this view not only with Hume but also with early Buddhist thinkers. Yet the epistemological and ontological implications of this denial of personal identity for the "Gospel of Self-Approval" are not pursued. (If there is no *I*, if it is an illusion, then the Master Impulse surely must be illusory, too.)

Throughout the dialogue, the Old Man's young apprentice blinks away these questions, and we are willing to momentarily put them aside because in Chapter IV it becomes clear that the elder speaker has patched together these different ideas in order to bring us to more pressing ethical concerns, the moral issue of "right living," that no doubt brought Twain to compose *What Is Man?* in the first place. In "Admonition," he says to the Young Man, "Diligently train your ideals *upward* and *still upward* toward a summit where you will find your chiefest pleasure in conduct which, while contenting you, will be sure to confer benefits upon your neighbor and the community." It is, he admits, a prescription taught by "all the great religions—all the great gospels," but with this difference: there are no delusions about why moral acts are performed—men put their comfort first always and the good of others second. But what other "gospels" is the Old Man referring to? I would guess one to be the Utilitarian social philosophy of Jeremy Bentham, whose "moral calculus" and Principle of Utility the Old Man seems to echo on several points.

"Nature has placed mankind under the governance of two soverign masters, *Pleasure and Pain*," wrote Bentham. "To them . . . we refer all our decisions, every resolve that we make in life. The man who affects to have withdrawn himself from their despotic sway does not know what he is talking about. To seek pleasure and to shun pain is his sole aim, even at the moment when he is denying himself the greatest enjoyment and courting penalties the most severe. . . . The *Principle of Utility*, accordingly, consists in taking as our starting-point, in every process of ordered reasoning, the calculus or comparative estimate of pains and pleasures."

And this principle is said to insure, as the Old Man hopes, a man's pursuit of pleasure will result in some measure of good for others.

It cannot be said that Twain was an original or groundbreaking thinker in *What Is Man?* (Mencken attributes the bulk of his ideas to a long-forgotten writer named Ingersoll). He overreaches when he takes on one of the most difficult questions in intellectual history, a question for which we do not have a satisfactory answer to this very day. But his motives, it seems to me, are ultimately ethical ones, even religious and political ones.

The Young Man sees it otherwise, lamenting at the end of their conversation that the Old Man has set forth "a desolating doctrine; it is not inspiring, enthusing, uplifting. It takes the glory out of man, it takes the pride out of him, it takes the heroism out of him, it denies him all personal credit, all applause; it not only degrades him to a machine, but allows him no control over the machine; makes a mere coffee-mill of him, and neither permits him to supply the coffee nor turn the crank; his sole and piteously humble function being to grind coarse or fine, according to his make, outside impulses doing all the rest."

He does not see that what the Old Man has taken from humankind he has given to God, though he should have been alerted to the spiritual *telos* of their conversation when in the section entitled "Not Two Values, But Only One," the Old Man, despite his seemingly materialist and mechanistic perspective, declares, "There are no *material* values, there are only spiritual ones." "The whole credit," he says, "belongs to the Maker. They (men and rats) are entitled to no honors, no praises, no monuments when they die, no remembrance." For all its playfulness with ideas, *What Is Man?* boils down, in the final analysis, to a scathing critique of human vanity, a subject Twain turned to often in his fiction. His entire argument, one might say, is encapsulated in a single, revealing exchange:

> o.m. . . . does man manufacture any one of those seeds, or are they all born in him?
> y.m. Born in him.
> o.m. Who manufactures them, then?
> y.m. God.
> o.m. Where does the credit of it belong?
> y.m. To God.
> o.m. And the glory of which you spoke, and the applause?

Y.M. To God.

O.M. Then it is *you* who degrade man. You make him claim glory, praise, flattery, for every valuable thing he possesses—*borrowed* finery, the whole of it; no rag of it earned by himself, not a detail of it produced by his own labor. *You* make man a humbug; have I done worse of him?

Y.M. You have made a machine of him.

O.M. Who devised that cunning and beautiful mechanism, a man's hand?

Y.M. God.

O.M. Who devised the law by which it automatically hammers out of a piano an elaborate piece of music, without error, while the man is thinking about something else, or talking to a friend?

Y.M. God.

O.M. Who devised the blood? Who devised the wonderful machinery which automatically drives its renewing and refreshing streams through the body, day and night, without assistance or advice from the man? Who devised the man's mind, whose machinery works automatically, interests itself in what it pleases, regardless of his will or desire, labors all night when it likes, deaf to his appeals for mercy. God devised all these things. *I* have not made man a machine. God made him a machine. . . .

Not once in *What Is Man?* does the Old Man apply his reductive, empirical logic to the existence of God, as he did to the soul, the *I*, and the virtues. For both interlocutors the Maker is a given to whom all praises belong, as in the biblical words "Not I but the Father within me doeth the works." But once he opens *this* door in their conversation, the conclusions—and intellectual quandaries—become all too evident, whether the Old Man admits them or not. "Temperament" and "make," all the external influences of the world that create the conditions for man as a machine, have come from the Maker. No form of determinism could be greater than this. All the internal evidence in the dialogue suggests that the Old Man's portrait of God is that of the watchmaker who has created in man and the world a delicate mechanism left to run on its own ("God makes a man with honest and dishonest *possibilities* in him and stops there," the Old Man tells us), and this empirically unacceptable resting place for the Old Man's "drunken theories" summarily deposits a reader in the realm of theological dilemmas two millenniums old—why has God chosen to make men like machines? What evidence is there even for a Maker?—that the dialogue does not wish to confront. In the end, *What Is Man?* impales itself on *both* horns of the conflicting views described by W. T. Jones—the mechanistic *and* the ethical and religious—yet does real justice to neither.

On the other hand, the Humean conclusion concerning the *I* is, while hardly a new idea, certainly a daring, even revolutionary one for an author releasing his work to American audiences in 1906. Similarly, we can work with and endlessly revisit the dour "Gospel of Self-Approval" and respect it for its cantankerous honesty. Just as we can respect the Old Man's pessimism about institutional religion and government, which makes him rail in the book's final speech about "a thousand wild and tame religions, every kind of government that can be thought of, from tiger to housecat, each nation *knowing* it has the only true religion and the only sane system of government, each despising all the others, each an ass and not suspecting it, each proud of its fancied supremacy, each perfectly sure it is the pet of God, each with undoubting confidence summoning Him to take command in war, each surprised when He goes over to the enemy . . . in a word, the whole human race content, always content, persistently content, indestructibly content, happy, thankful, proud, *no matter what its religion is, nor whether its master be a tiger or housecat.*"

Nevertheless, one comes to the end of Twain's dialogue wishing the author had been better acquainted with Western and Eastern intellectual history, saddened that he paid so little attention to contradictory statements in his text; and in our ears we hear Mencken's harsh judgment: "There is more to the making of literature than the mere depiction of human beings at their obscene follies; there is also the play of ideas." Mencken faulted Twain for his timidity in not publishing this book and for not trusting his own ideas, seeing that as a lapse in courage, which led him to conclude that "the weakness takes a good deal from his stature. It leaves him radiating a subtle flavor of the second-rate. With more courage, he would have gone a great deal further, and left a far deeper mark upon the intellectual history of his time."

To his credit, however, Twain leavens his philosophical dialogue with rich moments of humor, anecdotes that amuse us, and in Chapter V he wonderfully turns this entire book on its head when the Old Man, distancing himself from Diogenes, confesses, "I said I have *been* a Truth-Seeker. . . . I am not that now." True to his eccentric belief that men are like automatons, he does not exclude himself from his philosophy's condemnations. "Having found the Truth; perceiving that beyond question man has but one moving impulse—the contenting of his own spirit—and is merely a machine and entitled to no personal merit for anything he does, it is not humanly possible for me to seek further. The rest of my days will be spent in patching and painting and puttying and caulking my priceless possession and in looking the other way when an imploring argument or a damaging fact approaches."

There is little here that we can accept as self-evident, unarguable, or seminal for philosophic thought. But while the brilliant author of fiction masterpieces like *Huckleberry Finn* and *A Connecticut Yankee in King Arthur's Court* may not have been able to unveil man's nature in intellectually acceptable terms, as a novelist he was true in *What Is Man?* to the creation of two memorable and thoroughly consistent characters who entertain us from the first page to the last and, more important, force us to ponder—as Twain apparently did for much of his life—one of the enduring mysteries of man's life on earth.

Journal Entries on the
Death of John Gardner

A Word on These Entries

Since the age of 12 I've kept diaries and journals, writing pretty much every day in them since 1960. My association with John Gardner spans the years 1972 (fall) until his death ten years ago. Almost a decade to the day. As one might expect, my filing cabinet of old journals are filled with references to John. For this piece, however, I've chosen simply to fiercely edit some of the entries from the day after his motorcycle accident. Re-reading these journals, I realize what a transitional moment the time of his death was for me. My second novel, *Oxherding Tale* (1982), a story about slavery and Eastern philosophy that I argued back and forth about with John for five years during its period of composition, was about to be released (I believe John initially wanted me to do a replay of my first novel, which is filled with black folklore); I'd just returned from a six-month job as a producer/writer for the PBS black, dramatic series, *Up and Coming*, filmed in San Francisco (John thought I was writing too much television), where I'd spent the better part of 1981 training in the Choy Li Fut kung-fu school of grandmaster Doc-Fai Wong (he was a bit suspicious of my martial arts interests) and renewing my personal commitment to Buddhism and meditation. (He once told me, flat out, that he thought Buddhism was "wrong.") Inevitably, many of these emotional and intellectual threads flow together in the entries that follow.

September 15, 1982   3 A.M.

John Gardner is dead. At 2 P.M. yesterday, while riding on his motor-cycle, he had an "accident." No one knows the details, only that he went through a guard-rail. I had just pulled into the driveway at home when Joan stepped outside and said, "Something terrible has hap-pened." I held my breath, expecting her to say one of our children had been injured somehow (I knew it couldn't be fatal because she was too composed). Then she let it drop, "John Gardner is dead." At first I thought she was joking. John *dead?* Impossible! Not *him.* He'd always seemed indestructible, able to bounce back from injuries, mindless criticism of his work, even from cancer. I called Milton Kessler's home in Binghamton, where a woman verified John's death, and later novelist John McClusky Jr., called me with this news. The fact was again con-firmed by G. W. Hawkes, one of my former students at Washington who traveled to Binghamton to study with John.

But I could not—would not—believe it at first. This giant of con-temporary literature, this man who in 1972 (before he became too fa-mous and too busy) looked over my shoulder as I wrote *Faith and the Good Thing* and kept that novel on course; who probably saved me six years of development on my own as a writer of philosophical fic-tion; who was one of my best friends and supporters in the literary community—is dead at 49. Something in me feels a great numbness, a loneliness now. The loss his death represents to American literature and to thousands of people is tremendous, staggering, yet—and yet—how unhappy a life it sometimes seemed! He lived for art and love, but at his life's end he was, in some circles, the object of abuse and ridi-cule. Ten years of spectacular fame, international celebrity, honors and glory—so brief—and now his relentless service to American art and artists has ended *decades* before it should have. Why?

12:10 P.M.

I just spoke to Anne Borchardt, Gardner's agent who, thanks to him, is also mine. He will be buried after a Sunday funeral in the Presbyterian church in Batavia, N.Y.

All this is extraordinarily painful. No author has given more to the theory and practice of contemporary fiction. As a matter of fact, John was one of the two or three (if that many) American novelists who even *had* an aesthetic vision; he was certainly the only fiction writer I've ever known with whom I could seriously discuss philosophy from the pre-Socratics to Collingwood, from Gilgamesh to Whitehead. A gifted, gen-erous man in American literature, a *force* who devoted himself to art and to helping other artists, black and white, here in America and Japan, and now he is dead. Although it's a non sequitur, I can't help but feel that the suddenness of his death is related in some way or other (everything is connected, as John loved to say) to his personal life being in shambles toward the end, and that the literary mafia, as some call it, took it upon itself to dismantle his work, his life, his beliefs, on the occasion of his last book. He *did* say he was "hurt" by the reviews—he'd thought this was his best novel, his "novel for the '80's."

What did he say to me in the last letter I received from him, the one that asked me to accept a teaching position at Binghamton? He said, *I'm so lonely* . . . He wanted, I believe, to surround himself with old friends.

It's almost too much to believe, too terrible—and demoralizing—to think about.

September 16   1:25 A.M.

. . . a call from poet Richard Speakes about Gardner's death. It is so nice that friends who knew of my admiration for John should call.

But what does it *mean* that two and a half weeks before the publication of my best novel, *Oxherding Tale*, my teacher, friend, and a man I deeply admired, has died? I had very much wanted him to see this finished book that we argued so much about when I was writing it—it would have been a way to extend our often heated conversation through the mails on the nature of selfhood and (black) identity. Can any meaning be found here at all? As with my mother's death last year just two months before the birth of Elizabeth, this is a powerful, an awful transition for me.

September 17   2:20 A.M.

Gardner's death still makes me gloomy, sad. The loss to so many is so great. He was a total writer, in his way; he lived for art, and wanted so badly to be loved and respected for his products—and yet at the end he was troubled financially, divorced again, ridiculed in the press by reviewers who caricatured his position. It was so ugly, so unfair—he was bending over backwards to please them, I think, apologizing for *On Moral Fiction*. I think they fucked with his spirit. I think they wore him down. I think he was tired of carrying this fight for Goodness, Truth and Beauty (as he saw them) pretty much alone. The "nay-sayers," to use Nietzsche's term, brought down an American heavy-weight, a genuine "original" . . . In a way, Gardner never grew up—that is, he never gave in to fashionable "adult" cynicism, negativity, fatalism, and self-love; he remained at heart a farmboy who believed in love, great sacrifice, Christ, patriotism, the primacy of art, literature, and music. He hated pop existentialism and Sartre (yet admired Sartre too, oddly enough); he adored Homer, Chaucer, Shakespeare, the Greeks, Dickens, and all forms of what he saw as human nobility. He was loyal. And he was reckless, sometimes insensitive to the feelings of other artists when he made judgments, even occasionally cruel—they picked him apart, some of these people in the book world, looked relentlessly for flaws, found a few, then hounded him like harpies wherever he went. Will they *see* that now that he's dead? Will they see the sort of damage they did to John—and to those of us for whom he made American literature *interesting* again?

ඊඊ ඊඊ ඊඊ

A quick note: In 1973 I remember going to his Carbondale home to pick up pages of *Faith* he'd gone over for me. The house was empty, shadowy inside during late afternoon. John sat alone at the long dining room table, peering into a film-editing machine as he spliced together a movie—a comic cowboy film—he and members of his family had written and performed in. If I'm not mistaken, he'd been drinking. He was gloomy. Some reviews of *Jason and Medeia*, published that spring after the commercial success of *Sunlight Dialogues*, had savaged him as an academic, a "bright student" at best but not a great writer. I remember saying something about those reviews. And John, who was way inside himself at that moment, dismissed them all, saying, "They just try to keep you from getting to heaven."

6:15 P.M.

No sleep last night, and this was a long day.

I called Liz Rosenberg, John's second wife, and spoke a while, learned that John loved *Oxherding Tale* (but didn't like the cover), felt I was "coming into my own," and was showing it around. Shortly after I spoke with her, Bernie Rosenthal, Binghamton University's English Department chairman, called. His office has been swamped by media people asking about John. Binghamton will have a memorial on Wednesday—Bernie offered to pay my way there, but I still can't go, as much as I'd like to. And he urged me again to teach at Binghamton. One ghoulish note: people have already begun calling Bernie to ask if they could interview for Gardner's job.

From Art Washington, my screenwriter friend and buddy, I received a one-sentence message on my tape-machine after he learned of John's death: *"Anything you need, man."*

September 19   6:45 P.M.

There is the faintest twinge of "uneasiness" as I think that two weeks from tomorrow *Oxherding Tale* will be officially published and possibly in the hands of some of the same inept "reviewers" (if they can be called that) who were so unkind, so brutal to John on his last novel. At this time, I must take these events, each and every one, into formal meditation, that powerful medicine, that always centering practice that should, if one is wise, precede all significant judgment and social action. It is so necessary, so vital an experience, especially when one is living between the polarities of art and death, facing another publication—a public act with all the responsibilities and consequences that implies—and must live with the loss of a loyal friend and teacher. Perhaps that is how I should approach this coming week: namely, by tripling the time I spend in meditation, going deeper—the last few sessions have been, I think, as deep and deeply transformative as any I've experienced, but I've not hit bottom by any means.

September 23   1:17 A.M.

Just completed "The Six O'Clock News Game," a 30-minute espisode for a KQED PBS series—a first draft in just a little over 24 hours. Next: Revisions and final typing.

Richard Hart, my old friend from our days as Ph.D. philosophy students at SUNY-Stony Brook, sent me New York newspaper obituaries on Gardner. Indiana University Press sends its regrets over his death, and also in the mails I received a beautiful letter from Hilma Wolitzer about *Oxherding Tale*.

Despite the shock and sorrow I feel over Gardner's death, I continue to write and meditate strongly, perhaps *because* of his death. Within a few days I must turn my energies toward the one-hour show I promised to do for Fred Barzyk at WGBH/Boston, which is only 20% completed. But this is what I feel I need more than ever: namely, creative assignments, the challenge of "writing as yoga,"—yet another form of sacrifice and self-surrender . . .

October 11   11:50 P.M.

. . . I purchased, at last, Gardner's *Mickelsson's Ghosts* and John Howell's SIU bibliography on Gardner's works. His last novel, yes, *is* an ambitious work, full of narrative and dramatic sweat. It is grim, dark, pessimistic—the first 100 pages—and packed shamelessly with painful, autobiographical details, philosophical hypotheses: a philosophical novel in the form of a ghost story/college novel that tries in its opening to outdo the modern novel of *angst* and *ennui* and *despair*. He'd written, or at least published, nothing like *Mickelsson's Ghosts* before: It is filled, sadly, with defeat and futility, uncertainty and "depression," a word mentioned at least 20 times in the first 100 pages. There's so little light. So little of the old Gardneresque positivity, optimism, and courage in the beginning. All that is gone, replaced by a strange (for him) exhaustion, an end-of-the-road wheezing. It is saturated with the fear of death, entropy, pointlessness, so much of the pop existential tripe he railed so against in *Grendel*. How strange! His life is fascinating, painful, brilliant, noisy, and tragic. My reading of his last novel—so large in its broodings!—is filled with delight and sadness, fascination and gloominess.

October 27   10:40 P.M.

Received a call from Bernie Rosenthal, who still expresses interest in my teaching at SUNY-Binghamton. Always it is hard to talk about John—the suddenness of his death makes it difficult to truly believe he is gone, unreachable except through his many complex and highly diversified works.

November 4   12:50 P.M.

3 A.M. is an odd time to be awake and thinking about death, but so I was—Gardner's death, my mother's, and thinking about how brief our time is here. Joan and I are 34 (our birthdays exactly one week apart) my father is sixty, my colleagues in the Writing Program at Washington are middle-aged and beyond, my first students at UW are approaching 30, with children, or divorced, and out of work. So many of my colleagues seem to be aging so fast . . .

November 24   11 P.M.

From Karen Craig, editor at Indiana University Press, I received a postcard mentioning Sunday's *New York Times Review of Books* review of Gardner's volume for *Best American Short Stories*, which—I'm happy to hear—praises this special man's efforts.

December 26   1:30 A.M.

Managed to write a comment on John Gardner's life and work for the tribute to him being prepared in South Carolina.

January 28, 1983   4 A.M.

Why I'm up at this hour I don't know—napped after going to martial arts practice, then got up at 3AM to read a few essays in preparation for class tomorrow.

From Liz Rosenberg I received a letter, one that hoped I might be able to convince the TV people I know to film a few short stories by Gardner. I had a different idea—namely, a definitive documentary on the man's life and times; I immediately shot a letter off to Fred Barzyk at WGBH, suggesting this. My thoughts remain on this letter; I intend to shoot another one off to Fred tomorrow, one I shall write in a moment or two, further refining my ideas.

March 13, 1983

Gary Hawkes is at work on his tribute to Gardner for *The Seattle Review*; he's shown me two drafts, and it should be good, appropriate. Just now I am feeling gratified that (1) we can honor this man and Richard Hugo in the magazine, and (2) especially glad that WGBH/Boston is moving forward with the proposed film tribute to Gardner and his contemporaries, which is really Liz's idea. It doesn't matter to me if I write this as long as it gets written, as long as this project—a genuine labor of love—reaches completion.

May 3, 1983   3:50 A.M.

Just read John Gardner's *On Becoming a Novelist*, which his editor finally sent me: a lovely book, really. Sane, inspirational at turns, and quite instructive for the young, beginning writer.

Reviews &

Cultural Criticism

One Meaning of *Mo' Better Blues*

Two concepts—the "new Negro" and cultural nationalism—must be understood if we wish to unlock the artistic logic behind Spike Lee's fourth film, *Mo' Better Blues* (1990), and understand the position he has taken as a pro-black film director. Both concepts come from black people, one from Alain Locke, the Harlem Renaissance critic, and the other from the more important theoreticians of the black arts movement in the late 1960s.

In his essay "The New Negro" (1925), Locke describes the emergence of a new black art after World War I, a creative explosion brought about by a unique ensemble of social changes. The most important of these occurred when southern blacks fled racial violence and Jim Crow in the South by traveling to northern cities like New York's Harlem, where they interacted with Africans, West Indians, blacks free since the founding of the republic, and liberals—many of Jewish descent—fascinated, during the Roaring Twenties, with black folkways. All the elements were present, in this new black cauldron, for the creation of a progressive, international black consciousness and culture, and it was Locke who attempted to identify the new forms of black life emerging from the old. "The day of 'aunties,' 'uncles,' and 'mammies' is equally gone," he wrote. "Uncle Tom and Sambo have passed on. . . . In the very process of being transported the Negro is being transformed." One important feature of this new Negro of the 1920s, he said, was the appropriation by writers like Langston Hughes, Jean Toomer, and Zora

Neale Hurston of hitherto unrecorded black folk sources for artistic inspiration. In the work of many Renaissance writers it was the everyday life of the ordinary black man and woman—our mothers and fathers, kin and friends—whom few (if any) white artists could depict, that became the subject of exploration and celebration.

For all the outpouring of creativity during the Harlem Renaissance, however, two forces brought the movement to an end—or to a forty-year interruption, if we consider the 1960s (and later the 1980s) to be its continuation, as many critics argue. One force was, as one might expect, the Great Depression. The other was a fickleness by the movement's white patrons, such as arts promoter and novelist Carl Van Vechten, who encouraged the Renaissance writers because they considered the Negro to be an exotic creature free of white men's cares and hang-ups— in other words, the patrons' sense of black life was as one-dimensional as that of earlier writers during the Joel Chandler Harris plantation school era. Not until the 1960s would we see a broad-based return by black artists to the pivotal theme of the Renaissance—the celebration of the folk—and by then it would assume a more political, Pan-Africanist form.

Black theoreticians of the black arts movement, the cultural wing of the black power movement, not only encouraged a return to the celebration of the common folk, but also emphasized the importance of the artists' sense of *community*. Authors such as Amiri Baraka (LeRoi Jones), the late Larry Neal, the late John Oliver Killens, and Gwendolyn Brooks expressed their belief that black artists—and especially the black musician—are the servants of their people, men and women who spring from the folk, draw their inspiration from them, and, most important, *return* to them for spiritual renewal. This cultural nationalist concept influenced an entire generation of young black creators. It's easy to see how this concept differs from the romantic tradition of the late nineteenth century, in which the artist is often portrayed as standing *separate* from his community—a genius or freak torn by his lonely talent from the context of family and friends. In this tradition, and in the films and books influenced by it, such as the film *Amadeus* and the Herman Hesse novel *Narcissus and Goldmund*, only the artist can hear the Muses; only he, like one of Plato's philosopher-kings in *The Republic*, sees clearly the essential forms of the world (recall the remark, in *Mo' Better Blues*, made sarcastically by would-be singer Clarke when her lover Bleek Gilliam is too absorbed in his music to even hear her: "Let me leave the artist at work alone. The muse is visiting and Bleek is truly inspired. Then he will share his newest, latest gift to the world. Hallelujah").

Unlike the lonely artist of the Western romantic tradition, the cultural nationalist creator was seen as being *of* his people, and the highest regard was given to the men who produced jazz. Check out Henry Dumas's short story, "Will the Circle Be Unbroken?" (1966), in which the musician Probe plays music so anchored to the black world that it kills white members in the audience. The jazz-man, according to some 1960s critics, plays *with* others, and his work is a product of improvisation and spontaneity. If music is a "thing" in the Western tradition, fixed and made permanent by a text, in the black world it is deliberately short-lived, something that is mindful of its mortality, of the brief time that we have on this earth together: a music that happens at *this* moment only (if not recorded) and arises from the special interplay and dialectic of the jazz-man, his brothers on stage, and the audience *that* night. Black art, therefore, was seen as a We-relation. Such modern artists as John Coltrane (the guiding spirit of *Mo' Better*), Sonny Rollins, and Sun Ra were figures to emulate for the artists of the 1960s.

And so we come to the work of Spike Lee.

From his first film, *She's Gotta Have It* (1986), to *School Doze* (1988), to the highly controversial (and commercially successful) *Do the Right Thing* (1989), Mr. Lee reveals himself to be a director-writer-actor influenced by the principal thinkers of the black arts movement. He is, he says, a filmmaker who makes movies for black people (a position taken by poets like Neal and Baraka in their writing twenty-five years ago)— movies intended to counteract the negative and racist stereotyping of blacks found in films stretching from *Birth of a Nation* (1915) to the recent *Mississippi Burning* (1988). He is not, of course, our first black filmmaker, but in contrast to recent directors like Gordon Parks, Melvin Van Peebles, and the prolific Stan Lathan, he has established a style— part nationalist, part whimsy—that is clearly his own. In his films the *texture* of everyday black life is center stage—the feelings, rhythms, and unique panache of the common (black) man and woman are given full play. He achieves this, in part, by giving talented entertainers like the late Robin Harris, as comic Butterbean in *Mo' Better*, a great deal of latitude in bringing their own material to the set and, in part, by introducing memorable moments and flashes—the series of black men hitting on women in *She's Gotta Have It*, the three laid-back brothers signifying on the Korean fruit-and-vegetable stand in *Do the Right Thing*, the encounter between street bloods and college students at a Kentucky Fried Chicken in *School Daze*, and the band members ragging the perpetually late Left Hand Lacey about his French (white) girlfriend in *Mo' Better*. These moments come about because Mr. Lee listens, and listens extremely well, to what the folk are saying when they don't think anyone is watching them. For example, the scene in which the band members rag Left Hand Lacey has more the feel of being "caught" than planned; the actors, once they start to roll, step on one another's lines as in a real conversation, their joviality and ease as unmannered (and undirected) as if they were longtime buddies playing to a camcorder or to a hidden Candid Camera during a party.

Mr. Lee's films are built on these moments, not on Aristotelian dramatic principles. His approach, if I'm not mistaken, is to let textural moments of black life *happen* when he makes a motion picture, to let them accumulate slowly, so that by the film's end we have not so much the pleasant exhaustion that comes from a movie that propels us from the first frame to the last (as does any George Lucas film) but instead a collection of strong, black images and voices in our head when we leave the theater.

Few movie reviewers I read were kind to *Mo' Better Blues*. Inevitably, they drew comparisons—as did Mr. Lee himself—to other films about black musicians, specifically to *Round Midnight* (1986) and *Bird* (1988). In the companion volume to the film, *Mo' Better Blues* (New York: Simon & Schuster, 1990), Mr. Lee criticized both films for being "narrow depictions of the lives of Black musicians as seen through the eyes of White screenwriters and White directors. Two of the main characters in *Bird* are White. And of all the accounts of [Charlie] Parker's life that [Clint] Eastwood could have based his film on, he chose a book written by Bird's White wife, Chan Parker" (p. 39). Once he read that Woody Allen was also planning a film on jazz, Mr. Lee, the son of an accomplished bass player who has scored all his pictures, felt an even greater sense of urgency in portraying this subject from a black point of view. "You know I couldn't let Woody Allen do a jazz film before I did. I was on a mission."

Thus, he sets his fourth film—a work inspired by the black writer's determination to set the record straight—in 1969, when young Bleek Gilliam is ordered by his mother, Lillian, to continue practicing his trumpet when his friends arrive on their Brooklyn doorstep and want him to play:

> LILLIAN: Bleek, didn't I tell you to tell your hoodlum friends not to come around here?
> BIG STOP: Aw, Gem! Leave the boy alone.
> BLEEK: Can I go outside now?
> LILLIAN: Not until you finish your practice.
> BLEEK: What about then?
> LILLIAN: We'll see.
> BIG STOP: Let the boy be a boy, have some fun.
> LILLIAN: He could be a bum for all you care. Running the streets with those wild kids.

Lillian Gilliam (Abbey Lincoln) seems, to my eye, unnecessarily harsh and one-dimensional. Why, for example, is she so lacking in sympathy and only Bleek's father, Big Stop (Dick Anthony Williams), able to understand a child's desire to be with his friends? Although her shrillness mars this scene, the child actor, Zakee Howze, who plays Bleek, shows spunk and spirit when he shouts back at his friends that his practice time is important, then confides to his parents:

> BLEEK: Mommy, I never get to play with my friends. Now they call me a sissy. I ain't no sissy.

LILLIAN: Don't pay those fools no mind.
BIG STOP: A SISSY!
BLEEK: I'm sick and tired of this trumpet. I hate the trumpet.
(Big Stop looks at his son, gets up from in front of the TV, and goes to him.)
BIG STOP: Don't say that, Bleek. You'll have a lot of time to play with your friends. Don't hate that instrument; it's also your friend. We'll go to a ballgame. Just you and me. I'll make it up to you.
(CLOSE—BLEEK)
BLEEK: I still hate it.
(Bleek sticks the trumpet into his mouth.)

Much like young Charles Foster Kane, pulled away from his sled in *Citizen Kane*, Bleek Gilliam seems at first to resent the future planned for him by an insensitive grown-up. Whether he has true musical genius or progresses in his craft through sheer doggedness and dint of will is something we're never told. Unlike Milos Forman, who developed the character of Mozart in *Amadeus*, Mr. Lee does not provide us with material that helps us gauge the talent of his musician. In *Amadeus*, we see Mozart not only memorize another musician's composition after hearing it only once but effortlessly improve on it right before the other man's eyes; we hear him re-create the style and sound of other artists at a party for the entertainment of his friends; and, finally, we watch him produce first drafts of operas that seem flawless, even on his death-bed, where he dictates to a lesser artist a masterpiece that has the baffled scribe shouting, "Wait! What's that? You're going too fast!" These are, just maybe, the earmarks of musical genius, of a God-given talent so great, so mysterious it nearly tears apart the (Western) artist, who is always at pains to control these demons that whisper to him in a language of beauty and light few others can hear. Is Bleek so torn? We don't have enough insight into him to say. Yet it's clear that he *does* learn his mother's lesson about being dedicated to music and that during this learning process he also develops a staggering sense of self-regard and a selfishness that lay the foundation for the conflicts he will have twenty years later in his life—which Mr. Lee "smash-cuts" to, covering two decades of potential character development in the blink of an eye—with another musician in his band, Shadow Henderson (Wesley Snipes), his two lovers, Clarke (Cynda Williams) and Indigo (Joie Lee), and his manager, Giant, played by Mr. Lee himself.

The world of Bleek Gilliam, played as an adult by heartthrob Denzel Washington, centers on the smoky, below-ground *Beneath the Underdog* (the title refers to Charles Mingus's autobiography), an incongruously spacious nightclub (since it's in a basement) built in the late 1930s and usually packed with, as its name and design suggest, New York City's underdogs. In effect, the nightclub is a stage for Bleek's ego. It is *his* band, and no one else is allowed to perform original music. Giant, a gambler who can't get the group a better contract, often enrages the other artists, but he is Bleek's childhood friend since the third grade and, therefore, won't be replaced. And, perhaps worst of all, Bleek refuses to give Clarke the break she needs as a singer to make it in show business. Mr. Lee creates, as a backdrop for Bleek, a world of hauntingly beautiful music, of black performers who imitate the dress of their idols from decades past and look *good* on stage, of admiring women as different as Clarke and Indigo (a schoolteacher), and of white club owners—Moe and Josh Flatbush (John and Nicholas Turturro)—who exploit black talent. And within the band itself, Mr. Lee creates competition among other artists who feel they have not received the recognition that is their due. In *Mo' Better Blues*, the formidable antagonist is Shadow, who provides, I believe, a charismatic depiction of a talented, "overshadowed" black man who, by turns, can be sinister then consoling, crisply intelligent then goofy (the scene in which he talks about condoms with Giant), coolly professional then hot tempered. Shadow, in short, is unpredictable, and we watch him closely whenever he enters and threatens to take over a scene. One of Bleek's problems is that he doesn't watch Shadow enough.

During their sets, Shadow plays grandstanding solos that, according to Bleek, take "all day and night." It is Shadow who, potentially, can take it all away from Bleek—his band, his woman. Their differences are highlighted when, at a party, Bleek gives vent to his frustration as a black artist:

> BLEEK: I'm convinced Black folks are ignorant. We just plain are. I'm sick and tired of playing before everybody but my own people. They don't come out. We don't support our own. If Black artists, if I had to rely on niggers to eat, I'd starve to death. Jazz is our music, but we don't support it. It's sad, but true.
> SHADOW: Bleek, you're fulla shit. People like what they like. If grandiose motherfuckers like you presented the music in a way that they like it, motherfuckers would come.
> BLEEK: Oh yeah!
> SHADOW: Yeah! That's the way I'm gonna do it. Black folks will come. You watch.

I wondered how to interpret this exchange. On one level, Bleek is articulating the frustration many musicians feel when jazz is such a rage with whites and lately with Asians, yet responded to with indifference by many African-Americans, especially of the last generation. (Perhaps *Round Midnight* didn't get this entirely wrong.) But because these words come from Bleek, they reveal something about the inner discomfort he has felt since childhood toward his craft. No such friction between artist and audience seems to apply to Shadow, whose only goal appears to be providing others (including Clarke) with whatever brings them pleasure. We tend to agree with him when he says, "All Bleek cares about is Bleek." Shadow's evaluation of Bleek is especially harsh when it's clear that the band's leader won't give Clarke a shot at singing with the quintet: "Anything that might overshadow him, he blocks, like myself. I should be leader of this motherfucker, not Bleek."

But despite these professional conflicts in the life of Bleek Gilliam, and despite Mr. Lee's statement that "I always knew I would do a movie about music," the plot of *Mo' Better Blues* unfolds less in the direction of an artist's struggle with his craft (or his audience) than as a love triangle. "This time out," Mr. Lee said, "I chose to explore male-female relationships. All artists are driven by love for their art, and great artists are selfish in their devotion to it." He continued:

> This is Bleek Gilliam to a T. His music is his number one. So where do the women (two) in his life fit in? How do Clarke and Indigo deal with the fact that he is seeing both of them at the same time? And how does he tell them that they will always be second fiddle to his trumpet? That's some cold shit, and it takes a strong woman to stay with a man like that (p. 31).

To a great extent, then, *Mo' Better Blues* is a movie thematically at war with itself, alternating from the goal of addressing a black musician's life from a black perspective to dwelling on the sex life of Bleek Gilliam. As things turn out, the love story wins out, claiming more dramatic time in the movie than the tale of the artist's life.

There are scenes with Bleek making love to Clarke, Shadow doing the do with Clarke, and Bleek and Indigo engaging in foreplay, which takes the form of the artist pretending to be Dracula descending, his cape fluttering, on his latest victim. Once the story settles into this direction, *Mo' Better Blues* doesn't return to the initial question raised about the relationship of the musician to his craft. Instead, Bleek Gilliam's energy is consumed by the dilemma of having both Clarke and Indigo turn up at the club on the same night wearing identical dresses he bought for them in Paris. As Bleek tries to maintain his relationship with these women, he finds himself calling Clarke by Indigo's name (and vice versa) and mistaking one woman for the other during the act of making love—the contours of the women's individual lives blurring before his eyes as the two romances unravel, Clarke opting to fall in with Shadow and Indigo finally washing her hands of Bleek altogether. He has a shoving match with Shadow after Giant informs him that his chief competitor is boning Clarke. But it is not this conflict that Mr. Lee chooses for Bleek's ultimate demise. No, the coup de grace is provided by the worsening gambling debts incurred by Giant and by the loyalty of Bleek to his old friend.

Mr. Lee gives himself, as Woody Allen might, the role of comic foil for the other actors. Although he is called Giant, Shadow refers to him as midget and, in the movie's most devastating example of the Dozens, berates his work as manager (and his size) by remarking, "You keep coming up *short*." Which is true, for as a gambler, Giant is losing big.

While biking one afternoon, he is pulled into a car by two thugs, Rod (Leonard Thomas) and Madlock (Samuel L. Jackson), who tell him, "We don't believe in killing our brothers and sisters," then proceed to break the fingers on Giant's left hand. Mr. Lee gives these two sinister gangsters a touch of self-mockery. They pursue Giant to the nightclub on the very night Bleek has promised to help pay off his gambling debts, and drag him outside into an alley for another beating. When Bleek intervenes to help Giant, Madlock busts him full in his face with his trumpet, effectively bringing the musician's career to an end.

If Madlock and Rod are portrayed as caricatures of criminal types, the same must be said of other, secondary characters in *Mo' Better Blues.* Mr. Lee enjoys presenting them in pairs: the black bouncers Eggy and Born Knowledge (the latter breaks into a rap about the Black Man being God that at first glance might please many cultural nationalists, then make them knit their brows when they realize how they've been lampooned). And in yet another comic pairing, which led to some controversy for the film, we have the club owners Josh and Moe. When we are first introduced to these entrepreneurs, who inherited Beneath the Underdog from their father, they are singing praises to money—how numbers will never let you down, how you can count (literally) on the unwavering certainty of digits (a cash register ringing, say) more than you can on other people. For some critics, Josh and Moe are stereotypes of Jewish people whose presence is so widely felt in the entertainment business. A viewer must admit that they are offered to us in one dimension only, not as sympathetically rendered characters (for example, as Clarke is presented) but as clones of one another, making identical gestures at the same moment and completing each other's sentences as if they were Siamese twins, or two halves of the same person. They refuse to renegotiate the contract for the Bleek Quintet after the band becomes one of the club's hottest acts; Moe threatens, with a laugh, to sue Bleek if he tries to take his band elsewhere, and after Giant and Bleek take the beating of their lives in the alley, Moe tries to convince Shadow and the other musicians to go back inside and play. (Shadow refuses, swearing never to work for them again.) Nowhere does Mr. Lee say the Flatbush brothers are Jewish, but a few cultural eccentricities associated with the stereotype of Jewish businessmen are clearly present in these portrayals. A viewer is forced to conclude that, unlike Eggy and Born Knowledge (a lampoon of an idea), these comic club owners (a lampoon of an ethnic group) are less successful—and just maybe offensive to black and white audiences alike.

After the alleyway beating, Bleek Gilliam goes into hiding for a year. He is visited in the hospital by Big Stop. Back in his loft, which looks as if a tornado has passed through, he heals slowly and, apparently, reflects on the errors he's made that transformed his talent from a blessing into a curse and drove away the people closest to him. A full year passes before Giant, now working as a doorman and taking self-help classes to cure his gambling, sees Bleek again, this time on the street outside the Dizzy Club, which is featuring the Shadow Henderson Quartet, with Clarke as its singer. We learn that old wounds have healed. Former adversaries—and hurt lovers—are capable of forgiveness. Shadow has invited Bleek to sit in with his new band. As Bleek enters the nightclub, he is greeted warmly by applause. These people *do* care about him, no matter how badly he'd behaved in the past. Clarke gives him a kiss. No question she will remain with Shadow; the tenderness in her kiss suggests that you don't have to make love to everyone you love. The other musicians embrace Bleek, welcoming him back from the exile to which he was condemned by his own ego. Sadly, though, when he begins to play it's clear to everyone, most of all Bleek, that he's lost his gift. The gods, you might say, have taken it back because he abused it, and there's no sense in his trying to fool himself. Quietly, he—a figure of tragedy—leaves the stage and strides past the audience and then out onto the street, with Giant chasing behind him. "I'll never play again," he says, handing his trumpet to his oldest friend. Giant shouts at him as his figure recedes in the rain, "I won't sell it!"

The next scene occurs when Bleek, sopping wet, turns up at Indigo's apartment. Naturally, she's furious that she hasn't heard from him in over a year. But by now Bleek is not "too proud to beg" for her love.

BLEEK: You gotta let me redeem myself.
INDIGO: Redemption. The only reason you're here is because you can't play anymore and Clarke is with Shadow.
(He puts his hands on Indigo's shoulders.)
INDIGO: Don't, Bleek.
BLEEK: I once read, I forget where, a married couple was on a plane and it was going down into the sea. Without thinking, they tore off their clothes and began to make love ferociously, right there in their seats, oblivious to anyone and everything. They didn't care. The plane was about to crash and they all would be dead.
INDIGO: Get off me, Bleek.
BLEEK: They loved each other dearly and wanted to be together if they had to go. That plane, by some miracle, avoided crashing, but how were they to know?
(Bleek is now pressed up against Indigo as she struggles.)

Bleek's anecdote here, delivered at a crucial moment in a pivotal scene, is misleading. It says that in order "to be together" the couple on the airplane have to strip and start screwing. If I understand Bleek's story to Indigo, they are *already* together on the plane. By choosing this story to tell, the musician suggests, I'm afraid, that intercourse is the only way for two people to express their genuine devotion to each other. Nevertheless, the anecdote and his sincerity have the desired effect on Indigo. They make love, not the "mo' better" sort of sex after which the movie is named, not a simple "dick thing," as Bleek called his earlier affairs, but instead a surrender to each other. For Bleek, it is also a surrender of himself to others, a return to the world of the folk and family. In his script for *Mo' Better*, Mr. Lee writes that the end of the film was to be exactly seven minutes and forty-six seconds, which is the length of John Coltrane's "A Love Supreme." That composition plays over the montage that covers the next eight years in the life of Bleek and Indigo: their marriage, the day a son is born to them, the happy parents taking their child to an apartment in Brooklyn; the boy (named Miles) growing up; and Miles practicing the trumpet as Bleek himself had done in 1969. The budding musician's friends come to the house, shouting for him to come down and play. Indigo, now in the role of Lillian, says Miles must finish practicing first. We have cycled back to the movie's exact beginning—a contrivance to be sure, and the dialogue is the same, but with one difference. Bleek tells his wife, "Let the boy have some fun." Together in the window, with Indigo leaning into her husband, whose face registers a quiet maturity and peace we haven't seen before, they watch Miles race off, enjoying the freedom of childhood that Bleek was denied.

In *Mo' Better Blues* we end where we begin, with the black family. The life of the black artist is saved, Mr. Lee seems to be saying, by friends and kin—by Coltrane's sense of a love supreme—when his talent is lost and he has no refuge other than the family to restore his dignity. It is a movie that emphasizes the social side of the artist's life, a life with others, as black arts movement theoreticians urged us to embrace in the very year—1969—the movie opens. No one can deny that there are technical and thematic problems galore in Mr. Lee's fourth outing as a filmmaker. It is far too loose in structure to generate suspense. It needs, in nearly every scene, more attention to character. Although it is a far quieter and gentler film than *Do the Right Thing*, at its heart is the love-triangle idea that formed the basis of *She's Gotta Have It*, but in that movie the central theme does not have to compete with a host of other issues ranging from the exploitation of black creativity to replacing white images of black musicians with black ones. And, personally, I object to the notion that "great artists are selfish in their devotion" to their art, because we have too many examples of artists of the first rank who did not sacrifice their family lives, fidelity to their spouses, and loyalty to their friends to create beauty—authors such as Wallace Stevens and Ralph Ellison leap immediately to mind.

But the thought that Mr. Lee has used as a thread through this picture has a meaning every black artist—musician, painter, actor, or writer—knows only too well if he has plied his trade in the world and come wearily back home, not as a celebrated creator, just as a homeboy hoping to draw strength from those who love him even if he fails, even if his talent flees, even if he has nowhere else to turn. That meaning in *Mo' Better Blues* does not leave us: *You can't do it alone.* And, more important, *You don't have to.*

Review of *Richard Wright: Works*

Fifty-one years after the publication of "Native Son," the first best-selling novel by a black American, we are still struggling to take full measure of Richard Wright. He was a prolific poet, essayist, autobiographer, novelist, short story writer and social critic who overcame staggering obstacles—prejudice, poverty, a poor education—to become, as he has often been called, "the father of modern black fiction." In 1947, Jean-Paul Sartre could write, "The books of Richard Wright will remain alive as long as the negro question is raised in the United States." "Everything before and after Wright is different," novelist Margaret Walker, author of "Jubilee" and a friend of Wright in the '30s, reports in "Daemonic Genius," her controversial 1988 study, but adds, "When Wright died, his books were out of print."

Virtually every question important to 20th Century black—and American—culture runs through his restless life and even more restless literature. His personal odyssey from Natchez, Miss. to South Side Chicago, from America to Paris and the Third World, as well as his aesthetic journey from naturalism to "poetic realism," and explorations of Marxism, existential phenomenology and black nationalism, inspired authors as diverse as James Baldwin, Chester Himes and Ralph Ellison—hardcore realists together with surrealists, integrationists alongside black separatists.

Yet, as with any complex author who defies easy categorization, Wright's literary fortunes have soared and fallen in the last half century.

Civil rights activists in the '50s criticized Wright for relocating to France, far from the front lines of racial conflict in the United States. Black power militants in the late '60s saw him as prescient for rejecting the Communist Party and advocating a return to black folk sources in his famous essay, "Blue Print for Negro Writing." And in the '70s and '80s, feminists like Walker condemned Wright, claiming, "There is not one whole black woman in Wright's fiction whom he feels deserves respect. . . ."

Now, with the appearance of the two-volume "Richard Wright: Works," published by the Library of America and edited and annotated by Arnold Rampersad, we have a new opportunity to assess Wright's formidable and lasting contribution to American literature. But this time we have texts intended as the author originally wished them to be read. The works that millions know are, as it turns out, expurged and abbreviated versions of what Wright submitted for publication. By returning to typescripts, galleys and page proofs, the editors have restored deletions and changes demanded by Wright's publisher, Harper & Bros., and by the Book of the Month Club.

Volume One includes Wright's first novel, "Lawd Today," the story of a day in the life of a black postal worker, told in a montage of news-bulletins, songs and wordplay, which went unpublished until three years after his death in 1963; his first collection of short stories, "Uncle Tom's Children"; the highly successful "Native Son" (it sold 215,000 copies in three weeks); and the text for "How 'Bigger' Was Born." The Library of America has restored "Lawd Today" to the revised typescript prepared by Wright in 1937–38. They have returned to the 1940 second printing of "Uncle Tom's Children," which included one additional story, "Bright and Morning Star," and "The Ethics of Jim Crow," thus offering us all the selections Wright wished the collection to have. However, the major and most interesting change concerns one full scene and a handful of descriptive lines and speeches that the Book of the Month Club found too sexually explicit in "Native Son."

As it stands, "Native Son" is not simply a brutal thriller about a black chauffeur who accidentally murders his employer's daughter. It was also the birth of the black proletarian protest novel. Its central character, Bigger Thomas, is easily the best known character in black American fiction.

What Wright achieved in "Native Son," and what no American writer has done quite so well since (including Wright), was the construction of a fictive universe where everything is charged by the broken mind and broken heart of a black boy reduced to a state of thinghood. It is we, the readers, whom Wright turns into murderers, who he sends fleeing across frosty rooftops in Chicago and finds guilty for both the crimes against Mary Dalton and Bigger's girlfriend Bessie and this country's crimes against all the Bigger Thomases condemned to a life of frustration, invisibility and fear.

What could be missing from such a powerful work? The omission in question takes place in the first section, called "Fear," when Bigger and his friend Jack go the the Regal Theater and masturbate in their seats. It takes a full page before they finish, and Wright plays the scene with bawdy, Rabelasian exuberance. As might be expected, they decide to change seats, but once they've settled down again, Bigger and Jack see not only the racist film "Trader Horn" but also a titillating newsreel about the children of the rich. The focus of this feature is Mary Dalton, who is caught "accepting the attentions of a well-known radical while on her recent winter vacation in Florida. . . . "

"That gal there in that guy's arms," Bigger says, "That's the daughter of the guy I'm going to work for. . . . That's where I'm going to see about that job."

In Wright's original manuscript, Mary's legs and those of her lover are shown in close-up as she strains on her toes to kiss him. Jack advises Bigger, "Ah, them rich white women'll go to bed with anybody, from a poodle on up. They even have their chauffeurs."

Wright intended this heavy-handed scene mixing masturbation and an early glimpse of Mary to function as foreshadowing. But once the Book Club urged him to cut it, other passages had to go as well because to excise anything in Wright's fiction is equivalent to severing a limb from a living organism.

The cutting of the masturbation scene forced him to scale back another scene in Mr. Dalton's car, where Bigger, Mary and Jan share a bottle, and Bigger "looked at the mirror; Mary was lying flat on her back in the rear seat and Jan was bent over her. He saw a faint sweep of white thigh."

Gone, too, is a nerve-wracking moment when Bigger is helping a nearly unconscious Mary upstairs to her bedroom; he embraces her roughly in Wright's pre-cut manuscript, then completes a kiss, the absence of which in the version of "Native Son" I've taught for two decades, always troubled me. Was Bigger's encounter with Mary really as chaste as it reads in the Book Club version? And, if so, then why is he so frightened when Mrs. Dalton bursts in upon them? In the original, we read: "the sharp bones of [Mary's] hips moved in a hard and veritable grind. Her mouth was open and her breath came slow and deep."

Now, that is the realism we've come to expect from Wright.

There is also more sex between Bigger and Bessie, in the section called "Flight." But it is not until we reach the deletions in the third section, "Fate," when Bigger is on trial, that we see how Wright was at pains to double back upon himself and undo a thread in the novel that he thought important. The manager of the Regal Theater testifies about Bigger and other boys masturbating in the theater. Even Bigger's lawyer Max refers to that scene in his defence: "Was not Bigger Thomas' relationship with his girl [Bessie] a masturbatory one?" asks Max. "Was not his relationship to the whole world on the same plane?"

Wright struggled mightily and with only partial success to make Bigger's brief moment of masturbation work as social metaphor. Compared to the other "objective correlatives" in the novel—the relentless Chicago snow depicted as a symbol of the white world beating down upon Bigger; the redhot furnace in the Dalton's basement, which contains Mary's body and serves as a sign of his own burning guilt—this additional detail hardly seems essential to the meaning of his masterpiece. It's omission is, perhaps, an example of how a good editor can save a great writer from belaboring his point.

Approximately 14 pages and several passages were thrown out of Wright's 1953 novel, "The Outsider," a stunning adventure story about Cross Damon, a black postal clerk who is freed from his life of racial and personal misery in Chicago by a train wreck and then must face the existential dilemma of creating the meaning of his life from scratch. Inspired by his reading of Camus' "The Stranger," Wright created in this fast-paced, riveting narrative, which appears in Volume Two, one of the most complex characters in African-American fiction: a black intellectual, freed of his past, who plays out the Sartrean belief that "Existence precedes essence."

But Wright's agent and editor thought "The Outsider" was too long at 741 pages. They made suggestions; he complied. Then, without his knowledge, the publisher cut an entire scene of 12 pages, a lengthy encounter between Damon and a black woman being cheated out of her home by two con-men. These passages have now been restored.

Volume Two also includes the second half of Wright's famous autobiography, "Black Boy," called "American Hunger," which was not published until 1977. Again, it was Book of the Month Club that intervened, telling Wright in 1945 that they were interested in publishing the first half, originally called, "Southern Night," about his early life, but not the second, "The Horror and the Glory," about his Chicago experiences with the Communist Party and efforts to make himself a writer. Placed together now, "Black Boy" (another best-seller) and "American Hunger" (which is far less known) complete the finest story of an artist's personal odyssey that we have in black literature.

Young Wright in 1927 is the boy who policies his behavior in public, afraid that he will violate, even up North, some Jim Crow law. He is the boy who cannot relax, whose questions about the moral chaos of black life become not only a critique of capitalism and racism but also ethical probes into the hedonistic excesses of American culture. Working as a dishwasher in a North Side cafe, peering up from the American Mercury he hides behind a newspaper (Negroes who read are a novelty in the 1920s), he watches white waitresses whose "lust for trash" is paralleled by similarly truncated drives for alcohol, cheap thrills and consumer goods in the black community. He writes, "It seemed to me that for the Negro to try to save himself, he would have to forget himself and try to save a confused, materialistic nation from its own drift to self-destruction."

It is not a happy progress that Wright presents here. He is drawn, like many black intellectuals of this period, toward the Chicago John Reed Club. "I had lived so utterly isolated a life that the club filled for me a need that could not be imagined by the white members who were becoming disgusted with it." Unfortunately, though, his high degree of individualism and freedom of thought led the others to brand him a Trotskyite, an "intellectual" suspicious because he "talks like a book" and reads bourgeois literature. Although he grows more and more distant from his communist friends, he does retain his belief in their cause of social justice.

"God," he groans at one point, "I love these people, but I'm glad they're not in power, or they'd shoot me . . . Politics was not my game; the human heart was my game; but it was only in the realm of politics that I could see the depths of the human heart."

Throughout his portrayal of these "hungry days" in Chicago—days, really, of spiritual starvation— we also hear Wright's aunt finding fault with his reading and accusing him of wasting electricity. But the first glimmerings of the literary world he wants is there—in Stein's "Three Lives," Crane's "The Red Badge of Courage," Proust's "Remembrance of Things Past" and Dostoyevsky's "The Possessed." He experiments with Negro dialect and stream-of-consciousness in his fledgling efforts and writes revealingly of himself: "I strove to master words, to melt them into a rising spiral of emotional stimuli, each greater than the other, each feeding and reinforcing the other, and all ending in an emotional climax that would drench the reader with a sense of a new world."

Richard Wright accomplished this again and again during his furious passage among us. We owe a debt to the Library of America, and to Arnold Rampersad, for making available in these two handsome volumes a fuller vision of an artist—an explorer of culture and consciousness—who truly gave us "a new world" we are still trying to chart.

Spike Lee Does the Right Thing

The Malcolm X movie has by now generated more publicity without getting made than most films that do get made," writes novelist David Bradley (*The Chaneyville Incident*) in "Malcolm's Mythmaking," which appears in the current issue of *Transition*, devoted to the rediscovery of Malcolm X. Bradley's bristling article described the troubled history of this project in Hollywood, and how two novelists—himself and Calder Willingham (*Eternal Fire*)—as well as two Pulitzer Prize-winning dramatists—Charles Fuller and David Mamet—"bit the dust trying to produce a viable script."

Any writer familiar with scripting docudramas can sympathize with the obstacles they faced. The Malcolm X story is too large, as Bradley points out, for the traditional three-act structure, too rich for a motion picture that runs only 120 minutes, and too full of contradictions in a life that encompasses episodes of racial oppression in childhood, criminality in Detroit, religious conversion in prison, celebrity as the prototypical black nationalist of the 1960s, and a final turn toward orthodox Moslem brotherhood for what Hollywood values most: a simple "through-line" of action and emotion. And what do you do with the fact that, like any cultural hero (and for some, villain), Malcolm X means so many things to so many people that, as director Reginald Hudlin said recently to me, any picture about him has to be a "no-win issue?"

Well, the unfilmable film of all time *has* been made. Writing credit is shared by Arnold Perl and the controversial, neo-nationalist director

Spike Lee, who has been somewhat less than masterful in scripting his last five movies, particularly *Mo' Better Blues* (which I discussed at Lee's request in his 1991 book, *Five for Five*). While even the uncompromising critic Stanley Crouch has admitted that "Lee's control of the contemporary cinematic language . . . has been found impressive" in films like *Do the Right Thing*, no one has been eager to credit him with being a cracker-jack storyteller.

Given the excesses in his first five movies, his Madonna-like manipulation of the media, his insistence on not only directing but also writing and performing in all his pictures (a miscalculation for many filmmakers because there's no one to call you on your mistakes), and flat-out racist statements in his interviews, many people—myself included—could not conceive of how Malcolm's complex, unusual spiritual odyssey from hustling to humanism would turn out when director Norman Lewison threw up his hands because he couldn't "get a handle" on the story and it passed to Lee, who insisted no white man could tell this epic better than he could.

But those who were worried can relax. Lee was right. This is his best work to date. The magnitude of the problems involved in telling *X*, the hefty budget attached to it ($30 million), and everything at stake in this project for those who admire Malcolm and for the future of other black films, to say nothing of Lee's career itself, have led him to the wisdom of seeing that at least this time out he can't do it all himself. It couldn't be *his* vision. Or a platform for his views. Interpretation in a project such as this is an invitation to disaster. And where do we find Malcolm most clearly as Malcolm but in Alex Haley's "as-told-to" classic, *The Autobiography of Malcolm X*, which Lee, to his credit, has accepted as his bible or Koran for numerous scenes, speeches, and shots in this, the longest-running film in African-American cinema.

If there is grumbling about *Malcolm X*, it certainly can't arise from Lee's (and Denzel Washington's) faithfulness to the text that Malcolm himself hand-corrected. On the contrary, some might complain that Lee shows too much restraint in his slavish fidelity to the autobiography, giving us a celluloid transcription of the book's most dramatic moments. You watch this picture with a sense of déjà vu. There is Elijah Muhammad telling Malcolm how to win converts to the Nation of Islam by way of the "dirty glass of water" illustration. Here is pajama'd West Indian Archie in his rented room in the Bronx, a broken-down hustler contrite for once trying to kill Malcolm. And here is Malcolm copying out the entire dictionary when at Norfolk Prison Colony in 1948—but wait, isn't that scene placed in Charlestown State Prison in the movie? And, hold on, in the autobiography Malcolm's cellmate helps him get high on nutmeg, and *another* guy, named Bimbi, gets his respect for being intelligent and for the way he uses words. But in *X* both minor characters are fused into one, a Muslim named Baines who—as Lee's invention—introduces Malcolm to the teachings of Elijah Muhammad and later becomes his enemy.

In point of fact, it was Malcolm's brother Reginald who introduced him to the NOI, was later suspended by Muhammad for "carrying on improper relations with the then-secretary of the New York Temple," and wound up in a mental institution—a story that frightfully foreshadows Malcolm's problems to come when Elijah impregnates two of his young secretaries and exhibits moral failures that intensify Malcolm's public fight with the NOI and leads to his death.

So, yes, scenes from the autobiography are here, but adjusted for dramatic purposes. Example: Malcolm speaks of seeing the apparition of a man with "an Asiatic cast of countenance" appear in his prison cell; he decides this vision must be Master W. D. Fard, the messiah who taught Elijah Muhammad. In *X*, the benign specter is Elijah himself. Throughout the film, Lee takes artistic license in this way to bend Malcolm's history, which overflows with fascinating people famous and little-known, toward greater dramatic unity.

On the other hand, some omissions can only be seen as a conscious effort to sidestep the Muslim cult's racial dogmas in the 1950s. In the autobiography, Malcolm speaks at length of the fantastic notion that Muhammad gave his followers—and which Malcolm taught for years—that a black scientist created "a devil race—a bleached-out, white race of people," by genetically manipulating the genes of the "original" black race.

༒ ༒ ༒

Unlike the young people who have recently embraced Malcolm and, as his daughter says, "are inspired by pieces of him instead of the entire man," those of us old enough to recall "the angriest man in America" cannot forget the blistering hatred of whites that fueled some of Muhammad's followers 40 years ago, or their separatist call (and Malcolm's) for the United States government to give black Americans several states for the purpose of migration, or that bigots such as George Lincoln Rockwell of the American Nazi Party approved of their brand of segregation (as the Klan heartily supported Marcus Garvey's "back-to-Africa" movement in the 1920s). Ultimately, this was a position too little (pun intended) for a man of Malcolm's great love of truth. Days before his death he confessed to photographer Gordon Parks, as Parks reports in his autobiography, *Voices in the Mirror*, that "I did things as a Muslim that I regret now. I was a zombie—like all the rest of them. I was hypnotized, pointed in a certain direction and told to march."

As Lee's film makes clear, the Nation of Islam was for Malcolm the only means he had in prison—the lowest point in his life—to lift himself up from physical and spiritual degradation. It had 400 members,

Malcolm says, when he joined, but thousands after he left, people who came aboard because he briefly flowered in its fold and brought the group national attention after the 1959 Mike Wallace show "The Hate That Hate Produced." But Muhammad's race-tailored Islam was not, Malcolm saw after his trip to Mecca, in the global spirit of brotherhood that made this a religion of universal appeal. It was not, finally, *moral* enough (nor was Elijah) for a man who became so upright that an FBI agent tapping his phone in *X* is forced to admit, "Compared to King, this guy is a monk."

Happily, Spike Lee's *Malcolm X* steers close enough to the autobiography that he captures the essence of Malcolm's life as that of a black man's journey from racial tragedy to spiritual triumph. That trajectory toward greater truth and morality is, in the end, the "through-line" of this remarkable man's time on earth. And it is why even today he rightly stands, like King and Ghandi and Nelson Mandela (who appears in the film), for the best aspirations in us all.

Review of Kwame Anthony Appiah's *In My Father's House: Africa in the Philosophy of Culture*

Much like John Locke, who, in "An Essay Concerning Human Under-standing," saw himself "employed as an underlabourer in clearing ground a little, and removing some of the rubbish that lies in the way of knowledge," Kwame Anthony Appiah, a politically engaged Ghanaian intellectual, offers us a ground-breaking—as well as ground-clearing—analysis of absurdities and damaging presuppositions that have clouded our discussions on race, Africa and nationalism since the 19th century.

By carefully examining the concepts behind such emotional issues as Pan-Africanism and "African indentity," and by applying precision of thought—indeed, the entire history of Western philosophy—through-out the interdisciplinary essays that constitute "In My Father's House," Mr. Appiah delivers what may very well be one of the handful of theo-retical works on race that will help preserve our humanity and guide us gracefully into the next century.

"There is nothing in the world that can do all we ask race to do for us," Mr. Appiah writes in this well-researched and beautifully argued book. Yet as a concept, "race" is—like the notion of "force"—a phe-nomenon so culturally sedimented and overworked that it seems to resist systematic investigation, and we lament, as Augustine did when pondering the nature of time, "If no one ask me, I know; if I wish to explain to him who asks, I know not."

But Mr. Appiah, a Cambridge-educated philosopher who is now a professor of African-American studies at Harvard University, understands that every idea has its biography. So he returns us in his opening essays, "The Invention of Africa" and "Illusions of Race," to the seeds of Pan-Africanism sown in the 19th century by two African-Americans, Alexander Crummell and W. E. B. Du Bois. Analyzing their most important speeches, Mr. Appiah concludes that both men accepted a conventional notion of racial nationalism based on a romantic, European definition of the Negro.

"The very invention of Africa (as something more than a geographical entity) must be understood, ultimately, as an outgrowth of European racialism," Mr. Appiah writes. "The notion of Pan-Africanism was founded on the notion of the African, which was, in turn, founded not on any genuine cultural commonality but . . . on the very European concept of the Negro. . . . The very category of the Negro is at root a European product: for the 'whites' invented the Negroes in order to dominate them."

ᕦ ᕦ ᕦ

Accepting the illusion of race as a classificatory notion, Du Bois concluded in "The Conservation of Races" that each race has its unique "message" for civilization, and he wondered—and kept us wondering for nearly a century—what the mission of the Negro might be. For Mr. Appiah, this search for a unique racial destiny is much like the 19th-century quest for phlogiston, or the recent furor over cold fusion. Du Bois and Crummell began, he says, with an "ennobling lie" that may satisfy the heart's yearning for black unity but ignores all we have learned from genetics and flies in the face of what Mr. Appiah, as an African, intuitively knows: "Whatever Africans share, we do not have a common traditional culture, common languages, a common religious or conceptual vocabulary. . . . We do not even belong to a common race."

Mr. Appiah's repeated denial that race is the unifying trait of the African diaspora, and his jettisoning of all attempts to find a universal characteristic defining "black" people, doubtlessly will bother anyone who has a personal or professional investment in the idea of racial differences. Given today's race industry, we are talking about millions of individuals—politicians, preachers, professors and poets among them—who can no more budge from their belief in racial (and gender) differences than the Inquisition could give a fair hearing to Galileo. But Mr. Appiah offers a brilliant, and irrefutable, argument about postcolonialism in which he concludes, "We are all already contaminated by each other" in a complex, interdependent human world that is ill-served, finally, by the dead-end effort of engaging in "the manufacture of Otherness."

"I think it is clear enough," he writes, "that a biologically rooted conception of race is both dangerous in practice and misleading in theory: African unity, African identity, need securer foundations than race."

Mr. Appiah agrees with Chinua Achebe, the Nigerian novelist, who has said that "African identity is still in the making." For this reason, the burden of "In My Father's House" must be to replace the ideas we have operated on—of the tribe, the African, the nation—for so long.

Before Mr. Appiah can do that, however, he must clear away what he considers the seductive errors made by those who say Africa should find (or create) a black philosophy equal to the ones found in Europe. These writers and thinkers include Cheikh Anta Diop, the Senegalese scholar who looked to ancient Egypt for intellectual guidance for today's Africa, and Wole Soyinka, the Nobel Prize-winning Nigerian author who suggests that "Africa's cultures are an open book to each other." Mr. Soyinka's contention is erroneous, says Mr. Appiah, and gives us an "African worldview" that does not exist in a diverse continent of more than 30 nations and numerous tongues.

Mr. Appiah rejects the call for creating a black philosophy, which presumably would entail some form of uniquely Negro truth, because this position is "in danger of falling into racism." It is quite enough, he feels, for African philosophers to see their endeavor, first and foremost, as a *human* enterprise that will enrich "the one race to which we *all* belong." In the same vein, he writes that the Egyptianists like Diop "require us to see the past as the moment of wholeness and unity. [They] thus divert us . . . from the problems of the present and the hopes of the future."

The flaws in these positions and also in Mr. Soyinka's Yoruba myth making ("nativist nostalgia . . . largely fueled by that Western sentimentalism so familiar after Rousseau") are expressed succinctly by the author in his final essay, "African Identities": "If an African identity is to empower us, so it seems to me, what is required is not so much that we throw out falsehood but that we acknowledge first of all that race and history and metaphysics do not enforce an identity: that we can choose, within broad limits set by ecological, political and economic realities, what it will mean to be African in the coming years."

ॐ ॐ ॐ

Here, at last, we recognize the underlying intention behind Mr. Appiah's sweeping critique of the mystifications and mythologies of Africa. It is the desire to keep *open* the possibilities for Africa's future—a future that for Mr. Appiah blends modernization with a respect for the "old gods," that mixes the machinery and medicine and philosophy of the colonizers with traditional oral culture. In Mr. Appiah's Africa there is a role in society for the scientist and intellectual to challenge the authority of what the ancestors have (vaguely) said. "If you postulate an either-or choice between Africa and the West, there is no place for you in the real world of politics," he writes.

Mr. Appiah's humanism strikes this reviewer as human and humane.

"We will only solve our problems," he states, "if we see them as human problems arising out of a special situation, and we shall not solve them if we see them as African problems, generated by our being somehow unlike others."

But I think it is unfortunate that such an important analysis of race does not seem destined for a wide audience, though what serious work of philosophy is? Mr. Appiah's prose is dense, his sentences prolix and sprinkled with parenthetical qualifications that will make "In My Father's House" tough going even for the academics who are his primary audience. Mr. Appiah acknowledges this, suggesting: "What we in the academy *can* contribute—even if only slowly and marginally—is a disruption of the discourse of 'racial' and 'tribal' differences."

We can only hope those in the academy he is addressing do listen—and that, as with other works of philosophy, Mr. Appiah's formidable achievement will influence his colleagues, who in turn may have some impact on their students, so that what he modestly calls his "perfectly unoriginal opinion" will eventually gain as much popular currency as the intellectually naïve positions of those he criticizes. For, as Mr. Appiah must surely know, the truths initially disclosed by the philosopher are all already public. Not *his* truths. Not "white" or "black," but instead the rewards of reasoning available to anyone who makes the effort, as he does so well here, to "remove the rubbish that lies in the way of knowledge."

Review of Dinesh D'Souza's
The End of Racism:
Principles for a Multiracial Society

Even before its official publication, Dinesh D'Souza's "The End of Racism" was destined to become this fall's lightning rod for controversy. Two black conservatives, Glenn Loury and Robert L. Woodson, terminated their affiliation with the American Enterprise Institute, where D'Souza is a fellow, and held a press conference to denounce the book in, as Loury put it, their own "self-defense." Reporting recently on Loury's scramble to disassociate himself from a work in which he is favorably quoted, columnist William Raspberry compared "The End of Racism" to last year's "The Bell Curve" by Charles Murray and Richard Herrnstein. "It strikes me as a book," says Raspberry, "that only racists could cheer."

Ultimately, what "The End of Racism" has to say may well turn out to be far less important than who said it and why. Dinesh D'Souza is a 34-year-old "self-described conservative" born in East India. A former domestic policy analyst for the Reagan Administration who came to this country in 1978, he assaulted the political correctness on its college campuses with his contentious 1991 book "Illiberal Education." With "The End Of Racism," it seems safe to predict that, if nothing else, he will succeed in widening the circle of liberals who would love to see him tarred and feathered.

Personally, I'm not for riding anyone out of town on a rail. But after reading this book's 700-plus pages, I felt troubled enough, and gloomy enough, to phone a few close black friends for their reaction to D'Souza's proposed "principles for a multiracial society." None disagreed with the author's sense that "the task ahead is one of rebuilding broken families, developing educational and job skills, fostering black entrepreneurship and curbing the epidemic of violence in the inner cities," and none argued against D'Souza's belief that "the primary responsibility for cultural restoration undoubtedly lies with the black community itself."

What did enrage my friends was the route D'Souza took to reach these conclusions, his smug tone of cultural and intellectual superiority and the glibness of his solutions: e.g., repeal the Civil Rights Act of 1964 and create public policy that is race-neutral. While D'Souza claims to battle against "enemies of equal rights," he is in fact providing them with ammunition.

For D'Souza, America is engaged not so much in a culture war as in a "civilizational crisis," a societal breakdown at the center of which is the barbaric behavior of black America. "At every socioeconomic level," he writes, "blacks are uncompetitive on those measures of achievement that are essential to modern industrial society. Many middle-class African Americans are, by their own account, distorted in their social relations by the consuming passion of black rage. And nothing strengthens racism in this country more than the behavior of the African American under-class, which flagrantly violates and scandalizes basic codes of responsibility, decency and civility."

Because he sees "black failure" everywhere, and also empirical evidence to support the racial stereotypes of black violence and illegitimacy, D'Souza argues that whites are justified in practicing "rational discrimination" toward blacks. He does not hesitate before citing the controversial 1974 study of slavery, "Time on the Cross," to suggest that antebellum slavery was generally benign ("The American slave was treated like property, which is to say, pretty well"); he is at great pains to prove that blacks also committed the sin of slavery ("In 1830 there were more than 3,500 American black slave owners who collectively owned more than 10,000 slaves"); he does his level best to vindicate the efforts of 18th-Century and 19th-Century scientists who used quantitative methods for the purpose of racial classifications; and he revisits "The Bell Curve" in order to place squarely in the middle of our racial dialogue the oft-stated 15-point I.Q. differential between blacks and whites on standardized tests.

This dwelling on I.Q. differences leads directly to D'Souza's most scornful chapter, "Uncle Tom's Dilemma: Pathologies of Black Culture." "Black culture," he says, " . . . has a vicious, self-defeating and repellent underside that is no longer possible to ignore or euphemize. . . . No good is achieved by dressing these pathologies in sociological cant." For D'Souza, the most serious of these pathologies are, in order: (1) racial paranoia ("Many blacks seem to live in the haunted house of the past, apparently patrolled by the ghosts of white racism"); (2) middle-class rage ("We have to conclude that we are dealing with cases of people who live in a world of make-believe, in mental prisons of their own construction"): (3) dependence on government; (4) the cult of the "bad nigger" lionized in rap music, and (5) illegitimacy.

Correcting these "pathologies," D'Souza believes, requires a program of self-help along the lines offered 100 years ago by Booker T. Washington, or by people he identifies today as black, conservative reformers. "What blacks need to do," lectures D'Souza, "is to 'act white' which is to say, abandon idiotic back-to-Africa schemes and embrace mainstream cultural norms, so that they can effectively compete with other groups."

"America," he adds, "will never liberate itself from the shackles of the past until the government gets out of the race business." He urges black Americans to solve their own problems and then, incredibly, agrees with legal scholar Richard Epstein that "people should be free to hire and fire others for good reason, bad reason or no reason at all. . . . It is not unjust for an employer to refuse even the most qualified black because the job is the employer's to give and the applicant is no worse off."

No worse off?

D'Souza's vision of America after "the end of racism" is, one begins to suspect, the pre-New Deal era of the 1920s when segregated blacks minded their own business, were out of sight and out of mind, and the federal government allowed white businessmen to do pretty much whatever they pleased.

There is no question that D'Souza's subject is of vital importance to our future, and that on a few matters, such as the need for a new American (not just black) "ethic of responsibility," he is right. He has read an entire library of literature devoted to race.

But knowing what one has read and knowing America's racial history are two very different things. That D'Souza still has much to learn about this country explains his bizarre attempt to reintroduce racial stereotyping into our discourse when these are noxious ideas that Americans of goodwill have no choice but to reject, regardless of how pervasive such thinking may be. Furthermore, D'Souza seems oblivious to the countless contributions blacks have made to this republic. He also downplays the systematic disenfranchisement of blacks, who from the end of Reconstruction to the present have exhibited the very entrepreneurial, self-help moral philosophy he is calling for but saw their property, businesses and loved ones destroyed by envious whites. It is wrong, I am saying, to minimize the triumphs and courage that black Americans have demonstrated in the face of incredible adversity and just as wrong to blink at the fact that without the presence of black people on this continent for 376 years, American history would be unimaginable.

D'Souza's naivete and arrogance are revealed most in the statement that concludes his book: "It will be blacks themselves who will finally discredit racism, solve the American dilemma, and become the truest and noblest exemplars of Western civilization."

D'Souza's lack of familiarity with his subject prevents him from realizing the obvious, namely that generations of blacks already have proved themselves to be the most thoroughly American of our citizens, as the unprecedented popularity of Colin Powell shows. In "The End of Racism," readers will find wide-ranging and sometimes useful research, but D'Souza's frequently biased readings of the one-sided information he has assembled must be vigorously challenged by debate, factual corrections and discourse more civil than the author himself seems capable of delivering.

The King We Left Behind

"There are some who are color-consumed and they see a kind of mystique in being colored and anything noncolored is condemned."

—Martin Luther King, Jr.

It was said he could recite passages from Plato whole cloth from his head. His learning ranged over the cultures of both the East and West. He was twenty-five years old, and by all accounts he was a remarkably driven young man. At 5'7", he dressed so meticulously during his undergraduate days his college friends nicknamed him "Tweed." Yes, he cut a striking, handsome—and scholarly—figure from the pulpit of Detroit's Second Baptist Church on February 28, 1954, and Martin Luther King Jr.'s sermon that day, "Rediscovering Lost Values," brimmed with emotion and erudition.

He retold the story of Jesus' disappearance in Luke 2:41–52. Joseph and Mary had traveled to Jerusalem for the Passover feast. After it was done, they started back home to Nazareth, but discovered their son was missing. They paused. They searched among their kinfolk, then hied back to Jerusalem, where they found Jesus in the Temple with the doctors of the law. "That," said King, "is the thing that has happened in America. That we have unconsciously left God behind. . . . It wasn't a conscious process. You see, we didn't grow up and say, 'Now, good-bye God, we're going to leave you now. . . .' We just became so involved in getting our big bank accounts that we unconsciously forgot about God—we didn't mean to do it."

Ironically, some forty years later we are guilty of the same forgetfulness with Martin Luther King, Jr. Without our consciously rejecting him, he has been left behind. In a way, images of King have never been more ubiquitous, but his vision suffers from the curse of canonization. Across America his photograph is on display in elementary and secondary schools. It's difficult to visit a major American city and not find a street or a public building named after him. Most of our states honor the national holiday established in his name. Six-inch plastic King dolls, along with plastic podiums, can be purchased in toy stores, and his family has recently approved the manufacture of small, kitschy statues in his likeness, arguing that if anyone should profit from his commercialization, let it be them. Come every January 15 the airwaves carry his "I Have A Dream" speech, digitally compressed to fit into one-minute time slots. And at depressingly earnest ceremonies from coast to coast fourth-graders are encouraged to honor this nation's most preeminent moral philosopher by talking about their personal "dreams."

Can anyone doubt that this hagiographic presence is hollow? That it diminishes the pith and power of King's message to us during his fourteen-year public ministry? More importantly, does his vision of America—one of peace and brotherhood—still instruct us when liberals and conservatives alike, Democrats and Republicans, Louis Farrakhan and even pro-gun advocates in Washington state, cite his words to support their vastly differing political agendas?

Almost thirty years after King's death the tragedy of his absence is acutely felt in every fiber of our public and personal lives. For black America, this could well be called a crisis. A dialogue that is adrift. In the vacuum left by King no spokesman has emerged to electrify us with the tough-minded message that segregation and separatism, whether they arise from black or white communities, cripple our potential as social beings. Or that the methods we use to achieve justice must be quite as moral—as clean—as our goals. Or that the eventual goal itself cannot simply be the pursuit of power, or worship of Mammon, if our hope is to transcend the failed attempts at social and racial evolution in the past.

♨ ♨ ♨

No objective could have a greater practical urgency than King's compelling belief in a "beloved community" when almost weekly we are bombarded by news articles detailing public incivility, new depths of vulgarity in popular culture, worsening poverty in the inner cities, and the new status of young black men as "an endangered species." With each new terrible statistic, each new normalization of enmity in civic life, King's impassioned warnings—"If you sow the seeds of violence in your struggle, unborn generations will reap the whirlwind of social disintegration"—echo ever more strongly in our ears like the admonitions of a wise yet demanding elder who upset and angered us during his life—"Hate scars and distorts the personality"—and whose prophetic vision and clear voice return to haunt us late at night when we confront the ethnically balkanized character of our times.

But the descent—the degeneration—from King's belief in universal brotherhood to the tribal notion of my brother as someone who physically "looks like me," as Louis Farrakhan puts it, was not the work of a day but of three racially tempestuous decades. In the late-1960s, after summer riots in more than one hundred cities and the inflammatory, anti-white rhetoric of H. "Rap" Brown, an entire generation frustrated by the intractability of racism began to slip—politically and culturally— away from King's belief in "a power as old as the insights of Jesus of Nazareth and as modern as the techniques of Mahatma Gandhi" toward a smorgasbord of oppositional agendas. Other "leaders" came along with more militant voices. Times had changed, some said. Gandhi-esque nonviolence died at the Lorraine Motel.

The stage vacated by King on April 4, 1968 was promptly filled by gun-wielding Black Panthers waving Chairman Mao's "little red book," and fiery cultural nationalists like Amiri Baraka and Ron Karenga of US (who later invented the rituals of "Kwaanza"). Older leaders, among them men like the NAACP's Roy Wilkins and King, were dismissed by younger activists (poet Larry Neal called them "the New Breed") as Uncle Toms, or derided for being hopelessly assimilationist, old-fangled and bourgeois. Gradually, our preferred black spokesmen—the "authentic" black voices we listened to—became streetwise, ex-rapists like Eldridge Cleaver, or Huey Newton (who died in a drug deal that turned sour), or severe critics of the entire Eurocentric enterprise of Judeo-Christian civilization such as Malcolm X, of whom King said, "I feel that Malcolm has done himself and our people a great disservice": these are the true spiritual fathers of today's Crips and Bloods.

It was only a short step indeed from Karenga's cultural nationalism in the 1960s to Professor Leonard Jeffries of the City College of New York describing Europeans as cold, individualistic "ice people" (in contrast to the warm, communalistic "sun people" of Africa), and teaching in his CCNY courses that "rich Jews" financed the slave trade. Gradually over a period of twenty years, the profoundest aspects of King's vision, *satyagraha* ("truth force"), and his admonition that "We must be sure that our hands are clean in the struggle," faded before the Afrocentrists and separatists, whose strident voices and viewpoints came to dominate virtually every aspect of our discourse on race, especially in education. Just consider this conversation from Lola Franklin's third-grade class at J. S. Chick Elementary School in Kansas City, reported in *Time* magazine's April 29 cover story on "The End of Integration."

"Who can name an African-American comedian?" inquires Franklin.
"Eddie Murphy!" "Bill Cosby!"
"And some American comedians?"

"Whoopi Goldberg!"

"No, an American comedian," she corrects them.

"Roseanne!" a boy calls out.

"Good," says Franklin.

In this equation, American equals white, despite the fundamental role blacks have played since the time of the colonists in shaping this country's politics and culture. Toward the end of his life, King feared this situation might arise; he grasped instantly that the goal of the separatists was to divorce black people from a nation of their own creation.

And now we have the scandal of Afrocentrists—specifically Nation of Islam spokesmen—who have injected anti-Semitism into public discourse, most notably Louis Farrakhan and Khalid Muhammad, who told a Howard University audience that his hero was Colin Ferguson, the black gunman who emptied his weapon on whites and Asians on a Long Island train. His mentor, Farrakhan, draws stadium-sized crowds to hear him deliver a separatist doctrine fashioned by Elijah Muhammad in the 1930s, one that explains the origin of the white race with the fantastic myth of Yacub, a black scientist who created a "beast" destined to become the first European.

Contrast that to King being so convinced our goal was empathy he could say, "Strangely enough, I can never be what I ought to be until you are what you ought to be. You can never be what you ought to be until I am what I ought to be." From this desire to share each other's fate, the alliance of blacks and Jews of goodwill was formed, producing thirty years ago this country's finest (yet fragile) attempt at brotherhood, one that some of our present "leaders" have fractured by singling out Jews as their adversaries.

☽ ☽ ☽

The popularity of race-baiting anti-Semites in black American communities is not new, though it can be perplexing until, remembering King, we realize that hatred, anger and racial mythology are easy. They reveal a frame of mind best known by its astonishing mediocrity. And for its betrayal of the great humanity that inspired the civil rights movement. No moral, intellectual, or spiritual work is involved. And that, of course, may be the problem with Americans across the board in the 1990s. A reluctance to be challenged, to change one's prejudices, or to live nobly. The inability to see, as King saw, that the rallying cry of "Black Power" was born with a frightening blemish that might grow uglier with age. "I think it would be very dangerous and even tragic," he said, "if the struggle in the United States for civil rights degenerated to a racial struggle of blacks against whites."

Yet each and every one of us is an apostate. We are all responsible for this sea change in race relations, and the substitution of the "beloved community" with "identity politics." In my case, I cannot say I rejected

King, but as a young man I knew his philosophy only by its reflections and refractions. My parents, a quietly pious Methodist couple, kept a portrait of him displayed in our home, so I was respectful of the racial battles he fought and the personal courage he demonstrated again and again from Montgomery to Mississippi. In fact, I was a child of integration. It was an ideal I took for granted all throughout high school and college. But like other baby boomers I came of age in the years when King's greatest triumphs—the Nobel Peace Prize and Civil Rights Act of 1964—were behind him, his leadership was being challenged, and the Zeitgeist among young blacks shifted from focusing on the ninety-nine percent of our lives that we all share in common to the one percent of differences that divide us.

On July 2, 1964, when King stood behind Lyndon Johnson as he signed the Civil Rights Act, I was fourteen, living not in the South but in a Chicago suburb where many young black men viewed non-violence as unmanly and listened with greater interest to the speeches of Malcolm X than to the apostle of forgiveness who said, "Nonviolence . . . does not seek to defeat or humiliate the opponent, but to win his friendship and understanding." During a Mississippi march in the summer of 1966, Stokely Carmichael proclaimed, "What we need is Black Power!" and his words rang deeper with my black friends and me than King's plea that "Our destinies are tied together; none of us can make it alone. . . . There is no separate black path to power and fulfillment that does not have to intersect with white roots."

So yes, I thought of him less often and less clearly throughout the '70s. Then, during the Reagan years and early '90s, I watched my son and daughter growing up in a social minefield, one seeded—by whites and blacks alike—with dangers unknown to my friends and me in the 1950s or, for that matter, by my parents and their predecessors. Something had gone terribly wrong since my twenties. As an author, I discovered when I visited bookstores, or sat on panels with other writers, that the term "brotherhood" had become passé and love—with its bottomless duties and demands—was a positively antediluvian idea. Yet their omission was obvious everywhere. Recently visiting a Seattle lockup facility for youths under 18 awaiting trial, I stood nearly speechless before an audience of boys and girls no older than my own children, dressed in differently colored jailhouse jumpsuits, their faces emptied of hope for their futures, their eyes filled with years of betrayal. In Chicago last year my first novel, *Faith and the Good Thing*, was adapted for the stage by City Lit Theatre and the Chicago Theatre Company. I saw a morning performance, one attended by seventy-eight pregnant teenage girls all under the age of eighteen. To be honest, I watched them more closely than I did the play itself. They were herded in by their counselors. They were told how to "behave" in a theater, which they did until the point in the story when its protagonist, a young woman their age, is raped. The girls howled. Some urged the rapist on. At that instant I understood what had taken place among the black children who reportedly laughed when a Jewish woman is shot in *Schindler's List.*

After the play, I spoke with the young black actors whose energy brought this novel to life. Whenever they performed the rape scene for teenagers, they said, the reaction was the same, and they were troubled by it. I asked who has gotten these girls pregnant? Their mothers' boyfriends, I was told. Or older men in the southside buildings where they lived.

During that trip to Chicago I discovered how many black communities (including the one in my own hometown) have fallen into a condition my old friends and I now find as heartbreaking as the residual effects of racism. By now we all know the egregious news stories about black crime, drugs and illegitimacy, but I wondered: How did we allow this to happen? Between my generation and that of so many of the children I've seen there has been no transmission of the triumphs, personal and political, that strengthened black Americans for centuries, allowing our predecessors to overcome staggering obstacles in the pre-civil rights era and raise strong, resourceful sons and daughters—like King and countless others before him.

More and more, I found myself revisiting King to discern the genesis of our present dilemmas. I have made him my meditation for five years, studying his sermons, history, speeches, even his college papers in order to capture something of his life in an in-progress novel, but more importantly to understand—as I believe Congressman John Lewis does—the essence of the elder we left behind.

"If King could speak to us today," Lewis said in 1994, "he would say, in addition to doing something about guns, he would say there needs to be a revolution of values, a revolution of ideas in the black community. He would say we need to accept non-violence not simply as a technique or as a means to bring about social and political change, but we need to make it a way of life, *a way of living.*"

ॐ ॐ ॐ

I came to see that for King what we should do was inexorably linked to what we hope to be. He was insistent that "The great problem facing modern man is that the means by which we live have outdistanced the spiritual ends for which we live." Underpinning his belief in love's primacy was the sense that our lives constitute an "inescapable network of mutuality" that binds all people in a single "garment of destiny." The separatist's goal is illusory for King, a failure of sight. The segregationist, steeped in dualisms racial, sexual and otherwise, is blind to the fact that if he traced back his genes to A.D. 700, he would discover he shared a common ancestor with everyone on earth. None of us can be less closely related than fiftieth cousins. The sponge "Bull" Conner bathed with came from the Pacific Islands, his towel was spun in Turkey, his coffee traveled all the way from South America, his tea from China, his cocoa from West Africa. Every time he wrote his name he used ink evolved from India, an alphabet inherited from Romans who derived it from the Greeks after they'd borrowed it from Phoenicians who received their symbols from Semites living on the Sinai Peninsula between Egypt and Palestine. Whether we like it or not, our lives are intertwined and, as King observed, "We must all learn to live together as brothers or we will perish together as fools."

This is the root of King's revolutionary fervor. He agreed with the Marxist critique of capital, yes; but he could not forgive Marx for his atheism, because King believed that "Racial justice . . . will come neither by our frail and often misguided efforts nor by God imposing his will on wayward men, but when enough people open their lives to God to allow him to pour his triumphant, divine energy into their souls." Thus effective social change requires effort on two "fronts," one directed externally to eliminate injustice in the political realm, the other directed inwardly toward refining our character and cultural values. "We must set out to do a good job, irrespective of race," he said, "and do it so well that nobody can do it better."

As if peering into a crystal ball disclosing the dilemma of black life at century's end, King stated, "We must work on two fronts. On the one hand, we must continually resist the system of segregation—the system which is the basic cause of our lagging standards; on the other hand, we must work constructively to improve the lagging standards which are the effects of segregation. There must be a rhythm of alteration between attacking the cause and healing the effects. . . . We are often too loud and boisterous, and spend too much on alcoholic beverages. These are some of the shortcomings we can improve here and now. . . . Even the most poverty stricken among us can be clean, even the most uneducated among us can have high morals. By improving these standards, we will go a long way in breaking down some of the arguments of the segregationists."

If we had heeded King's warnings in the late 1950s, especially when he declared "We shall have to create leaders who embody virtues we can respect," perhaps today we would not be struggling to close the widening racial divide in American society, or to repair the dialogue between blacks and Jews. All these matters King broached long ago. If he were with us now, standing in the pulpit before a forest of black microphones, I believe he would take his sermons in the '90s from Proverbs 29:18, gently yet emphatically reminding us that brotherhood was our goal, love our method, generosity and forgiveness our rule, peace our way of life, and, finally, that where there is no vision, the people perish.

Charlie's Pad

A Capsule History of Blacks in Comics

One of the invaluable features of *Still I Rise*, the first cartoon history of black America, is the wealth of information its writers, Roland Laird and Taneshia Laird, and its artist Elihu Bey, provide about the marginalized—and often suppressed—political, economic and cultural contributions black people have made on this continent since the seventeenth century. Using the most basic means of communication we have—pictures—they transport us back through time, enabling us literally to see how dependent American colonists were on the agricultural sophistication of African slaves and indentured servants; how blacks fought and died for freedom during the Revolutionary and Civil Wars; and how, in ways both small and large, black genius shaped the evolution of democracy, the arts and sciences, and the English language in America, despite staggering racial and social obstacles.

As a contribution to illustrated history from a black point of view, *Still I Rise* is a unique achievement, one that will be valued—like Art Spiegelman's *Maus: A Survivor's Tale* and Larry Gonick's *A Cartoon History of the Universe*—by students, educators, collectors, and general readers for a long time to come. Yet it presents an interesting paradox. Although the book chronicles the often "invisible" history of black America in Elihu Bey's energetic and uncompromising drawings, the black men and women who were pioneers in the field of American comic art are noticeably absent. As a rule, cartoonists of any color often labor in obscurity. Except for a handful of current celebrities, among them Matt Groening ("The Simpsons"), Robert Crumb ("Fritz the Cat"), and Gary Larson ("The Far Side"), they are an unnamed, largely unrewarded tribe of ink-stained storytellers expressing themselves in a medium as ancient as that used by the Paleolithic painter who left images of reindeer grazing on the walls of a cave in Font-de-Gaume, France thirty thousand years ago. Remember: we think in pictures. Like music, the content of a drawing can be universally recognized; it cuts across language barriers, is "worth a thousand words," and has long been employed for tale-telling and propaganda. Regardless of age, nearly everyone recognizes the images of highly merchandized characters like Popeye and Superman, but how many of us can identify Elzie Segar, Joe Shuster and Jerry Siegal as their creators, or tell you much about them? This anonymity is, sad to say, even greater for the black comic artists who prepared the way for *Still I Rise*, although some of their creations have won an enduring place in America's popular imagination.

During a 1989 lecture trip in Germany for the United States Information Agency, I met one of those pioneers: the late, great Ollie Harrington, who died on November 2, 1995. Once called "America's favorite Negro cartoonist" by Langston Hughes, Harrington's weekly cartoon panel, "Dark Laughter," began its appearance in the *Amsterdam News* on May 25, 1935. By December 28, it was featuring Bootsie, a

"Doctor Jenkins, before you read us your paper on inter-stellar gravitational tensions in thermo-nuclear propulsion, would you sing us a good old spiritual?"

bald, pot bellied and witty observer of racial life (he could be the brother of Hughes's Jesse B. Semple) in one-panel drawings memorable not only for the crisp humor with which they laid bare social injustice but also for Harrington's delicate, detailed draftsmanship. (Vintage Harrington can be found in his cartoon depicting an elderly black scholar about to present his scientific research to white colleagues, one of whom benignly rests a hand on the scholar's shoulder, and says, "Doctor Jenkins, before you read us your paper on inter-stellar gravitational tensions in thermonuclear propulsion, would you sing us a good old spiritual?")

Among Harrington's circle of friends during the Harlem Renaissance were writers Arna Bontemps, Rudolph Fisher and Wallace Thurman. He was the art director for Adam Clayton Powell's newspaper, the *People's Voice*, and, for the NAACP, he was a spokesman who assailed the lynchings of blacks in the south, a stance that brought him under the scrutiny of the F.B.I. In 1951, Harrington left America, joining a now legendary group of black expatriate artists that included Chester Himes and his close friend Richard Wright. But in 1961, a year after Wright's death, Harrington went to Berlin in August to speak with publishers about translating American classics and found himself trapped in East Berlin. In his essay, "Why I Left America," he wrote, "I couldn't leave because I didn't have the proper visas. . . . I was a virtual prisoner. I lost my French apartment. I lost everything. I had to stay there."[1] Yet still he worked for twenty years, placing his political drawings in the *Daily Worker* and East German magazines.

When the wall came down in the winter of 1989, East Berliners were flocking to the West. I learned Harrington was among them. Brimming with questions, I arranged to meet him at a cafe. An affable, friendly man, he arrived wearing a green turtleneck sweater, a brown leather jacket, and black-rimmed spectacles. Sipping coffee, we discussed Richard Wright's haiku and the situation of black cartoonists before he left the States. "Where," I asked, "did you publish your work?"

"That's the point," replied Harrington. "There wasn't anywhere to publish."

Of course, he was telling the truth. Before the 1960s, the great bulk of work by black cartoonists could be found only in black newspapers and magazines, and much of their effort has been lost or forgotten. To be sure, there were blacks in comics from nearly the beginning of the genre, which kicked off in America in 1896 with R. F. Outcault's "Yellow Kid." (Comic books came later, in May of 1933, the first being *Famous Funnies*.) But these black characters were grotesques—their faces, as Harrington once put it, "a circle, black with two hot dogs in the middle for a mouth."[2] There was Ebony, the buffoonish sidekick in Will Eisner's syndicated 1940s strip "The Spirit"; or the hulking Lothar, a black aide to "Phantom"-creator Lee Falk's "Mandrake the Magician." On and on from the late nineteenth century through the 1950s there were hideous, bubble-lipped Sambos penned by white illustrators influenced by Al Jolson and the minstrel tradition, and it was these vicious stereotypes that black comic artists, working primarily in the Negro press, fought mightily to correct.

Among these nearly forgotten creators is Jackie Ormes, one of the few black women cartoonists from the pre–Civil Rights era. Thanks to the research of comics historian Trina Robbins, author of *A Century of Women Cartoonists*, we know that Ormes's "Torchy Brown in Dixie and Harlem" premiered in 1937 on the pages of the *Pittsburgh Courier*, when she was twenty-two years old, and lasted until 1940, presenting over a three-year period the "Brenda Starr"–inspired adventures of her young heroine after she sells her farm and travels to New York City. For the *Chicago Daily Defender*, Ormes worked as a reporter in the 1940s and contributed an unpaid strip about a black maid called "Candy." Her single panel cartoon "Patty Jo 'n Ginger" was distributed by the Smith-Mann syndicate and in 1948 inspired Patty Jo dolls produced by the Terri Lee Co. in Nebraska; they were the first black character dolls in this country, Robbins reports, and are collector's items today. Ormes revived Torchy for the *Pittsburgh Courier* in a 1950 strip called "Torchy Brown Heartbeat," and in its panels tackled issues such as bigotry and pollution before the feature expired in 1955. Ormes died at age seventy in January 1987.[3]

To her credit, Robbins also unearthed the work of a second black woman cartoonist of the 1950s, Doris McClarty, whose one-page strip "Fireball Freddie" appeared in the black magazine *Hep*.[4] Its characters, slang-spouting hipsters, seemed drawn from the world of Cab Calloway. ("Well Pops," says one, "Kate gave me the gate. Now I'm doing the town brown.") However, students of the genre may find McClarty's work less interesting for its draftsmanship or ideas than for its linguistic curiosi-ties—the discovery, for example, that black argot like "bust a cap" and "cop a plea" dates from the 1950s.

So yes, Harrington is correct about black cartoonists earlier in this century being confined largely to the black press. But was the reason simply the artists' race? Or was it that white editors and readers would not accept black content presented from a black point of view?[5] The evidence suggests the latter to be the case, at least in part, since black artists Russell Patterson and Matt Baker drew white characters in com-ics for mainstream publishers, and one of the most successful panel car-toonists of the 1940s and 1950s, E. Simms Campbell, published erotic humor so regularly in *Esquire* and *Playboy* that his elegant, painterly cartoons and clever gag lines significantly contributed to the urbane tone and visual style of those magazines. (In a quintessential Campbell drawing we find a smiling, sexually pleased white maid taking the fur wrap of her young, high society mistress, remarking, "While you were out, your Mr. Drake called—let's just call him our Mr. Drake from now on.") And to this list of black artists producing before the 1960s we

"Krazy Kat" cartoon reprinted with special permission of King Features Syndicate.

must add the man whom art critic Gilbert Seldes identified in his 1924 book *The Seven Lively Arts* as being responsible for "the most amusing and fantastic and satisfying work of art produced in America today"[6]: George Herriman, the creator of "Krazy Kat."

For many readers and critics, among them E. E. Cummings, "Krazy Kat" was the greatest comic strip there ever was or would be. Pablo Picasso was a fan. Often described as the strip most preferred by intellectuals and savants, it ran in only about thirty-five newspapers (at its peak) from October 28,1913, until Herriman's death on April 25, 1944. Yet for many fans "Krazy Kat" represented not merely the highest attainment of American comic art but a triumph of poetry, metaphysics, and democracy as well. Its premise was simple enough: Krazy, a black cat of indeterminate sex (but usually seen as female), loves Ignatz Mouse. But Ignatz hates Krazy and beans the Kat on her noggin with a brick at every opportunity—an act the Kat always interprets as love ("a missil of affection"), thereby transcending the Mouse's hostility, even spiritualizing it in a way that would please both Mohandas K. Gandhi and Martin Luther King Jr. Completing this vaudevillian love triangle is Offissa Pupp, who loves Krazy, protects her from Ignatz, and frequently hauls the Mouse off to jail.

As with all great art, the simplicity of its premise conceals the many-layered complexities of "Krazy Kat." For poet Cummings this comic strip "reveals the ultimate meaning of existence."[7] In Ignatz he sees the spirit of free will tilting toward anarchy; in Offissa Pupp, the power of society and authority; and in Krazy he finds "a living ideal . . . the only original and authentic revolutionary protagonist. . . . She is a spiritual force," one who proved day after day in the papers of her most preeminent admirer, William Randolph Hearst, the truth of the adage "Love will find a way." And what has all this to do with democracy? Well, let us hear Cummings's own words: "The meteoric burlesk melodrama of democracy is a struggle between society (Offissa Pupp) and the individual (Ignatz Mouse) over an ideal (our heroine)—a struggle from which, again and again and again, emerges one stupendous fact: namely, that the ideal of democracy fulfills herself only if, and whenever, society fails to suppress the individual."[8]

Politics and metaphysics aside, Herriman's "Krazy Kat" was as revolutionary in its inventive compositions as in its ideas. Located in the dreamlike world of Coconino County, which recalls the artist's fondness for Monument Valley in the desert of southeastern Utah, Herriman's characters performed against a constantly transmogrifying background—in the space of two panels, their external world fluidly changed from surrealistic mesas and cactuses to forest scenery and seascapes, ever blurring the border between appearance and reality.

Herriman, a mulatto born in New Orleans in 1880, who according to reports never took off his hat,[9] indoors or out, because he had black, kinky hair, was a genuine American original. He experimented with the layouts for the Sunday panels of his strip, breaking down the conventional—and experiential—boundaries in the image area, a technique cartoonists would widely adopt thereafter. His scritchy penwork was joyously self-conscious, his characters aware that they lived in a comic strip—perhaps today we would call them "postmoderns," and his oeuvre "metacomic." He invested Krazy's voice with puns, poetry and linguistic playfulness, which usually earned her a brick on the head from Ignatz.

As so many have said, "Krazy Kat" cannot be explained; it simply must be experienced. And millions have absorbed this product of Herriman's genius; it was adapted as a ballet in 1922 by Adolph Bolm; inspired John Alden Carpenter's "jazz pantomime" for piano, numerous critical articles and anthologies, and Jay Cantor's 1988 *Krazy Kat: A novel in five panels*; and was included among the twenty groundbreaking "Comic Strip Classics" stamps issued by the U.S. Postal Service in 1995.

But if there is "black" content in "Krazy Kat," it is symbolic and covert. Not until the late 1960s, after the Civil Rights Movement and close on the heels of Stokely Carmichael's 1966 call for "Black Power" during a Mississippi march, do we witness an entire generation of black comic artists grappling with black content and themes.

According to grandmaster Harrington, one of the first to accept this challenge was Brumsic Brandon Jr. In his syndicated comic strip "Luther," Harrington says in a 1976 article, Brandon dared "to create non-white characters or even poor white characters who are human, sympathetic and even lovable. And what better stage setting could he devise than the schools and the kids they're trying to educate? Brandon buses his kids to the Alabaster Avenue Elementary School for their daily duels with Miss Backlash."[10]

In the 1960s and early 70s, however, the undisputed leader among syndicated black cartoonists was Morrie Turner, creator of "Wee Pals," a gentle, interracial comic strip about precocious children styled along the lines of (yet never as successful as) Charles Schulz's "Peanuts." By 1972 "Wee Pals" was appearing in seventy newspapers in the United States and abroad. But like the work of Harrington's generation, Turner's more biting social and racial cartoon commentary in the late 1960s and early 1970s was published—often in a panel called "Humor in Hue"— on the pages of the black-owned press, in publications like the never financially profitable *Negro Digest* (later renamed *Black World* before its demise). A 1971 cartoon shows an elderly black man reading his newspaper at home. Then he notices a sinister-looking white man peering into his window and asks, "Are you the F.B.I., the C.I.A., Army intelligence or the welfare investigator?"

Turner was featured in the August 1972 issue of *Black World*. His work often kicked off that magazine's annual "cartoon festival," which frequently included work by younger cartoonists who signed their drawings with the names Pollard, Winners, Herb Roberts, Ham (who, if I'm not mistaken, also drew a panel for the Nation of Islam's *Muhammad Speaks*, creating white characters with devilish tails and horns), Dave Farmer, or Walt Carr (a highly versatile comic artist profiled in *Black World's* July 1973 issue), as well as cartoons of my own creation. Of all these contributors, Carr, a ten-year contributor to *Jet, Ebony*, and *Playboy* (which had the best rates for panel cartoonists at the time) was the most technically accomplished. Always his compositions were balanced, his lines bold and clean and economical like those of Hank Ketcham ("Dennis the Menace"), with a startlingly effective use of solid black shapes to pull a viewer's eye to his drawing's focal point. A typical Carr cartoon might show a seven-foot, militant, black high school student sitting on the sofa in his parents' home beside a white, baffled-looking college recruiter and saying, "Never mind the $100 a week job, new clothes and car, rent free apartment and job for father—will I get a degree?"

The early 70s was for black cartoonists, as it was for black people in general, a tumultuous, creative period. Some black gag-cartoonists like Buck Brown found steady work on the pages of *Playboy*.[11] New black magazines burst on the stands—providing new markets—and just as quickly disappeared. In that period, Tom Floyd, an Indiana-based editorial cartoonist who operated his own advertising firm, published *Integration Is a Bitch!* (1969), 116 pages of panel cartoons based on his experiences as a designer at Inland Steel Company. These were scathingly satirical drawings that explored the humiliations and pain endured by a black, white-collar worker decades before *Time* magazine devoted one of its covers to "The Rage of the Black Middle-Class." In one representative cartoon, a white employee shows his company's new black worker around the office as two white men from a mental institution drag off a Negro in a straitjacket. Says the white employee, "You'll be our second attempt at integration."

It was at this time that I worked full-time as a cartoonist, publishing around one thousand cartoons in the black press, in *Players*, the *Chicago Tribune* and other newspapers and selling one-page scripts to Charlton Comics. I also created two books, *Black Humor* (1970) and *Half-Past*

Nation Time (1972), and created, hosted, and coproduced an early PBS how-to-draw series, "Charlie's Pad," which was broadcast nationally in 1970.

But what I shall call Harrington's Rule still applied—black content-cartoons in the 1970s were still difficult to place outside the black "special interest press," as some called it, and that rule is alive and well today. (Consider the *New Yorker's* special 1996 "Black in America" double issue, which featured the work of 13 "gag artists," only one of whom was black; eight blacks who submitted work were rejected, and the magazine's cartoon editor, Lee Lorenz, regretfully admits that the *New Yorker's* stable of cartoonists is still entirely white.)[12]

It would take another decade or two before we saw the efflorescence of an exciting new "Black Age of Comics," following or sprouting from the rise of so-called graphic novels (and Japanese manga) and stores devoted exclusively to comics, skyrocketing prices for comic art from the Golden and Silver Ages (on June 29, 1996, one of the fifty remaining copies of 1938's Action Comics #1, containing the first appearance of Superman, sold for $61,900 at Sotheby's), and the coming of age of a new generation of independent, Afrocentric, entrepreneurial cartoonist/publishers (there were about twenty nationwide in 1993) determined to market their own works directly to black readers. The names of these artists may be unknown to the larger public, but there can be no question that their products have propelled the long tradition of black cartooning into fresh, hitherto unexplored realms of the imagination.

A stroll through any well-stocked comics store in the 1990s might bring you into contact with the storytelling of Canadian artist Ho Che Anderson in *Black Dogs*, a meditation on the slaying of fifteen-year-old Latasha Harlins by a Korean storekeeper, the Rodney King beating, and Los Angeles riots; and his even more ambitious *King* (1993), a graphic novel about America's most preeminent Civil Rights leader. You may find Craig Rex Perry's *Hip Hop Heaven*, tales about black teenagers; or Brian and Wayne Cash's portrait of police brutality in *Harry the Cop*; or Turtel Onli's *Malcolm 10*, a comic about a clone possessing the brain of the slain Muslim leader (Onli also coined the term "Black Age of Comics"). If your luck prevails, there will be heroic adventure tides from ANIA, a consortium of black independent publishers who release Eric Griffith's *Ebony Warrior*; Rober Barnes's *Heru, Son of Ausar*; and *Zwanna, Son of Zulu*, by Nabile Hage, who, to promote his company, Dark Zulu, climbed the Georgia State Capitol building wearing a leopard-skin loincloth and tossed down comic books. Jason and David Sims's *Brotherman* may be on the shelves alongside issues of *Icon, Hardware*, and *Blood Syndicate*, superhero stories bearing the "Milestone" imprint, produced by black independents but distributed by D.C. comics.[13] If you can find them (or order them directly from their publishers), there is an embarrassment of black creative products to choose from—everything from Clint Walker's Christian "Faithwalker" comic strip to "Where I'm Coming From," a Jules Feiffer-esque syndicated feature by Barbara Brandon, daughter of the creator of "Luther"[14]; filmmaker Reginald Hudlin's *Bebe's Kids*, the first black feature-length animated film (based on characters by comedian Robin Harris); and the ubiquitous Spike Lee's book *Floaters* produced with Dark Horse Comics.

Which brings us to Roland Laird's Posro Komics, founded in 1988 in Edison, N.J. The name "Posro" is a twist on "Negro," pointing to Laird's desire to bring a positive spirit to black comics production.[15] There are nine artists working in his stable to produce "MC Squared: A Man With a Serious Game Plan," a slice-of-life, hip-hop book featuring a young Harlem barber/computer hacker named Earl Terrel. In March 1993 Posro launched "The Griots," a witty strip about a black newspaper-owning family that was picked up by twenty newspapers. In one representative strip a black mother hears her daughter talking out loud, she thinks, about the notorious Middle Passage: "Parents and children separated . . . human beings packed together and transported like cattle." The girl's mother is pleased, and thinks, "Wonderful . . . eleven years old and she already understands the horrors of slavery." Then she is mortified when her daughter continues: "A school bus can be a horrible experience."

Laird has stated, "We want to do the comic book equivalent of Invisible Man by Ralph Ellison, something that strong."[16] *Still I Rise* may very well be the realization of Posro's dream. Teamed with Elihu Bey, whose concern it is "to show the beauty in things that are not beautiful,"[17] Laird has contributed an epic to the field of American comic art, a transgenerational story that spans three centuries of racial and political oppression and the quest for freedom, a story inspired by Olaudah Equiano's declaration that "When you make men slaves you compel them to live with you in a state of war."

Their task was formidable. Laird's script required exhaustive research, endless revisions, and was reviewed—one draft after another—by a team of historians and editors. But this challenge of compressing the broad, essential outlines of black American history into comic book format was only the first stage in creating *Still I Rise*. Regardless of how artful the script might be, the text for comic art must be seen as similar to a screenplay—it is essentially the starting point, or springboard, for stimulating the visual imagination of the illustrator, Elihu Bey, who, like a film director, must realize in images the writer's words one panel (or shot) at a time.

In film, before the cameras roll there is the storyboard, the director's carefully rendered "comic strip" that sketches out the possible sequence of shots in a movie. With a writer's script in hand, the illustrator's task closely resembles that of the director (and some filmmakers, such as Federico Fellini, came to film after first working as cartoonists). But for the comic artist there is no division of labor as in a film; he must be the director, cameraman, actors, set designer, make-up artist, hairdresser, and prop person all at once when he touches pencil to paper. Like a cameraman, he must decide which panels will provide "establishing shots," which will be close-ups or middle-distance, and where to locate the point of view—a bird's-eye angle looking down, or peering up from the floor, or reflecting the scene in a character's wine-glass or in a mirror, or from any unusual angle that will powerfully bring the writer's words to life. (As a playful exercise, compare the camerawork in *Citizen Kane* to the best draftsmanship of Will Eisner's "The Spirit" comics in the 1940s). Moreover, if he is inventive, there will be *movement* between his panels as he lays them out on the page, a kinetic feel or sense of flow that dynamically pulls the reader's eye from one panel to the next, a technique borrowed from the way many directors edit their shots. The movement of action (or "lines of force") in one shot may pull the viewer's eye from left to right, then in the following shot this direction may be immediately reversed, creating energy and tension (a device used often by James Cameron). Even before we read the text, we should feel excitement from the explosion of pictures on each page. We should find each panel so richly drawn, so charged with emotion in its smallest details, and so generous in the way the artist "fills the frame" that we constantly resist reading on too quickly in order to stop and study the panel for small revelations we might have missed at first glance.

Achieving this is every comic artist's dream, but such magic requires nothing less than throwing out reams of sketches before the illustrator settles on his final pencils for each page. He may do the inking himself, or rely on another artist's pen and brush work, for such collaborations often result in a startlingly elegant blend of visual styles (as when Wallace Wood brought his distinctive inking work to the pencils of Jack Kirby's comic strips in the 1950s). Then comes the lettering, which again the artist may farm out or do himself. Being an illustrator of many talents, young Elihu Bey chooses to draw, ink, and letter his own pages in this one-of-a-kind book.

Scenes of racial conflict are plentiful on the pages of *Still I Rise*, but as an illustration of American history from a black (and faintly Afrocentric) viewpoint we also find here a cornucopia of seldom-reported events, facts, and experiences of African-Americans that enriches our understanding of this nation's past. More than a comic book or graphic novel (though it is indebted to both), *Still I Rise* is popular entertainment that enlightens. And permeating its encyclopedic research is Posro's recognition of the beauty, resilience, and spiritual endurance of black Americans who, refusing to lose faith in themselves and in the ideal of liberty, forced this republic time and again to live up to its principles of equality and justice.

Notes

1. Oliver W. Harrington, *Why I Left America and Other Essays* (Jackson: University Press of Mississippi, 1993).

2. Mel Watkins, "From Harlem to East Berlin," *N.Y. Times Book Review*, December 19, 1993.

3. All research on Jackie Ormes is from Trina Robbins, "Hidden Treasure," in *Comics Journal* (June 1993).

4. Trina Robbins, *A Century of Women Cartoonists* (Northampton, Mass.: Kitchen Sink Press, 1993).

5. Robbins, "Hidden Treasure."

6. Robert C. Harvey, *The Art of the Funnies: An Aesthetic History* (Jackson: University Press of Mississippi, 1994).

7. George Herriman, *Krazy Kat* (New York: Grosset & Dunlap, 1969).

8. Ibid.

9. Harvey, *The Art of the Funnies.*

10. Harrington, *Why I Left America.*

11. Richard Goldstein, "The Spin," *Village Voice*, May 7, 1996.

12. Ibid.

13. All research on black comic books is from Jeffrey Winbush's "The New Black Age of Comics," *Comics Journal* (June 1993).

14. Robbins, *A Century of Women Cartoonists.*

15. "At Posro Komics, Hip-Hop Heroes Battle Stereotypes," *New York Times*, July 12, 1993.

16. "Hip! Hop! Pow! The New Black Superheroes," *Washington Post*, October 13, 1991.

17. Gary Dauphin, "To Be Young, Superpowered, and Black," *Village Voice*, May 17, 1994.

Selected Cartoons

"Believe me, Richard, I've been in publishing for thirty years,
and I can assure you a book about black anger will simply never sell . . ."

"The best we can figure, Mrs. Reed, is that your husband Ishmael accidentally summoned the loas and they took him away."

"We read his book and saw the opinion polls, so we shouldn't be surprised . . . "

"Oh, maybe I should have told you not to mention Spike Lee or Toni Morrison."

"Mrs. Mosley, I'm not sure it's such a good idea for little Walter
to spend so much time reading crime fiction . . ."

"Psst, boss . . . Lighten up on the numerology, okay?"

"Sure, it's an honor to work for Dr. Carver, but the pay here is peanuts."

"Oh, no, we don't want to meet your leader.
We just came for the Octavia Butler book party."

Interviews &

Conversations

An Interview with Charles Johnson
Conducted by Jonathan Little

Like his narrator in *Middle Passage* (1990), Charles Johnson charts a course through the vexed and volatile issues of multiculturalism and racial politics in America. The rush of publicity Johnson received after his best-selling novel *Middle Passage* won the National Book Award in 1990 drew attention to his versatile and prolific career as a cartoonist, novelist, short story writer, essayist, and screenwriter. Whatever the medium, Johnson continues to address the charged philosophical questions surrounding cultural and individual racial identity.

Johnson began his artistic career with two collections of political cartoons lampooning American race relations, *Black Humor* (1970) and *Half-Past Nation-Time* (1972). His interests then turned to writing. After completing six unpublished novels, Johnson published *Faith and the Good Thing* (1974). The novel reflects his primary interest in blending philosophy and fiction as he depicts Faith's search for the truth or the meaning of life, the "Good Thing." His next two novels, *Oxherding Tale* (1982) and *Middle Passage*, both set in the nineteenth century, also show African-American characters struggling to define themselves as they search for spiritual and metaphysical happiness in the face of difficult odds.

Johnson explains the link between philosophy and fiction in *Being and Race* (1988), his phenomenological study of African-American writing since 1970. In it he argues for the need for "aesthetically venturesome" and "wickedly diverse" philosophical African-American fiction that is not tied to any single genre or motivated by any single ideological or political agenda. Johnson's collection of short stories, *The Sorcerer's Apprentice* (1986), illuminates his range as he experiments with realism, allegory, fable, fantasy, and science fiction. His novel in progress concerns Martin Luther King, Jr., whose ability to draw from many different spiritual and cultural traditions has impressed and influenced Johnson.

Johnson's publishing career has coincided with an equally prolific career in television and film screenwriting. His credits include *Charlie Smith and the Fritter Tree* (1978), a dramatization of the life of a 135-year-old African-American for the PBS Vision series, and *Booker* (1988), a program about the childhood of Booker T. Washington for the Walt Disney channel. He has recently completed a screenplay adaptation of *Middle Passage* for Tri-Star Productions.

Johnson was an energetic and engaging host during my stay from July 31 to August 3, 1992, in Seattle, where he teaches creative writing at the University of Washington. He showed me around the city he calls "the social correlate of my soul," with its African-American mayor and harmonious mixture of Asian, African-American, white, Native American, and Latino-American populations. It seemed strikingly appropriate to Johnson's eclecticism that during our wanderings we toured an amphibious assault Navy vessel, a downtown bookstore where he has given several readings, a local artist's backyard studio, and, at Johnson's home, which was being remodeled, the boarded-up entrance to his home gym; he has for eleven years practiced Chinese *choy li fut kung fu*, and he now teaches it in a neighborhood center. As we walked, I had the uncanny feeling that I was momentarily participating in one of Johnson's fluidly polymorphic and international fictions.

Q. In all your novels it seems that your central characters are questing after some kind of enlightenment and that during this process they have to work through a variety of options embodied in other characters in the novel. Is this an accurate interpretation of the structure of your novels?

A. In each one of the novels there is a progression from ignorance to knowledge, or from a lack of understanding to some greater understanding. Certainly that's true of *Faith and the Good Thing*. I know it's true of *Middle Passage*. The last chapter is "Moksha" in *Oxherding Tale*, meaning "enlightenment" or "liberation." Yes, you're right. That is the structure of the books, probably the short stories too. There's usually a moment of awareness, an epiphany if you like, a place where the character is smashed into a larger vision under the pressure of events. Usually he goes through a lot of positions that other people hold, which are partial. It seems kind of Hegelian in that way. Not that the final position synthesizes all of them, but that the character goes through several moments.

Q. What happens to individual identity during the process of development your main characters go through?

A. I think it dissolves. "What is individual identity?" is a central question for me. I personally don't believe in the existence of the ego. I think it's a theoretical construct. There's no empirical verification for it at all. And if there is such a thing as identity, I don't think that it's fixed or static; it's a process. I think it's dominated by change and transformation, more so than by any static qualities. It is many identities over the course of a lifetime. That identity, if it is anything at all, is several things, a tissue of very often contradictory things, which is why I probably have a great deal of opposition to anything that looks like a fixed meaning for black America. I just don't believe it. It's ridiculous as a thought.

Q. Is this process of development similar to Ralph Ellison's statement, "Thus because jazz finds its very life in an endless improvisation upon traditional materials, the jazzman must lose his identity even as he finds it"?

A. That's a nice quote. I'm not sure what it means, but I'm certainly willing to give credit to Ellison for anything. It's very interesting to me where we get the notion of the self. Hume, with his radically empirical approach, looks into his experience to see if there's anything that corresponds to the idea of a self. What he finds are memories, impressions, sensations, but no self. For Hume the self is inferred as a thing that holds all of this together. It's much the same in Buddhism, where the self is an illusion. In Buddhism all you have is this flow of impressions and sensations. The self is one of those objects we talk about without having fully examined it. For me, if there's any way to talk about it, it's as a verb and not a noun. It's a process but not a product, and never is a product, unless it's dead, and then there's no more possibility for action and change. Once dead, it becomes somewhat like Whitehead's idea of the eternal object.

Q. So at the end of *Middle Passage*, Rutherford becomes a model for these ideas?

A. Andrew Hawkins's identity in *Oxherding Tale* is that of a free-floating creative force. That's true as well for Rutherford. What he's done is prehended or taken so much from all the people who are already on that ship, from the Allmuseri to the various members of the ship—but he's done that his entire life. That sort of tissue of world experience is what he is. He's become much more humble in terms of making assumptions about objects and others. He's more willing to listen and wait for them to speak, which is a very phenomenological position in the world. It's very simple. It's not a difficult idea.

Q. His identity, though, I would say, isn't lost; rather, there's an accretion.

A. It's cumulative, if you like. It's Whitmanesque in a particular sense. I'd like to talk about it in the same sense that Toomer does in the poem "Blue Meridian." Let's be more specific. When you say "his identity," what do you mean?

Q. Maybe I'm looking at calcified perceptions of identity, but I was thinking in terms of his development as a character. Does he lose himself, as Ellison would say, in the process of finding himself?

A. I like that formulation, yeah. There's a line by Husserl that's really very nice: "I lose myself in the objects and the others." Yes. I do think that's what it is. What he finds is not a fixed notion of the self. It's something that's very expansive. You've seen, for example, the Necker's cube? When I show it to my students, they always see the initial kinds of variations, tilting left, tilting right. We write them down, and we do this for about half an hour. Then someone begins to see things that nobody else did in the room. The others don't see them until that person has narrated and described it—"I see a . . . " Everybody else is looking and straining, then, "Oh yes! I see that now too."

We go through this, and we get maybe thirty possible disclosures of that one simple object in class, each based upon everybody's different backgrounds—where they're coming from and where they were born, how they grew up, the kind of mother they had, the father they had, the objects they looked at. All of that's brought to disclosing the object. But somebody will say, "I see a paper bag," and nobody else is able to see it. Only if that person describes it will the other people see it. So at one point, what is entirely subjective becomes intersubjective. We share an image. When we go down the line, looking at profiles of the Necker's cube, you can never really get two of those images at once.

One of the things that's interesting is that people are sure in the beginning when they first look at it. "Oh, it's got to be this, it's got to be that," they say. Then they become more humble as they get to the thirteenth profile, the fifteenth profile, the twentieth profile, and then if somebody new comes in the room there may be yet another disclosure of the object. If you said "What is it?" which is the final question I ask them, they know they can't answer that question, because it's a box leaning left, *hyphen* a box leaning right, *hyphen* a box leaning up, *hyphen* a box leaning forward; it's *hyphen* a fish tank, *hyphen* a paper bag, *hyphen* a stage, *hyphen* looking down at a pyramid. Its being is a hyphenated being, always open-ended. It is all of those perceptions, but only one of them can exist at a time before consciousness. Using Husserl's idea of consciousness, we must say that consciousness is always consciousness *of* something.

In much the same way, that is how I talk about every phenomenal object. Things are given to us in profiles. Sides, angles, but not the entire thing. We have to walk around, for example, that wall. That's given to us there. But empirically, we have no sense at all that there's a room on the other side. This all could be like a Hollywood movie set. Until you walk around and see the other side and confirm or refute that, you just don't know. That is much like where we find Andrew Hawkins and certainly Rutherford Calhoun at the ends of *Oxherding Tale* and *Middle Passage*. There have been so many profiles disclosed and revealed for the meaning of the world that one has a very humble attitude about making existential claims about it. You know that even if you've exhausted all the possible meanings at this moment, the next generation, given its experience and what it brings to that object's revelation, will find something new. Being is historical. I'm in agreement with what Merleau-Ponty says of perceptual experience, that the more revelations and disclosures and profiles you get for the object, the more ambiguous it's going to become, the more hazy. That's what interests me. The easiest images to get are the first two or three. Box left, box right, box forward, box back.

When I think about how we write it seems we always go with the first two or three perceptions. We don't go with the fifth or the fortieth, because you have to dig to get to those. You have to force the imagination. You have to go to the trouble of confirming with somebody else, "Did you see that?" Of course, all science begins that way too, with a first person seeing—the scientist looking into the microscope. It's one person, one consciousness and this object. He has to say to a colleague, "Come here, look at this, do you see that?" Then you have intersubjectivity. If you have three people, it's even better. That's what I believe in far more than objectivity. Intersubjectivity is shared meaning, a shared vision.

But the problem with our writing is that we reach for the first one or two meanings. The reason we don't dig deeper is because the resistance is so great. In other words, you may have to free up all your presuppositions, all the prejudices, all of your background to be able to get to the thirtieth or fortieth profile or disclosure of the object. Usually, I think that happens in the social context. Somebody else on the other side of the room coming from another part of the world, or world experience, will through language, as Heidegger says, allow this object to be disclosed for somebody else. If you do it by yourself you have to fight against all the presuppositions and prejudices. I think that's what fiction ought to be about. It ought to be about getting beneath those sedimented meanings, all the calcified, rigid perceptions of the object.

For the average person, doing this, letting meaning flower in this way, can be frustrating. It doesn't allow them to *use* the object as they'd like to. For utilitarian reasons, they say, "That's a Necker's cube leaning left, or a Necker's cube leaning right." But that's not good enough for the artist or the philosopher. I think we have to bracket the whole idea of utility if any object—or the world—is going to disclose whatever meaning it has. I think the same thing is true of racial phenomena. Very often we only deal with surface images, the most easily graspable meaning, which is usually the meaning we've inherited, or somebody else's vision, now our own. For the sake of progress, we have to go much, much deeper. Metaphor allows us to do that.

Q. You seem heavily postmodern in your emphasis on parody and intertextuality. There's a sense of creative theft or borrowing in your works, Rutherford perhaps being the best example of this, as he "trespasses" on other identities and becomes interpenetrated by them.

A. What do you mean by "borrowing"?

Q. In terms of the structure—Homer's *Odyssey*, for example. You not only borrow structural elements but historical detail from sea narratives, slave narratives. You obviously spent a lot of time doing research for *Middle Passage*.

A. I did in fact. Let me see if I can make sense of that in terms of where we just were in our discussion. What I didn't have when I got to *Middle Passage* was knowledge of the sea, so I spent six years reading every book and rereading every book I could on that subject, anything relating to sea adventure. I read Homer, Apollonius of Rhodes, the Sinbad stories, slave narratives, Gustavus Vasa, and some material that was sent to me from Werner Sollors at Harvard. I looked at all of Melville again, Conrad. You name it, anything I could.
  Why do that? Well, for two reasons. One is very writerly. I needed to know the parts of ships; I needed to know what that whole universe was like. But I needed to know the literary universe of the sea as well. What I needed to know were the profiles, again, the disclosures, the meanings that other writers for two thousand years have had for this particular phenomenon, the sea. I needed, in so many words, to look at that Necker's cube and see the phenomena of the sea disclosed over and over again. If one looks, and this is a simple matter, I guess, at any author who's written about the sea, whoever it is, the sea means something quite specific in the way that it is disclosed and experienced.
  But why, why did I do that? Is that borrowing, is that stealing, is that intertextuality? I think it's something else. I think it's the fact that all knowledge, all disclosure, all revelation from the past, from our predecessors, black, white, and otherwise, is our inheritance, and most of the time we just don't know it. Seriously, we just don't know it. That's why we do research. Any sense that other human beings have made out of the world, any sense that they have pulled out of this universe of

non-sense as Merleau-Ponty would say, any judgments—all that is what we have inherited as human beings. And in a way, that's how I have to write. I have to know that. We are perpetually indebted to our predecessors for that. It's not something I can ignore or something I can abandon. I may come upon a disclosure of the object that's different from anything that's come before, but I think it's predicated on all that came before. In the same way, I don't think you can get the Einsteinian universe without first the Newtonian universe. It's all a long conversation, and the writer does not come into this discussion *ex nihilo*, born with nothing behind him.

Does that make sense in terms of how *Middle Passage* came together, and why research? It isn't just to do a historical novel. It's not that. It's to understand what others have brought to the rendering and disclosure of the subject. You could call it borrowing, I suppose. My intention is somewhat different, a very synthetic technique.

Q. I think you install the reference, but you also subvert it, or you do something new with it.

A. Yes, if I'm doing it, it's again much as we discussed that Necker's cube. I'm trying to say, "Yes, the sea is this, as so and so said, yes, the sea is that, as so and so said, but it's also *this*." It keeps opening up, I hope, as we progress through the book. The same thing happens with the major characters. We're seeing sides of them disclosed in dramatic situations in the course of the novel as they interact with different people. They learn things about themselves that they could not have known except through these encounters.

Q. In terms of African-American fiction now, where would you come down with Toni Morrison when she seems to rework the Black Aesthetic and the Black Arts Movement? She seems to reject political prescriptiveness but at the same time holds on to the aesthetic principles of black art. She identifies them as non-Western and oral.

A. Let me say a few things. I don't want to be unfair to Toni. I understand what the Black Arts Movement was and why it came about. It was very interesting and very exciting. It had a big impact on me when I was a cartoonist. But in *Being and Race*, I try to trace through some of the limitations that are imposed on creative freedom by that particular orientation, and also on intellectual freedom. If we were going through our Necker's cube and all those profiles, we would probably have to stop at a certain point if we had a Black Nationalist orientation or a Black Aesthetic position. That's why I had to move away from it. It just wasn't answering enough questions. It wasn't going deep enough in terms of investigating phenomena. People in the Black Arts Movement do not seem to be widely interested in questions that are crucial to all of us. Our relationship to the environment, for example, our relationship to technology. All the human questions. I do think it's a narrower focus.

Morrison is an extremely talented prose stylist. I happen to think that the earlier books are better than the later ones. *Sula* is a very interesting book. And in *Beloved* she achieves something I would talk about this way: I would say it is the penultimate or final fruit of the Black Arts Movement. It's extremely poetic. You can look and see that for six years she spent time revising and rewriting those lines. And she's very good at that. But on the other hand, I have real problems with the vision that animates that book. Again it has the problems that you find in the Black Arts Movement. I could take you through the book step by step and say why that's so. It's an interesting, middle-brow book. I don't think it's an intellectual achievement, because I'm not sure where the intellectual probing is going on. The last book, *Jazz*, is really—I don't know what to say about it. There are no characters, there's no story, there's no plot, and even the poetry which Morrison is so good at is not there. It just isn't there. I'm not sure why she released that book at all.

We still have to address the Black Arts Movement as an ideology and speak about it in those terms. There are wonderful things that came out of that period, and important things, but I'm not sure it led to very much literature that we would consider to be lasting. I've got first editions on my shelf of books from that period that I'm sure most people have never heard of. I found them to be interesting when I read them, but, unfortunately, they did not meet the standard that Ralph Ellison set in 1952 with *Invisible Man*, or the standards set by Albert Murray with his remarkable essays in *The Hero and the Blues*.

The question is this: Are there two aesthetics? Is there a white aesthetic and is there a black aesthetic? What constitutes a black aesthetic? The oral tradition? What's that? Take call and response, for instance. Everybody says that. Where is call and response in the novel? This is my question. I know what it is. It occurs in the black church when the minister and the congregation respond back and forth. Sure. As my friend Stanley Crouch points out, you can tell a story orally, but when you get to the novel you have to do things that are particular to the novel as a form for that story to come to life.

There's a lot of easy, simplistic thought that goes on in our discussion of black literature. A certain voice is supposed to represent the oral tradition. Well, there are lots of voices in the black community, lots of voices. Why is one selected over another? We have the voice of Du Bois, we have the voice of Douglass, we have the voice of Harriet Tubman, we have the voice of Malcolm X. Why is one voice chosen to represent the oral tradition? I also get really tired of people saying, well, black people have been telling stories for years and years. *Everybody's* been telling stories for years and years. Some of those are wonderful stories, such as when Julius Lester collected black folktales. They are beautiful, wonderful stories that were told orally and finally set down. But when you compose them on the page in one of the literary traditions that we inherit, you have to do things to those stories to make them effective as literature. Character development, connections, transitions, all kinds of things.

We have a way of talking about these so-called differences between the white and black aesthetic that do not make a great deal of sense. Skip Gates has this idea of signifying as somehow being a part of this. But again, if that's a general aesthetic proposition, then you should be able to go to any black literary work of art and find that it signifies in the way that Skip is talking about. You can't do that. All these works will defy that very simple notion of how you go about it. And the same thing with the oral tradition. I just don't believe it. I don't believe that there are two aesthetics. It cannot be universally demonstrated for all black literature.

Q. So you would also reject Morrison's idea that literature should be used as a means of African-American empowerment?

A. What does she mean by that? What does that mean? African-American empowerment through literature? How does a book do that? Does a book empower me to vote? I don't get it. How do you interpret that?

Q. It seems to me that she and others feel that you can maintain connection with a heritage, an ethnic identity that might be lost or appropriated by mainstream culture. Writers can use literature as a means of counteracting oppression and historical conditions.

A. That sounds great, but I still don't get it. We need a definition of empowerment. We need a definition of identity. I want a definition of how something is appropriated by something else and what that means.

First of all, as a writer, I don't believe that art imitates. There is a mimetic element, but I really think that what a writer does is create an experience on the pages of the book for the reader. You're creating experience. You're not transcribing experience. If you talk about the African-American past in your work, you're obviously interpreting an experience. Language will distort and transform, as William Gass points out. It's all filtered through a consciousness, and the consciousness obviously of the author.

I think that these claims about black writing are simplistic. I kind of understand the intention behind them, but I don't think they make a great deal of sense. How does *Jazz* counteract oppression and historical conditions? How does any literature do that? There are certain instances and times when books have a huge impact, as with *Uncle Tom's Cabin* during the abolitionist movement. There are direct connections—this led to that in the public sphere—but claims are being made here for literature that have not been demonstrated at all. Is *The Great Gatsby* about empowering white people, is that what that's doing?

Q. Is that necessary? The privileged whites are already being represented. I think Morrison and Alice Walker, for example, are talking about people who have been left out of the tradition, left out of the representation. As writers they are celebrating an identity that had previously been silenced.

A. I think that's what they say they are doing. I think to put it that way, however, is really coded. People who were left out, silenced, marginalized. Yes, I buy that. You can write about people and publish works about individuals who have never had a story told about them before, or who have never been allowed to tell their own story. Of course, it's still Morrison telling the story, it's not that person. It's her imagining that person. Or Clarence Major can do that in his book *Such Was the Season*, where the protagonist is a black woman matriarch in an Atlanta political family. That does bring something new to our literature. It brings a new angle, a new perception, a new character's perspective to our literature. It may bring a different voice to our literature as well.

I'm not sure that American literature hasn't always done that. Bill Gass has an unusual and interesting analysis of character in fiction. He says that what we are dealing with on the page are concepts. And from Gass I have to go to Sartre. Characters are constructs, mental beings, who have more in common with mathematical entities than real people. They are not real people, but nevertheless, it is the act of consciousness that brings them to life during the reading experience, that creates a "fictional dream in the mind," to use a phrase from John Gardner.

These are created objects. We draw and prehend from the world in the creation of any particular art work, and that means you draw things you've heard from other people, their behavior and so forth. But when someone makes the claim that what we've done is empowered a certain class of people by giving a representation of them on the page, I'm not sure what that means. I sort of say, yeah, that seems to be a little bit of what's going on. Ten percent of what you're saying sounds right, but I'm not sure that claim can be made as strongly as some people would like to make it.

Beloved is about a woman who kills her kids. How representative is that of women during the period of slavery? I have no idea. Morrison says that it's based on a real woman. I would have to say that woman is probably, if not psychotic, then someone who needs a lot of help. If black people had done that en masse, we would not be here today.

People killing their kids to save them from slavery? Come on, we're still talking the sixties here, and certain very clever, cute ideas that I just don't think were the case. I don't think that the historical record confirms that.

Q. So you don't feel that African-American literature has a social obligation or function?

A. I do, but not that one necessarily. I do think that art should be socially responsible. I do halfway believe most of the time in John Gardner's notion of moral fiction. Where social responsibility comes into play is in the simple fact that whatever the work is, whatever the book is, whatever the product is, it's something that we interject into the public space. It's a public act. It's our human expression, and we are responsible for all our forms of human expression, all our deeds and actions, of which art is one. The artist has a tremendous degree of responsibility. Whether it's the responsibility of promoting or supporting certain political ideas, I really don't know about that. I don't know if that's what art should be about. Somebody can write a book that is a political indictment, but should he or she write every book like that?

I would like for people to look at my books and feel that they are socially responsible. I say that because I try my very best to be fair to every character on one level. I remember when I used to pass drafts of things by John Gardner. I was still young, and I would set a certain character up to say and do things I didn't like, just so I could slap him around, and thereby slap around some people I knew who behaved like that. He would write in the margins of the manuscripts, "Shame on you. Why are you doing this? Why are you presenting this straw man to me? What am I supposed to do with this character, dislike him?" I really had to think about that aspect of John's criticism. I find that the most reprehensible characters, like a Captain Falcon, have to be characters I find enormously interesting, somebody I would like to poke at and get under the skin of and see as many sides of as I possibly can during the course of this fiction. That character must be subjected to the same kinds of things that everybody else is. Every major character for me is a character of evolution and change. They are not the same at the end of the book as when we first saw them. The ideal novel would be one in which there are no minor characters, where there are no flat characters. Everybody is in this situation of process and change. Everybody is being forced and pressured, as the main characters are, to move forward in their lives, to have their perceptions changed, to react differently in different situations. That would be the ideal novel. What I want is the process novel where everybody mentioned is a main character in the process of evolution. That would be the ultimate moral fiction.

Q. Couldn't you also say that you and Morrison have different political visions?

A. What is her political vision? Can it be stated? We know that Baraka at various times said he was a nationalist, and later he was a scientific socialist, and he explained what that meant. What's Morrison's political vision?

Q. I guess I was speaking more aesthetically, with her ties to the Black Arts Movement.

A. The Black Arts Movement, if you look at it as an ensemble of ideas, is contradictory. What was the Black Arts Movement? You've got to look at Larry Neal, you've got to look at Baraka, you've got to look at John Oliver Killens. Was there a systematic body of beliefs? No, there wasn't. Look at Malcolm X, who had a big impact on my generation. At the end of Malcolm's life, someone asked him what his philosophy was, and he said, "I don't know." He was very honest. This was after his trip to Mecca. No, this was not systematic thought. Not in terms of having empirical evidence for what you're talking about. Not in terms of ethics hooking up in a systematic, intelligible way with epistemology and with ontology. No, it wasn't that. It was a passionate literary movement, in many ways, with a couple of ideas which took different form among different writers. If you talk about the Black Arts Movement, you need to look at just what that was for different sorts of people. Let's take Ishmael Reed. He says he first began to write in cultural nationalist workshops. When I read Reed's work, I see a particular spin on cultural nationalism. He's said things that are quite different from Baraka and from Larry Neal. You have to ask the question, If he comes out of cultural nationalism, and has some belief in the Black Aesthetic, what is the relationship of that to what Morrison is talking about? Where are the points of similarity and where are the points of difference? I'm sure people are doing extensive work on both of those authors to see the variations. I don't think the Black Arts Movement, as a body of thought, is coherent, consistent, or complete. By complete, I mean taking in as much as possible, taking in all the available profiles of phenomena. It's not philosophy, it's ideology.

I try in *Being and Race* to distinguish between philosophy and ideology. A philosopher is somebody who is perpetually asking questions. One who always goes back to his initial premise and presuppositions and is willing, if necessary, in the face of contrary evidence, to abandon them if he has to and start all over again from scratch. Ideological positions can't do that. They can't afford to do that. That's the problem I have with them. No philosopher can be comfortable with ideology. And I don't think everything is ideology. I don't think that every idea that we have, every ensemble of beliefs, must necessarily be ideology, whether in the scientific sphere or the philosophical sphere. Phenomenology, if I'm not mistaken, does not build up an architecture of propositions but rather goes back to try to eke out an understanding of what we think we already know. You're always standing in an interrogative mode toward the world.

I would like to believe that I could write book after book after book and someone could believe that they had been written by different people. In this book over here, *Faith and the Good Thing*, black folklore has this particular function. But over there, there's none of that in *Middle Passage*. The sea has this particular meaning there, but in the next book the sea might have an entirely different meaning, given the fictive universe that has evolved out of its unique set of characters. Things could absolutely change in terms of the overall experiential effect, from book to book. That's the kind of freedom I would like to see from novel to novel, from story to story.

Q. Let's say you are writing a novel on King and you are showing the inherent benefits of his position. Isn't that an ideological stance?

A. Why?

Q. Because it's imbued with a political application.

A. A political application? You mean I'm promoting King?

Q. You could be.

A. I'm interested in King. I think he's a very complex figure. I actually think we don't know enough about King. What I'm really interested in is the man, the evolution of the individual. I'm interested in a number of other things too, of a political-philosophical nature about the man. The vision of the civil rights movement—specifically integration—as it applies to King is there because that's part of the man. But I have to say of this man, that, when he first encountered racism, he wanted to hate white people. That's part of who he was. I have to have characters in there who represent the Black Nationalist position, because they're part of his world. All of the stuff that was there, as much as possible, I have to have it. I'm not sure that's an ideological position.

Someone will say, "Well, why did you write about this guy rather than Malcolm X?" I think we have a whole lot of popular material about Malcolm X, and very little on Martin. People don't really understand King, other than a couple of clichéd ideas about him, phrases and sound bytes. But I want to understand what his life was like after he led the Montgomery bus boycott at age twenty-six. I want to know that evolution, that history, up to his assassination. I want to know what a human being has to do to rise to that level of public service. He received fifty death threats. That's what interests me.

Why not Malcolm X? Other people have taken from Malcolm a number of things that they find interesting about him that aren't even true of the man. Even his daughter says that they don't take the whole man, and they've used him for political purposes that even Malcolm probably wouldn't agree with. Malcolm's just too much with us, and King not enough these days. I want people to see King in all his particularity and texture. I want to know how he shaved when he got up in the morning. He used a depilatory powder because he had very sensitive skin. The stuff stinks, I know exactly what it is. I want to know how much sugar he put in his coffee. That's what interests me.

If I did Malcolm, I'd do one different from the cliché. It would be about this unusual individual who goes from being a hustler to prison to the Nation of Islam to a break with the Nation of Islam, and a bloody public break at that. Nobody talks about the animosity between him and Elijah Muhammad's people. People forget that. And it almost spelled the end of the Nation of Islam. Things got very shaky. I'd go after what Malcolm's broader vision of Islam was about. It wouldn't be a couple of phrases or statements from Malcolm X. It would be his life in evolution, with all kinds of ideas and contradictions. As when he first joins the Nation of Islam, and he says, since he has a Jewish friend, "Do I have to hate Himey too?" This is a life in process. It isn't just one thing. That is the way I would do Malcolm X.

Q. In *Being and Race*, while you recognize the achievement of contemporary African-American women writers, you also qualify this by saying that their writing is "more at the stage of criticism of social crimes." In *Possessing the Secret of Joy*, Alice Walker dwells on the physical and mental mutilation of black women and its result—insanity. Would Gardner call this vision "responsible" and "moral"? Would you?

A. Alice is talking about clitoridectomy. There's a social crime for you. I shouldn't speak for John here. Some of the portraits of black men in those books are so limited and so one-profiled, as opposed to thirty or forty images of black men, that they don't seem moral to me. It's not just Walker. You could also talk about Morrison. You do not see black men like Colin Powell or W. E. B. Du Bois or astronaut Ron McNair or Frederick Douglass. It's an extremely narrow range of human beings. You basically see black men who are fuck-ups. And there's a lot that can be said about black men who are fuck-ups. But how does that tap into the general negative images we have of black males in the eighties, coming from the Reagan administration, with Willy Horton and Bush, and these comic images of black men in film and on television? Where, finally, are the images of human beings who are black and male and lead responsible lives? You don't see anybody like the mayor of Seattle, Norman Rice, who's a remarkable human being. Those are not characters in our books. Stanley Crouch is of the opinion that that is going to be the next wave.

If we're going to talk about politics and black writing, then we've really got to talk about politics. You can talk about Jesse, who won't run for office because it's a lot easier to get in front of the cameras. Or you can talk about Ron Brown, or Norm Rice, who will indeed go through what the political process is. You present yourself to people, you have a list of proposals, you get elected, and you go in day after day to confront all manner of problems to serve the greatest number of people at any given moment. That's politics. The other stuff, with the rhetoric, that's not politics. Even if that gets someone elected, that human being, like Norm Rice and the other black mayors, is going to have to go in every day and deal with all kinds of interest groups. Politics is the art of compromise. That's real politics. It's not rhetoric. It's not about ideology. It's about solving problems on a daily basis.

Stanley is right. Someday we're going to have to get those kinds of black people into our fiction. All those workers in the NAACP, all those people, year in, year out, going to every one of the civil rights hearings in Washington. The work is boring, it's dull, it's everyday, it's pedestrian. But that's how you get the passage of civil rights legislation. Somebody can get in front of a crowd and microphones and scream at the top of his voice, but I have to say, for all my feeling for that, it's not politics. We need portraits of lives like that of Norm Rice in our literature to really understand politics. The problem is those lives aren't flashy. They lack sensational drama. King used to say that, even with all the attention focused on him. He was certainly charismatic, and so was Malcolm—but what about the thousands of people who made King possible? That's what's also interesting. The people in the background, in the shadows.

Q. In a recent paper you gave at a conference for the National Council of Teacher Educators you cited Allan Bloom and Dinesh D'Souza and others who warn against the Balkanization of American society through multiculturalism. How do you feel about their ideas?

A. I first gave that paper as a way of providing an overview to foreign audiences of what the debate is in America, and I wanted to make it pro and con. I started out talking about the sixties, especially in historical terms, including Malcolm X and Martin Luther King, and the ideals of integration, and how we shifted to the Black Power Movement. It's about literature for the most part, the emergence of different authors of color during the last twenty or thirty years. And I quote D'Souza and

Bloom to indicate that there is a counterargument, that there is opposition to what is called multiculturalism. I even quote President Bush, who gave that talk at Michigan a year ago. It came right out of Roger Kimball, *Tenured Radicals*. He used the phraseology of that book and D'Souza's book. My paper was descriptive, not promotional. I ended with a quote from Julius Lester, who is a writer I deeply admire. He speaks about his education at Fisk. It involved the canon. He didn't have any problem with it. To be honest, I don't have any problem with it either. I have no problem with reading the pre-Socratics anymore than I do with reading the Vedas. We should read all those things.

One of the things we have to emphasize is that no student can hold the elementary school, high school, and university he attends responsible for his intellectual life. The only person responsible for someone's intellectual life is that person. The only thing we can do in the schools is create an atmosphere of curiosity so that people, after they get out of school, continue to be students to the very end of their days, and that's going to involve cross-cultural understanding.

I'm not sure I like the way the whole multiculturalism question is formulated. As I've said, I've been a student of Eastern philosophy since I was nineteen, when I got involved in the martial arts. All black students obviously are students of Western culture, if they are in America, right? So they're already multicultural. If you begin to look at the history of an idea, because all ideas have a history or biography, you find it threading back through time and all groups of people. For example, if you are going to study Aristotle, you've got to be able to look at what happened to Aristotle when he wasn't available in the Middle Ages but was very present in Arab countries. I think globally in that sense. I don't like some of the ways the arguments about multiculturalism have been formulated, although I think at heart they're absolutely right.

We should read as much as we possibly can from all cultures. It's that simple. For me, it never has been something I had to be noisy about. In the classes I taught, the texts were already from all sorts of different people and places. D'Souza's book pisses off a lot of people. But in a sense, he does say one or two things in there that are not all that bad. He's all for having study groups look at the work of W. E. B. Du Bois. I think we should all be looking at *The Souls of Black Folks,* and all that Du Bois did that was ground breaking in the area of sociology. Even look at his fiction. Du Bois is a major thinker of the twentieth century. But I'm not sure D'Souza would be happy if we have to look at Iceberg Slim. I don't know if you know Iceberg Slim. There are works within black literature and black culture that are definitive and important and should be looked at, but D'Souza is griping about mediocrity, about books that are not worth our attention. I can't help but agree with that.

Q. Wouldn't you draw a distinction between D'Souza and Bloom? Bloom has his traditional great books canon.

A. He does. The thing that's interesting about Bloom is that he was a philosopher. A whole lot of that book is about Plato. I have philosopher friends who like what he does with philosophy in there, but his claims are pretty extreme about women and blacks, about black studies and women's studies. It's a book that feels threatened. It's amazing that it sold as many copies as it did. But he has one line in there that really made a lot of sense to me. He says our task is to understand how Plato saw the world. That was always my sense of philosophy. I wanted to understand how Schopenhauer saw the world. I wanted to understand how Nagarjuna, among the Buddhists, saw the world. The issue is not my going to school to get images of myself, because I don't need that. I don't need a feel-good education. As Julius Lester says, you go to school to learn everything that you are not. Of course, that's ironic, because finally we are all those things, but we are not aware that we're all those things.

I'm not talking about multiculturalism so much as I am about Afro-centricism—the idea that a black student will say something like, "I'm going to study myself." I'm not sure what that means. The whole question of selfhood is a very large one. If you go back fifty generations in the life of any human being, you will discover that they share an ancestor with everybody else on the planet. Race breaks down fifty generations back. Alex Haley could trace his roots back to Africa following one side of his family—I think it was his mother's side. But if he followed his father's side, he would have ended up probably back in Europe. As a matter of fact, the book he didn't get a chance to write and was talking about doing was about how genetically mongrelized all Americans are. That, he felt, would be an even more powerful book than *Roots*. It will never get written now. That, you see, is the issue, the fact that we are a tissue of cultures. We are a tissue of races already; the concept of race, as Kwame Appiah points out, is false. Certainly in modern America there is mongrelization. So if the multiculturalists are using an outmoded notion of race, then their categories are problematic for me. I'm not going to read a book simply because it's by an Asian writer. I'm not going to read a book just because it's by a Native American, or just because it's by a black American. I want to read finely articulated thought, by whoever it is, anywhere on the planet, any culture. But it has to be something that meets the standards I bring to all literature, which means it has to disclose, reveal, and it needs to be worked over a lot in terms of revision and polishing. But I'm not interested in any work because it's by somebody from a particular race. That doesn't mean anything, finally.

Q. I find your arguments about the fluid, intersubjective nature of education and knowledge fascinating. But you don't want to use those arguments to keep out nontraditional texts, or to construct an elitist canon.

A. What do you mean by "elitist canon"?

Q. I mean in terms of Bloom's Eurocentricism.

A. Oh no. I don't believe that. You should have Confucius, Chuang-Tse, and Lao-tse, and you should have the *Ten Ox-herding Pictures*, and you should have the great documents out of the Hindu tradition. But those works have been around for a long time. You could go over to the philosophy department and get some of them, or you could go over to the Far Eastern departments and get other ones. They've been translated for a long, long time. They just weren't in the English departments, which were basically white male in their curriculum. Those texts are there, and the scholars are there to tell you about them, people who have devoted their entire lives to translations and interpretations. I feel extraordinarily enriched by their efforts. I couldn't have gotten it otherwise, prior to the rise of multiculturalism. That movement didn't bring those books into existence.

Now, when you say an elitist canon, I'm not sure what you're saying exactly. Some people would throw the canon out entirely. Why do we need a canon? I don't know about using the term "canon," but I do think there are certain works that have been valuable to human beings for five hundred years. Some of those works still speak to us. I finally went back and looked at Thomas a Kempis's *The Imitation of Christ*. Believe me, it *does* speak to contemporary life. The elegance of his thought, the way he delves into the human situation—it is beautiful. There are certain texts that we need to know because of the vast influence they've had on other people. That's why I say we need to know the teachings of Confucius, because they have influenced so much that people have done. We need to know the principal texts of Buddhism. We need to know the great literary works of China, India, Japan, Africa.

I do think that art is elitist. It is an elitist activity. That may sound like a strange thing to say, but I will say it. When I sit down to write a book I put in the best thought, the best feeling, the best technique and skill I can muster. I'll go over it twenty-five times over five or ten years, I don't care. Because this may be the last utterance I make to any human beings, my last statement in language. I have to be able to stand behind it. I push the language so that it's far above pedestrian, laundromat speech, or language you would overhear in the supermarket, because I care about the language. When I'm talking I can't revise my words over and over and over until they are as precise as I can make them. Also, when I write I can rethink my feelings, so that if I might hurt somebody I can look at that feeling again and try to create something that won't be harmful to others. I do believe in the masterpiece. I believe that a great work of art is a special appearance in our lives. There are works that do not have that intention. They are written for popular or commercial reasons. Some journalism has to be written too quickly for it to develop those layers of thought and feeling you find in masterworks, to reach that level where no sentence can be pulled out without disturbing the sentence in front of it, the sentence behind it, thereby making the paragraph in front of it and behind it collapse. That's the kind of art I'm talking about.

I do think art is elitist. I don't think you can substitute, just because it's a "text," an African-American comic book for Melville's *Benito Cereno*. I used to be a cartoonist; I know how comic books are done. I know how much work goes into one and how much work goes into great fiction. That doesn't mean socially that I am elitist, because I'm not. But the reason I left journalism was because I couldn't do this in that field. The reason I left behind being a cartoonist was because I was looking for the means that would allow me to express the most I could. When I say best thought, best feeling, best skill, I mean even more than that. I mean the book will pull me to a new level of skill. It will demand that of me. When I start it, I will have to learn new things in order to finish it. I'm going to have to develop techniques I've never dreamed of to complete it. A great work of fiction has the same importance to me as a great work of philosophy. That's why I say it's elitist.

Critic, Not Cynic
Charles Johnson talks with Stanley Crouch

Charles Johnson: There have been a lot of claims recently for an intellectual renaissance taking place among black writers and academics, people like Henry Gates, Cornel West, bell hooks, and others. Is this a real intellectual flowering?

Stanley Crouch: I don't really consider bell hooks an intellectual. She's a person who has a job in academic circumstances, but her work, and what I've heard her say, is quite worthy of the fact that she spells her name with lower-case letters. Cornel West has a certain kind of eloquence but I'm not yet struck by anything that he's said, and I was very disappointed in his hobbling along behind Louis Farrakhan in the Million Man March. Skip Gates' greatest contribution in the long run might be that high-quality profile he did of Colin Powell in *The New Yorker*.

Johnson: But it seems to me that doesn't constitute an intellectual renaissance. Because if Cornel West is a significant philosopher there should be a work of philosophy that is a watershed work within his oeuvre, right? And then, the same should be said of bell hooks and Henry Louis Gates as a literary critic.

Crouch: I'm not sure these people represent what some people mean when they're talking about the real renaissance. The stack of books that Albert Murray has written surely constitute a major contribution to American letters and thought. I would say that Leon Forrest's novel *Divine Days* is a rather extraordinary effort. I'm actually more interested in some of the films of people like the Hughes brothers [*Menace II Society, Dead Presidents*] in terms of the potential they suggest for probing some of the urban dilemmas we see playing themselves out in the Negro American working and lower class.

Johnson: What are your thought on the Million Man March?

Crouch: I thought it was a rather timid little example of post-black power Negro American confusion. On the one hand people were supposed to be going to Washington to atone for not having upheld their roles as men—but the overwhelming majority of people who turned out insisted they had nothing to atone for at all. It was like gathering smokers to talk about not smoking, and then 95 percent of the people who arrive don't smoke in the first place.

Johnson: You write a lot about democracy in *The All-American Skin Game*. What's the greatest threat to American democracy in 1995?

Crouch: I think it's the religion of bad faith that has developed since the McCarthy era, when people began to lose faith in the government. After that came the Vietnam War, the hanky-panky of the FBI and the CIA, Watergate, the Iran Contra controversy, and so on. People have developed a condition that I call paralytic cynicism, which results from this bad faith. That is the greatest threat to democracy because people just throw their hands up and say, Gee whiz, things aren't perfect.

Johnson: Is that the reason for the large public support to draft Colin Powell?

Crouch: Definitely, Powell's popularity was based on the fact that people wanted someone to go into the Oval Office who could lead across race and class. Someone who could reiterate, convincingly, allegiance to the greatness of the United States but who wouldn't be incapable of getting people to recognize that the sacrifices necessary to address our problems are not just another con job to better the position of one group or another in society.

Johnson: You have never declared yourself liberal or conservative; as you write in your book, you don't care if the cow comes from the left side or the right side of the field, you care whether the milk is sour. But Powell declared himself a Republican.

Crouch: Yeah, but I don't think being a Republican means he wouldn't have come up with solutions that people might have agreed upon. The fact that people like William Kristol and William Buckley and others were starting to say, Well, OK the guy's pro-choice but he's not so bad—what that suggested to me is that had Powell pursued the nomination, he could have pushed people like Louis Farrakhan, Pat Robertson, Pat Buchanan, and Ralph Reed into the political margins where they belong.

Johnson: Well, I guess though, the question I'm chasing with Powell declaring himself a Republican has to do with the rise of black-conservative thought as represented by publications like *National Minority Politics*, to which you contributed a recent piece on the image of blacks in films, and the predominance of writers like Shelby Steele in terms of interpreting black American experience. There are a whole host of others. Is this a minority of people in the black community or is it really representative of where most people have always been, despite the black power movement of the '60s?

Crouch: Well, a number of people have said that black people are for civil rights not civil liberties, that the Afro-American community has never accepted the justification that people act irresponsibly because they are poor. I saw an interesting thing on television where they were discussing Jesse Jackson's complaint about the difference in sentencing for possession of crack cocaine as opposed to powder cocaine. They went into one of these communities and they asked one of these black women what she thought. She said, 'Look, all I want is to get these dealers out of here and if they never come back that's soon enough.' I mean, her thing was, these people are selling this crack and shooting people and all this; I don't care how long they go to jail. The longer the better.

Johnson: Earlier you mentioned Albert Murray. Why is the work of Murray and Ralph Ellison so important to you?

Crouch: For my money those are the two guys that have had the most insightful and thorough understanding of the Negro American tradition and how implacably it fits within the epic of American history and culture. There is far more depth to what they have to say about the Afro-American relationship to this culture in this country than anyone else writing.

I think it's unfortunate that Ellison's novel, *Invisible Man*, is greatly celebrated but that the remarkable mind that exhibits itself in his books of essays—*Shadow and Act* and *Going to the Territory*—tends to be neglected. Those essays contain profound insights: about the Afro-American tale in the context of American fiction or music, about American law, about the legal and social philosophy that arose in this country from having to address this part of America that has come up from chattel slavery through all kinds of difficulties, about how Afro-Americans have continually redefined our attitude towards the myth and ideals of this country. What Ellison has to say hasn't really been taken up by American intellectuals, nor has a book of the importance of Albert Murray's *South to a Very Old Place*, because they're far too removed from current conventions of thinking about American society.

My major ambition is to clarify the difficulties and the possibilities of being black in America, in a way that will bring about more recognition of the ongoing struggle between the noble and the ignoble traditions of American life. When the chips are down, our human commonality is the thing that has always brought us through our greatest difficulties in the United States. The commonality that stretches across race and class is best utilized when people do not have an unrealistic sense of the nature of human life. That is, that disappointment and decay are fundamental, but so are friendship, faith, family, romance, and heroic figures. It is our job to develop in the United States a sufficiently mature vision that will allow us not to be overwhelmed by difficulty, not to pretend that those things which are difficult don't exist.

Johnson: Do you think we'll evolve beyond racism?

Crouch: I think it will become less and less of a factor in human affairs. As it is now. We have black mayors in so many cities, black men and women in the tops of administrations, we see a greater presence in American life whether it's in our soap operas or on our sporting teams. There are so many renditions of multiracial cooperation and multiracial complexity in our society that have no precedent that it seems to me we're moving closer to the time when the individual will become more significant than the group that the individual comes from.

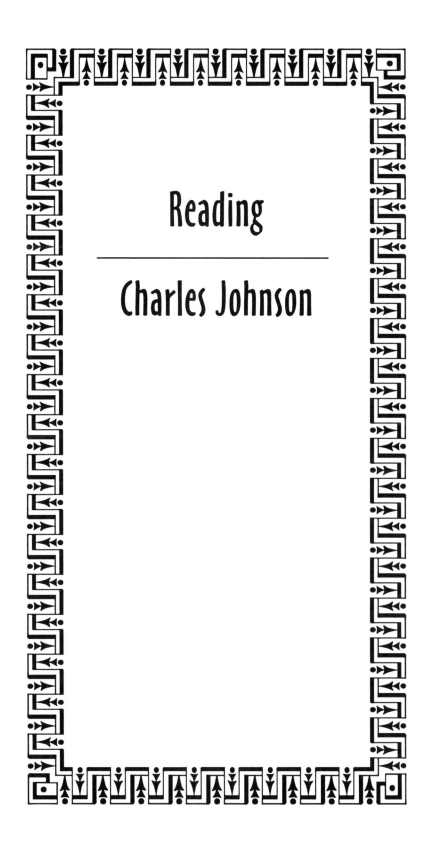

Reading

Charles Johnson

Philosophy and Hydrology

Situating Discourse in Charles Johnson's
Faith and the Good Thing

John McCumber

Panta, said Thales, *hydor*: in the usual translation, "all things are water." If philosophy for Thales had been a thing,[1] and if he had known about syllogisms, he would have stood before the following:

All things are water.
Philosophy is a thing.
Therefore, philosophy is water.

Silly indeed. But it is only by way of this conclusion, perhaps, that philosophy can seek (to say nothing of find) its origin. For if in the original philosophical dictum, which is Thales', the nature of all things is said to be water, then philosophy cannot return to that dictum without confronting the question of what it would be like to be, itself, water. What it would mean for the *logos* to be *hydor*, which will here be called the possibility of hydrology, is indicated, I will argue, in Charles Johnson's novel, *Faith and the Good Thing*.

Water was given its most rigorous philosophical treatment not by Thales or even by Aristotle but by that thirstiest of thinkers, Hegel. In his *Philosophy of Nature*,[2] Hegel is able to provide a philosophical account of the following features of water:

1. It is an opposition which has returned into itself, i.e., which has become a merely neutral medium.
2. It is "internally indeterminate," i.e., homogeneous throughout.
3. It has a merely passive being-for-others, from which follows that:

4. It adheres to its containers, making them wet, and
5. It cannot be compressed, since compression would be a prius to further action (expansion).

But if philosophy is, as we like to believe today, nothing more than
one particularly brittle complex of ancient and would-be-eternal conceptual structures, these traits do not, it seems, describe philosophy at
all—certainly not as it appears in *Faith*. What I have described is, in
fact, Faith Cross herself: uncomplicated whore and plaything of every
man who encounters her; repository of myths and tales which remain
with and heal those she encounters; rejector of all oppositions and
finally of hope—except for the one incompressible urge to seek out the
Good Thing, as if it were her level.

What does Faith have to do with philosophy, and how could water
ever be the middle term between them? For there is no lack of other
candidates for such status, at first glance better than water. One of
these, congenial to philosophy at least, is universal conceptuality itself. Humanity is one species, and Faith is descended from the ancestors of her own oppressors (p. 66), including those Europeans who
dragged her across the ocean into slavery. Among what she shares with
them may be the universal structures of human life that philosophy
has traditionally sought to articulate and justify. This certainly is part
of Johnson's argument, for few writers—and certainly few American
ones—have been as insistent that philosophy does capture and articulate the meanings of our lives in a way indispensable to the novelist. In
his *Being and Race*, for example, Johnson points out that Senghor's philosophy of *négritude* is close to Neoplatonism, while Eldridge Cleaver
was, in his most radical days, in some respects an inverted Cartesian.[3]
What seem at first blush to be non-European thought patterns often,
Johnson notes, turn out to inhabit the philosophical enterprise somewhere; for though philosophy has always been primarily European, it
has also always been diverse.[4] And this is especially true, he suggests,
for African American literature, because the immediate political implications that always crowd in upon African American writing push it
beyond the comfortable confines of the aesthetic into other domains,
transgressions which are in some respects necessarily philosophical.[5]

But it does not follow that European philosophy, *as Europeans have
conceived it*, applies directly to African American (or even to European
American) experience. For the common ancestry of Faith and her
(white) oppressors is very remote indeed, so distant that its site has
sunk into the sea, and the paths have diverged widely since. Consider
Hegel's famous "Battle to the Death," from his *Phenomenology*, a section which deeply inspired Marx and whose centrality to Hegel's own
thought was established by Alexandre Kojève.[6] In it, two conscious-
nesses, each seeking to assert abstract superiority over all that lives,
encounter each other and engage in a battle that neither really needs.

The winner becomes the Master in the *Phenomenology*'s ensuing section, "Lordship and Bondage"; the loser becomes the bondsman who, in the depths of his misery, turns in on himself and eventually comes to realize his own capacity for thought, thus providing—and becoming—a crucial stage in the onward push of Spirit. Now hear this retold in an African American version, by the unnamed minister of the Church of Continual Light:

> "You think you're the center of the whole world at first, you think it whorls around you like the planets around the sun—don't you?"
> "Yes, Lord!" a woman shouted.
> "But one day, you come across someone else who thinks just the very same thing. You've got to fight then, to do battle over who's going to be supreme, you or that other fellah, 'cause that's the way we men are. . . . " The minister's mouth opened, Faith caught her breath. His mouth was bright red inside, the color of fresh blood. "And you both lose!" he boomed. "You both see neither one of you have *any* thin' to do with what pushes the world along. What, then?" he said.

What, indeed? The possibility of such an outcome, where both battlers live but both lose because *neither* can relate in any way to the onward push of the world, is nowhere entertained by Hegel, nor so far as I know by any commentator on him. It is simply too desperate to be part of any philosophy—an "expenditure without reserve" far more ghastly, for example, than the laughter with which Bataille thought to stave off the march of Hegel's dialectic at this point.[7]

And yet Hegel is "relevant" to Johnson's passage. We understand it differently and better when we learn what it so specifically does not echo. What must happen to Hegel in order for this nonechoing to take place, in order for him to show up through a fragment of a sermon supposedly uttered by an inauthentic minister holding forth at 64th and Stony Island, Chicago, Illinois? Must Hegel not be somehow made fluid, his thought rendered capable of dissolution and reinstatement in a discourse definitively, perhaps unimaginably, other to it? How is such liquefaction possible? What are the implications of that possibility?

ॐ ॐ ॐ

Faith, being a good novel, is not about philosophical ideas (p. 92). But it presents philosophical phenomena, experiences about which philosophers have traditionally thought and worried. One of the most philosophical of phenomena is time, and *Faith* presents it in complex ways, often recurring to a very traditionally threefold rubric, whose three individual folds are very untraditional indeed.

The most readily understandable fold in the traditional rubric is the present: time is understood in terms of the now, as what stands given and allows other things to manifest themselves. The reason this is so readily understandable is that it is so widespread in modern culture. *Faith* locates it in both religion and science. When, for example, Faith is undergoing her childhood "marriage" to Christ she has a mystical vision of infinite presence, or eternity,

> There on the ground . . . she saw it clearly—all the possible number of things in space, all forms that had ever existed in time reflected back into time like a man's image trapped in a room of mirrors—she, herself, Faith Cross, fading back and forth on the continuum of time until she . . . screamed it—"Thank Yooou!"—sang it—"Thank You"—and finally believed in its healing grace—"Thank You!" (P. 12)

But this perfect religious vision does not last, and neither does the very imperfect vision of the scientist, Dr. Lynch, according to whom the universe is nothing but swirls in space-time and life is simply tension and release, and not worth living because the three transcendent values of the Western tradition have fallen apart: "The truth isn't beautiful and it doesn't make me feel good" (p. 39). "Truth," in the dominant strain of the philosophical tradition, is allowed to be nothing other than the simultaneous *presence* of fact and sentence or belief, the presence in or to the mind of some object or state of affairs that exists independently of it: a presence for which Lynch has, at enormous cost, sacrificed the other two values.

Since presence grounds truth, it is (again traditionally) the foundation of knowledge. Faith is saved from the constrictions and compressions of religion and science because she is able to locate the extravagance of their knowledge-claims; science cannot explain why we should live, and religion cannot explain how it is that we die: "The silent kitchen said so" (p. 12). The questions which expose that extravagance are imposed on Faith by her mother's death. The silent kitchen testifies to what Heidegger calls the worldhood of the world, the gathering together into a significant whole of what would otherwise be, in Reverend Brown's phrase, "a lot of empty things that keep bumpin'into each other in the dark" (p. 14):

> The kitchen had changed. You could locate nothing misplaced, nothing out of the ordinary, for as a housekeeper Lavidia was meticulous; but the kitchen's former gloss of permanence was gone. Its smell was still that of the dry cotton fields just outside the open window above the sink, of browning bread Lavidia had baked just two nights before; yet Lavidia was gone. Though old, dissipated, sometimes evil, she had been the focus of the farmhouse. . . . Without her the kitchen, the house, the world beyond fell apart. (P. 5)

As Heidegger points out, world is always, as here, given as something already there, an *immer schon*. What Heidegger does not deal with is the capacity of a world, a whole of significance, suddenly to be *entirely* past, irretrievably gone, because the person—the Dasein—who inhabited it has died.[8] And that is what has happened to Faith, rendering childish both the gloried consolations of Brown's religion and the courageous pain of Lynch's science. Forced by nothing less than human mortality to put away the things of the child, Faith undergoes what Heidegger, in *Being and Time*, cannot recognize: the *simultaneous* disclosure of a world, of a significant whole established in and through the past, and the rupture and receding of that very world before the question of the future—before Reverend Brown's simple, devastating "What will you do now, child?" (p. 5).

In this, we see time presented very differently from the standard view of it as a succession of present moments. It is a field of play in which connections are established (the past) and simultaneously undone (the future). It has not tenses but rubrics: connecting and rupturing. None occurs before or after the others—and so all are, it seems, "present" together.

On one of its levels (and I do not pretend to discuss here more than a small part of this very complex book), *Faith and the Good Thing* is an extended and powerful argument against that impression, against the view that connecting and rupturing are to be conceived in terms of the "present," indeed as "present" themselves. And this is directly related to philosophy, for is not truth the dominant notion of all philosophy? And what is truth if not the intellectual presence of the present?

It is important to name our villain. It is not, as so often, "presence" that is at fault but the dominating drive that beats in the heart of presence, not, as the Greeks would say, *parousia* that is the problem, but *ousia* itself.[9] In what I will call the "substantialistic" approach to a domain, that domain is divided into two kinds of thing: those which are themselves (at least relatively) independent of other things and dominate the rest and those which are dependent on, dominated by, those independent entities. Substance is thus an abstract conceptualization of dominance, and it is the dominance (for example, of presence) that causes problems. In what has traditionally been called "metaphysics," a substantialistic approach is taken to all that exists, as in the broadly Aristotelian dictum that everything that is has Being and intelligibility only in virtue of its identity as a substance or its relation to substance. As articulated by Aristotle, this substantialism has remained basic to the West; the degree of its sway over us today is shown by *Being and Race*'s terse formulation of one of its contemporary corollaries: "To *be* is to be white."[10]

If we take a substantialistic approach to time, we will seek to find some one subsection of it which is independent and upon which everything else depends for its existence and intelligibility. And this, since Descartes anyway, has been the "now"—the present moment.[11] For the "now" is utterly divorced from and hence independent of all that went before, so much so for Descartes that the universe requires God's action to sustain it at each instant, and that effort is exactly the same as His original action in creating it; the movement from each moment to the

next is a full *creatio ex nihilo*. The past and the future, in a substantialistic approach, will depend on the present for both their existence and
their intelligibility. The past exists only because it was once present and
the future because it will be. Each is intelligible only because it can be
conceived as a present of a different kind, as belonging to a genus of
which the present is the dominant member, as species of the "now."
The problem, again, is not with the "now," of which nonmetaphysical
accounts have been available since Aristotle. If the "now" as present
dominates, we have the rule of truth. But the "now" as past and future
can also be given that sort of dominance and can exercise it over the
present itself.

Faith and the Good Thing undertakes, I suggest, to show that the past
and the future can be appropriated in ways which escape the conceptual
of the present, as other than "nows." It does this not by philosophical
argumentation but by showing us characters who achieve and fail at
such appropriation. Those who fail—Arnold T. Tippis, Kujichagulia, and
Alpha Omega Holmes—are presented as inauthentic, men who cannot
be true to themselves and who cause trouble for others, especially Faith.
Those who succeed—Todd Cross and Richard Barrett—are, in spite of
their terrible fates, true to themselves and enriching for Faith. And
behind them all, commenting and reflecting, stirring her cauldron into
a (veritable) Thaumaturgic Mirror and conjuring truth from blood, is
the Swamp Woman. Let us consider them in turn.

ʤ ʤ ʤ

Let us begin with the past and with Arnold T. Tippis. To conceive
the past substantialistically means, according to my previous account,
to conceive of it as a "now," one which is independent of all else, utterly
unchangeable because previous—and as able, in its independence, to
dominate the rest of time's domain: the present and the future. The
traditional philosophical name for this relation of dominance is "causality," according to which what is present is a mere effect of previous
"nows," its causes, which themselves (for the purposes of the moment)
are taken as uncaused. Tippis is excellent at reducing complex phenomena to such causality:

> "You can't escape history [says Tippis], or the needs and neuroses you've
> picked up like layers and layers of tartar on your teeth. . . . Your every
> past action and thought have made you what you are. Am I right or
> wrong?" His words troubled Faith. The past, remote and distorted by the
> mercy of waning memories, had the terrible power to be present at all
> times in its effects; this was true. (P. 58)

Tippis believes in causality, a concept powerful enough to effect his
extraordinary *rapprochement* between history and tooth decay. Moreover, he actually lives by that belief. This means that, for him, the life

is the production of causal effects on the world: it is a matter of satisfying instinctual needs, themselves unquestioned. Unfortunately, this
means turning people into objects you can use:

> Objectifying a thing, making it no more than an object so it can be
> grasped, manipulated, and ruled is, obviously, dehumanizing. . . . But too
> many of your drives can only be satisfied, and only then temporarily,
> in this way. There *is* no other way unless you kill off your feelings . . .
> (P. 58)

No effect can resist its cause, because it is what its cause makes it
be. But Tippis, by his own account, is also an object and therefore is
himself prey to causal forces from outside, which have the capacity to
enter into him and make him what he is. It is only consistent, then,
that his self-definition depend utterly on the situations that may offer
themselves to him, generally in the form of want ads: dentist, porter,
salesman, usher, nurse—he tries them all, and his changes are "never
from within, only catalyzed from without" (p. 83). It is also, more omi-
nously, only consistent that Tippis should reduce his relation to Faith
as well to one of causality, the exercise of total power over her objectified
being—power which itself comes from nowhere but his own desire and
a being which is nothing more, or less, than her body. This means rape,
to which Tippis proceeds at length, making Faith a "thing in which to
unload" his energy (p. 153).

To approach the past with the notion of truth, we see, is not only
misleading but evil, for you will set it up as substantial, as independent
itself, dominating the rest. Since part of the rest it dominates is your
own present situation, you become a mere effect, a receptacle for its
tensions and releases. By a simple transformation, when *ego* becomes
the past and *alters* the present, I can reduce another person to my effect:
in effect, rape that person. Causality is not merely violent; it is violation, intimately bound (in ways still far too mysterious) to the practice
of rape.

Is there, then, a way of relating to the past without appeal to causality—a way that does not reduce the present to its effect? Which can
even, perhaps, allow the present to exercise some power over the past?
We exercise power over something by changing it, and to change the
past is to lose faith in its brute facticity, to reinvent it. Faith's father,
Todd Cross, is presented as a master of such invention: his calling is to
produce "stunning fictions and well-meant lies" as needed (p. 14). Not
that his stories are all determinable as false; his tale of his life, as Faith
gathers it from him (p. 44f), is not so much invented (though parts of
it seem to be) as dreamlike, pieced together out of images that offer
themselves as distorted and incomplete and hence untrue, however
imaginary they may or may not be. If the tales are untrue to the past,
they are also unfalse to it.

It eventually becomes impossible for Faith to separate the true from the false in Todd's stories (p. 88); but such separation is not necessary. Though his stories are "outrageous" and essentially strange (pp. 43, 41), they do their job. However much trouble Todd Cross occasionally makes for himself with his inventions (he causes himself everlasting misery by telling his wife, before their marriage, that he is rich, p. 45), he is able recurrently to triumph by conjuring up another story. His tales create a bearable, even joyous, and certainly wise world for a poor share-cropper, fated to die at the hands of white thugs, and for his small daughter, whose fate will be less definitive but certainly no less painful. They do this even when, in addition to being false, they are not even Todd's; at least one of his tales (the one on p. 42) in fact comes directly from Plato's *Symposium*. The healing power, in other words, is not Todd's; it belongs to the stories themselves.

Since Todd's stories are not exactly false, they do have a relation to whatever it may be that actually happened in the past; since they are not exactly true, the relation is an unfaithful one. The past is deprived of the solid independence of substance and becomes a mere shadowed background, lit up at will by the stories we tell about it. Untrue to the past, such stories play with it: because they play with it, it does not dominate them; because it cannot dominate them, it cannot dominate the present, insofar as these stories are part of it (and Todd himself tries to crawl entirely inside his stories; while he never even bothers to discover his own birthdate, he names his pots and pans—pp. 16, 44, 64). The way out of nihilistic determinism is by telling tales neither false nor true. Even if, in truth, the only relations between past and present are causal ones.

The excellence of such tales is, we read, beauty: as the Swamp Woman says, "all good stories (and true ones too) have to be pretty, even the ugly ones" (p. 28). If the virtue of the present is truth, that of the past is beauty, the establishing of the right connections. Only by viewing the past as the background of beauty can it be approached in a way independent of truth, the temporal schema of which is presence. The possibility of such independence already shatters the dominance of the present, its ability to provoke substantialistic accounts of time, and instead delivers time not as a series of "nows" but as the unfaithful play of present and past—of connection and its absence. The Swamp Woman generalizes this: "Before you ask if *anythin*'s true, first ask y'self if it's good, and if it's beautiful" (p. 30, emphasis added).

A similar doubleness, between "now"-oriented and non-"now"-oriented, can also be found in ways of encountering the future. Consider, first, the legendary Kujichagulia, husband of Imani. Kujichagulia, the Swamp Woman tells Faith, should never have been born: he asked too many questions, and in that sense remained a child forever (p. 28). His questions led him to break from the established harmony of African village life. This was not exactly a willful decision; even after he settled down with Imani and apparently forgot his quest for the Good Thing, he still felt longing and deeply incomplete (p. 29). But such incompleteness merely places him before the future; for we have seen that, as Faith learns from her mother's death, the future is rupture, loss of connection previously established, the abyss that yawns when beauty is broken; and to stand before the future is to be, as Kujichagulia remained, a child.

What calls Kujichagulia out of his mythical harmony, what changes him from a kid with a lot of questions into a homeless seeker, is the Good Thing itself; for the pure, unreflected presence of that is what he seeks on top of Mount Kilimanjaro (p. 29). The idea that it is the Good that tears us from the everyday, again, inhabits the philosophical tradition. For Kant, the good action is one performed through freedom, and freedom is defined by him as an act performed not from inclinations (anything which belongs in the law-governed totality that he calls "nature") but from respect for the (eternal) moral low as a break in the causal chain.[12] But Kujichagulia cannot actually find the Good Thing; he loses it as he comes upon it, by dying (p. 189).

A similar fate awaits Alpha Omega Holmes, the lover whom Faith, rightly, never quite trusts (pp. 7, 102, 148). He bears some resemblances to Todd Cross, both physically and in his ability to conjure up the right lie for the moment. But unlike Todd Cross, whose stories are educational and save not only Faith but others whom she encounters (p. 71f), Alpha Omega Holmes lies for his own advantage, to save himself (and Faith) from the angry farmer Cragg and to win Faith (pp. 144f, 155): he tells good tales, but self-serving ones.

The resemblance is deeper with Kujichagulia, for Alpha Omega Holmes is also concerned with the difference between things as they seem and as they really are (p. 154), and this has involved him too in a quest—a quest which tears him away from daily life and sends him off on a variety of pursuits, including jail and the solitary, impoverished life of a painter who gives away his paintings. Indeed, sudden departure is second nature to him: he never calls his parole officer after he leaves jail, a dangerous dereliction, and twice vanishes, without a word, from Faith's life—the second time after rejecting her and their unborn child (pp. 54, 146, 182). But whereas Kujichagulia was concerned with *finding* something, Alpha Omega Holmes seeks to *create* something: himself. His paintings are merely a means to this end:

> But someday when I've got hit all together, there won't be a dime's worth of difference between what I'm creatin' and myself—you won't be able to separate me from my work by space, or by a difference in materials, because—and I *know* it sounds crazy—my life'll be the finished work . . . (p. 159)

It is in no trivial, or even ordinarily egoistical, sense that Alpha Omega Holmes's lies are self-serving. They are part of a life which, in all respects, is a service to self—to the future, true self he hopes, one day, to be able to create (pp. 157, 159, 164). It is in the name of this self that he turns Faith away when she tells him of her pregnancy and her willingness to leave her husband, the odious Maxwell (p. 165).

Both Kujichagulia and Alpha Omega Holmes, then, are in the service of the Good Thing, of that which tears us from our established harmonies and liberates us from our past. But both conceive of the Good as, strictly, a *thing*, one which belongs to their futures; and in this they are the temporal mirror images of Arnold T. Tippis. For Alpha Omega Holmes, the thing in question is his future self, the existence of which he hopes to achieve to the full. For the sake of this, he lives and paints—does everything, in fact, that he does (except, perhaps, make love to Faith); whereas for Tippis the past dominated the present, for Alpha Omega Holmes the future does, and every bit as completely. The same is true for Kujichagulia, who finally gives up his life in the pure presence of the Good Thing, when, in its presence, his quest ends and he loses his future.

If the philosophical name for the dominance of the past over the present is causality, that for the dominance of the future is "teleology." For teleology, which Aristotle conceived as a sort of complement to what we today call causality (and what he calls "moving cause"), conceptualizes the fact that a future state, though not yet existing, can explain and thus dominate the present while being itself in no need (for the purposes of the moment) of explanation. Thus we cannot understand what the acorn is without understanding the oak; but the oak has no further purposes and does not exist (so Aristotle) for the sake of the acorn.[13] Teleology thus conceptualizes the substantialization of the future. In it, the future "now" becomes dominant and independent, controlling the present.

Both Alpha Omega Holmes and Kujichagulia lead lives of nearly perfect teleology, utterly dominated by a single determinate purpose, which itself is not challenged or explained. And this leads them, as with Tippis, into unfaithfulness to self. Kujichagulia abandons his quest for the Good Thing and resides for decades with Imani, to whom he cannot in the end remain faithful. Alpha Omega Holmes cannot make proper use of his own talent for stories and turns them into something to hide behind. Both, moreover, abandon their women—Kujichagulia in the night, Alpha Omega Holmes in all the brutality of daylight. If the paradigm of causality is rape, that of teleology is abandonment.

In opposition to Kujichagulia and Alpha Omega Holmes, somewhat as Todd Cross stood to Arnold Tippis, is Richard M. Barrett. Like the lives of Kujichagulia and Alpha Omega Holmes, Barrett's life has been a quest for the Good Thing, as well as a life of radical changes. By his own testimony he had already, in his youth, "experimented with everything under the sun" (p. 90); his further background includes marriage and a professorship at Princeton, the loss of these, and stints as a thief and a penitent. When he reappears in Faith's life, begging forgiveness for having mugged her as she arrived in Chicago, he stands before the most radical departure of all: death itself. She frees him for it not with an answer but with a question: "Will you look with me?" (p. 94).

But unlike the quests of Kujichagulia and Alpha Omega Holmes, Barrett's quest is not for a "thing." His Doomsday Book bears the results of his lifetime of incessant inquiry, "the sum total of every truth I have come to know and believe" (p. 87). It is perfectly empty. Whereas for Kujichagulia the Good Thing existed atop Mount Kilimanjaro (and nowhere else)) and for Alpha Omega Holmes was his idea of himself (no other idea, no other self), Barrett insists that it is not a "thing" at all. Only in the early stages does it appear to be, of necessity, something thingly—pure, unsullied, and out there—such as a thing on a mountaintop, apart from its modular reflections, or one's own best self, apart from others (p. 91f). In truth, all we have by way of the Good Thing is the ongoing proliferation of quests and inquiries into it—"*the* human adventure," according to Barrett, one which, in the last analysis, is unending (p. 91). When life's connections are broken, the living transform themselves; they turn out to be not the unified sources of action and knowledge that "the tradition" has always wanted them to be but ways or paths: stories that lead for a while, then exhaust themselves, and end: "We operate on beginnings, middles, and ends," says Barrett. "When you reach the end of one road, say, as a professor, you begin another" (p. 91).

Hence, Barrett's life—though certainly a demanding one—is not harnessed to any set purpose. No goal is prescribed for his "constant questioning," and even mugging Faith is part of the quest—for as he does so he ruminates, pushing his reflections just a little further than they have gone before (p. 52). It is not that Barrett, lacking a determinate purpose, is reduced to acquiescence in the present, much less enjoyment of it. Quite the contrary: the indeterminacy of his goal, which nonetheless remains a goal, means that anything and everything can be otherwise. And in that "otherwise" yawns the gap of a nonsubstantialistic future, a future that, like Heidegger's "call of conscience,"[14] is too empty to prescribe to or dominate the present but calls us out of it by breaking the connections between it and the past connections, so beautiful they can be seductive.

Barrett's future, in other words, is truly open; assuming the form of no thing—or, in his final moments on the park bench, of nothing—it is the future only in that it is a space of unformed possibility, the breaking of whatever connections are relevant, including, as it is formed, the connection to Faith. Empty as death, the future cannot dominate; it can only remind the present of its own finitude, that it is not everything. The future, then, is the rupture of the bonds, dating from the past, which threaten to overwhelm the present. The search for the Good

Thing, ending in such emptiness, is ultimately less a quest than a path-way—what Heidegger called a *Holzweg*, which the French translate as "chemins qui ne mènent nulle part."

All this, again, is underwritten by the Swamp Woman, for whom the Good Thing is like the nonsubstantialist future: "How can it be over when ya only been on *one* path—and a silly one at that? . . . There ain't no beginnin' and there ain't no end. . . . There ain't nothing but searchin' and sufferin' too" (p. 189). And Faith accepts it in the book's final pages:

> She was more than any one path, or the total of them all. She would glean from each its store of the Good Thing, would conjure it up. . . . And when she'd traveled the existing paths, she would create a new, untrodden one. That was progress. If she discovered X number of paths and traveled them all, then she, before she died, would leave X-plus-1. That was responsibility: factoring the possible number of paths to the Good Thing, but not becoming fixed, or held to those paths in her history, or the history of the race. Moving always on. . . . (P. 195)

Outside of substantialism we have, then, these three, which cannot be reduced to each other: the presence of the present, the undeniable truth of science; the beauty of the right connections, or the past rein-vented by tales neither true nor false; and the good itself, the rupturing emptiness beyond (in Plato's words) Being and essence.[15]

$$\text{�™ ☙ ☙}$$

And we need all three. I have elsewhere styled the establishment of connections via the telling of untrue, unfalse tales as "narrative" and the opening of gaps in such narrative as "demarcation."[16] According to *Being and Race*, the novel has a kind of temporality which makes it exhibit both.

Narrative is most obviously evident in a novel's plot.[17] But the plot of a novel, the connected sequence of events it relates, is not an untrue/unfalse tale; it takes a determinate stand with respect to truth, for it claims, as fictional, to be false. In any case, as Johnson notes, "plot" is an originally Aristotelian concept, grounded in the demand of his meta-physics for *energeia*, which is the highest state of being for a substance; when a substance reaches *energeia*, its form totally dominates its mat-ter.[18] Dominated by its plot, the novel would be a substantialistic totality, in which what Johnson specifies as "Western esthetic logic" prescribes that earlier events cause later ones and that the whole be seen as the un-folding of a single large purpose, presumably that of the author. Caught in the categories of causality and purpose, the novel would be entirely captured by substantialistic categories.

That such is not the case is due in part to the nature of kitsch, which Johnson (following Karsten Harries) defines as the retreat from ambiguity, from the fact that "no experience is raw. None is *given* to us as meaningful, or as meaning only one thing."[19] This dictum holds, in its globality, for works of art, including novels; and it entails that we cannot locate the novel within the traditional, substantialistic conception of time.

If, to begin with, the novel passes from writer to reader, it does not originate with a writer alone in space or from any other single, independent cause. It begins, Johnson tells us in *Being and Race*, from a writer who is already within a life-world and language, object and medium, which themselves are already bursting with meaning which it is up to the writer to appropriate and order with her linear (and other) devices (pp. 11, 13, 23, 44). Not, of course, that the writer is completely true to the life-world from which she starts, for then her work would not be fiction. Nor is she completely false to it either, for then what she creates would be a completely self-contained linguistic whole. And that, however seductive to substantialistically minded critics, is impossible as long as a literary work is written in a language common to, indeed created by and learned from, others (p. 34ff).

Any novelist is also connected to those specific human beings who will be her readers. If her novel is not kitsch, it can be understood in a variety of ways. The novel, then, needs its readers to be itself. The beginning, middle, and end of a plot exist in the world "only to the extent that they are structures of you and me" (p. 31). The connections explored in the plot are to some extent established by the readers themselves as they link their memories of the book's beginnings with what is now on the page; to read is, to some extent, to reinvent. The novel does not "cause" certain effects in its readers, the way his past causes changes in Arnold T. Tippis, but is a field of latent connections, certain of which each reader brings forth.

Any novel also involves ruptures. It begins not only with the life-world that one's predecessors have shaped but with a certain distance from, even contempt for, at least some of those predecessors (p. 4). Like any work of art, a novel is immediately perceived as inhabiting a space which is precisely not that of the ordinary life-world, of daily experience; it is an event within a certain sort of phenomenological *epochê*, the suspension of everyday pursuits and attitudes (pp. 5, 23). Only by rupturing such everyday connectedness can the novel provide itself with space in which to grow and develop on its own terms, as an "internal perfection" and unity (p. 36). Hence, at the same time that the novel reaches out to the life-world it describes and to the language in which it is written, it alienates itself from both; it conducts a simultaneous demarcation and narrative.

There are also breaks between the novel and its audience. For when the novel develops its internal perfection to the full and its plot comes to an end, the individual reading it does not. She simply finishes it and, presumably, picks up another novel (or does something else). This is made clear from some words I omitted from one of the quotes, from Richard Barrett:

> "People are somewhat like novels (don't make *too* much of that simile)— we operate on beginnings, middles, and ends; subjective aims depositing in ongoing history to be prehended by other subjective aims. When you reach the end of one road . . . you begin another." (P. 91)

So people are ways, and novels are ways; but since they begin and end at different times, the end of the novel differs from, demarcates itself from, the person reading it. The novel can, like Barrett on his bench, die away into a world where its possibilities are so broad as to be nonexistent. It may also, via its distance from the ordinary life-world of a person, open up gaps and possibilities that are more or less specific, as when a novel "changes my life." But again this effect, though what the novel is after, is not determinate, for it depends to some extent on how the reader reinvents the novel. The novel, in other words, is an indeterminate quest for readers, for its own reinvention. If it begins with a gap (as well as a continuity) between its own writing and the life-world and language which preexist it, it ends with a gap as well (and with continuity) between itself and its readers. The future is open at each stage.

Any novel thus describes a trajectory that, in a broader sense than Aristotle's, is a narrative, one beginning with the life-world and language, passing through the writer, and ending with the reader. According to substantialist views of time, the novel—that which I see on the page before me—would have a past: it was written by someone, caused by her desire to create it. It also would have a future, because when I read it it will cause certain effects in me. But this account, we have seen, ignores the aspects of reinvention and distance that enter in at each stage. In truth the novel must, as a temporal being, be located within the other temporality that Faith so consistently works out. It makes no truth-claim about its own past, about its author, language, and life-world, but from time to time illuminates all three, each functioning not as cause but as background to that illumination. Nor does it have a set purpose, a determinate effect it is to produce in the reader—though that it is to have some effect, fit into its readers' lives somehow, is very clear. The novel's timeline is a trajectory of faithlessness rather than truth, of invention rather than causality: what I have called a nonsubstantialistic one. The question now is that of how the novel, conceived in terms of this sort of time, can make use and sense of philosophy.

There are various channels by which philosophy makes its way into Faith's southern rural world and then into the emptiness and pain that is her Chicago. Those channels are, mainly, characters. I have mentioned the unnamed preacher who parodies, and destroys, Hegel. But there are others. Reverend Brown applies Plato's cave-myth to Faith (p. 14), and Todd Cross tells her Aristophanes' story from the *Symposium* (p. 42). Beaumont Gaines decides to check out the empirical validity of the Barbara syllogism ("all men are mortal" p. 35); Dr. Lynch presents a philosophical cosmology (p. 36ff); and Arnold T. Tippis summarizes his version of Freud (p. 57f). Richard Barrett fairly bursts with philosophical insights and quotes, and even Maxwell, Faith's hapless husband, lives out a pale vision of Nietzsche and Hobbes, seeing the world as a series of collisions of wills to power (p. 99f).

But the champion of this is the Swamp Lady, who never speaks without dragging through her words half the great philosophers of history, as in this passage on the nature of the Good Thing:

> " . . . I figure it must be the right functionin' of an organism as it participates in a form, or the fulfillment of a teleological principle inherent in all matter, or gettin' in the right relationship with the Lord (or Lords, or y'self, dependin' upon your persuasion), or followin' the Hedonistic Calculus in all matters of equally appealing desires, or doin' unto others as you would have them do unto you, or a leap o' faith, or abolishin' private property, or maybe avoidin' Bad Faith." The Swamp Woman giggled obscenely, as if she'd told a joke. "Take your pick, sweetheart." (P. 24)

This list presents, *in chronological order*, the views of Plato, Aristotle, Augustine (Proclus, Skepticism), Bentham, Kant (phrased in the words of the Golden Rule which inspire the first formulation of the Categorical Imperative),[20] Kierkegaard, Marx, and Sartre. A number of characteristics of the list are, in fact, shared by the other characters who channel philosophy to Faith.

1. Each element in the series is accurate. Though a couple of my assignments of names to doctrines may be doubtful, in the main each formulation is an elegant distillation of the single most basic ethical thought of a major philosopher. So, in general, Johnson's channels get their philosophy right.
2. Each idea is cut away from its context within the thought of the philosopher who uttered it. The Swamp Woman's reference to Plato contains no account of what a "form" is, nor any of functioning, to say nothing of right functioning: there is no examination of what was most important for Plato, which is how these ideas hang rationally together. It is as if she has, delicately but ruthlessly, cut away the entire Platonic system except for the single element she needs at the moment. The elements thus produced are smaller than what the French might call "philosophemes," or even "gestures": they are philosophical atoms, single phrases, which cannot it would appear be reduced any further in size.
3. The series as a whole recapitulates the history of philosophy. The philosophers are referred to in their historical order, from which it follows that
4. The Swamp Woman, like the other channels of philosophy in the book, is not an autodidact; this list is not the kind that could be compiled by someone who found a couple of philosophy books in a

shopping mall bookstore. Like Dr. Lynch (who, we are told, had "attended all the great schools," p. 33), Richard Barrett (professor at Princeton), and even Arnold T. Tippis (informed by his psychoanalyst), the Swamp Woman has a *systematic* knowledge of philosophy. That is why she leaves out of her list no thinker of major relevance.

One further point is that this channeling, whose nature we have yet to examine in any sort of detail, is not the activity merely of the characters within the book. The main channeler is Johnson himself, who, writing the novel, shows the same relentless application of philosophical insights to the African American life-world that his characters aim at. This gives us a clue to the nature of what I call channeling: is it possible that what the Swamp Woman is doing to philosophy is of a piece with what a novelist does with the life-world?

Philosophy presents itself *to philosophers* as a series of systems, of internally coherent but mutually contradictory attempts to model the universe and its basic features. The first step in what I call channeling is to bracket what makes these systems contradict one another, and that is their respective claims to truth. The philosopher for Johnson is apparently to be viewed as operating the way William Gass, by Johnson's account, thinks the novelist does: like a mathematician, "who, in a carefully wrought, coherent, internally consistent theorem, creates a beautiful architecture of meaning that may or may not have anything to do with the world of everyday existence" (*Being and Race,* p. 35)

Don't ask if it's true; ask if it's beautiful.

But in thus bracketing the truth claims of traditional philosophers, we are wrenching their thought out of its most basic human context: that of the search for (some kind of) truth. Indeed, as I suggested, the Swamp Woman goes further: she freely and radically dissociates philosophical ideas from even their most immediate contexts within the thought of those who propound them. And, in that the isolated remarks remain basically accurate, she shows that *those ideas cannot resist.* You can take Plato's idea of the healthy functioning of an organism as it participates in a form, fail completely to discuss what a Platonic Form is, and still have said something intelligible. You can take his account of the cave and put it into the mouth of a rural clergyman trying to explain to a young woman why religion is important. You can take Hegel's account of the "Battle to the Death" out of his *Phenomenology,* revise it radically, and have another preacher tell it. You can have a six-year-old southern girl achieve the Spinozistic vision of the world *sub specie aeternitas* on the floor of her country church. And so on, throughout the book.

And you can take these freely dissociated philosophical elements and place them into your own narrative—indeed, into your plot. For at least some of these philosophical elements help drive the plot forward. The Heideggerean vision of the silent kitchen begins it, for example;

the Spinozistic vision of all things defines Faith's childhood; Maxwell's Nietzschean Hobbesianism sums up her spiritual location in Chicago. Cut off from their original context, the philosophical elements take up positions in a narrative, positions which are neither wholly true to their original loci within philosophy (for the context and use are foreign) nor wholly false to them (for the elements retain accuracy). Philosophy, in other words, is for Johnson as novelist just like any other part of the life-world: something from which he distances himself and about which he tells tales at once untrue and unfalse. Philosophy, then, is both nar-ratable and demarcatable; it can be dissolved into its elements and inserted into a variety of narratives other than its own.

And what is philosophy, if it can be treated in such ways? Certainly not the ageless, articulated, conceptual structures that philosophers like to talk about. The contradictions among its historical components are now gone; it has returned from such opposition into a merely neutral medium. Unable to resist this loss of structure, it shows itself to be "internally indeterminate," homogeneous throughout. And it manifests in this its purely passive being for others—for Charles Johnson, its other as novelist, and for the tales he tells. It adheres to, inheres within, those tales, and makes them somehow accurately philosophical. And in all this, it cannot be compressed; its elements cannot finally be deprived of meaning in relation to the life-world. For Charles Johnson, fiction, like all art, has a larger duty to that world (in the Heideggerean sense of that complex of human concerns which crystallize around the work of art; *Being and Race*, p. 35ff). The philosophical elements redeposited in his novel have the capacity to restore, seek out, their own relation to the life-world. Not that they describe it, the way they claimed to in their previous philosophical lives; but in that they light up the past (which in their case is philosophy) and open up the future.

Philosophy has now come to have the five characteristics I located in Hegel's treatment of "water." Johnson has shown, in other words, that philosophy is indeed liquefiable, that it makes sense to conceive of the *logos* in terms that the *logos* itself has traditionally applied to *hydor*. Not that this is wholly unfaithful to the past; philosophical elements con-tinually seep into our lives, and their role in conceptually consolidating such practices as rape, abandonment, and domination is perhaps more implacable and intimate than we have dared think. In any case, this deep role of philosophy in constituting our lives remains invisible as long as we remain fixated upon philosophy as merely the search for truth. For from that sort of perspective, we are finished with "to be is to be white" the moment we have declared it false.

Undoing that perspective, in fact, is the *philosophical* side of the future that Johnson's use of philosophy opens up. Since that future, like all futures, is room for change, possibility, a sort of emptiness which makes empty space possible, it is impossible to delineate it; indeed, the future has no unity, and there is no reason to think that philosophy will

ever have a unified essence. But what Charles Johnson's use of philosophy suggests, if I am right in what I have written here, is that our
Western heritage, with all its faults—with, indeed, its still unexamined
habit of conceptually consolidating such unsavory, not to say horrid,
practices as domination, rape, and abandonment—is still susceptible
of modification, of expanding and demoting its currently dominant concern with truth and the present into multiple concerns with the past
(accessible, even to philosophy, only through unfaithful narratives) and
the future (opened up through demarcations). Such philosophy, which
I have elsewhere called "situating reason," would operate out of a temporality much like that explored and evinced by *Faith and the Good
Thing.* And in adopting such novelistic temporality, it would be taking up again the hydrological possibilities latent in but passed over by
Thales' original dictum. In this respect, philosophy would, for better or
worse, do anything but disappear. It would continue to permeate us as
it has always done, only we would know how it did so. In what may be
his most profound depiction of liquefied philosophy, its triumph, and
its overcoming (p. 47f), Johnson shows us how:

> She tipped her cauldron over; its contents oozed to the sloping floor and
> spread like something sentient out of the crooked shanty door, filling
> the swamp, choking spiny catfish and snails. . . . Around the shanty the
> swamp bubbled, and overflowed the borders of the bog and slid over the
> forests and hills of Hatten Country. . . . It covered the countryside, de-
> luged the cities; it covered the world. Billions were covered with the
> brew. And when they managed to smear it all off, they looked like her:
> the Swamp Woman. Their limbs had become gnarled oak sprouting yel-
> low boils, their flesh was as black as the ink of a squid. And all around
> the world people looked at each other, winked their clear yellow eyes
> evilly, and squealed in harmony: *"Hee hee!"*

Notes

1. It apparently was not: legendarily, the word *philosopher* was not coined
until Pythagoras; just what those activities are which distinguish the philosopher from other humans has never been satisfactorily specified.

2. G. W. F. Hegel. *Enzyklopädie der philosophischen Wissenschaften im
Grundrisse,* in Hegel, *Werke,* ed. Eva Modenhauer and Karl Markus Michel
(Frankfurt am Main: Suhrkamp, 1970–71), vol. 9, 284, and *Zusatz,* p. 140ff;
English translation in Hegel, *Hegel's Philosophy of Nature,* trans. A. V. Miller,
(Oxford: Clarendon Press, 1970), pp. 111ff.

3. Charles Johnson, *Being and Race: Black Writing since 1970* (Bloomington: Indiana University Press, 1988), pp. 19, 27.

4. Ibid., p. 26.

5. Ibid., p. 7.

6. Alexandre Kojève, *Introduction à la lecture de Hegel* (Paris: Gallimard,
1947).

7. Georges Bataille, "Hegel, Death, and Sacrifice," trans. Jonathan Strauss, *Yale French Studies* 78 (1990; special issued on Bataille), pp. 9–28.

8. Martin Heidegger, *Being and Time*, trans. John Macquarrie and Edward Robinson (New York: Harper & Row, 1962), p. 105f. The book discusses death (p. 349ff) only insofar as it is one's own, the possibility of which cuts one off from others.

9. The Greek language wears this on its face: "presence" (*'h paroysîa*) is compounded out of *par*—, meaning "by" or "at," and *'oysîa*, meaning "substance": presence is something that happens to a substance, namely that it finds itself "at" or "by" something else. There is thus no presence, in Greek, without substance. This is clear, for example, in Plato: *'oysîa* for him is of course the Forms, which alone are present or, indeed, "are" anything at all. Only they, in his standard parlance, can have "presence" with respect to anything else; see *Gorgias* 497c, *Republic* IV 437d, *Phaedo* 100d, and *Sophist* 247a; the latter specifically remarks that in order to be present, a thing must first wholly be (*pântvw 'einaî ti*).

10. Johnson, *Being and Race*, p. 14.

11. René Descartes, *Principles of Philosophy*, in *The Philosophical Works of Descartes*, trans. Elizabeth S. Haldane and G. R. T. Ross (Cambridge: Cambridge University Press, 1931), vol. 1, p. 227f.

12. Not in a narrative, because for Kant, who could never fully accord independent worth to beauty, narrative has only a subsidiary function in the good life; see "An Old Question Raised Again: Is the Human Race Constantly Progressing?" trans. Robert E. Anchor, in Immanuel Kant, *On History*, ed. Lewis White Beck (Indianapolis: Bobbs-Merrill, 1963), pp. 137–154.

13. Aristotle, *Metaphysics* II 994b8ff, VI 1021b21ff.

14. Heidegger, *Being and Time*, p. 317f.

15. Plato, *Republic* VI 509b.

16. John McCumber, *Poetic Interaction* (Chicago: University of Chicago Press, 1989); see esp. the General Introduction.

17. See Johnson, *Being and Race*, pp. 31f, 40.

18. See McCumber, *Poetic Interaction*, pp. 205–217, for this account of Aristotle.

19. Johnson, *Being and Race*, p. 31.

20. This formulation, given in the *Grundlegung der Metaphysik der Sitten*, can be found in the Berlin academy edition of Kant's works, vol. 4, p. 429.

Charles Johnson: Free at Last!
July 19, 1983

Stanley Crouch

Since most contemporary novels involving race are scandals of contrivance, unwheeled wagons hitched to cardboard horses, it's a particular pleasure to read Charles Johnson's *Oxherding Tale*. This is his second novel and, being a long ball past his first, *Faith and the Good Thing* (1974), it separates him even further from conventional sensibilities. In *Faith*, Johnson told the tall tale of a black girl's search for meaning— What is the good life? What is good?—and soaked it through with skills he had developed as a cartoonist, television writer, journalist, and student of philosophy. This time out, he has written a novel made important by his artful use of the slave narrative's structure to examine the narrator's developing consciousness, a consciousness that must painfully evaluate both the master and slave cultures.

The primary theme is freedom and the responsibility that comes with it. Given the time of the novel, 1838 to 1860, one would expect such a theme, but Johnson makes it clear in the most human—and often hilarious—terms that the question of freedom in a democratic society is essentially moral, and that social revolution pivots on an expanding redefinition of citizenry and its relationship to law. The adventure of escape only partially prepares Andrew Hawkins, the narrator, for the courage and commitment that come with moral comprehension. Andrew's growth is thrilling because Johnson skillfully avoids melodramatic platitudes while creating suspense and comedy, pathos and nostalgia. In the process, he invents a fresh set of variations on questions about race, sex, and freedom.

Though only 176 pages, *Oxherding Tale* is so rich that Johnson's contrapuntal developments of character and theme gain epic resonance. He expands his tale with adventures of style that span the work of Melville and Ellison, Twain and Bradbury, opting for everything from the facetious philosopical treatise to a variation on *The Illustrated Man*. Like a jazz musicians' high-handed use of harmony, Johnson's prose pivots between the language of the novel's time and terms from contemporary slang, regional vernacular, folklore, the blues, academia, and Madison Avenue. The technique recalls American film comedians' pushing the talk and attitudes of the day into period situations, lampooning the conventions of the past and the present. But Johnson is essentially a gallows humorist who manipulates microscopic realism to sober and control the reader's response, just as he takes narrative liberties to create an echoing, circular tension in which characters and dangers rhyme and contrast.

Johnson models his book on the work of Frederick Douglass, especially *Narrative of the Life of Frederick Douglass, An American Slave,* published in 1845. Douglass was an epic hero if there ever was one, and his work spans experience that moves from slavery to partial freedom to escape and eventual celebrity. His greatest importance to Johnson, however, is that he took Hawthorne's assault on New England hypocrisy south. In order to assert his humanity, Douglass questioned the Southern social order and everything that upheld it, from force to compliance, superstition to imposed illiteracy. He continually attacked the amoral sexual practices of the slaveholders and the distortions of American ideals caused by their defense of the chattel system. Douglass's native intelligence allowed for insights that only our finest novelists have been able to extend—the often dangerous nature of personal responsibility, the mutual infantilization of master and slave, the roles of religion and folklore, music and humor, risk and victory. In effect, Douglass is the figure who provides the moral passageway between Hawthorne and Melville and supplies the foundation for *Huckleberry Finn*.

By using Douglass's achievement as a model, Johnson perforates the lays of canvas-thick clichés that block our access to the human realities of American slavery. He also creates a successful metaphor for the 1960s, when black militants and intellectuals (students mostly) rejected Christianity and capitalism, and collided head-on with elements of black culture as basic as food (familial conflicts between emulation of Islam's disdain for pork and the hippie concern with health foods are symbolized by Andrew's embracing vegetarianism in imitation of his first white guru). The metaphor's impact comes from Johnson's sense of the play among history, cultural convention, and the assertion of identity in personal and ethnic terms.

Like Douglass, Andrew Hawkins is a mulatto. Unlike Douglass, he can pass for white, a fact that adds complexity to the moral choices he must make when he becomes a runaway. That fact also places him between what seem only two worlds but are actually many, and it adds the texture of an espionage tale in which "passing" is essential to suspense and victory. To thicken the plot, Johnson introduces a transcendentalist who supplies Andrew with a set of Eastern references and a pursuit of "The Whole"—though all systems of thought the hero encounters are satirized mercilessly. These devices allow Johnson to undercut Andrew's theorizing with concrete summonings of the worlds through which he passes—even inserting, as Melville might, a two-page treatise on the nature of slave narratives!

Johnson's ironic humor resounds at the novel's beginning as he pushes the master's wife into the position of slave woman by proxy. Just as "Benito Cereno" explained the behavior of slaves by reversing the situation, showing white men acting strangely—often "childlike"— because of their slaves' disguised rebellion, Johnson creates a bumbling Kingfish and a sullen, desexualized Sapphire in the master's house. As the novel opens, a drinking session is in progress. Jonathan Polkinghorne, master of Cripplegate, and his butler, George Hawkins, who is also his favorite slave, are indulging in a distinctly male camaraderie that seems to transcend their races and stations—each catches hell from his spouse when he comes home drunk. Literally inebriated with power, Jonathan proposes that they exchange wives for the evening in order to avoid static in the bedroom. George follows orders after the master makes it clear that he intends for them to be carried out.

Wobbling from the effects of wine and anticipation, George crosses the territory of *Invisible Man* and *The Odyssey*. In Ellison's novel, the narrator is upbraided and expelled from a Southern Negro college for following orders rather than pretending to, for not knowing he should give white people what they *want*, rather than what they ask for. George makes a parallel mistake and proves himself an even bigger fool by revealing his identity. As he makes love to Anna Polkinghorne in the darkness, she yowls with delight, calling him "Jonathan," but George can't resist telling her who's doing the satisfying, just as Odysseus couldn't resist shouting his name to the Cyclops. Like Odysseus, George is humbled by losing almost everything: as Anna swells, pregnant with George's child, his social position diminishes. He falls to the position of field hand—oxherd—outcast and laughing-stock of the slave quarters, given his come-uppance for ever having felt secure and superior to his fellow slaves. Though George's wife, Mattie, accepts Andrew as her own after Anna refuses to see him, she is forever fighting with George, a mad battle in which their mutual needs are persistently camouflaged by complaint and derision.

Faced with Anna's hatred of being treated like a slave—a beast of the field to whom mates can be assigned—Jonathan's explanation includes the popular justification for rape: "Anna, you wanted George, not me, to be there, didn't you?" Like Benito Cereno, Anna is forever changed by experiencing the other side of slavery and becomes a variation on the now standard black shrew who rejects her husband for what he has "let" happen to her. As if writing an improvisation on Cleaver's "Allegory of the Black Eunuch," Johnson describes her transformation:

> What had been a comfortable, cushiony marriage with only minor flare-ups, easily fixed by flowers or Anna's favorite chocolates, was now a truce with his wife denying him access to the common room, top floors, and dining area (he slept in his study); what was once a beautiful woman whose voice sang as lovely as any in this world when she sat at the black, boatlike piano in the parlor, one foot gently vibrating on the sostenuto pedal, was now an irascible old woman who haunted the place like a dead man demanding justice. . . .

Jonathan is estranged from Anna because of the immoral nature of the order he gave George, and because he is a victim of a system in which immoral power choices can also ricochet. George's problems with Mattie stem from something only he knows—that his action could be explained as the result of many things, including cowardice, but when he felt lust for Anna and rationalized his act as an expression of God's will, he was using the order for his own purposes, embracing the slaveholder's self-justifications, and was culpable. Just as Jonathan and George mirror and provide contrast to each other, so do Anna and Mattie. Anna rejects Andrew because he complicates her identity in a way she finds repulsive, while Mattie, however embittered, saves her outrage for the men responsible and loves the child. While Mattie becomes more contentious, Anna becomes a voluntary spinster whose desexualization by slavery will be echoed by Minty, Andrew's first love and the daughter of a womanizing mulatto slave. Minty is introduced with a naïve but fearful lyricism:

> . . . I saw her eyes—eyes green as icy mountain meltwater, with a hint of blue shadow and a drowse of sensuality that made her seem voluptuously sleepy, distant, as though she had been lifted long ago from a melancholy African landscape overrich with the colors and warm smells of autumn—a sad, out-of-season beauty suddenly precious to me because it was imperfect and perhaps illusory like moonlight on pond water, sensuously alive, but delivering itself over, as if in sacrifice, to inevitable slow death in the fields.

Minty is seen a few years later, after Andrew has escaped and is passing himself off as a white man at a slave auction.

> . . . I stood trying to recognize something of the girl at Cripplegate, in whom the world once chose to concretize its possibilities in the casements of her skin. . . . If you looked, without sentiment, you could see that her dress was too small and crawled up when she moved, flashing work-scorched stretches of skin and a latticework of whipmarks. Her belly pushed forward. From the cholesterol-high, nutritionless diet of the quarters, or a child, I could not tell. She was unlovely, drudgelike, sexless, the farm tool squeezed . . . for every ounce of surplus value, then put on

sale for whatever price she could bring. She was, like my stepmother, perhaps doubly denied—in both caste and gender—and driven to Christ (she wore a cross) as the only decent man who would have her.

The road to that hideous epiphany is a long one, taking Andrew through continual redefinitions of his identity and the nature of his surroundings. When Anna demands that Andrew be sent away because he symbolizes her humiliation, Jonathan refuses and makes provisions for his education. From Ezekiel William Sykes-Withers, Andrew gets a classical education expanded to include the teachings of the Eastern philosophers and mystics. Andrew embraces the idea of the universe as the Great Mother, becomes an intellectual fop, and makes pompous evaluations of the problems of man. Ezekiel, with his head ever in the clouds, and George, with his pushed into the earth, give Andrew anti-thetical perspectives experience will allow him to synthesize. George's bitterness at his fall from grace shapes an overview that defines anything connected with white people as bad:

> Too much imagination, he decided, was unwholesome. And white. If you were George Hawkins, you were coldly courteous to a Master who banished you to the bleakest life possible, a life spent among animals, away from the center of culture at Cripplegate; but wasn't his exile a blessing? Didn't it prove that whites were not, morally, Nature's last word on Man? They were, George swore after three fingers' worth of stump liquor—his eyes like torches—Devils or, worse, derived in some way he couldn't explain from Africans, who were a practical, down-to-earth people.

That homemade ethnic nationalism is the spiritual tragedy of Andrew's father, a man who sustains his hurt and sands down the universe to fit his disappointment: "Grief was the grillwork—the emotional grid—through which George Hawkins sifted and sorted events, simplified a world so overrich in sense it outstripped him. . . . " George had no knowledge of the threat that education and imagination posed.

Andrew's schooling will later make it possible for him to read and forge documents, to make language work for him, just as the slaves had made Christianity function as religion, self-expression, style, political editorial, and code of revolt. And because of his learning, Andrew, for all his naïveté, comes to realize he must ask for his freedom: "Consider the fact: Like a man who had fallen or been rudely flung into the world, I owned nothing. My knowledge, my clothes, my language, even, were shamefully second-hand, made by, and perhaps for, other men. . . . My argument was: Whatever my origin, I would be wholly responsible for the shape I gave myself in the future, for shirting myself handsomely with a new life that called me like a siren to possibilities that were real but forever out of reach."

The oblique references to Caliban and Odysseus are apt: the runaway slave that Andrew will soon become is a man whose knowledge must be used to free him from teachers as he looks for home—except that the home for which slaves felt nostalgia was more the dream of freedom than an actual place. But before Andrew chooses to pursue freedom in concrete geographical terms, he floats along in the philosophical clouds he shares with Ezekiel. Too mystical to trust sensuality, Ezekiel longs for a system that will explain everything and sends Karl Marx the money to visit America. Johnson brilliantly satirizes the relationship between a revolutionary's self-obsession and his theories: "As of late, political affairs affected Marx physically. When he felt a headcold coming on, a toothache, he looked immediately for its social cause. A new tax law had cost Marx a molar. Nearby at a button factory a strike that failed brought on an attack of asthma. These things were dialectical."

Marx's appearance signals Andrew's first awareness that ideas have human sources or targets; Marx, a jolly family man and sensualist, has as his credo. "Everything I've vritten has been for a voman—is *one* vay to view Socialism, no?" Marx's boredom inspires Andrew to look more closely at the stern Ezekiel: "Abruptly, I saw my tutor through his eyes: a lonely, unsocial creature unused to visitors, awkward with people as a recluse. Not a Socialist, as he fancied himself. No, his rejection of society, his radicalism, was not, as he thought, due to some rareness of the soul. It was stinginess. Resentment for the richness of things. A smoke screen for his own social shortcomings." What Andrew had thought the opposite of George's vision was substantially the same—a world view created out of bitterness. Yet Andrew, the pampered mulatto, has still to taste the sourness and terror of slavery, the black world beyond abstraction. His decision to ask for his freedom will bring him cheek to jowl with sexual decadence, drugs, and death.

Andrew's second white mentor is Flo Hatfield, a ruthless voluptuary on whose plantation Andrew expects to earn money that will buy freedom for George, Mattie, and Minty. Middle-aged and beautiful, Flo Hatfield has been infantilized by her power over others, but Johnson makes her as sympathetic as she is repulsive, self-obsessed, and petulant. Good at business and something of a feminist, Hatfield's resentment of male privilege becomes a justification for her appetites. She dresses her lovers, all of whom are slaves, as gigolos; when she tires of them, they're sent to work in her mines, where death is certain. Though she seems sexually free at first, a cosmopolitan upper-class white woman beyond the erotic provincialism of Negro women, she is actually so much a slave to sensation that Andrew's job as sexual servant results in addiction to opium, her favorite aphrodisiac. When Johnson writes that her lovers had "died and gone to Heaven, you might say," he is playing on the black dictum: "A colored man with a white woman is a Negro who has died and gone to heaven," but he is also creating a metaphor for the inevitable fall that follows the spiritual death of decadence.

No more than a tool of Hatfield's narcissism, Andrew falls for her hedonistic heaven when he strikes her in anger after she refuses to allow him to earn his freedom. Andrew is sent to the Yellow Dog Mine, where the landscape echoes Bessie Smith: "Wild country so tough the hootowls all sang bass." With him is Reb, his second father figure. En route, Andrew asserts his white features and they escape, pretending to be master and slave. In the process, they must outwit the Soul-catcher, Horace Bannon, a man who psychologically *becomes* a slave, then goes where slaves would hide. Bannon's technique is close to the one Reb preaches—a slave must learn exactly how masters think so that he can control their relationship as much as possible. Bannon is a psychopath whose "collage of features" suggests mixed ancestry and whose blood-lust is allowed free rein by the constant flight of slaves. Perhaps the greatest condemnation of the chattel system is that it instituted sadistic behavior for the maintenance of injustice. From Reb, Andrew learns what historian Forrest G. Wood meant when he said that what had been endured by the vast majority of Negro slaves exceeded the suffering of even the most oppressed white group. A captured African slave whose name has been changed twice by different masters, Reb is himself a harsh lesson in the stoicism born of tragedy. He no longer dreams of Africa, where Islam was as much an imposition of slavery as Christianity was in America. Reb faces his fate, raising his fists in his own way.

All that Andrew has learned, both intellectual and moral, is put to the test when he decides to marry a white woman—or she decides for him. Once Andrew enters that world, the theme of espionage, of assumed identity that allows for information about the opposition, also allows for a fantastic parody of the liberal wing of the town. One of the bridesmaids at Andrew's marriage comments, "*My* problem is that whenever someone gives me a quick feel in a crowded room, I wheel round, naturally, and slug him, then I realize he's Indian, black, or Mexican, and I feel simply dreadful for the rest of the day because I've hurt someone disadvantaged." From there, Johnson moves to a climax remarkable for its brutality and humbling tenderness; Andrew must dive into the briar patch of his identity and risk destruction in order to express his humanity.

That a work of such courage and compassion, virtuosity and intelligence, has been published by a university press is further proof that commercial houses have a very circumscribed notion of African-American writing. But then, any black writer who chooses human nature over platitudes, opportunism, or trends faces probable rejection. Charles Johnson has enriched contemporary American fiction as few young writers can, and it is difficult to imagine that such a talented artist will forever miss the big time that is equal to his gifts.

Johnson Revises Johnson

Oxherding Tale and
The Autobiography of an Ex-Coloured Man

Vera Kutzinski

A man's story is his gris-gris.
—Ishmael Reed, *Flight to Canada*

Autobiography is often called the most problematic of literary genres, if indeed it can be classified as a literary genre at all. That precarious status may well have made autobiography particularly attractive to Afro-American and other marginalized writers who, for obvious social and historical reasons, have had special stakes in questions of self-writing. But their interest cannot be justified on the grounds that autobiography offers greater possibilities for reliable self-knowledge than do other, es-tablished genres; it does not. On the contrary, since all autobiographies are, in some way, portraits of the writer as a reader, usually a young, inexperienced and thus unreliable reader, they draw attention precisely to their own unreliability and thus to their inherent instability as a cog-nitive paradigm. I am interested here particularly in so-called fictional autobiographies because they tend to emphasize that unreliability and instability to the point of making it a central theme. This is the case with both James Weldon Johnson's *The Autobiography of an Ex-Coloured Man* (1912 and 1927)[1] and Charles Johnson's recent *Oxherding Tale* (1984).

Both novels adopt the autobiographical form in order to tell us about the dangers of certain kinds of readings and explore the possibilities of others. Let me elaborate on this by drawing a by now perhaps familiar distinction between interpretation and reading: being literate enables us to interpret, to assign a particular meaning to a text; reading, in contrast, enables us to entertain the possibility of a variety of meanings or significances, to acknowledge the simultaneous existence of differing interpretations of the same text and thus the impossibility of reducing it to a single meaning. Reading, then, presupposes an awareness of form, of language as mediation. In this sense, reading is a special kind of literacy, an awareness of language, of linguistic/rhetorical relationships and their historical, cultural and social dimensions. Interpretation, on the other hand, is a form of illiteracy, of what Wilson Harris has called "illiterate imagination" (Harris, *Womb* 32). To give an example, Frederick Douglas's 1845 *Narrative* can be said to chronicle the movement from illiteracy to literacy, from an unawareness to an awareness of language, which, as we shall see in my comparison of *The Autobiography of an Ex-Coloured Man* and *Oxherding Tale*, is analogous to the movement from slavery to freedom.

In addition to sharing a common ancestor, the slave narrative, the two novels are also linked by a common theme, which distinguishes them both from the classic slave narrative and from other fictional performances of Afro-American autobiography such as Ralph Ellison's *Invisible Man* (1952), LeRoi Jones's *The System of Dante's Hell* (1965), Ernest Gaines's *The Autobiography of Miss Jane Pittman* (1971), Octavia E. Butler's *Kindred* (1979), David Bradley's *The Chaneysville Incident* (1981), or Alice Walker's *The Color Purple* (1982)[2]: that theme is "passing," which is closely linked to each novel's preoccupation with acts of reading, or better, misreading.[3] The lives of both narrator-protagonists, the Ex-Coloured Man and Andrew Hawkins, are characterized by a particular kind of illiteracy, that is, their actions revolve around misreadings of cultural signs and/or texts, including themselves. But whereas Andrew ultimately, almost in spite of himself, acquires the ability to read and gains his freedom (or "moksha," the title of the novel's final chapter), which, in turn, manifests itself in the way in which he shapes his autobiography, the Ex-Coloured Man remains imprisoned in illiteracy and thus, in a sense, enslaved.[4] His passing into another world, an internalization of the slave autobiographer's journey from the South to the North, is an endless odyssey: it leads nowhere. Each of his "passages" represents a preoccupation with surfaces: he defines the difference between freedom and slavery either in terms of a specific geographical location or in terms of external appearances, that is, skin color. According to Andrew Hawkins, the narrator-protagonist of *Oxherding Tale*, this mode of perception is the very essence of slavery:

> Although nearly anything you said about slavery could be denied in the same breath, this much struck me as true: the wretchedness of being colonized was not that slavery created feelings of guilt and indebtedness, though I did feel guilt and debt; nor that it created a long, lurid dream of multiplicity and separateness, which it did indeed create, but the fact that man had epidermalized Being. (*OT* 52)

To externalize freedom, to make it dependent either on geography or on physical appearance, is to validate that epidermalization of Being and thus to commit the same error, to be guilty of the same misreading of surfaces, as one's enslavers. Slavery, then, can be defined as a "way of seeing," specifically as *"seeing distinctions"* (*OT* 172).

This mode of perception is characteristic of the Ex-Coloured Man and symptomatic of his illiteracy, which can be more specifically defined as a denial of history. Robert Stepto has described the Ex-Coloured Man as a "seer of surfaces . . . : When he sees a mule stuck in the mud road or a terrified black man burning while chained to a post, he can identify with the victim but not see *through* the victim—even in retrospect—to the underlying historical and racial tropes" (Stepto, *Veil* 116–117). The point, however, is not that the Ex-Coloured Man cannot see through the surface, but that he *misreads* the surface itself. He is unaware that the surface itself can be read, that what appears to be surface is already composed of layers of meaning; in short, that inside and outside are inseparable. This is precisely why he can call *Uncle Tom's Cabin* "a fair and truthful panorama of slavery" (*A* 42) and why he never once sees himself as black, not even in the highly specular moment of self-examination prompted by the racist slurs of his fellow pupils:

> I noticed the ivory whiteness of my skin, the beauty of my mouth, the size and liquid darkness of my eyes, and how the long black lashes that fringed and shaded them produced an effect that was strangely fascinating even to me. I noticed the softness and glossiness of my dark hair that fell in waves over my temples, making my forehead appear lighter than it really was. (*A* 17)

He sees himself as an image without being able to read that image: he does not realize that the whiteness of the image has traces of blackness, "shades" and "fringes." Without understanding that inside and outside are but aspects of the same thing and that the inside can be traced on the surface, he has no way of recognizing that he cannot lock away his inner life as he can lock away his old manuscripts in a box and place them at a safe distance.

The real tragedy of the Ex-Coloured Man's life is that he is imprisoned by his own erroneous definition of freedom, which is a direct result of his inability to comprehend the nature of surfaces. For him, surfaces are masks that hide the inside instead of revealing it. He does not understand the intricate entwining of inside and outside, their meshing in language. This is why we as readers can see on the surface of his present autobiographical discourse traces of the hidden manuscript pages to which he himself is blind. Perhaps most indicative of the Ex-Coloured Man's misreadings is the seemingly innocuous childhood incident he describes at the beginning of his narrative:

> At times I can close my eyes and call up in a dreamlike way things that seem to have happened ages ago in some other world. I can see in this half vision a little house . . . I can remember that flowers grew in the front yard, and that around each flower bed was a hedge of varicolored glass bottles stuck in the ground neck down. I remember that once, while play-

ing around in the sand, I became curious to know whether or not the bottles grew as the flowers did, and I proceeded to dig them up to find out; the investigation brought me a terrific spanking, which indelibly fixed the incident in my mind. (*A* 4)

As Stepto has suggested, the digging up of the bottles constitutes "an innocent yet devastating act of assault upon a considerable portion of his heritage," which prefigures the Ex-Coloured Man's "misdirected attempts to approach, let alone embrace, black American culture" (Stepto, *Veil* 100–101). Important here is that the Ex-Coloured Man cannot see the surface as a pattern to be read, so that he attempts to find meaning by "digging," by penetrating the surface, which of course destroys the pattern. As a result of dismantling this "text," an image of kin that represents his cultural history and an important part of his identity, he is displaced, exiled from his origins. The fact that he still does not understand the tropological significance of this childhood incident even as he narrates it indicates that his exile is indeed a permanent condition.

The Ex-Coloured Man does not understand that all lives carry within them indelible traces of other lives, and that these traces must be deciphered, because in comprehending the ever-shifting patterns they constitute lies the key to one's identity. The young Andrew Hawkins reveals a similar kind of incomprehension or illiteracy when he comments on his future life:

> Like a man who had fallen or been rudely flung into the world, I owned nothing. My knowledge, my clothes, my language, even, were shamefully second-hand, made by, and perhaps for, other men. I was living a lie, that was the heart of it. My argument was: Whatever my origin, I would be wholly responsible for the shape I gave myself in the future, for shirting myself handsomely with a new life that called me like a siren to possibilities that were real but forever out of reach. (*OT* 16–17)

These remarks anticipate Andrew's later attempts to escape not only slavery but his origins as embodied in his father, George Hawkins, by passing for white, changing his name to William Harris and even inventing a new history for himself.

Interestingly enough, the major turning point in his new life is brought about by an act of misreading. What he misreads is a present sent to him by Horace Bannon, the Soulcatcher ("Shiva's hitman," *OT* 147), whose presence in the novel ironically serves as a constant reminder of the origins Andrew is trying to erase. Bannon's present is a ring that belonged to another ex-slave, Reb the Coffinmaker, who, unlike Andrew, completed the traditional journey to the North on which they had embarked together.

> Onto the table clattered a dull ring (orichalc) that twirled on its side, then clinked against the candlestand. A trinket that from time out of mind was the ornament of the Allmuseri *osuo*. Metal worked painfully,

like scarification, into the skin during infancy and, like skin, was im-
pleached until cartilage and metal melted back into a common field.
(*OT* 148)

Particularly interesting about this description is the comparison of metal
and skin, which is suggestive in a number of ways. On the one hand,
"metal worked painfully . . . into the skin" evokes images of slavery and
bondage (the ring as chain), in which case the shedding of the ring
would be a rather conventional figure of liberation. On the other hand,
however, the ring, as much a part of Reb as his skin, is already a representation of freedom, a synecdoche of Reb's psychological and intellectual independence, which is derived precisely from his awareness of
being part of a tradition, of embodying that tradition to the point of
being able to divest himself of its external trappings. The ring represents
the almost alchemical impleachment of cartilage and metal, of organic
and inorganic substances, of subject and object, of inside and outside,
of individual self and community. The ring is like skin, a piece of parchment that can be read. Andrew, however, interprets it as a sign of Reb's
death and thus as a signal that the Soulcatcher has now begun his hunt
for him. He is unaware of the ring's tropological complexities because
he lacks a sense of history. One is reminded here of Michael Harper's
dictum that "where there is no history, there is no metaphor" (Harper,
Images 70). Similarly, one might add, without a sense of history, there
is no reading, only interpretation, or misreading.

   An intriguing feature of *Oxherding Tale*, something that underscores
its fictionality, is the explicit counterpoint between the voice of the
narrator-protagonist and another authorial voice that twice interrupts
Andrew's narrative to comment on it. This counterpoint is important
not only because it signals the extreme self-consciousness of Johnson's
writing, but because it identifies Andrew's perception of himself, his
new life and his relation to the other characters as misreadings. (The
only, but much less obvious, equivalents to this in *The Autobiography of
an Ex-Coloured Man* are the traces of previous texts, such as DuBois's
The Souls of Black Folk, that suggest the presence of an authorial consciousness other than the narrator's.[5]) Charles Johnson reminds us, as
he digresses to meditate on the nature of slave narratives, that "no form
. . . *loses* its ancestry; rather, these meanings accumulate in layers of
tissue as the form [in this case, the slave narrative] evolves" (*OT* 119).
This definition of (literary) ancestry as accumulation of meaning in
layers of tissue connects with a later comment on "The Manumission
of First-Person Viewpoint," where the Self, the perceiving Subject,
is described as "a palimpsest, interwoven with everything—literally
everything—that can be thought or felt" (*OT* 152). In other words, the
authorial Self, the first-person narrator, is a text that is made up of traces
of previous inscriptions, traces of its ancestry, its history, that accumulate like layers of tissue. In this sense, the narrating self is "less a reporter

than an opening through which the world is delivered: first person (if you wish) universal" (*OT* 153).

Reb's ring is such a palimpsest only Andrew does not see the traces, the accumulated layers of meaning, at least not yet. It is not until he is confronted, at the end of the novel, with Horace Bannon's tattoo, the quintessential palimpsest already prefigured by Reb's ring, that Andrew learns to read and, in doing so, to face his past instead of continuing to efface it. The following is a description of this tattoo which Bannon exposes in reply to Andrew's question about George Hawkins, his dead father, who has, in the meantime, been murdered by the Soulcatcher:

> I waited for the Soulcatcher's explanation, my gaze dropping from his face to his chest and forearms, where the intricately woven tattoos presented, in the brilliance of a silver-gray sky at dawn, an impossible flesh-tapestry of a thousand individualities no longer static, mere drawings, but if you looked at them long enough, bodies moving like Lilliputians over the surface of his skin. Not tattooes at all, I saw, but forms sardined in his contour, creatures Bannon had killed since childhood: spineless insects, flies he'd dewinged; yet even the tiniest of these thrashing within the body mosaic was, clearly, a society as complex as the higher forms, a concrescence of molecules cells atoms in concert, for nothing in the necropolis he'd filled stood alone, . . . , and . . . the profound mystery of the One and the Many gave me back my father again and again, his love, in every being, from grubworms to giant sumacs, for these too were my father and, in the final face I saw in the Soulcatcher, which shook tears from me—my own face, for he had duplicated portions of me during the early days of the hunt—I was my father's father, and he my child. (*OT* 175–76)

At this point Andrew realizes that he is indeed an opening through which the world, that is, history, is revealed: he sees himself as his father's father, and by implication as his own father. This insight, produced by the reading of the tattoo which shows him that "all is conserved; all" (*OT* 176), makes it possible for him to see autobiography not as an image of self, but as an image of kin, or, as de Man has suggested, a figure of reading.[6] To signal this change (in addition to the pleonastic proliferation of images in the above passage), Andrew starts his autobiography with a story told to him by his father, a radical break with a convention fostered by the slave narrative due to his peculiar historical context: the inscription of an absence, a lack of information about one's origins, one's history. The origin Andrew inscribes is still illegitimate in that it does not conform to traditional genealogical patterns—he is the illegitimate son of a black man and a white woman, yet another break with (literary and social) convention—but it is not so because he lacks information about his family, especially about his father. By inscribing his father's history, Andrew redeems, and legitimates, his history as well as redeems autobiography from the charge of *self*-indulgence. He reveals identity, selfhood, to be a function of kinship, not a function of "the private, egotistic interests that normally colored my vision" (*OT* 172). To inscribe one's Self is to efface it in the process of writing history, to realize that self and history are as inseparable as inside and outside, that in fact the self can only become a text once it reads, and reinscribes, the traces that are already part of its (sur)face. Freedom, then, is the ability to perform that kind of reading, one that acknowledges history instead of anxiously attempting to deny it. The tragedy of such a denial is revealed in the Ex-Coloured Man's story, a story of permanent exile encapsulated in his inability even to articulate the word "father." Unable to affirm his forefathers, biological and cultural, the Ex-Coloured Man is reduced, in his own mind, to what Ralph Ellison has called "a white man's inadequate . . . conception of human complexity" (Ellison, *Territory* 287).

I have shown earlier that the theme of passing in each novel is closely linked with certain acts of misreading. To pass for white is to submit oneself to an inadequate conception of human complexity, to misunderstand, in the sense of taking literally, the relationship between skin and kin. According to Charles Johnson, skin color (or the lack thereof) does not by itself function as an image of kin. What creates kinship, and thus selfhood, is the ability to read skin, to perceive it as a parchment, a palimpsest, as a text already inscribed with the traces of its history. To become literate, then, is to be able to see that the relationship between skin and kin is neither direct nor "natural" but always mediated by language. It is an ideological construct that simplifies human relations in order to construct social barriers and justify oppression. For the Afro-American writer (or any writer, for that matter) not to realize that skin color, in this case, blackness, is a trope, a figure of substitution that encodes social relations rather than representing a cultural essence or commodity, is to reenact the Ex-Coloured Man's fatal error. Autobiography, then, is indeed an act of (self-)reading, one that challenges closure and totalization and, in doing so, calls into question our entire system of generic (as well as social and racial) classification. To attempt to turn autobiography, in this case Afro-American autobiography, into a genre, a closed system, is to ignore this radical openness in favor of upholding categories that are ultimately as limiting, as oppressive and as devoid of human complexity as the literal substitution of skin color for kinship and tradition.

What both James Weldon Johnson and Charles Johnson endeavor in their respective novels is to scrutinize the tropology of literacy and self-writing, and with it the socio-cultural processes through which identity is negotiated. Their narrator-protagonists' act of misreading have important implications for our own practice of reading, not to mention our beliefs in the efficacy and truth-value of existing cognitive modes, literary and otherwise. In particular, they force us to take a closer look at

the complex and highly ambiguous relationship between literacy, freedom, and identity. What we come to realize is that not all forms and
practices of literacy necessarily lead to freedom, at least not as long as
freedom, much like identity, continues to be sought exclusively in essential definitions (of race *and* of gender) rather than in socially negotiated relations. In this respect, George Hawkins's parting words to his
"changeling" son also directly concern the contemporary reader of *Oxherding Tale* and other Afro-American texts, who, regardless of his or
her skin color and/or racial origins, may well share Andrew's peculiar
predicament: "Be y'self . . . That's all I'm askin'. . . ." (*OT* 35).

Notes

1. The 1912 edition was published anonymously.
2. I am excluding from this list other "modern" slave narratives such as
Margaret Walker's *Jubilee* (1965), Ishmael Reed's *Flight to Canada* (1976), and
Shirley Anne Williams's *Dessa Rose* (1986) since they do not employ first-person
narrative. It should, however, be acknowledged that *Oxherding Tale* appears to
be greatly indebted to Reed's satirical novel in other ways.
3. Similar concerns can be found in other novels that dramatize "passing,"
from William Wells Brown, Frances Harper, and Charles Chesnutt to Jessie
Fauset and Nella Larsen. But in none of those texts does the thematic preoccupation with the boundaries of selfhood and identity find distinct formal reso-
nances.
4. Werner Sollors has argued that the figure of the successful musician in
The Autobiography of an Ex-Coloured Man embodies a possible resolution of
the conflict between consent and descent, that a fusion or synthesis of these
two sets of social/cultural relations and their accompanying conscriptions of
identity "is seen possible in the process of aesthetic creation, which the [novel
itself] represents but which [its narrator] abandoned" (*Beyond Ethnicity* 172–
173). What Sollors does not consider, however, is that the musical trope of
harmony or *harmonization* also locates identity and self-knowledge in an aesthetic creation *outside* of the text and, in fact, outside of literature.
5. See Stepto, *Veil* 111–114. Sollors describes the Ex-Coloured Man as
James Weldon Johnson's ironically inverted anti-self, whose dreams of what he
should have been have been clearly point in the direction of his creator's real life (*Beyond
Ethnicity* 171). In the case of *Oxherding Tale,* however, no such simple inversion
would explain the relationship between narrator and author.
6. Paul de Man explains: "Autobiography . . . is not a genre or a mode, but
a figure of reading or of understanding that occurs, to some degree, in all texts.
The autobiographical moment happens as an alignment between two subjects
involved in the process of reading in which they determine each other by mutual
reflexive substitutions. . . . The difficulties of generic definition that affect the
study of autobiography repeat an inherent instability that undoes the model as
soon as it is established. . . . The interest of autobiography, then is . . . that it
demonstrates in a striking way the impossibility of closure and of totalization
(that is the impossibility of coming into being) of all textual systems made up
of tropological substitutions" ("Autobiography" 70–71).

Works Cited

de Man, Paul. "Autobiography as De-facement." *The Rhetoric of Romanticism.* New York: Columbia UP, 1984.

Ellison, Ralph. "A Very Stern Discipline." *Going to the Territory.* New York: Random, 1986.

Harper, Michael. *Images of Kin.* Urbana: Illinois UP, 1977.

Harris, Wilson. *The Womb of Space: The Cross-Cultural Imagination.* Westport, CT: Greenwood, 1983.

Johnson, Charles. *Oxherding Tale.* New York: Grove, 1984.

Johnson, James Weldon. *The Autobiography of an Ex-Coloured Man.* New York: Hill and Wang, 1960.

Sollors, Werner. *Beyond Ethnicity: Consent and Descent in American Culture.* New York: Oxford UP, 1986.

Stepto, Robert B. *From Behind the Veil: A Study of Afro-American Narrative.* Urbana: Illinois UP, 1979.

Wrestling with Desire
Slavery and Black Masculinity
in Charles Johnson's *Oxherding Tale*

Jeffrey B. Leak

In 1970 Toni Morrison published her first novel, *The Bluest Eye*, and Alice Walker published her first novel, *The Third Life of Grange Copeland*. In the next decade, Walker won the Pulitzer Prize for *The Color Purple* (1982) and Morrison received the same honor for *Beloved* (1987). Thus the freedom struggle of the 1960s has in some ways necessitated the fictional exploration of black female experience in the second half of this century. As the second wave of the modern feminist movement has taken hold, black women have prompted us to explore gender in all of its ambiguity and complexity. Indeed, as William L. Andrews reminds us, "the much-celebrated renaissance of Black American women's writing that has taken place in the 1980s may be read as testimony to a continuing and vital discourse about the meaning of gender and the nature of male and female roles in African American culture and society."[1]

Given the ways in which black women novelists are exploring the "meaning of gender," we must analyze gender identity and its constructions in the fiction written by black men. As scholar and novelist Sherley Anne Williams asserts, "in order to understand that problem [gender relations] more fully, we must turn to what black men have written about themselves."[2] In this vein, Charles Johnson's second and most ambitious historical novel, *Oxherding Tale* (1982), which unfolds in the antebellum South, represents a thematic and technical innovation crucial to the ongoing dialogue on gender in the African American novel.[3]

As the fiction of novelists such as Zora Neale Hurston, Alice Walker, and Toni Morrison illuminates the experiences of black women, in *Oxherding Tale* Johnson illuminates the dilemmas and possibilities of black male experience within the context of American slavery and freedom.[4]

In the case of Andrew Hawkins, the narrator and protagonist in *Oxherding Tale*, I am interested in his masculinity, in what French feminist theorist Elisabeth Badinter refers to as the "quality of a man."[5] While there are many themes and philosophical concerns in *Oxherding Tale*, the principal concern, the one that directs the narrative, revolves around what Andrew Hawkins refers to as a "crisis in the male spirit" (28). The early reviews of *Oxherding Tale* focused on its postmodern sensibility and its numerous philosophical allusions, and in most instances downplayed the question of gender that lies at the heart of this novel. In his laudatory review of the novel, Stanley Crouch does state that Johnson "invents a fresh set of variations on race, sex, and freedom."[6] But even more specifically, Andrew reveals to us the fact that he feels compelled "to know, in this age of sexual warfare, [his] heart, make it [his] meditation, and be forever creating some meaning for what it [means] to be male, though with what real satisfaction, and with how much resemblance to the promise of [his] gender, [he does] not know" (28).

As Andrew ponders his position as a black male of biracial ancestry in the antebellum South, he gives voice to certain issues and questions of gender identity. He seeks, in his words, to create "some meaning for what it means to be male" (28), though uncertain as to how his maleness relates to his gender. Through his first-person narrative, Andrew provides us with a meditation on the tenuous relationship between black masculinity and desire. In Andrew, his father, George Hawkins, his tutor, Ezekiel Sykes-Withers, and the Coffinmaker Reb, we find black men who engage desire in antagonistic terms within the context of bondage. This antagonistic engagement of desire has roots in the debilitating dynamics of slave experience and the complexity of gender identity. One must ask, then, what is the relationship between the body and the performance of the body? How does one's sex or biology influence the formation of one's gender, as well as one's attitude toward desire? How is the question of desire and identity resolved for men, both black and white, within the framework of slavery? These and other related questions have an immediate relevance in terms of contemporary gender studies, as well as for the male figures in Johnson's fictional slave narrative.

Judith Butler, in her work on the materiality of the body, theorizes more broadly about the gender issues which are the subject of Andrew's meditation. Race does not figure prominently in her analysis, but the way in which she distinguishes between sex and gender will clarify and further problematize Andrew's racial and gender identity:

The category of "sex" is, from the start, normative, it is what Foucault has called a "regulating ideal." In this sense, then, "sex" not only functions as a norm, but is a part of a regulating practice that produces the bodies it governs, that is, whose regulatory force is made clear as a kind of productive power, the power to produce—demarcate, circulate, differentiate—the bodies it controls. Thus "sex" is a regulating ideal whose materialization is compelled, and this materialization takes place (or fails to take place) through certain highly regulated practices. In other words, "sex" is an ideal construct which is forcibly materialized through time. It is not a simple fact or static condition of a body, but a process whereby regulating norms materialize "sex" and achieve this materialization through a forcible reiteration of those norms. That this reiteration is necessary is a sign that materialization is never quite complete, that bodies never quite comply with the norms by which their materialization is impelled.[7]

If I understand Butler correctly, sex has to do with the designations male and female, and these designations are determined by anatomical realities and differences. Thus one inherits a "regulating ideal" or a socially constructed gender narrative in relation to one's sex. With Andrew, we must discern the degree to which the realization of gender is compelled or resisted in relation to the "regulating ideal of sex" (2). To complicate matters further, just as social constructions of "sex" serve as a "regulating ideal" (2), so too do social constructions of race.

Oxherding Tale begins with Andrew's recollection of his origins, establishing from the start his relationship with his father. "Long ago my father and I were servants at Cripplegate," he reveals, "a cotton plantation in South Carolina" (3). The way in which Andrew enters the world is but one of many moments where we witness Johnson writing against the grain, that is, in contrast to the conventions of the slave narrative. One night master Polkinghorne and his house-slave George Hawkins are enjoying home-brewed beer on the front porch. When inebriation sets in, neither wishes to return to his respective abode to face his prudish and pious wife, respectively, the mistress Anna Polkinghorne or the slave woman Mattie. At the command of the Master, the two men switch places—that is, exchange wives for the evening. The net result of this female commodity exchange is Andrew having been born to Anna Polkinghorne, the plantation mistress, who in her outrage never acknowledges him as her child.

Unlike most slave narratives in which the narrator has a slave mother and a white father, Andrew has a slave father, George Hawkins, and a white mother who denies their maternal relationship. Moreover, according to nineteenth-century law, the child of a master-slave sexual encounter would inherit the social and legal condition of the mother. Legally speaking, Andrew should be free, but blackness in either its literal or figurative manifestation makes even the law subject to unfair and racialized mutations. This scenario and others characterizing Andrew's movement from slavery to freedom contribute to the novel's unconventional character.

From the beginning of his tale, we know that Andrew values his relationship with his father, George Hawkins. Having impregnated the plantation mistress, Hawkins suffers the ultimate descent in the slave community. Now relegated to the status of a field slave who functions as a "shepherd of oxen and sheep" (7), Hawkins has plenty of time to lament his expulsion from the relatively privileged confines of the plantation house. Keenly aware of his father's dubious status and of the complex relationship between physical and psychic liberation, Andrew petitions Master Polkinghorne for the chance to purchase freedom for his family and his beloved Minty, a slave girl.

In response to Andrew's bold but naive request, Master Polkinghorne feigns acquiescence. With a letter addressed to Flo Hatfield, mistress of the plantation Leviathan, the adolescent slave Andrew begins his journey toward freedom.[8] Unaware of the sexual exploitation that awaits him, he proceeds to Leviathan with his father. As they embark on their journey, he contemplates the generational differences between himself and his father. Unlike his naive son, Hawkins is acutely aware of Flo Hatfield's deadly reputation: "I don't spect to see you again 'til Judgment Day" (20). He then seeks assurance from his ivory- complexioned son that he will not commit what he perceives to be the ultimate sin—passing into the white world. Notwithstanding the shaping realities of slavery, for the elder Hawkins racial identity is the primary component governing his world. Accepting the binary conception of race, he is a nineteenth-century black nationalist, one for whom intellectual engagement and whiteness are synonymous. Moreover, Hawkins would have Andrew define himself within a chronic racial binary which denies the white or European part of Andrew's ancestry.

Indifferent to Andrew's biracial ancestry, an ancestry for which he is half responsible, his father implores him to clad himself in the cloak of the "Race Man" (21). This racial cloak signifies allegiance to the race, despite multiple racial and cultural points of origin. For Hawkins, all thought and actions become racialized with no possibility for realization outside the racialized epidermis. Then, in a gesture which reveals the absurd logic of his racial chauvinism, Hawkins admonishes his son to "be y'self" (21). Ironically, in order for Andrew to be himself, he must claim that part of himself which his father refuses to acknowledge. This racial ideology denies the existence and possibilities of a hybrid identity. As Andrew reflects upon his father's ideological position, he realizes that

> I wanted my father's approval—I did, in fact, clomp along in his boots when I was a child, but he was so bitter. And his obsession with the world historical mission of Africa? I didn't want this obligation! How strange that my father, the skillful, shrewd, funny, and wisest butler at

Cripplegate—so faithful on the surface, that he was even permitted to keep a shotgun before the Fall, and still had it—was beneath his mask of good humor and harmlessness a flinty old Race Man who wouldn't cook, wouldn't clean, who left his bedpans unemptied, who loosened his belt after my stepmother's meals, broke wind loudly, and, as often as not, fell asleep in the middle of her conversations. (21–22).

For Hawkins, one's manhood is rooted in racial loyalty, a loyalty which dictates that men of African descent must embrace a racially exclusive form of identity. Thus manhood, even for his biracial son, should constitute allegiance to the "world historical mission of Africa" (21). Although Africa is a continent with a plurality of cultures, Hawkins views it and his racial identity monolithically. This mythic homeland, one which to our knowledge neither father nor son has seen, is where the enslaved African man can reclaim his lost paternalism.

Clearly, Hawkins's definition of manhood is characterized by a certain rigidity in racial and gender terms. In contrast, his son adopts a more fluid species of male identity. As readers, we must be mindful of the ways in which traditional notions of European American manhood have influenced historical and fictional constructions of black manhood. Traditionally, European American manhood has focused on a historical notion of citizenship which is predicated on the figurative and literal emasculation of African American men. Black film scholar Ed Guerrero reminds us of the "contradictions" which attend the realization of black manhood:

One must also consider the social contradiction and hoax inflicted on black men, which originates in the very definitions of self-worth and manhood in our society. It has come to be a cruel joke that in a culture driven by media fantasies of sex, violence, and power; a culture where material wealth is the highest measure of self-worth; a culture that defines "manhood" by the ability to provide economic survival for one's self and family—in this culture, the very means of achieving "manhood" are systemically and institutionally kept out of the grasp of all too many black men.[9]

Given the complex legacy of slavery and the historical emasculation of black men, the ability to achieve "material wealth" and thus "manhood" is a highly complex, though not impossible, proposition. Moreover, while black men have attempted historically to conform to the prevailing model of white manhood, there are certain ways in which they are distinctly different from their white counterparts. According to Sherley Anne Williams, in terms of black literary and autobiographical texts, the "black male patriarch in the nineteenth century has more to do with providing for and protecting his 'dependents' than with wielding authority or exploiting their dependency so as to achieve his own privilege."[10]

White manhood, in other words, has been constructed historically in relation to material wealth and property, but the claim to manhood of which every white man could boast—from white peasants to plantation owners—originates in the epidermis. As historian Bertram Wyatt-Brown reveals, white manhood in the antebellum South was rooted in a fallacious but nonetheless unequivocal notion of whiteness:

> In early colonial America, few could boast of exalted station. Even thereafter, by European standards, the great Southern families could not claim to belong to the nobility, as distinct from the gentry class. . . . From first to last, there was the honor of having a white skin—what one historian has called "herrenvolk democracy," the fraternity of all whites against all blacks. Its importance never ceased, and even grew in strength as other forms of privilege fell away.[11]

Thus black male identity has been forged historically within a cauldron of whiteness. In addition, from a social and political perspective, black manhood has been achieved in approximate terms; for the ultimate litmus test of manhood in the dominant culture has been that of having white skin. Unlike black women, who, as a result of racism and sexism, have been compelled to define themselves in relation to the private sphere, black men have sought an affirmation of identity through institutional affiliations that would create a space for them in the public sphere.

While material well-being and whiteness inform the construction of manhood in the nineteenth century, it would be remiss to focus solely on these particular aspects of male identity, for material wealth and racial composition are but two of the numerous factors that inform masculine development. Andrew's use of the term *gender* (28) connotes a more expansive notion of black male identity, one that moves beyond the traditional criteria of manhood. Such a discursive gesture was unavailable to historical slave narrators such as Frederick Douglass. In other words, the very language Andrew employs to articulate his thoughts is postmodern in sensibility, reminding the reader of the rhetorical limits of nineteenth-century racial and gender discourse.

The difference between Hawkins and Andrew is that the son possesses a greater capacity for self-critique which enables him to examine critically his father's preoccupation with racial binaries and his own tendency to evade desire through intellectual posturing: "For men of my [Andrew's] period the dream of contributing to the Race, of Great Sacrifice and glory, drew us back from desire. We wanted to do something difficult—see?—like tame the West, spearhead a Revolution, or pin the universe down like a butterfly on the pages of a book" (43). Operating at times with a sparse understanding of social reality, Andrew observes in his father a context for living that is confined by race. Hawkins's racial ideology leads him to be "suspicious of pleasure as a final cause" (43), preventing him from engaging the world in its totality.

Ironically, the elder Hawkins uses race to remove himself from the world. In his view, one's identity is rooted in race which begs the question: does race determine one's capacity to fully engage the world, or is race but one of many factors that contribute to the formation of identity within the world? Andrew, an enslaved adolescent, engages this question, one which his father is incapable of engaging.

This interrogation of his father's dubious race and gender philosophy reaches its apex during a deer hunt. Furious with his wife, Mattie, for having imposed a vegetarian diet on the family, Hawkins is determined to eat, to kill, meat: "Death in the form of George Hawkins tracked down a deer and dropped it" (26). Emotionally and physically fatigued, Hawkins orders Andrew to skin the deer. As Andrew adheres to his father's instructions, he recalls a conversation between himself and his eccentric tutor, Ezekiel Sykes-Withers, regarding the merits of vegetarianism. In this conversation, they discuss the nature and origin of violence. This recollection causes Andrew to reconsider his actions during the deer hunt:

> What if all Ezekiel's talk about how poleaxing preceded porkchops was saying that violence of the shotgun blast, the instant before the final explosion of dust, stayed sealed inside like a particle, trapped in the dying tissues, and wound up on the dinner table—as if everything was mysteriously blended into everything else, and somehow all the violence wars slavery crime and suffering in the world had, as Ezekiel suggested, its beginning in what went into our bellies? (27)

With this ontological question flooding his mind and tears in his eyes, Andrew implores his father to dress the deer, lamenting, "It's all wrong" (27). For Hawkins this tearful retort constitutes the ultimate rejection, for in this refusal Andrew forsakes his father's restrictive form of manhood. In Hawkins's view, Andrew's refutation of violence and affirmation of vegetarianism signifies an allegiance to Mattie and Ezekiel, the black woman and white man—both of whom, in terms of Hawkins's narrow constructions of race and gender, seek to emasculate the black man. Unable to interpret an action or person in its singularity, Hawkins feels betrayed by Andrew, who aligns himself with the very forces that, in his mind, seek to annihilate him.

Thus Hawkins's precocious son correctly concludes that his father suffers from racial paranoia, an affliction which according to Andrew "simplified a world so overrich in sense it outstripped him, and all that was necessary to break this spell of hatred, this self-inflicted segregation from the Whole, was to acknowledge, once and for all, that what he allowed to be determinant for his life depended on himself and no one else" (142). Such a posture would transform the world of Hawkins from that of comfortable stagnation rooted in chronic racial binaries to possibilities predicated on individual initiative. The onus for transformation, moreover, lies with the individual, in this case the African American male. In this moment we find crystallized an exploration of the generational conflicts between African American men.

By creating such a complicated relationship between Andrew and his father, Johnson departs from Douglass and other slave narrators who could not explore—given the conventions of the slave narrative—the historical conflicts and relations between enslaved fathers and sons. Indeed, this intergenerational conflict is a prominent feature in African American men's autobiographies. David L. Dudley informs us that an "autobiographer seeking to displace an older writer whom he sees as a father figure wrestles not only with making his own artistic space but also with his identity in relation to the literary and cultural tradition in which he lives and writes."[12]

While Dudley's comments relate to autobiography and figurative father-son relationships, his observations are applicable, with certain amendments, to actual and fictional father-son relationships. Andrew seeks a space in which he can exist absent his father's narrow definition of racial identity, one in which he does not feel compelled to deny the white or any other part of himself. He seeks an identity in which the myriad elements of his person may be integrated, elements which include his biracial heritage but which also include intellectual and spiritual freedom, states of being that, in theory at least, transcend narrow definitions of race and gender.

Moreover, Andrew does not simply refute the figure of the "Race Man" (21) as embodied by his father; he seeks to remove himself from a cycle in which African American men serve as a metonym for violence. As heroic as Frederick Douglass emerges after his battle with the slave-breaker Edward Covey (one in which he acts in self-defense), part of Douglass's self-fashioned image is rooted in a certain bravado or machismo which reinscribes more conventional attributes of male identity such as physical prowess. As Douglass's figurative heir, the adolescent Hawkins seeks to refute any construction of male identity rooted in violent action. For Andrew, his sense of masculinity emerges from a number of overlapping spheres and intellectual traditions: the world of the slave, the world of the master, and the Asian and Continental philosophies introduced to him by his tutor, Ezekiel. Andrew's broad intellectual training and experiences enable him to imagine black masculinity in terms of possibilities rather than negations. Unlike his father, he refuses to be governed by static notions of identity.

The "crisis in the male spirit" (28) that emerges in the slave George Hawkins manifests itself in other ways in men of European descent. In Andrew's tutor, Ezekiel Sykes-Withers, we have a European American man who also stands in conflict with his gender. Seemingly destined to a life of emotional sterility, Ezekiel, much like his student, has inherited a dubious legacy of manhood from his father. Shortly after his arrival at Cripplegate, we learn that Ezekiel, whose sole aim in life is to fathom "how the heart might find peace in a world where the spirit [seems] exiled" (29), carries with him a legacy of filial despair. As he and Master Polkinghorne discuss the terms of his tutorial duties, he reveals that his family was murdered by his father: "He shot my mother and sister, and would have blown me to Kingdom Come, too, I assure you, had I not been away that evening" (11).

If we recall the way in which Guerrero establishes the relationship between "material wealth" and "manhood," Ezekiel's father is another victim of this oppressive and reductive ideology. In a conversation with Andrew, Ezekiel elucidates the rationale for his father's decision to kill his family and himself:

> "My father spent twelve, maybe fifteen hours a day in a brass foundry, where I was employed for a time when I was fifteen, and for a pitiful wage. If all he could expect was poverty—if, I say, Andrew, all he could see ahead was sixty years of bad news, the breakdown of his family, debts and disappointment, without hope of change, without consolation, wasn't it better to be done once and for all with the person feeling, eh? It is not easy to be a grown man Andrew. We are not like women. . . . We are weaker." (30)

Ezekiel inherits a narrow vision of manhood from his father, one in which men are judged by material production, and when production is deficient, the exigencies of poverty lead to the disintegration of the traditional family. This economic and domestic disintegration calls into question one's manhood. We are privy, however, to only part of Ezekiel's violent domestic history. While we know the details of his father's psychic collapse, we have no sense of how his mother was affected by stifling economic and social conditions. She certainly functions in some capacity as mother and wife, but Ezekiel excludes her from his recollection. In light of how women have been socialized in Western cultures, it would seem that his mother played a pivotal role in domestic affairs. Moreover, as Badinter argues, gender identity does not occur in singular terms—that is, men and women are influenced by each other. Ezekiel's silence with regard to his mother anticipates that of Andrew with regard to his stepmother, Mattie.

Just as George Hawkins's perception of the world is rooted in racial monoliths, Ezekiel embraces the notion of gender polarity which asserts that men "are weaker" (30) than women. In effect, Ezekiel's construction of the masculine and feminine precludes men and women from engaging identities that resist, to return to Butler, "regulatory practices" (1). Although he argues for the eternal strength of women, Andrew's tutor nonetheless theorizes gender in essentialist terms. Given the absence of his mother's story, Ezekiel engages in a form of gender erasure. As Butler notes:

> Indeed, the construction of gender operates through *exclusionary* means, such that the human is not only produced over and against the inhu-

298	Reading Charles Johnson

man, but through a set of foreclosures, radical erasures, that are, strictly speaking, refused the possibility of cultural articulation. Hence, it is not enough to claim that human subjects are constructed, for the construction of the human is a differential operation that produces the more and the less "human," the inhuman, the humanly unthinkable. These excluded sites come to "bound" the human as its constitutive outside, and to haunt those boundaries as the persistent possibility of their disruption and rearticulation. (8)

Ezekiel's problem lies in perception. Though intellectually astute, he perceives only the problematic aspects of his father's experience. By excluding his mother from his oral history, he erases her experience as a gendered being. As he refers to the psychic strength of women, Ezekiel's silence with regard to his mother's struggles gives heft to the fallacious assumption that men are actually weaker than women. Such a posture is predicated on biological difference, but according to anthropologist Andrea Cornwall, the "male/female dichotomy has no intrinsic biological or other essential reality. Rather, this dichotomy is a potent metaphor for difference in western cultures whose import must be understood in terms of historical and ethnographic specificities."[13]

Ezekiel's silence regarding his mother constitutes, in Butler's words, a "radical erasure" (8), a gesture which foreshadows perceptions of femininity which Andrew will adopt. If, for the sake of argument, men "are weaker" than women, this weakness is less a result of biological or genetic difference and more a result of emotional deficits. Historically, men have viewed their relationship to women and nature in terms of superiority, unable to humble themselves in relation to the cosmos. While the men in *Oxherding Tale* view women and nature as active participants in their lives, women nonetheless remain cast in essentialist terms. This, in fine, is Ezekiel's dilemma. Perhaps Ezekiel's struggle with women is rooted in the need for men to establish themselves in opposition to women. As Badinter has suggested, being born in the belly of the opposite sex complicates male identity formation; and "as long as women give birth to men, as long as the XY develops with an XX, it will always take a little longer and be a little more difficult to make a man than to make a woman."[14]

While Ezekiel initiates Andrew into the pleasures of the intellectual life, he is nonetheless plagued by static constructions of gender, as opposed to race. When he suggests to Andrew that "we are not like women. . . . We are weaker" (30), the tone, if not the content, of his observation recalls the binary race logic of George Hawkins: "Too much imagination, he [George] decided was unwholesome. And white" (23). For the introspective Andrew, this assertion cannot escape interrogation, as he seeks "to [create] some meaning for what it [means] to be male . . . " (28). Andrew's constructions of masculinity and femininity are in some ways problematic, but his rhetoric and actions at least speak to an awareness on his part of the ambiguous nature of both phenomena. This level of receptivity and flexibility distinguishes Andrew from his father and Ezekiel, both of whom too often revert to a Way of Being predicated upon dichotomy.

In Ezekiel's view, men are a nuisance in the history of humankind and women the essence of all human experience. Continuing his conversation with Andrew regarding the nature of women, Ezekiel explains further his philosophy of gender and the basis for his belief that men are weaker than women, to which Andrew replied, "How are we weaker?":

> "Spiritually, I think. Perhaps all philosophy boils down to the simple fear that the universe has no need for us—men I mean, because women are, in a strange sense, more essential to Being than we are. Have you never felt that? . . . " "In the East," he said, "men believe themselves to be offspring of the sun, creatures of light, made of the same stuff that powers stars. They worship Being as a female, the Mother. But we in Europe and the Americas have settled for something else. Something less, I daresay. We build machines, Andrew, create tribal languages in philosophy— like little boys with secret codes in their clubhouse—to get back at the universe because she has failed to give us a function." (31)

As Ezekiel reflects upon the way in which women are "more essential to Being than [men] are" (31), we find that his gender formulations are rooted in a kind of philosophical narrowness. At the core of Ezekiel's assertion is the notion that women are more emotional, in harmony with the natural elements, and that men, given their preoccupation with rationality and violence, cannot know the world as women do. There is certainly a rationale for Ezekiel's comments, given the manner in which men and women have been socialized historically. We must distinguish, however, between socialization and essentialism.

If Ezekiel has influenced Andrew to the point of inspiring awe, the next male whom Andrew encounters inspires emulation. In the slave Reb, the Coffinmaker at Leviathan, we find a man who, unlike George Hawkins and Ezekiel Sykes-Withers, fears nothing. As he reluctantly befriends Andrew, Reb becomes aware of and irritated by Andrew's ignorance regarding the perils of slavery. After Andrew asks the Coffinmaker for directions to the plantation house, Reb queries, "You folks, I say, or white people?" Andrew answers the query with confidence and says, "Definitely folks" (36). Unaware of his future status as Flo Hatfield's concubine, Andrew does not fully understand the culture of Leviathan: "You ain't folks or white," Reb intimates to the young initiate. "You fresh meat, boy" (36). With his son Patrick presently serving as Hatfield's concubine, Reb is painfully familiar with the sexual exploitation and possible death which await Andrew. After meeting Reb, a member of Johnson's fictional tribe the Allmuseri, Andrew wonders if he, too, is "as scarred by slavery as my father? As unfirm in his gender as Ezekiel?" (46).

We learn that Reb's spiritual and philosophical orientations depart from those of George and Ezekiel, both of whom seem to dichotomize certain aspects of racial and gender experience. In the case of Reb, the tendency to dichotomize is replaced with a kind of spiritual stoicism. The fear of difference which undergirds George Hawkins's narrow conception of race and Ezekiel Sykes-Withers's narrow conception of gender is replaced in Reb by a marked degree of fearlessness. This fearlessness has become part of plantation lore:

> It was said that when he first arrived at Leviathan he found himself confronted by two white hunters on a backroad. They'd caught no game that day. They leveled their shotgun at Reb. When he failed to run, one hunter said, "Nigguh, you lookin at somebody who kin blow off yo head without battin' an eye." It is said that the Coffinmaker blinked, pushed aside both shotguns like treelimbs in his path, and, passing on, replied, "You lookin' at someone who can be shot without blinkin' an eyelash." (46–47)

For the Coffinmaker, death represents the transition from one form of Being to another. Whereas George and Ezekiel fear both life and death, Reb views the body as the vessel through which both phenomena are enacted and reconciled. Unlike a Frederick Douglass, who faces the slavebreaker Edward Covey in self-defense, Reb's defense lies in understanding the relationship between the finite body and the infinite Spirit. He embodies the values celebrated in the *Bhagavad Gita*: "weapons cannot hurt the Spirit and fire can never burn him. Untouched is he by drenching waters, untouched is he by drenching winds."[15] Moreover, as the great-grandson of Rakhal, a "powerful osuo," Reb is also the master of "Yaka powders and Yohimby roots" (49). Put another way, he is a root doctor, a conjurer, possessing the ability to send his "kra forth to dwell in the cattle kraals. It took up ten thousand hosts, this I, slipped into men, women, giraffes, gibbering monkeys, perished, pilgramaged in the animal and spirit worlds, dwelling peacefully in baobab trees" (49).

Reb stands as a complete anomaly for Andrew, expanding even further the possibilities of black masculine identity. He embodies the level of self-awareness which Andrew seeks. If Andrew admires Ezekiel's penchant for contemplation, then he views Reb in heroic terms—an affection so profound that he begins to perceive Reb as his surrogate father: "I was, or felt myself to be, several selves, like the Coffinmaker's polyhedral kra, which suffered all possible forms. Absorbed sin in all its subtle variations. And sojourned still" (61). Andrew perceives himself in "polyhedral" terms, not exclusively black or even male but open to the forms and possibilities of his "kra," or spirit.

As much as Andrew admires and respects Reb, he realizes that he cannot fully adopt his spiritual stoicism, for ultimately this Way of Being is, in his words, "dead to hope" (77). Having suffered through the death of his wife and witnessed his daughter's physical deterioration as a result of pellagra, the enslaved Coffinmaker resigns himself to a life in which he desires nothing. In other words, for Reb a life absent of desire produces no pain. During this period of profound despair, Reb adopts the only strategy available: "accepting—said the Coffinmaker—the shock of nihilation" (76). As Andrew reflects upon Reb's history, we learn that

> so deep was the experience of sacrifice engraved in him—his forty or fifty years adjustment to self-denial—that even in his eating he was wont to make sacrifice, saying, "Lawd, you *better* take this food!" So often had food, property, and loved ones been snatched away that now he treated whatever he had as someone else's property, with the care and attention that another's property deserved. Reward he did not expect. Nor pleasure. Desire was painful. Duty was everything. . . . This was his Way. It was, I thought, a Way of strength and spiritual heroism—doing what must be done, dead to hope—but like Flo Hatfield's path of the senses, it was not my Way. (76–77)

Although Reb is not fluent in formal philosophical discourse, his view of life resembles that of Ezekiel. In their respective lives, they view love and desire in antagonistic terms. That Reb is unable to love freely is certainly understandable, in light of the exorbitant realities of slavery, realities which in part lead Andrew to view him in heroic terms.

We finally come to understand the depth and discipline of Reb's character at the end of the novel, as the Slavecatcher Horace Bannon offers Andrew information about George Hawkins and Reb. Both men have assumed vastly different fates, and their respective destinies, in one way or another, involve a struggle with desire. As a man who has profited from the capture and resale of black bodies, Bannon provides Andrew with an assessment of the two men who have influenced his flight to freedom. Now passing in the white world as William Harris, Andrew must learn the truth about his biological father and his surrogate father:

> "And what," my voice floundered, "did Reb want?" The Soulcatcher laughed. "Nothin'! That's hit right there—what threw me off, why hit took so long to run him down: yo friend didn't want nothin'. How the hell you gonna catch a negro like that? He can't be caught, he's already free. Not legally, but you know what Ah'm sayin'. Well suh, Ah had to think a spell about strategy. Ah's always worked on the principle that the thing what destroys a man, what finally unstrings him, starts off first as an appetite. Yo friend had no appetites. There wasn't no way Ah could git a handhold on the nigguh, he was like smoke. So Ah went back to Square One, so to speak: Ah studied him, lookin' fo' a weakness, a flaw somewhere, so Ah could squiggle inside and take root, like Ah did with yo Daddy—now he was an easy kill, oh yeah, Ah did indeed snuff George Hawkins after the Cripplegate uprisin', but he was carryin' fifty-leven pockets of death in him anyways, l'il pools of corruption that kept him

so miserable he begged me, when I caught up to him in Calhoun Falls, to blow out his lights—." (173–74)

The destinies of George and Reb, in Andrew's mind, revolve around desire. Much to his credit, George Hawkins feels both love and desire, but he is unable to benefit in a fruitful way from these emotions. On the other hand, Reb resigns himself to a life absent of desire, which enables him to view death with indifference. Reb's commitment to a life of stoicism is, for Andrew, a form of existence that is "dead to hope" (76). As Andrew contemplates the lives of these two men, he is aware that his ability to establish emotional ties with men and women will determine the depth and quality of his life, as well as the depth and quality of his manhood.

In Andrew's view, each individual inherits the privilege and responsibility of creating his "Way" (77). Andrew does not seek complete separation from his male forebears but simply the space to develop his "Way" absent chronic binaries, emotional sterility, or spiritual stoicism. In one way or another, these three men with whom Andrew is most intimate have found themselves in conflict with desire. For George Hawkins, desire is forsaken in the name of racial chauvinism and nationalism; for Ezekiel, desire is displaced in the name of gender polarity; and for Reb, desire is forfeited for spiritual stoicism.

For Andrew, desire and the imagination are central to his conception of manhood. In this narrative there are Ellisonian overtones which suggest the possibilities of fruitful and diverse forms of black masculinity. As Ralph Ellison reminds us in *Going to the Territory* "often we've been in such haste to express our anger and our pain as to allow the single tree of race [and gender] to obscure our view of the magic forest of art" (278). Certainly, Johnson would embrace this notion. Moreover, while our narrator is not, formally speaking, an artist, his life, and every human life, can be construed as an evolving work of art. Put another way, Andrew embraces the ambiguities of life—slavery and freedom, birth and death, reason and emotion. Andrew's view is represented in the Taoist maxim: "a way can be a guide, but not a fixed path; names can be given, but not permanent labels."[16] As Andrew finds his "Way," he realizes that the diverse models of male experience to which he has been exposed speak to the complexities and nuances of black male experience.

In what sense, finally, can we characterize Andrew's "Way," his journey toward self-realization? Andrew stands as a work in progress, an unfinished project as we consider his new life at the end of the novel. While we may not know all that Andrew will become, we have a profound understanding of the forms of human identity he has chosen to reject. He rejects any form of male consciousness absent love, desire, and their attendant complexities. In this instance, our understanding of Andrew Hawkins is rooted in his unequivocal rejection of constructions of masculinity that deny him the possibility of growth and transcendence.

In Andrew and his male trio, Johnson has provided us with an exploration of black masculinity in which these men wrestle with the fundamental emotion which slavery sought to destroy: chiefly the ability to desire and love, to invest passion and sympathy into other human beings. As we continue to explore constructions of black masculinity in African American literature, our questions and concerns should focus on the degree to which black male protagonists affirm or deny their capacity for desire and love. As readers, we also need to explore the extent to which these male characters are able to engage the beauty and complexity of love: the ultimate form of human expression, which determines the "quality of a man" as well as the outcome of what Johnson terms the "crisis of the male spirit."

Notes

1. William L. Andrews, "The Black Male in American Literature," *The American Black Male* (Chicago: Nelson Hall, 1994), p. 66.

2. Sherley Anne Williams, "Some Implications of Womanist Theory," in *Reading Black, Reading Feminist*, ed. Henry Louis Gates, Jr. (New York: Meridian, 1990), p. 70.

3. While I find value in Williams's assertion, I am interested in the novels of Toni Morrison and William Faulkner, for they provide a certain kind of plurality of meanings and readings of black masculinity.

4. Charles Johnson, *Oxherding Tale* (New York: Grove Press, 1982). All further references to this novel will be made parenthetically.

5. Elisabeth Badinter, *XY: On Masculine Identity*, trans. Lydia Davis (New York: Columbia University Press, 1995), p. 9.

6. Stanley Crouch, *Notes of a Hanging Judge: Essays and Reviews* (New York: Oxford University Press, 1990), p. 136.

7. Judith Butler, *Bodies That Matter: On the Discursive Limits of "Sex"* (New York: Routledge, 1993), p. 2.

8. Johnson's fiction is filled with philosophical allusions. For a thorough exploration of the philosophical dimensions of *Oxherding Tale*, see Rudolph P. Byrd, "*Oxherding Tale* and *Siddartha*: Philosophy, Fiction, and the Emergence of a Hidden Tradition," in this volume.

9. Ed Guerrero, "The Black Man on Our Screens and the Empty Space in Representation," *Callaloo* 18, no. 2 (Winter 1995), p. 397.

10. Williams, "Some Implications," p. 72.

11. Bertram Wyatt-Brown, *Southern Honor: Ethics and Behavior in the Old South* (New York: Oxford University Press, 1982), p. 65.

12. David L. Dudley, *My Father's Shadow: Intergenerational Conflict in African American Men's Autobiography* (Philadelphia: University of Pennsylvania Press, 1991), p. 2.

13. Andrea Cornwell, in Cornwall and Nancy Lindisfarne, eds., *Dislocating Masculinity: Comparative Ethnologies* (New York: Routledge, 1994), p. 9.

14. Badinter, *XY*, p. 185.

15. *Bhagavad Gita*, chap. 2.

16. "Every art and science is called a tao, or a way; but the source of everything, the fountain of all art and science, is called the Tao, or the Way." This definition comes from Thomas Cleary, *The Essential Tao: An Initiation into the Heart of Taoism through the Authentic Tao Te Ching and the Inner Teachings of Chuang Tzu* (New York: Harper Collins, 1991), p. 9.

Works Cited

Cornwall, Andrea, and Nancy Lindisfarne, eds. *Dislocating Masculinity, Comparative Ethnologies*. New York: Routledge, 1994.

Douglass, Frederick. *Narrative of the Life of Frederick Douglass*. New York: Penguin, 1982.

Ellison, Ralph. *Going to the Territory*. New York: Random House, 1986.

Hurston, Zora Neale. *Their Eyes Were Watching God*. New York: Harper & Row, 1990.

Johnson, Charles. *Being and Race: Black Writing since 1970*. Bloomington: Indiana University Press, 1988.

Morrison, Toni. *The Bluest Eye*. New York: Washington Square Press, 1970.

——. *Beloved*. New York: Plume, 1987.

Walker, Alice. *The Third Life of Grange Copeland*. New York: Pocket Books, 1970.

——. *The Color Purple*. New York: Washington Square Press, 1982.

Oxherding Tale and Siddhartha

Philosophy, Fiction, and the

Emergence of a Hidden Tradition

Rudolph P. Byrd

Charles Johnson has written a searching introduction to the Plume edition of *Oxherding Tale*, originally published in 1982, in which he carefully sets forth the genesis and publishing history of his second novel. This edition of *Oxherding Tale* is the first instance in which Johnson, within the framework of introductory or prefatory remarks, has chosen to reflect upon the processes, both hostile and nurturing, undergirding the writing of a particular work of fiction. Given the novels that bracket *Oxherding Tale, Faith and the Good Thing* (1974) and *Middle Passage* (1990), respectively, it is significant that Johnson chooses to begin this much welcomed public reflection upon the setbacks and advances of literary production with *Oxherding Tale*. There are, I believe, certain motivations for Johnson's decision to bring, as it were, his enlarging readership into his confidence.

Oxherding Tale is perhaps the most widely taught and admired of Johnson's novels, and the author regards it as his "platform" book (xvii). He adds that *platform* is a "playful reference" to *The Platform Sutra of the Sixth Patriarch*, a canonical work in Zen Buddhism. *Oxherding Tale* is Johnson's "platform" book in the sense, as he writes in the introduction, "that everything else I attempted to do would in one way or another be based upon and refer to it" (xvii). As the pivotal work of fiction that constituted the greatest challenge in intellectual and artistic terms, *Oxherding Tale* had far-reaching influence on Johnson's subsequent fiction. For example, in *Oxherding Tale* Johnson begins his exploration of the physical and metaphysical nature of slavery within the framework of Buddhism, Taoism, and Hinduism. Beyond the painful and patent fact of chattel slavery, in what other ways, ruminates Johnson in *Oxherding Tale*, can we be enslaved? This is the central question in this metaphysical slave narrative whose title-page, Johnson notes, bears the imprint of the "Taoist symbol for a man travelling on the Way" (xvii). Further, and related to this systematic exploration of the various species of slavery within the framework of Eastern philosophy, the Allmuseri, a fictional African clan, is a *defining* presence through the character of Reb, the Coffinmaker, in *Oxherding Tale*, but a *dominant* presence through the character of Ngonyama in *Middle Passage*. Plainly, in these and other ways *Oxherding Tale* has had a profound impact upon the content and intellectual concerns of Johnson's subsequent fiction. It is for this reason that he has taken such pains to reconstruct the context and process of *Oxherding Tale*'s composition and publication.

Certainly, Johnson's foray into literary criticism is, in some sense, a response to certain personal and historical exigencies; that is, a desire to make his own past as an artist visible, coherent, and accessible. *Being & Race: Black Writing since 1970* (1988), Johnson's only book of literary criticism, is, in part, an earlier and extended elaboration of this desire. Johnson's more recent and much welcomed public reflection springs, however, from yet another source. There is in his introduction a desire to assess and weigh the aesthetic value of *Oxherding Tale* in relationship to his other novels. And, in my view, *Oxherding Tale* remains the work of fiction in which Johnson's artistic and intellectual vision is most fully realized. While *Faith and the Good Thing* and *Middle Passage* are unified, coherent, and complex works of art, there is, I believe, a degree of depth, strangeness, and power in *Oxherding Tale* that is unequaled in the other novels. Johnson himself holds a similar view of the value of his "platform" book. In comparing *Oxherding Tale* with *Middle Passage*, the novel for which he was awarded the National Book Award in 1990, Johnson writes that his prize-winning third novel "contains only a fraction of its predecessor's complexity" (xvii). Johnson's candor and lack of sentimentality regarding the artistic achievement of his novels is unusual and admirable. As an artist, it is evident that the value he assigns to a particular work is linked neither to encomia nor to prestigious literary prizes, but rather to his own independent evaluative standard. It seems that Johnson, like Jean Toomer in the writing of *Cane*, and Gabriel García Márquez in the writing of *One Hundred Years of Solitude*, wrote his most important and influential work of fiction to date early in his artistic career.[1]

In 1975, Johnson undertook the difficult but meaningful work of writing his most highly esteemed novel with, in his words, "absolutely no encouragement" (xiii)—neither polite interest from colleagues nor advances from publishers. This spite work, for in one sense it is plain that Johnson embarked upon this ambitious literary experiment in defiance of his detractors, would take five years to complete. Of the many writers whose works sustained and influenced him during the long and lonely period of *Oxherding Tale*'s composition, Johnson acknowledges an intellectual debt to Herman Melville, Henry Fielding, Laurence Sterne, and most importantly Hermann Hesse. Of the several writers mentioned in the introduction to the Plume edition of *Oxherding Tale*, Hesse's influence is the most profound.

While Johnson read and studied all of the novels by the German writer who was awarded the Nobel Prize for Literature in 1946, Hesse's *Siddhartha* (1951) exercised a decisive influence on *Oxherding Tale*. Indeed, it is not an exaggeration to assert that *Siddhartha*, in the conceptualization of *Oxherding Tale*, occupies a position of co-equality with *The Ten Oxherding Pictures* by Kaku-an Shi-en, a foundational work of Zen Buddhism, and the conversion and slave narratives of American and African American literature.

In what specific ways can we discern the imprint of *Siddhartha* upon *Oxherding Tale*? As an artist who is self-consciously creating a distinctive body of work that reflects the influence of a range of literary ancestors, what did Johnson imbibe from his immersion in the fictional universe of Hesse that has endowed *Oxherding Tale* and the other fictions which so forcefully emanate from it with their particular intellectual cast and trajectory? These are the central questions I wish to explore within this essay.

ʊ̈ ʊ̈ ʊ̈

Of the several points of convergence between *Siddhartha* and *Oxherding Tale*, structure and intellectual concerns are preeminent. Like *Siddhartha*, *Oxherding Tale* is a novel in two parts in which *compression* is the operative word. Both are densely layered works, *Oxherding Tale* even more so than *Siddhartha*, in which arcane knowledge constitutes the core concern. As artists, Hesse and Johnson are engaged in an experiment whose objective is to join philosophy and literature. While I will have more to say about this shared intellectual endeavor later in this essay, for the moment I would like to emphasize the centrality of Buddhism for both novels, although Johnson extends his zone of inquiry to include Hinduism and Taoism.

In addition to sharing structural and intellectual preoccupations, *Siddhartha* and *Oxherding Tale* are both historical novels. Hesse's emphasis is upon an historical figure, while Johnson's emphasis is upon an historical era. Siddhartha, Hesse's questing and questioning protagonist, is in many ways the fictional counterpart to the Buddha himself, who, according to scholars, was Sakyamani Gautama, born in India in the sixth century B.C.E. Like Gautama, Siddhartha is a member of the Indian élite, a Brahmin born to luxury and power. Hesse writes that the "handsome Brahmin's son" was expected to become a "great learned man, a priest, a prince among Brahmins." "Love stirred in the hearts of the young Brahmins' daughters when Siddhartha," writes Hesse, "walked through the streets of the town, with his lofty brow, his king-like eyes and his slim figure" (3–4). Inevitably, Siddhartha, like Gautama, becomes disillusioned with his privileged existence. Both men discover that an existence framed by temporal realities is meaningless. After encountering a group of Samanas, peripatetic renunciates, "lean jackals in the world of men" around whom "hovered an atmosphere of still passion, of devastating service, of unpitying self-denial" (9), Siddhartha makes the fateful decision to leave his father's palace and to join them. While his commitment to the Samana's life of self-denial is genuine and deep, Siddhartha remains dissatisfied. He does not discover in ascetism the much sought after release from *samsara*, or the cyclical nature of existence. In these particulars, Hesse remains faithful to the fragmented history in which Gautama, the Buddha, is enshrouded.

Hesse introduces, however, a significant variation in a novel based in large measure upon the life of Gautama. While Siddhartha's life corresponds in many ways to the life of this historic figure, Hesse's protagonist is not, it seems, the Buddha. Doubtless anticipating the injunctions and denunciations from scholars and practioners of Buddhism, Hesse creates the character of Gotama, who is called "the Illustrious, the Buddha" (120). While Siddhartha recognizes that Gotama is a holy man, for never had he "esteemed a man so much, never had he loved a man so much," he does not, like his friend and companion Govinda, become a disciple of Gotama, whose name and divine attributes recall Gautama. While respectfully acknowledging the patently enlightened state of the "Illustrious One," Siddhartha apprehends the flaw in the otherwise flawless teachings of Gotama. The teachings do not contain, so the Brahmin's son asserts in conversation with Gotama, " 'the secret of what the Illustrious One himself experienced' " at the moment of enlightenment (34). While the teachings or doctrine are important, individual effort is more important in attaining *moksha*, or release from *samsara*. In his artful reconstruction of aspects of the life of the Buddha, Hesse illustrates one of the fundamental tenets of Buddhism. And in the process, he avoids the censure of the purists who would doubtless find the freedom of the artist in the domain of history problematic, and he invests his novel with the dramatic tension and conflict so essential to its sense of unity and coherence.

While Hesse is engaged in a selective retelling of the life and experiences of the Buddha, Johnson is engaged in a selective reconstruction of an epoch through the creation of a fictionalized antebellum slave narrative. The narrator of this metaphysical slave narrative is Andrew Hawkins, who assumes the identity of William Harris by the novel's conclusion. In contrast to Siddhartha, Johnson's questing and questioning narrator is a mulatto fugitive slave in whose life we apprehend patterns that recall the lives of such fugitive slaves as Frederick

Douglass and Harriet Jacobs. Hawkins's dense narrative is the vehicle for a journey whose destination is not Hesse's fabled East, but the world of the antebellum South of Spartenburg, South Carolina. Like Arna Bontemps's *Black Thunder*, Margaret Walker's *Jubilee*, Ernest J. Gaines's *The Autobiography of Miss Jane Pittman*, Ishmael Reed's *Flight to Canada*, Octavia Butler's *Kindred*, Toni Morrison's *Beloved*, Sherley Anne Williams's *Dessa Rose*, and most recently John Edgar Wideman's *The Cattle Killing*, Johnson has created a fictional universe set in motion by the paradoxes and actualities of slavery in a purportedly democratic republic.

"Although nearly anything you said about slavery could be denied in the same breath," muses Andrew Hawkins in a state of freedom, "this much struck me as true: the wretchedness of being colonized was not that slavery created feelings of guilt and indebtedness, though I did feel guilt and debt; nor that it created a long, lurid dream of multiplicity and separateness, which it did indeed create, but the fact that men had epidermalized Being" (52). This important passage, which is an example of the fine writing everywhere in evidence in *Oxherding Tale*, is a kind of expansive synecdoche in which we apprehend the various ways in which slavery has shaped the life and sensibility of Andrew Hawkins.

Certainly, Hawkins feels "guilt and debt" because he fails to realize the important goals to which he had committed himself when setting out from Cripplegate to Leviathan: to earn enough money to purchase his own freedom as well as that of his father George Hawkins, his stepmother Mattie Hawkins, and his betrothed Minty, all of whom make certain sacrifices in order to make his slave existence endurable. Certainly, Hawkins is immersed in a "lurid dream of multiplicity and separateness," for with the exception of the friendship he establishes with Reb, Leviathan's Coffinmaker, he remains, for significant periods, either a sexual slave or a fugitive slave seeking meaning and safety in a culture and economy that would deny him, at every turn, such fundamental needs of human existence. And in Hawkins's use of the rich and resonant phrase *epidermalized Being* is expressed the ultimate paradox of slavery in a democratic republic which values, theoretically, the humanity of each individual. The sole objective of slavery in the United States, and more specifically the slavery so deeply entrenched at Cripplegate and Leviathan, was the grotesque reduction of human beings into matter, into chattel for personal profit. In the writing of this historical novel, Johnson remains faithful to his artistic goal of fully illustrating the dispiriting actualities which supported and advanced this capitalistic enterprise.

While masterfully reconstructing aspects of an enterprise and an epoch, Johnson, in contrast to Hesse, destabilizes our expectations of historical fiction by writing against the conventions of this genre. The many instances of modern colloquialisms, the decision to place Karl Marx in dialogue with a transplanted New England abolitionist during a visit to a slave plantation, and the veiled and droll exchanges on political correctness and Affirmative Action are all instances in which Johnson exhibits a certain irreverence for conventions that presumably govern the writing of historical fiction. These calculated interpolations in a discourse centering upon the uses of history in fiction are occasions when Johnson advances an alternative view of history and the historical process; that is, neither is remote or static, and both are powerful forces shaping contemporary existence.

While the imprint of *Siddhartha* upon *Oxherding Tale* is discernible in such important domains as structure and genre, the influence of this German novel upon this American novel is also discernable in the patterning of experience and the ineluctable variations which this artistic process inspires. During the period in Siddhartha's life when he returns to his Brahmin existence, he develops a relationship with Kamala, the beautiful and wealthy courtesan skilled in the art of love. Hesse writes that Siddhartha "learned many things from her wise red lips" (66). A patient teacher with wide experience and high standards, Kamala, whose name recalls Kama, the deity who reigns in the sensuous realm of the Buddhist cosomology, lovingly initiates Hesse's disillusioned Brahmin into carnal mysteries. Impressed by the skill and sensitivity of her young and able student, Kamala remarks to Siddhartha after a session of sex: " 'You are the best lover that I have had. . . . You are stronger than others, more supple, more willing' " (73). Shifting now to *Oxherding Tale* we observe a fascinating variation. Again, after a session of sex of the most histrionic kind, Flo Hatfield, the sovereign of Leviathan and Kamala's fictional variation, remarks to Hawkins, her sexual slave: " 'La, Andrew, you are the best *servant* I have *ever* had. . . . You are the most willing to learn, the most promising' " (64–65; first emphasis mine).

While there are striking similarities in the language and situation between these corresponding episodes in *Siddhartha* and *Oxherding Tale*, Johnson's variations underscore the ways in which his artistic and intellectual concerns differ from those of Hesse. While Flo Hatfield shares Kamala's devotion to carnal mysteries, the sovereign of Leviathan is not motivated by love, which becomes the dominant force in Kamala's relationship with Siddhartha, but predictably by power. It is significant that Kamala describes Siddhartha as the " 'best lover' " she has had, while Flo Hatfield describes Hawkins as the " 'best servant' " she has ever had. Of course, *servant* is a genteel synonym for *slave*, and Johnson, through the fevered and narcoticized coupling of Hatfield and Hawkins, is able to explore a range of novel, complementary, and paradoxical themes: the domination of the slave by the master and, conversely, the peculiar domination of the master by the slave; the sexual exploitation of the slave by the master and the sexual exploitation of slave men by their masters; the slavery of the body and the slavery of the spirit. Unlike Hesse's Kamala, who renounces her life as a courtesan, Flo Hatfield remains a slave to sexual desire. As the Coffinmaker remarks to an incredulous Hawkins, Flo Hatfield is " 'a slave like you'n me' " (62). In this masterful inversion, slavery for the sovereign of Leviathan ironically assumes the form of an erect black phallus.

Along with the provocative metamorphosis of Kamala into Flo Hatfield, Johnson accomplishes other variations while also honoring Hesse's example and influence. In contrast to Flo Hatfield and Andrew Hawkins, the affectionate coupling between Kamala and Siddhartha produces a son. The discovery that he is a father inspires in Siddhartha a series of reflections and preoccupations regarding his proper relationship to his son. Sadly, Siddhartha's son rejects him as well as his contemplative existence. Ironically, he chooses instead the Brahmin existence that Siddhartha himself has rejected. The relationship between fathers and sons is also a central theme in *Oxherding Tale*. There is the ambivalence between George Hawkins and Andrew Hawkins which is registered in Andrew's rejection of his father's reductive racial theories. Further, there is the violence which so mangles the filial ties of the fathers of Ezekial Sykes-Withers and Horace Bannon. Finally, there is the great gulf of silence between Reb, Leviathan's Coffinmaker, and his doomed son Patrick.

While the dynamics between fathers and their sons is an important theme in *Siddhartha* and *Oxherding Tale*, so also is the theme of male friendship. In *Siddhartha* this theme is concretized in the deep friendship between Govinda and Siddhartha, and later between Siddhartha and Vasudeva, the ferryman. Correspondingly, in *Oxherding Tale*, there is a powerful friendship between Reb and Andrew Hawkins, which possesses both an avuncular and paternal cast. While Johnson shares Hesse's interest in male friendships, a defining characteristic of such novels as *Narcissis and Goldmund* and *Damien*, Johnson is also interested in exploring the basis for the failure of such important relationships, as evidenced in George Hawkins's betrayal by the philanderer Nate McKay. In fine, the world of men and the concerns that define this world are patterns central to both *Siddhartha* and *Oxherding Tale*. In Hesse's novel this pattern is reflected in the male world of the Samanas and their collective goal of asceticism and transcendence; in Johnson's novel this pattern is reflected in the fraternity of the slave men of Leviathan and their shared nihilism or "absence of life-assurance," which is counterpoised against the spiritual powers of Reb and the resilience of Andrew Hawkins. Above all, Hesse and Johnson are artists deeply interested in exploring the tensions between selfhood and manhood, between enlightenment and certain stultifying forms of masculinity. While these male friendships are metaphors for the human capacity for self-development, these friendships also suggest the very positive potentialities that exist among androcentric communities and relationships. Crucially, Johnson's meditations in this vein are, in contrast to Hesse's, explicit and deliberate, and they anticipate by many years the current and marked interrogation of masculinities. In the study of the construction of masculinities, *Oxherding Tale* is a canonical text occupying the place of Toni Morrison's *Beloved* in the study of the construction of femininities.

ᘓ ᘓ ᘓ

In these fictional worlds determined to a large degree by male interests, men are both competitors and allies, assassins and the vehicle for *moksha* or release, liberation, and enlightenment. It is to this last shared pattern in *Siddhartha* and *Oxherding Tale*, male friendships as the vehicle for *moksha*, that I now turn. In Hesse's classic, *moksha* is achieved within the framework of two powerful male friendships. In the first instance of this expansion of consciousness, Vasudeva is the catalyst for Siddhartha's achievement of enlightenment. In providing comfort to Siddhartha, who is pained by the failed relationship with his son, Vasudeva gently encourages his friend to merge his thoughts with the great river upon which they have been ferrymen. Completely trusting Vasudeva, Siddhartha's "wound" or grief over his son's repudiation of him becomes the path to a revelation as he listens to the "many-veiled song of the river," and studies the images flashing across the river's undulant surface:

> Siddhartha tried to listen better. The picture of his father, his own picture, and the picture of his son all flowed into each other. Kamala's picture also appeared and flowed on, and the picture of Govinda and others emerged and passed on. They all became part of the river. It was the goal of all of them, yearning, desiring, suffering; and the river's voice was full of longing, full of smarting woe, full of insatiable desire. . . . They all belonged to each other; the lament of those who yearn, the laughter of the wise, the cry of indignation and the groan of dying. They were all interwoven and interlocked, entwined in a thousand ways. And all the voices, all the goals, all the yearnings, all the sorrows, all the pleasures, all the good and evil, all of them together was the world. All of them together was the stream of events, the music of life. When Siddhartha listened attentively to this river, to this song of a thousand voices; when he did not bind his soul to any one particular voice and absorb it in his Self, but heard them all, the whole, the unity; then the great song of a thousand voices consisted of one word: Om—perfection. . . . From that hour Siddhartha ceased to fight against his destiny. There shone in his face the serenity of knowledge, of one who is no longer confronted with conflict of desires, who has found salvation, who is in harmony with the stream of events, with the stream of life, full of sympathy and compassion, surrendering himself to the stream, belonging to the unity of all things. (134–36)

Having performed the ultimate service as ferryman and friend in aiding Siddhartha to cross one realm of consciousness into another, Vasudeva departs, a luminous figure, in order to complete his own journey "into the unity of all things."[2]

Siddhartha closes with Siddhartha, now the ferryman, performing the same revelatory function for Govinda, who is on his way to the funeral of Gotama, the Buddha Siddhartha once acknowledged as a holy man but who, unlike Govinda, he refused to follow as a disciple. After renewing their friendship, Siddhartha launches into a critique of the dangers of yielding to dogma and the so-called "wisdom which a wise man tries to communicate" (142). It is worth noting that Johnson mounts a similar critique of teachers and dogma in the character of Ezekial Sykes-Withers, who is a slave to reason. Siddhartha's strong views on this subject set off a wave of anxiety, doubt, and suffering in Govinda, who throughout his life has been the follower, not the leader, the disciple not the teacher. Attuned to the upheaval within his friend which is registered so clearly in his countenance, Siddhartha, in a gesture of tenderness and regard that corresponds to the gesture made by Vesudeva during a corresponding crisis, invites Govinda to kiss him on the forehead. Surprised by this request, Govinda "was compelled by a great love and presentiment to obey him; he leaned close to him and touched his forehead with his lips. As he did this," writes Hesse, "something wonderful happened to him":

> He no longer saw the face of his friend Siddhartha. Instead he saw other faces, many faces, a long series, a continuous stream of faces—hundreds, thousands, which all came and disappeared and yet all seemed to be there at the same time, which all continually changed and renewed themselves and which were yet all Siddhartha. He saw the face of a fish, of a carp, with tremendous painfully opened mouth, a dying fish with dimmed eyes. He saw the face of a newly born child, red and full of wrinkles, ready to cry. He saw the face of a murderer, saw him plunge a knife into the body of a man; at the same moment he saw this criminal kneeling down, bound, and his head cut off by an executioner. He saw the naked bodies of men and women in the postures and transports of passionate love. He saw corpses stretched out, still, cold, empty. He saw the heads of animals—boars, crocodiles, elephants, oxen, birds. He saw Krishna and Agni. . . . And all these forms and faces rested, flowed, reproduced, swam past and merged into each other, and over them all there was continually something thin, unreal and yet existing, stretched across like thin glass or ice, like a transparent skin, shell, form or mask of water—and this mask was Siddhartha's smiling face which Govinda touched with his lips at that moment. And Govinda saw that this mask-like smile, this smile of unity over the flowing forms, this smile of simultaneousness over the thousands of births and deaths—this smile of Siddhartha—was exactly the same as the calm, delicate, impenetrable, perhaps gracious, perhaps mocking, wise, thousand-fold smile of Gotama, the Buddha. (150–51)

Hesse's novel closes with Govinda's achievement of *moksha*. Honoring the powerful symmetry that endows his novel with unity and force, Siddhartha is the vehicle for Govinda's release from *samsara*.

In the final chapter of *Oxherding Tale*, a chapter significantly entitled "Moksha," Andrew Hawkins, like Siddhartha and Govinda, achieves release from the double yoke of slave life and *samsara*, or the slavery of human existence. The vehicle for Hawkins's release—that is, his ferry-man—is Reb, Leviathan's Coffinmaker, and Horace Bannon, the Soulcatcher. In his asceticism and the practice of non-engagement, Reb embodies the values so central to Buddhism and Taoism. Through the practice of non-engagement and the extinguishing of desire, fear, and ego, Reb successfully eludes Horace Bannon, the Soulcatcher. Reb's seamless flight into freedom has profound consequences for both Hawkins and Bannon. Honoring a promise he made to Hawkins and Reb—"'If Ah ever meet a Negro Ah can't catch, Ah'll quit!'" (116)— Bannon renounces his vocation of assassin and slave catcher. In so doing, Hawkins, unlike his father George Hawkins, is spared a painful death at the hands of Bannon. Reb's example of asceticism and self-sacrifice has far-reaching and concrete consequences in the world of slavery: Reb is a free man; Bannon is a reformed man; and Andrew is a free man. Interestingly, the tripartite configuration of male friend-ships in *Siddhartha*—Govinda, Siddhartha, Vesudeva—is invoked and in part preserved through the shifting and complex relationship among Reb, Hawkins, and Bannon. Through his practice of non-engagement, Reb secures Hawkins's liberty; in his final metamorphosis into the Hindu God Krishna, Bannon is the vehicle for Hawkins's achievement of *moksha*:

> I waited for the Soulcatcher's explanation, my gaze dropping from his face to his chest and forearms, where the intricately woven brown tattoos presented, in the brilliance of a silver-gray sky at dawn, an impossible flesh tapestry of a thousand individualities no longer static, mere draw-ings, but if you looked at them long enough, bodies moving like Lillipu-tians over the surface of his skin. Not tattoos at all, I saw, but forms sardined in his contour, creatures Bannon had killed since childhood: spineless insects, flies he'd dewinged; yet even the tiniest of these thrash-ing within the body mosaic was, clearly, a society as complex as the higher forms, a concrescence of molecules cells atoms in concert, for nothing in the necropolis he'd filled stood alone, wished to stand alone, had to stand alone, and the commonwealth of the dead shape-shifted on his chest, his full belly, his fat shoulders, traded hand for claw, feet for hooves, legs for wings, their metamorphosis having no purpose beyond the delight the universe took in diversity for its own sake, the proliferation of beauty, and yet all were conserved in this process of doubling, nothing was lost in the masquerade, the cosmic costume ball, where behind every different mask at the party—behind snout beak nose and blossom—the selfsame face was uncovered at midnight. . . . (175)

Andrew Hawkins's achievement of *moksha* constitutes the climax of *Oxherding Tale*; this is the moment, the linchpin around which all thought and action in the novel revolve. Similarly, in *Siddhartha* Govinda's achievement of *moksha* also constitutes the climatic scene. While there are striking correspondences in language and imagery, the central difference is that Govinda and Siddhartha's dual achievement of *moksha* is beautifully translated into Hawkins's double release from the dual yoke of slavery and *samsara*. In this elegant instance of compression, Johnson, once again, exhibits an admirable degree of independence as an artist while concurrently honoring his own artistic intentions; that is, the very careful charting of his protagonist's achievement of both liberty and enlightenment. The result is that Andrew Hawkins, who at the novel's conclusion assumes the identity of William Harris, is the first protagonist in American literature to achieve *moksha*.

𝕌 𝕌 𝕌

The very deep imprint of *Siddhartha* upon *Oxherding Tale* should, by now, be quite evident, as well as the manner in which Johnson has maintained, through his masterful inversions and variations, the independence of his own artistic vision. While it is clear that *Siddhartha* occupies, as I asserted earlier, a position of co-equality with *The Ten Oxherding Pictures* and the conversion and slave narratives in the conceptualization of *Oxherding Tale*, in what other ways does Hesse, through his achievement in *Siddhartha*, influence Johnson's artistic choices? I now return to the second question driving this inquiry into Johnson's expanding fictional universe.

I would like to suggest here that Hesse's *Siddhartha* provided Johnson, during a period in his artistic development when he was most receptive to experimentation, with a model in art that he could adapt to meet his own developing intellectual and artistic ambitions. As an artist who is also a trained philosopher, Johnson found Hesse's integration of philosophy with fiction intriguing in the extreme. Clearly, Johnson regards *Siddhartha* as a beautiful book, a compelling book, and his admiration of it is reflected in the pages of *Oxherding Tale*. Hesse's example in *Siddhartha* not only provided Johnson with an artistic framework within which to address particular questions regarding a particular *artistic project*, but the German author and his masterpiece also provided Johnson with the path, and the means, to imagine an *artistic tradition* within which *Faith and the Good Thing, Oxherding Tale, Middle Passage*, and *Dreamer* could be situated and explained.

This rich tradition in letters is called philosophical black fiction, the elements of which Johnson has set forth in his essay "Philosophy and Black Fiction." In general terms, Johnson defines philosophical black fiction as art which interrogates experience. More specifically, it is a fiction that is first and foremost a mode of thought and a process of hermeneutics. It is also a fiction which works to suspend, shelve, and bracket all presuppositions regarding African American life. With this bracketing accomplished, African American experience becomes, Johnson theorizes, a pure field of appearances within two poles: consciousness, and the persons and phenomena to which consciousness is related intentionally. Drawing upon a range of philosophical systems, the writer of philosophical black fiction describes how these phenomena appear and observes that black subjectivity stains them with a particular sense. The principal themes of this fiction are, among many, identity, liberation, and enlightenment. Intent upon the liberation of perception, for the reader and the writer, philosophical black fiction produces what Johnson terms "whole sight"; that is, the calculated projection of a plurality of meanings across a shifting and expansive symbolic geography of forms, texts, and traditions.

This twentieth-century tradition in African American literature begins with W. E. B. Du Bois's *The Quest of the Silver Fleece* and includes Jean Toomer's *Cane*, Ralph Ellison's *Invisible Man*, Richard Wright's *The Man Who Lived Underground* and *The Outsider*, James Baldwin's *Go Tell It on the Mountain*, Toni Morrison's *The Bluest Eye*, Cyrus Colter's *The Hippodrome*, Gloria Naylor's *Bailey's Cafe*, and Samuel R. Delany's *The Mad Man*. To date, these are the writers who, in my view, comprise this hidden tradition in twentieth-century African American literature which Johnson has aptly termed *philosophical black fiction*. Inaugurated and dominated by male authors, this tradition of adapting complex philosophical systems—Platonism, Eastern Philosophy, Continental Philosophy, Christianity, and psychoanalytic theory—to construct a coherent fictional universe seems to be, with the exception of selected novels by John Gardner and Rebecca Goldstein, the sole province of African American writers.

Of the many writers in this dynamic tradition, Johnson is the only writer trained in philosophy. Moreover, he is the most self-conscious in terms of his stated goals of employing diverse philosophical systems to examine questions which have a moral cast, and which also endow his explorations of African American life with originality and force. The conceptualization of this emerging tradition reflects Johnson's commitment to combine his artistic goals and impulses with his broad intellectual interests while endowing the American novel with greater depth and force. Clearly, such a tradition was nurtured by Johnson's reading of Toomer, Wright, and most especially Ellison. The foundational writer, however, the writer whose skillful combining of philosophy and literature provided Johnson with both the impetus and the model, is Herman Hesse. One of the foundational texts in this evolving and hybrid tradition which Johnson has named and significantly increased through the force of his own imagination is, as I have argued, *Siddhartha*.

Notes

1. *Dreamer* promises to occupy an important place in the philosopher/novelist's expanding canon, thus potentially altering his present estimation of *Oxherding Tale*.

2. For commentary on the "doctrine of inner realization" or enlightenment, see Suzuki. There are fascinating correspondences between the ways in which the Buddha, Hesse, and Johnson describe this expansive state of consciousness.

Works Cited

Hesse, Hermann. *Siddhartha*. 1951. New York: Bantam, 1971.
Johnson, Charles. *Oxherding Tale*. 1982. New York: Plume, 1995.
——. "Philosophy and Black Fiction." *Obsidian* 6 (1980): 55–61.
Suzuki, D. T. "Zen as Chinese Interpretation of the Doctrine of Enlightenment." *Essays in Zen Buddhism*. New York: Grove Weidenfeld, 1961. 39–117.

Charles Johnson and the Philosopher's Ghost

The Phenomenological
Thinking in *Being and Race*

Michael Boccia

Charles Johnson is a phenomenal writer. In *Faith and the Good Thing*, he writes, "Children, there's nothing worse than being haunted by a philosopher's spirit" (98), and the philosopher's ghost that haunts him is the phenomenologist Merleau-Ponty. Johnson's collection of nonfiction essays *Being and Race: Black Writing since 1970* is required reading for anyone interested in understanding the philosophical underpinnings of his writing. *Being and Race* explains the linguistic and artistic thinking behind his work. He not only believes in the philosophies of the East and West, but finds his center in the middle with the linguistic philosophies associated with phenomenology. The essays contained in this book are divided into two parts: "First Philosophy," which I shall discuss at length, and "Black Writers since 1970," which is an elegant and informative discussion of writers of both genders. Most of my attention will focus on phenomenology, which impregnates all of Johnson's writing, but I will also discuss its relation to the forms he selects through imitation and parody. And no one reading these essays could fail to note not only his thoughts about the reader in relation to the text but also the relation of the artist to the text. In short, I will examine Johnson's views as to how phenomenology informs the content and form of his work, as well as his revelations about the reader and the writer.

Johnson steadfastly refuses to accept the dichotomy of form and content and, I think, even chooses the term *being* to show the connection between form and content. Language so defines how we think about the world that it determines how we experience our environment. He argues, "We live in language" (p. 23).[1] We might argue that the book is divided into two parts as delineated by its title. "Being" is about phenomenology and "Race" about the subcultural experience and meaning that has evolved in African American literature. But for the purposes of my discussion, I will accept the artificial distinction between form and content.

Lifeworld: Form and Function

I am humbled by Charles Johnson's wealth of knowledge and stylistic pyrotechnics. His ability to parody numerous literary traditions and styles tells us that he values enormously the form itself, but in the end he wishes to demonstrate his most important theme: fiction is experience. Because language is so integral to experience that it transforms experience, language in effect becomes experience. And since fiction is language, then fiction is experience. So no matter how much weight we place on his prodigious output, his depth of understanding of the literary forms, the emphasis in his own critical writing is on the fact that the form is inseparable from meaning. An equal but related factor is what Johnson calls the Lifeworld, a translation of the phenomenological term *Lebenswelt*, which may also be defined as a worldview or cultural bias. The Lifeworld is affected by one's subculture and locale, so that it may be seen as the culmination of all the forces that come into play in determining how we understand the world of experiences. The Lifeworld informs our experiences. Johnson emphasizes this relationship between form, meaning, and culture repeatedly but never more clearly than when he writes:

> No literary form is neutral. None is a value-empty vehicle into which we can simply pour the content of experience. Here the ancient form-content notion proves itself false. Each form, whether it be a fairy tale or a non-narrative work, reveals a *Lebenswelt*, or vision of the world that is appropriate to a particular universe, and the use of any form will transfigure with startling results the "content" one wishes to express through it. (p. 48)

Johnson also discusses at length the concept of *Lebenswelt*, or Lifeworld. Here he suggests that our interactions with experience are sifted through the worldview of our culture, which in fact determines how we comprehend and interpret the world. In the *Lebenswelt* of Johnson's literary world, form is content.

Artist's Philosophy: Phenomenology

Phenomenology is so important in understanding Johnson's literary work that he mentions it in the opening line of the preface, where he traces the dizzying history of phenomenology from the mathematician Edmund Husserl through the religious thinking of Max Scheler, passing Martin Heidegger and making a left turn at Jean-Paul Sartre, until stopping at Maurice Merleau-Ponty. In the latter, whom he cites as on par with Mikel Dufrenne, Johnson finds the most satisfying expression of his own views. He believes that the most significant contributions develop the idea that "language, perception, and the body as the foundation for all perceptual experience" (p. iix) are embodied in the concept of Lifeworld. The Lifeworld is the culmination of our sensory perceptions, our linguistic and cultural biases, and our experiences, even when the experience is a vicarious one, such as reading a novel. Of course the Lifeworld is discrete for each individual, but we would all share views propagated by our society and subcultures. Johnson credits Merleau-Ponty more than any other philosopher with significantly advancing arguments in phenomenology with the development of the concept of Lifeworld, which combines "dialectical theory, language, perception and the body as our foundation for all perceptual experience" (p. vii). If we understand this to mean that these views in combination create our worldview and determine even how we think about the world, then the next step is to explore Johnson's view on the relation between fiction as a vicarious experience and phenomenology.

Fiction as Experience

Willing participation as the audience for any art form creates an experience that the human mind perceives as equal to a "real" experience. This is especially true if we accept that audiences have Coleridge's "willing suspension of disbelief." The audience at a horror film has come expecting, even desiring, to be frightened by movie monsters on the giant screen. If for a single moment the moviegoers remember that they are sitting in the safety of a theater with hundreds of others watching nothing more than flickering lights passing through celluloid and projected on a silver screen, they will not be frightened by the cinematic experience. Such an experience may even be thought of as more "real" because it can be more intense. The artist creates an experience with a particular goal in mind, such as writing a joke with the expectation that the audience will laugh or a tragedy with the expectation that the audience will cry. Therefore the art form manipulates the audience in ways that everyday life does not. Not only is the experience of art more intense, but there is often an intended message for members of the audience, who are meant to be enlightened by the epiphany of the moment, as James Joyce suggested. Johnson too believes that literature can create that moment of enlightenment: "Fiction, in a funny Buddhist sense, might even be called a Way" (p. 45). Clearly he believes that the experience of reading may be tantamount to a learning experience in life.

The distinction between "real" experience and vicarious experience is one that has been discussed by such diverse thinkers as Plato, John Locke, Bishop Berkeley and Chuang Tzu. And whether or not reality is defined by Plato as a shadow cast on a wall or by Chuang Tzu as the dream of a butterfly, all of these philosophers agree that experience is filtered by our perceptions and cultural prejudices. As Johnson sees it, all human experience is filtered by our biochemical and philosophical limitations. There may be a single "truth" of the world, but we will never be able to separate ourselves from that "truth." So fiction shapes our beliefs in the same manner that religious or political views do.

Charles Johnson also believes, in a very Taoist sense, that there is no single correct interpretation of life's experiences. The same belief holds true for interpreting fiction—or any art, for that matter. Humans are conditioned by the art form itself into thinking in a particular way. Again giving us his chief source on this very complicated philosophical and linguistic issue, Johnson writes:

> phenomenologists such as Maurice Merleau-Ponty conclude that philosophy and fiction—both disciplines of language—are about, at bottom, the same business . . . making it clear in *Sense and Non-Sense* that our lives are inherently metaphysical insofar as each moment of perception . . . involves the activity of interpretation; perception is an *act*, and this observation puts the lie to that ancient stupidity that says the processes of philosophy and fiction are two different disciplines—they are sister disciplines. (p. 32)[2]

Both of these disciplines inform the participant how to understand and interpret the world. Nor is this process a simple black and white one. There is no single Lifeworld that all humans share; nor is there a single experience or interpretation of life's experiences. So the human experience is many faceted and complex, allowing for numerous valid interpretations. Johnson suggests, "Because no experience is 'raw.' None is given to us as meaningful, or as meaning only one thing" (p. 31). Thus, like life, literature always has several diverse explanations and meanings.

Johnson believes that form and style stem from the worldview of the author. He cites Linsey Abrams, "A Maximilist Novelist Looks at Some Minimalist Fiction" (1985), who writes that "style is never simply technical choice, but evolves from how a writer sees the world" (p. 6). Clearly Johnson's personal philosophy combines Asian philosophy and European phenomenology. He states that the martial arts are like phenomenology, "something you *do*" (p. ix). We can see the influence of Asian religious and philosophical thought throughout his fiction, but he makes this correlation very clear in *Being and Race*. Johnson compares literature and martial arts when he says that "in the traditional, Asian martial arts, we say of a student after he has brilliantly executed a kata, or prearranged set of fighting moves . . . that he has 'honored the form' " (p. 47). Just as Ishmael Reed compares boxing to writing in *Writin' Is*

Fightin', Johnson compares the discipline of learning the traditions in martial arts to that of learning literary traditions. In both cases one must imitate the conventions before one can fully understand the subject. He proposes that "it's fair to compare the severe discipline of the Asian martial arts to writing, emphasizing (1) the galaxy of forms we inherit, (2) the need of every apprentice to master forms through relentless practice, study and repetition; and (3) the duty incumbent on every apprentice to cultivate an attitude of 'honoring the form' . . . moving the form forward through his own interpretation of possibilities made real by this historical moment" (pp. 47–48). This process of learning the tradition and repeating the patterns of the convention is similar to a writer of sonnets learning his or her craft by reading sonnets and then imitating them. After all, why does a writer select a specific form and choose to fulfill the rules of a particular genre, except to honor the form by writing in the same tradition? Imitation is the highest form of flattery.

Not only does Johnson believe that there is a correlation between being and race, a correlation between being and fiction, and a correlation between being and form, but he also believes that Being is the Word. He argues that phenomenology is the "philosophy of experience" (p. ix) and fiction itself is experience, even though and maybe especially because it is vicarious and designed for an intentional purpose, to arouse particular feelings in the reader. For example, in Jerzy Kozinski's *Painted Bird*, the reader becomes inured to the terrible experiences of the boy, until the reader has the same deadened sensibilities. The repetition of the terrible tortures that the boy sees and suffers makes him feel no pathos for anyone's pain and suffering. The reader is transformed by the vicarious experience to share the same deadened emotions and null feelings as the protagonist. So the form of the book creates an experience that is meaningful for the audience.

Art: Fulfilling the Form

Charles Johnson's knowledge of fiction is as vast as his knowledge of philosophy, and he clearly owes a debt to T. S. Eliot's critical thinking about the importance of literary tradition. Johnson spends a good deal of time in defining literary forms, which in turn permits him to imitate them with great precision. In *Being and Race* he defines forms such as the sketch, fable, apologue, and everything else up to the novel. His own fiction includes all these forms, albeit often in outright parodies, such as *Oxherding Tale* and *Middle Passage*. But his parodies always go beyond a mere aping of a conventional form or device; they give meaning to the tale he tells.

We must remember that the linguistic philosophy that Johnson adheres to proposes that even the literary traditions teach us about the meaning of life by creating experience. So the models that our culture utilizes to educate us are especially significant. Eliot, whom Johnson paraphrases when he states that writers stand on the shoulders of their predecessors, argued that literary tradition teaches us how to communicate. Johnson connects the literary conventions of literature with the morals of their tales when he writes that the artist "must have models with which to agree, partly agree or outright oppose, and these can only come from the tradition of literature itself, for Nature seems to remain silent, providing no final text or court of judgment" (p. 5). Johnson is far too sophisticated to embrace any single narrow interpretation of literature or life.

Almost all elements of writing are discussed in *Being and Race*. Johnson speaks of character, plot, setting, and numerous other literary conventions, saying that each element of the fabric should be woven so that it is essential to the entire tapestry. He writes: "Every writer dreams of achieving this, I believe—a fictional world so fully rendered that even a single glove, as Prosper Merimee once said, has its theory and reinforces the unifying vision, the truth, of the novel as a whole" (p. 15). Johnson also speaks at great length of larger literary structures, such as novel plots, offering John Gardner's *Forms of Fiction* (1962) as his inspiration. Gardner suggested that writers submerge themselves in a genre until they intuitively know the form from repeated exposure, then "compose a new work satisfying this form, following its conventions, and ambitiously play variations upon them" (48). Of course, this concept is not original with Gardner. Johnson also credits Northrop Frye, "The Educated Imagination," for reminding us "how story plots in the air around us are as old as humanity itself. Correction: *are* humanity itself" (51). There cannot be enough emphasis put on the correlation between literary form and the enlightenment of the reader.

But all forms continually evolve as new writers build upon the work of authors who have fulfilled the form before. These writers defined the forms, but the forms are directions as well as definitions. Once again Johnson paraphrases Eliot when he writes that the literary tradition was "handed down by our predecessors, black and white, who provided a path to walk on but who could not themselves finish the journey" (51). They could not finish the journey. Nor shall we finish that journey, since the efflorescence of meaning is endless.

Audience

The audience of literature receives much attention in *Being and Race*, where Johnson discusses at length the effects of literature on the reader. There are two central ideas that he expresses. First there is a moral aspect to every tale, and second the structure of the tale affects how the audience responds. There can be little question of the significance of Eliot's "objective correlative" to Johnson. The objective correlative is defined by Eliot as an object in symbolic form, such as a metaphor in a poem, that correlates to an emotion and creates a specific emotional response in the reader. Nor can the influence of the pheno-menologists be ignored, because they suggest that our language and worldview determine how we understand the metaphor, and hence our world.

Johnson accepts the concept that the reader is transposed to the Lifeworld of the novel. The reader is immersed in a kind of transcen-dental ascendance that is similar to the concepts of the American Tran-scendentalists, such as Ralph Waldo Emerson, who believed that lan-guages and literature operate on many planes of consciousness. Johnson writes: "Language is transcendence. And so is fiction. They comport us 'out there' behind the eyes of others, into their hearts." And again: "Merleau-Ponty is our best guide for making clear how great is our debt to our predecessors and contemporaries whenever we use these com-mon cultural phenomena—language and literary form—to create fic-tion" (p. 39). Johnson is emphatic that there is a correlation between the written word and the reader that parallels the correlation between hu-mans and the "real" world of daily experience. He says, "writing doesn't so much record an experience—or even imitate or represent it—as it *creates* that experience" (pp. 5–6). So in the end the experience of the reader of a text is dependent not only on the text but also on the reader and his or her worldview.

As I suggested, phenomenologists argue that vicarious experience is more real than perceptions of "reality" because vicarious experience is carefully constructed to evoke emotions in the audience. In a comedy the elements are consciously arranged to make us laugh at life and to feel that all is well with the world. In a tragedy we are compelled to shed tears and feel sorrow.

The purpose of this manipulation through style and form is to teach. The reader is supposed to learn from the experience and perhaps be morally improved. Johnson finds a "workable middle ground" through John Gardner's views on the relation of language and thought and moral education in Leo Tolstoy's "What Is Art?" (1898). Johnson recognizes that one function of the arts is to educate humanity. He believes that this is accomplished by the emotion created by the vicarious experience provided by fiction. He quotes Tolstoy to make his point: "Art is a human activity, consisting in this, that man consciously, by means of certain external signs, hands on to others feelings that he has lived through, and that other people are infected by these feelings, and also experience them" (p. 37). And through this experience the reader is enlightened.

To sum up Johnson's complex thinking on these issues, he believes that the nature of human perception is such that our minds cannot distinguish between vicarious and nonvicarious experience. In addition, the prejudices of our language and our cultures determine how we de-fine and interpret our world. Most important, we must remember that "we speak of experience as something that 'happened' to us, . . . though this kind of talk shortchanges the enormous role played by imagination and language and cultural conditioning in our perception and assumes that meaning is *given* directly to us with little or no shaping necessary from our side" (p. 30). Indeed there is nothing but shaping from our cultural and personal biases. The Lifeworld is the confluence of the rivers of perception, cultural prejudice, and individual experience.

Culture and Subculture

To understand Johnson's writing in the context of society, we must understand how Johnson sees his own subculture and understand how African American literature is part of and affected by mass American culture. In *Being and Race*, he goes to great lengths to discuss African American traditions in literature and how these have changed the course of American society. Johnson does not envision two separate societies, one black and one white, but a multicultural society spanning numerous subcultures from city and country and every corner of the planet. This multifaceted perception of reality jibes nicely with his philosophical thinking. He demonstrates this when he writes that

> what we have, from the standpoint of phenomenology are not different worlds but instead innumerable perspectives on *one* world; and we know that, when it comes to the crunch, we share, all of us, the same cultural Lifeworld—a world layered with ancestors, predecessors and contemporaries. To think of this world properly is to find that all our perspectives take us directly to a common situation, a common history in which all meanings evolve. (p. 44)

So despite the fact that American society is often segregated, ultimately all the views of mainstream culture are influenced by all the subcultures and ultimately interact with and influence every individual.

African American literature is the central focus of the majority of the critical discussion in *Being and Race*. Johnson surveys most of the major black writers with great acumen. His historical viewpoint on African American literature, especially as a protest literature, is well developed in the pages of *Being and Race*. Although the book is subtitled *Black Writing since 1970*, Johnson explains his views on the eras before this date as well. He states that there are several schools of thought that contributed to the development of contemporary African American writing. The best example is his discussion of the concept of Negritude as a positive force for the voice of blacks.

The concept of Negritude was developed by Léopold Sédar Senghor, who argued that Negro reasoning was different from European reasoning because it was based on touch rather than sight. Johnson notes that Senghor, in "The Psychology of the African Negro," suggested that the Negro was "intuitive through participation." In fact he implied that the Negro experience of "reality" was superior to its European counterpart because the Negro had "a sympathetic, even magical grasp of the world"

(p. 18). There can be little doubt that this view developed in part in response to stereotypes of African Americans. Instead of African American religious traditions being considered superstition or mumbo jumbo, here blacks are in touch with gods and more "spiritual" than whites, therefore superior. Johnson bewails the fact that most of the literature of African Americans up to the 1960s tends to be one-dimensional, focusing on the issue of racial equality and human justice, both very noble topics indeed.

Johnson prefers to explore a multitude of themes in his writing and admires a writer who is not bound to a single genre or style or topic. He clearly does not want to be stereotyped as a black protest writer, although he writes about the same issues as many of the protest writers. He is troubled by what he sees as "the overwhelming technical and thematic one-dimensionality of much of black fiction published prior to 1970" (p. 119). But then there is a dramatic change in the direction of the themes among some fair percentage of black writers; after 1970, "black is beautiful" becomes the replacement for the protest literature that preceded it. Blacks argue not that they are equal to whites but that they are superior. In addition, there is a rise in the popularity of black literature which does not solely address issues of racial equality.

In Johnson's view, the Black Arts Movement and Cultural Nationalism are the key movements that effected this change in outlook. Speaking of the valuable contributions of the Cultural Nationalist movement, Johnson firmly believes that much of contemporary African American literature could exist only because of the groundbreaking work of this group. In *Being and Race*, he suggests how important both movements were:

> No one should doubt, not ever, the contribution of these men and women. Or their value. The truth, which is hardly said enough, is that black writing of the 1980s stands on the shoulders of the confrontationalist fiction of the Angry School. Without it we could not stand at all. (p. 83)

Indeed all of his own work contains an element, sometimes a central element, that focuses on racial issues. He also says that some of the credit for the new spirituality of American culture is due to the protest themes of the black writers before 1970. Even the counterculture of the sixties was influenced by these writers. Johnson may be critical of the limited nature of this writing, but he reveres and honors its contributions. This is most clear when he writes, "Cultural Nationalism and the Black Aesthetic have despite their numerous shortcomings as systematic thought, shaped much black American fiction" and have a "new American hunger for spirituality, moral values, breadth of vision, and a retreat from materialism. . . . the primary thrust of Cultural Nationalism is the reaffirmation of the hope of black men and women . . . that they can lead lives of deeper creativity and spirituality" (p. 120). These are the giants on whose shoulders Johnson stands when he explores the moral aspects of his own literature.

Why did this type of protest literature evolve? One answer, Johnson suggests, is that of Carolyn Gerald, who in "The Black Writer and His Role," *The Black Aesthetic*, argues that African Americans had encountered only a negative or "zero image" of themselves "and that a program for black cultural reconstruction is required to create positive images" (p. 17). The only way to overcome the negative stereotyping of blacks by generations of Americans was for African Americans to shout from the rooftops of their literary ivory towers that black is beautiful. And Johnson thinks a good deal of the work for improving society was done by women authors. In fact, he devotes a large portion of *Being and Race* to the works of women. Because women faced a different Lifeworld on a daily basis than men, their writing reflected numerous and diverse social issues. He writes, "It is against this depressing, perhaps even disastrous background of the black family's internal contradictions and near collapse that we must understand some of the angrier work of some black women authors" (p. 96). But Johnson is quick to assert that not all black women are angry protest writers. Many are joyous. He writes, "women writers of all colors have brought forth a new universal, or way of seeing" (p. 97). The other significant issue that Johnson repeatedly discusses is the purpose of art, which is to educate society. One way of accomplishing this is by exposing the ills of society. An early proponent of this who was a large influence on Johnson is Larry Neal, who in "The Black Arts Movement" (1968) says that the purpose of the arts is to teach. Johnson believes that art not only should teach but also entertain and explain life's complexities to us.

Artist Biography

Being and Race reveals much about Charles Johnson's personal life. He reveals a good deal about what he sees as the influences on African American culture. He explains that black American culture is heavily influenced by the literary traditions of religion. Like jazz, African American culture combined folk faith, Christianity, and African thinking into a new form. The black church provided a forum for black cultural creativity. He says that in his own experience the church was a "place where blacks could reinterpret Christianity and transform it into an instrument for worldly change" (p. 84). The other aspect of his life that Johnson reveals much about is his position as an African American in our society. He often lets an interesting idea slip out, as when he talks of the "artistic impulse." He asks, "Do we *begin* at the same place, writers black and white? (p. 3). The answer is clearly no.

Much to my surprise, Johnson speaks quite a bit about the influence that the Christian church had on his life and writing. Although I did not find it apparent in his fiction, Johnson gives great weight to the benefits that organized religion offered African Americans. The church was one place where black cultural activities could evolve communally and still remain separated from mainstream society. One example of the influence of the black church was the fostering of his sense of community. Johnson says:

> the richest, most enduring source of black American culture is found in the black church. And I can say, personally, that the community in which I was raised in the 1950s, one comprising black people transplanted from the south decades before, was bonded by the religious piety of my parents and the parents of my friends. (P. 83)

My own prejudice, formed strictly from reading his fiction, suggested to me that he had an Asian influence in his religious upbringing. I thought he was a child of zen, not of Baptists. But I was completely wrong. The other aspect of the church that affected Johnson was the beautiful language that can be found in the liturgy and gospel. He says he has the same love of the poetry of the Bible and the ministers as his father, who "loved the rich oratory of black preachers. The voices of his neighbors and relatives raised in song. The values of family life and hard work to help one's children and kinfolk" (pp. 83–84). In the confines of the church, African Americans could create a community to enrich their own lives, and this community extended beyond the confines of the church walls. We must remember that a great deal of the Civil Rights Movement grew from these beginnings of the African American community.

African American Subculture

The title *Being and Race* suggests the other aspect of Johnson's subculture that has profoundly affected his life: race. Johnson confesses, "Life is baffling enough for every novelist, and for writers of Afro-American fiction it presents even more artistic and philosophical questions than for writers who are white" (p. 3). Although I am not sure I can completely agree with this concept, clearly Johnson feels that his role in American society is strongly affected by his being an African American. There is ample evidence in his fiction that one of his chief concerns is the equality of the races and genders, but these are not his only concerns. His interest in other social issues and linguistic philosophies sets his work apart from the protest literature of what he calls the angry black writers dominant before 1970.

To understand the darker side of Charles Johnson, we must understand his views on black writing. That is, after all, part of the subtitle of *Being and Race*. He argues that the chief aim of much of African American literature was to criticize the injustices of society, including sexism and classism as well as racism. But there is more to literature than these issues, and the resulting limited focus of this protest literature was too confining for African American writers after the sixties. Johnson himself fits in the latter school. He loves life and words, which is apparent in the joyous nature of his writing. His work is still a social protest, but as an affirmative writer he wants his books to be an affirmation of life as well.

It is important to reach beyond the limits of social realism, to be not only a protest writer against racism, sexism, or classism but to be for peace, justice, and love. Johnson also sees African American writers as a very diverse group. They are multicultural and "benefit greatly from the revitalizing influences of cross-cultural fertilization" (p. 52). Black literature is like jazz, the only completely original American art form, which grew from the combination of African, Caribbean, and European music. In the same way, African American literature could draw upon sources from several cultures that were not available to white mainstream writers.

There can be little question that the tradition from social realism of escaped slave narratives to the Magical Realism of Ishmael Reed was a long and perilous one. African American literature was compelled by the *Lebenswelt* of the era to deal with the social injustices of slavery and racism. "From its beginnings," Johnson claims,

> in the poetry of Phillis Wheatley and the narrative of Gustavus Vassa, black fiction comprises, one must confess, an overwhelming tragic literature. It is full of failures. A catalogue of man's inhumanity to man and woman. Book after book discloses the desperate struggle of a people first to survive against stupendous odds and then to secure the most basic rights in a perpetually hostile environment. (P. 7)

Having survived such overwhelming difficulties, black literature was finally able to expand beyond being a protest literature to explore the joy of life that enabled African American culture to survive against vast odds in a hostile environment.

ʊ̈ ʊ̈ ʊ̈

As I stated at the beginning of this essay, *Being and Race* is required reading for anyone interested in better understanding the thinking of Charles Johnson. This book offers his contemplations on such diverse issues as phenomenology, African American literature, and the black church. He surveys his philosophical roots and clearly defines his indebtedness to Merleau-Ponty's synthesis of phenomenological arguments. Johnson also turns a thoughtful eye to literary traditions, discussing everything from basic conventions to genres, including discussion of race and gender. Almost as an extra added attraction, we can learn a lot about the personal experiences of Johnson that have influenced his life and writing. Seldom do we as readers find such a useful book for understanding so many perspectives of an author's thinking.

Phenomenology, or at least Johnson's views on this complex subject, is clearly laid out for the reader of this book. The crucial aspect to comprehend is that fiction is a way for humans to understand our lives and world. Johnson believes that our culture, through all the arts, shapes the way we think about the world. And this is a very human thing to do. In fact it may be what distinguishes us as humans. The importance of art is best expressed by Johnson when he writes, "Our faith in fiction comes from an ancient belief that language and literary art—all speaking and showing—clarify our experience" (p. 3). The clarity of experience is the epiphany, or moment of enlightenment, we receive from the experience of reading. So not only does the *Lebenswelt* shape the way we think of the world, but the writer shapes the *Lebenswelt*. Thus the writer creates the way we think about life. This is the moral aspect of literature that is so essential for a fuller, richer life and ultimately the improvement of society.

Formal aspects of art in general and fiction in particular are explored in great detail. Johnson offers views on how the elements of fiction may be used to create that *Lebenswelt*. And he repeatedly emphasizes that he does not want to be known as a one-dimensional writer of black protest literature. He demonstrates a broad knowledge of African American literature with often brilliant insights into the meaning and cultural significance of both men and women writers. But he makes clear that his highest praise is for those writers who have mastered the tradition and "honored the form." He writes:

> Still our greatest respect must be reserved for the protean writer, the performer like Chaucer or Shakespeare, who slides from genre to genre, style to style, leaving his or her distinctive signature on each form lovingly transfigured and pushed to new possibilities. No creator, black or white, can be exempt from this standard. No genuine artist would wish to be. (P. 53)

Johnson is one of those genuine artists who has pushed the limits of fiction to new and interesting possibilities.

Clearly Johnson reveals a great deal about himself and his culture in this book, which is deliciously written. As he writes, "literary art is at its best when it is a sumptuous act of imagination, invention and interpretation" (p. 31). *Being and Race* is a sumptuous feast of philosophical thinking that informs us about a great writer and his works.

Notes

1. All references are to *Being and Race: Black Writing since 1970* (Bloomington: Indiana University Press, 1988).

2. A chief influence cited by Johnson is Maurice Merleau-Ponty, "Metaphysics and the Novel," *Sense and Non-Sense*, trans. Hubert L. Dreyfus and Patricia Dreyfus (Evanston: Northwestern University Press, 1964), p. 26, and *The Phenomenology of Perception*, trans. Colin Smith (London: Routledge and Kegan Paul, 1962).

It Rests by Changing

Process in *The Sorcerer's Apprentice*

Rudolph P. Byrd

It rests by changing.

—Heraclitus

"That all things flow" is the first vague generalization which the un-
systematized, barely analyzed, intuition of man has produced. It is the
theme of some of the best Hebrew poetry in the Psalms; it appears as
one of the first generalizations of Greek philosophy in the form of the
saying of Heraclitus. . . . Without doubt, if we are to go back to that
ultimate, integral experience, unwarped by the sophistications of theory,
that experience whose elucidation is the final aim of philosophy, the flux
of things is one ultimate generalization around which we must weave
our philosophical system.

—Alfred North Whitehead, *Process and Reality*

The *Sorcerer's Apprentice: Tales and Conjuration* (1986) is the only collection to date of short fiction by Charles Johnson, though the author,
while working chiefly in the genre of the novel, has continued to write
and publish short fiction since the publication of this fine debut collection.[1] With the publication of *The Sorcerer's Apprentice*, Johnson joins
a long tradition of African American writers of short fiction, by which
I mean chiefly the short story. Inaugurated by the publication of Charles
Chesnutt's *Conjure Woman* (1899) and *Wife of His Youth* (1899), this
tradition includes such collections as Langston Hughes's *Ways of White
Folks* (1934), Richard Wright's *Uncle Tom's Children* (1938), Ernest J.

Gaines's *Bloodline* (1968), James Alan McPherson's *Hue and Cry* (1971) and *Elbow Room* (1981), Toni Cade Bambara's *Gorilla My Love* (1972), Alice Walker's *In Love and Trouble* (1973) and *You Can't Keep a Good Woman Down* (1981), Paule Marshall's *Reena and Other Stories* (1982), Randall Keenan's *Let the Dead Bury Their Dead* (1992), Anthony Groom's *Trouble No More* (1995), and Ralph Ellison's *Fly Away Home and Other Stories* (1996).

Of the collections mentioned, *The Sorcerer's Apprentice* shares the greatest number of affinities with Chesnutt's *Conjure Woman*. Chesnutt and Johnson share a deep preoccupation with slavery as a framework for interrogating relations of power, as well as questions of citizenship for an historically maligned and discredited black population. *The Sorcerer's Apprentice* opens with "The Education of Mingo" and closes with "The Sorcerer's Apprentice," stories that explore the shifting configurations of power between master and slave as well as aspects of slave culture within the antebellum and postbellum South. Further, as artists both Chesnutt and Johnson are drawn to the rich world of African American folklore, a world of sorcerers and spells, fabulations and conjurations, motherwit and lies which bear the imprint of truth: a world that is the foundation, as Richard Wright argues in "Blueprint for Negro Writing," for much that is enduring in African American literature.[2] Above all, Johnson and Chesnutt share an abiding preoccupation with the theme of change and transformation, a theme and organizing principle that links in deeply subtle ways *The Conjure Woman* with *The Sorcerer's Apprentice*. For Chesnutt, the theme of change and transformation constitutes the expanding floor of a critique of such southern apologists as Joel Chandler Harris, as well as an uncomprising argument regarding the centrality of African Americans in the reconstruction of a much-divided republic in the aftermath of the Civil War. As treated by Johnson, such a theme possesses certain correspondences to the progressive political views that enliven the stories of *The Conjure Woman*, and similarly it becomes the expanding floor for a meditation on the endless possibilities of humankind. Ultimately, in his treatment of the theme of change and transformation Johnson moves beyond slavery and the engulfing tragedies along the color line to a region in fiction defined above all by enduring human truths as they are articulated within the discipline of philosophy.

While Johnson wrote and assembled the stories of *The Sorcerer's Apprentice* fully cognizant of Chesnutt's achievement in *The Conjure Woman*, the work most central to his prestidigitations in the realm of short fiction is Alfred North Whitehead's *Process and Reality* (1929). Johnson's conception of change and transformation, in fine, his conception of *process*, is deeply stained by his reading and study of Whitehead's sometimes opaque but often instructive magnum opus. The stories of *The Sorcerer's Apprentice* are, in one sense, an expansive treatment and illustration of Whitehead's theory of organism set forth in

Process and Reality. While these stories were not originally conceived of as an integrated collection, nevertheless their coherence rests upon a thematic unity or a theory of process set forth not only in Whitehead's *Process and Reality* but also in his later and related collection of essays, *Adventures of Ideas* (1933). As an artist and trained philosopher, Johnson remains committed to creating "philosophically serious fiction," or more precisely what he terms philosophical black fiction, the principles of which are set forth in his essays "Where Philosophy and Fiction Meet," "Philosophy and Black Fiction," and "Whole Sight: Notes on New Black Fiction." In these essays, Johnson names a new a tradition in African American literature and identifies those writers— Jean Toomer, Richard Wright, and Ralph Ellison are his exemplars— whose corpus is the point of intersection between philosophy and fiction. As defined by Johnson, philosophical black fiction is "art that interrogates experience." Further, it is a species of fiction absent certain fictions, that is to say, the formulaic, overdetermined, essentialist castings of black experience. These reductive fictions are the antithesis of the objectives of philosophical black fiction which is the liberation of perception and the achievement of "whole sight," that is, the ability to apprehend the varieties of black experience in their dynamic and always shifting constellations.

Like the other works of fiction in Johnson's ever-enlarging oeuvre, *The Sorcerer's Apprentice* contains instances in which the questions of philosophy and the requirements of art are masterfully combined to produce "whole sight." In *Faith and the Good Thing*, Johnson employs the insights of Plato's *Republic* to deepen the meaning of the novel's central question: what is the nature of the good? In *Oxherding Tale*, Johnson plumbs a range of Asian philosophical systems and texts, including the *Ten Oxherding Pictures*, a classic in Zen Buddhism, to give weight to the question framing all thought and action in this metaphysical slave narrative: what are the ways in which we can be enslaved? In *Middle Passage*, Johnson mines Hegel's *Phenomenology of Mind* in his investigation of the various meanings occasioned by the question which vibrates at the core of this prize-winning novel: what is the nature of freedom? And what, precisely, is the relationship of *The Sorcerer's Apprentice* to these other works? Is there a question at the collection's center from which is born what Whitehead would term a "concrete unity"? I would like to suggest here that the eight stories of *The Sorcerer's Apprentice* constitute an advancement of Johnson's ambitious artistic project whose objective is to create fresh and original works of fiction grounded in philosophy that reveal the richness of the black world. Moreover, the stories of this collection gesture toward an answer to the question posed by Whitehead in his preface to *Process and Reality*. For Whitehead the vital question is "What does it all mean?" or, to rephrase this question: how can the operations of the world be explained? For both Whitehead and Johnson, the answer to this cosmological inter-

rogative is "process." Before proceeding to an analysis of Johnson's treatment and adaptation of Whitehead's question in *The Sorcerer's Apprentice*, it is necessary that I elaborate upon the conception of process so
central to Johnson's artistic project.

ψ̈ ψ̈ ψ̈

> The community of actual things is an organism; but it is not a static
> organism. It is an incompletion in process of production.
>
> —Alfred North Whitehead, *Process and Reality*

A mathematician and philosopher of science, Whitehead believed
in the innate dignity of humankind. In profound disagreement with
such thinkers as Galileo, Descartes, Newton, and Locke, who conceived of the universe as a series of complex mechanical operations, he
developed a theory in which the seemingly contradictory tenets of religion and science could be integrated. According to Whitehead, the
"best rendering of integral experience . . . is often to be found in the
utterances of religious aspiration." One reason for the thinness of so
much modern metaphysics, he argues, "is its neglect of this wealth
of expression of ultimate feeling."[3] Whitehead attributed much of the
"thinness" of modern metaphysics to Immanuel Kant. He rejected the
"Kantian doctrine of the objective world as a theoretical construct from
purely subjective experience" (p. xiii). Seeking to harmonize religion
with science while also vigorously contesting the antireligious current in
philosophy, Whitehead developed the theory of organism, which posits
that "relatedness has its foundation in the relatedness of actualities;
and such relatedness is wholly concerned with the appropriation of the
dead by the living—that is to say, with 'objective immortality' whereby
what is divested of its own living immediacy becomes a real component
in other living immediacies of becoming" (pp. xiii–xiv). In the theory of
organism, he also posits that "the creative advance of the world is the
becoming, the perishing, and the objective immortalities of those things
which jointly constitute *stubborn fact*" (p. xiv). According to Whitehead,
the theory "of organism is combined with that of 'process' in a twofold
manner. The community of actual things is an organism; but it is not a
static organism. It is an incompletion in process of production. Thus
the expansion of the universe in respect to actual things is the first
meaning of 'process'; and the universe in any stage of its expansion is
the first meaning of 'organism' " (pp. 214–15).

In his theory of organism, Whitehead maintains that "each actual
entity [or actual thing] is itself only describable as an organic process.
It repeats in microcosm what the universe is in macrocosm. It is a
process proceeding from phase to phase, each phase being the real basis
from which its successor proceeds towards the completion of the thing
in question" (p. 215). In other words, all of human experience and the

operations of nature, or what Whitehead terms "living immediacies," do not comprise isolated, independent phenomena but rather are organic, integrated, and dynamic operations that, in their changing totality, yield a meaningful, intelligible, and ultimately spiritual order. Hopeful and affirmative, Whitehead's theory of organism rejects fragmentation and dislocation as necessarily permanent conditions, for, as he theorizes, "to be something is to have the potentiality for acquiring real unity with other entities" (p. 212). For Whitehead, the dynamic interplay of these "living immediacies" or "organisms" within fluid environments constitutes the most advanced reading of the processes of the world. As one commentator observes, the world in all its complexity and variety is the issue of the "combination of these forces in a particular way. . . . [and] is the result of the selection and ordering of God. For Whitehead, the ultimate good is the perception of God as this unifying force behind the movement of the world process. Thus Whitehead constructed a metaphysical system which made room for the incorporation of all scientific theory and discovery, and which included as well all subjective experience."[4]

Committed to revealing the structural complexities embedded in what he posits as a "fluent world" of "living immediacies," Whitehead argues that there are two species of fluency or process: concrescence and transition. According to Whitehead, concrescence "is the name for the process in which the universe of many things acquires an individual unity in a determinate relegation of each item of the 'many' to its subordination in the constitution of the novel 'one'" (p. 211). Within the framework of his theory of organism, an instance of concrescence is termed an "actual entity" or an "actual occasion." Throughout the critical chapter entitled "Process" in *Process and Reality*, Whitehead uses these two terms interchangeably. They are synonyms for concrescence, or the process whereby an existent acquires a particular relationship with other existents and thus achieves a coherence—a "concrete unity." "There is not one completed set of things," argues Whitehead, "which are actual occasions" (p. 211). Further, he maintains that a "set of all actual occasions is by the nature of things a standpoint for another concrescence which elicits a concrete unity from those many actual occasions. Thus we can never survey the actual world, except from the standpoint of an immediate concrescence which is falsifying the presupposed completion" (p. 211). Ultimately, in Whitehead's theory of organism " 'the actual world' is always a relative term, and refers to that basis of presupposed actual occasions which is a datum for the novel concrescence" (p. 211).

The second species of fluency or process Whitehead terms "transition." In explaining the character and function of transition in relation to concrescence, Whitehead defines transition as the fluency or process whereby we observe and apprehend the movement from "particular existent to particular existent." Further, transition is the "perpetually perishing which is one aspect of the notion of time; and in another aspect the transition is the origination of the present in conformity with the power of the past" (p. 210). In his definition of transition, Whitehead introduces the concept of time. For Whitehead, transition achieves its reality chiefly within the divisions of the past and the present. As a fluency, transition seeks to explain and give meaning to the "perishing of the process," for the completion of a "particular existent constitutes that existent as an original element in the constitutions of other particular existents elicited by repetitions of process" (p. 210). Plainly, concrescence and transition are interrelated; one process does not occur without the other. At the precise moment when an existent enters the flow of existence and achieves concrescence or becomes an actual occasion bearing the particular imprint of previous actual occasions it is, in that same moment, perishing, assuming its place within the past which is, according to Whitehead, "a nexus of actualities [or actual occasions]" (p. 214). And what of the future? The attainment of concrescence possesses significance for the future only insofar as such actualities become components in what Whitehead terms "other living immediacies of becoming."

As Whitehead's theory of organism places great stress upon organic processes, a relation with the future and the achievement of what he terms "objective immortality" is, by the logic of his theory, assured though implicit. For Whitehead, the ultimate reality is not death but rather process: the infinite and subtle movement of existents from phase to phase toward the achievement of a unity which he terms "the satisfaction." The satisfaction is the "culmination of the concrescence into a completely determinate matter of fact, the attainment of the private ideal which is the final cause of the concrescence" (p. 212). In one sense, the satisfaction is the final phase of the becoming of any organism according to Whitehead's theory of organism. It is the defining moment in this dynamic process wherein an actual entity achieves its particular function or role. To adapt these terms to meet the outline of the individual human lives treated in Johnson's fiction, the satisfaction is the moment when an individual achieves, through the interplay of will in combination with historical and contemporary forces, a particular identity which is itself subject to endless permutations through repetitions of process.

And what, to return to Whitehead's question, does this all mean? Put most succinctly, Whitehead is suggesting that the permanency of the world, its thingness, its concreteness, is both a "stubborn fact" and an illusion. Yes, the solidity of the earth, its impressive girth and vastness, is indisputable, but we also know, to paraphrase Heraclitus, Whitehead's ancestor in the metaphysics of process, that it is impossible to "step twice into the same river, nor can one grasp any mortal substance in a stable condition, but rather it scatters and again gathers; it forms and dissolves, and approaches and departs."[5] Transformation and change, or concrescence and transition to return to the terms which propel Whitehead's theory of organism, are the constants in nature and human experience. Of course, what occurs at the macroscopic level also occurs at a microscopic level. In macroscopic terms, the obvious example is the earth and its evolutionary processes. In microscopic terms, a striking example would be the cyclical nature of the individual human life, from the moment of conception to the moment of death. In fine, a concrescence or an actual occasion is, as Whitehead stresses, an organic process whose meaning is reflected and concretized at both the macroscopic and microscopic levels of existence. It is a process, as Whitehead concludes in the pivotal chapter in *Process and Reality*, "proceeding from phase to phase, each phase being the real basis from which its successor proceeds towards the completion of the thing in question" (p. 215). Of course, it is the manifestation of Whitehead's theory of organism at the microscopic level, the deep and subtle impression of the operations of the cosmos upon the individual human life, that is of profound importance to an artist, a storyteller like Johnson.

ॐ ॐ ॐ

> The philosophical writer is simply the man or woman who . . . wishes only to be open to the world of culture and consciousness in all the fascinating, constantly changing forms it takes.
> —Charles Johnson, "Where Philosophy and Fiction Meet"

How, precisely, has Johnson translated the complexity of Whitehead's theory of organism into the fictional universe of *The Sorcerer's Apprentice*? In what manner does he adapt the features of Whitehead's theory of organism in the eight stories of this collection? First, individually and collectively the stories of *The Sorcerer's Apprentice* constitute a concrescence, or an actual occasion. As an artist who is fully appreciative of the relationship of compression and order to complexity, Johnson crafts discrete fictions in which, to summon Whitehead in this context of storytelling, "the universe of many things acquires an individual unity." In other words, the stories themselves constitute an "individual unity" in which we behold the "universe of many things." Second, Whitehead's definition of concrescence is a means of apprehending the "individual unity" or the richness and coherence of the eight stories of *The Sorcerer's Apprentice*. The interrelationship of these stories, or their "subordination in the constitution of the novel one," is a means of suggesting and framing the complex set of situations and thematic relationships which comprise the totality of the collection itself. Put another way, within the framework of this collection concrescence is a signifier for an individual story and for all eight stories. Third, the second species of process, the transition, which is the movement "from particular existent to particular existent," is reflected in the rapid degree of change in the lives of Johnson's masterfully drawn characters, as well as in the seductive and powerful progression of ideas that function as a bridge in thought between each of the eight stories. Fourth, while Whitehead believed that the operations of the world had their beginnings in the mind of God, thus establishing what he regarded as a harmony between science and religion, the stories of *The Sorcerer's Apprentice* are imbued with neither Christian pieties nor orthodoxies of any kind. The eight stories do possess, however, a moral center from which emerges an ethics by which the conduct and choices of characters may be evaluated and judged. Fifth and perhaps most important, Johnson and Whitehead take as their supreme subject the "flux of things," the dynamic and shifting operations of the world at both the macroscopic and the microscopic levels. As a philosopher, Whitehead theorizes about the "flux of things"; as an artist and storyteller, Johnson reveals the operations of "the flux of things" upon the individual within the protean worlds of fiction. And there is also this to say: just as the "community of actual things is an organism," as Whitehead asserts, so is it also, as Johnson would doubtless concur, a work of fiction. Like an organism, a work of fiction, and *The Sorcerer's Apprentice* is our ready example, possesses its own force, identity, strangeness, its own morphology, unity, and conflict, which are born of what Whitehead terms a "process of feeling" (p. 211). "An actual occasion is analyzable," Whitehead writes. So too are the eight stories of *The Sorcerer's Apprentice*, which are, as I have been suggesting here, individually and collectively a concrescence, or an actual occasion, and thus a daring translation of Whitehead's theory of organism into the realm of fiction. Certainly the power of Whitehead's theory of organism is registered in many other ways in *The Sorcerer's Apprentice*. At this juncture, my intention is to indicate the principal ways in which it assumes significance in Johnson's tales and conjurations. While the imprint of Whitehead's theory of organism is visible in all eight stories, for the purposes of this essay I will examine the translation of this philosophical concept in "The Education of Mingo," "Exchange Value," and "China."

"Mingo's education, to put it plainly," Johnson writes in "The Education of Mingo," involved the "evaporation of one coherent, consistent, complete universe and the embracing of another alien, contradictory, strange."[6] The education of Mingo, or rather his miseducation in the ad hoc school of bondage directed by his master Moses Green, is a striking illustration of the chief principal ordering the fluent world posited in Whitehead's theory of organism. Whitehead's emphasis upon fluent and shifting realities achieves its most concentrated expression in the relationship between Moses Green and his bondsman Mingo. Further, this emphasis upon fluidity registered in the relationship between master and slave complements the concerns so central to this story first published in 1977: the shifting and dynamic, alienated and alien world of the slave who at every turn is challenged to make meaning out of strangeness, and the corresponding condition of the reader who, in like fashion, is challenged to locate the meaning in the contradictory and initially alien universe of each story.

A bachelor and a curmudgeon, "without children, without kinfolk . . . Moses [Green] lived alone on sixty acres in southern Illinois." In his loneliness, Moses "felt the need," as Johnson writes, "for a field hand and helpmate—a friend, to speak the truth plainly" (p. 3). Notwithstanding his desire for companionship which humorously recalls the loneliness of God before the creation of the world, Moses Green is committed to the complete subordination of Mingo to his will as the master. Set on the landscape that also would serve as a stage for Rutherford Calhoun's evolving drama in *Middle Passage* some twenty years later, Johnson begins "The Education of Mingo" with an irony and a paradox. The irony is registered in the name he bestows upon the story's protagonist; Moses Green, unlike his namesake in the Old Testament, is far from interested in Mingo's liberation from bondage. The paradox emerges in Johnson's careful sounding of the curious dependency of the master upon the slave, which is given fuller treatment as the story gains momentum, as well as in two later and related works of fiction written after "The Education of Mingo": *Oxherding Tale* (1981) and *Middle Passage* (1990).

Putatively the "youngest son of the reigning king of the Allumseri, a tribe of wizards," Mingo is a member of the fictional African klan that produced Reb of *Oxherding Tale*, that transformed Rutherford Calhoun of *Middle Passage*, and to which the protagonist of *Dreamer* has ties of kinship. Described as a "dark boy . . . , wild [and] marshy-looking," Mingo is powerfully built with a "breastbone . . . broad as a barrel," and "thick hands that fell away from his wrists like weights" (p. 4). To underscore further the striking physical differences between master and slave, as well as the loss of nobility in this erstwhile African prince, Mingo's laughter, as Johnson writes, "sounded like barking" (p. 5).

The education of Mingo and its carefully calibrated process of change and revision would have both positive and negative consequences for Moses Green, whom Johnson derisively described as the " 'good Christian gentleman' committed to washing a Moor white in a single generation" (p. 5). By turns master, teacher, father, and creator, in the presence of Mingo Moses "constantly revised himself" and policed "all his gestures." In this experiment to remake a human life and in the process remake and elevate himself, Moses achieves a heightened degree of power as well as an exaggerated sense of his own importance: "He felt, late at night when he looked down at Mingo snoring loudly on his corn-shuck mattress, now like father, now like an artist fingering something fine and noble from a rude chump of foreign clay. It was like aiming a shotgun at the whole world through the African, blasting away all that Moses, according to his lights, tagged evil, and cultivating the good; like standing, you might say, on the sixth day, feet planted wide, trousers hitched, and remaking the world so it looked more familiar" (pp. 5–6). While this educational experiment sometimes frightened Moses, and while he became increasingly aware of the differences between himself and his pliable slave, nevertheless the instruction, as it were, continued. For a period of time Moses, a Pygmalion enthralled by his own art, could not have been more pleased with the results: "Slowly, Mingo conquered knife and spoon, then language. He picked up the old man's family name. Gradually, he learned—soaking them up like a sponge—Mose's gestures and idiosyncratic body language. . . . That African, Moses saw inside a year, was exactly the product of his own way of seeing, as much one of his products and judgements as his choice of tobacco; was, in a sense that both pleased and bumsquabbled the crusty old man, himself: a homunculus, or a distorted shadow, or—as Moses put it to his lady friend Harriet Bridgewater—his own spitting image" (pp. 6–7).

A loquacious and self-satisfied woman in the early stages of spinsterhood, Bridgewater warns Green about the dangers of his experiment with what she derisively terms a "salt-water African." Most disastrously for her, he ignores these warnings and protests. Unwavering in his commitment to realize the goals of this misguided educational experiment, Moses Green yields to no one. In time, Johnson writes, the "boy was all Moses wanted him to be, his own emanation, but still, he thought, himself. Different enough from Moses so that he could step back and admire him" (p. 11). As a concrescence or actual entity, Mingo has achieved the satisfaction: the defining moment in Whitehead's theory of organism. As stated before, at the moment of satisfaction an actual entity achieves what Whitehead terms the "private ideal which is the final cause of the concrescence" (Whitehead, p. 212). For our purposes, the satisfaction is the achievement or realization within the individual of a particular role, a particular identity. In the case of Mingo, this "final unity," as Whitehead also terms it, is a function of the effective projection of the will of Moses Green, and a corresponding collapse of an opposing will and purpose in his slave. In fine, Mingo has yielded to the will and superior position of Moses Green, and thus he has become even more completely not only his slave but also his "homunculus," Green's "distorted shadow" and "spitting image."

Exhibiting a pride and devotion to his work that recalls Pygmalion, Green is unfortunately robbed of the glory of his accomplishment through two acts of murder. Both murders are committed by Mingo, his Gallate, his prized student, his bondsman. The first victim is Isaiah Jenson, a friend of many years to Green, whom Mingo bludgeons with a meat cleaver. Jensen's murder is one of many instances of whimsy and humor in this tale. Not only does Jensen die with the "image of Mingo imprisoned on the retina of his eyes," an artful appropriation of embellishments common to grade B horror films, but the messy ax murder reveals the degree of slippage in Mingo's education: "Months ago, maybe five, he'd taught Mingo to kill chicken hawks and be courteous to strangers, but it got all turned around in the African's mind (how was he to know New World customs?), so he was courteous to chicken hawks (Moses groaned, full of gloom) and killed strangers" (pp. 13–14).

Ineluctably and ironically, the second victim is Harriet Bridgewater, whose murder is no less violent although the exact cause of death remains ambiguous: "By the wagon, by a chopping block near a pile of split faggots, by the ruin of an old handpump caked with rust, she lay on her side, the back fastenings of her dress burst open, her mouth a perfect O" (pp. 20–21). Bridgewater's death is ineluctable because Green, a man she had hoped to marry, failed to take heed of her many cautions. The spinster's death is ironic because her infatuation with Green precludes her from establishing a clear connection with the circumstances of Jensen's murder to "a recent tale of monstrosity and existential horror"—Mary Wollstonecraft Shelley's *Frankenstein*—she is in the process of reading, but sadly unable to finish because of the excesses committed by the Dr. Frankenstein in her midst.

The murders of Jensen and Bridgewater possess a dark symmetry. Mingo commits these murders on the same day: "October 7 of the year of grace 1855" (p. 21). Further, we discover that the murders are not arbitrary, uninformed instances of violence but rather baleful projections of Green's consciousness, which Mingo, Green's very own "emanation," has fully absorbed and actualized. Irritated by Jensen's habit of borrowing tools and not returning them, Green had hoped Jensen would "go to Ballyhack on a red-hot rail," in fine, he had wished to be rid of a nuisance, but he had not wished Jensen dead. In the case of Bridgewater, Mingo had divined Green's own ambivalence regarding marriage to a woman who possesses the temperament of a shrew: "You say—I'm quoting you now, suh—a man needs a quiet patient, uncomplaining woman, right?" (p. 21). Here again there is evidence of slippage in Mingo's education. In giving back the thoughts and words of his master, Mingo appears to display a kind of rigidity in his thinking that does not allow for nuance and, as we have seen, that possesses fatal consequences for those who fall within his circumscribed pattern of reality. Or is there something else afoot here? Is Mingo feigning idiocy as a mode of resistance, fully aware that ultimately he will not be held accountable for his violation of the codes of a community which defines him as subhuman? Here and in other instances Mingo emerges as "faintly innocent, faintly diabolical," in fine, a projection of the paradoxes that have shaped the personality and will of Moses Green. Finally, the murders of Jensen and Bridgewater are markers which register the rapid degree of change in the fluent world of Mingo and Green. While remaining in a subordinate position, Mingo has evolved from a position of ignorance and dependency to the attainment of an intelligence and agency which enables him to exercise, paradoxically, a degree of power over his master. Conversely, Green, while remaining in a dominant position, has assumed such roles as master, father, guardian, dependent, and most crucially an accomplice in murder in relation to his slave. "How strange that owner and owned magically dissolved into each other," Johnson writes, "like two crossing shafts of light (or, if he'd known this, which he did not, particles, subatomic, interconnected in a complex skein of relatedness)" (p. 19). Johnson's language recalls one of the fundamental principles of Whitehead's theory of organism, which maintains that "relatedness has its foundation in the relatedness of actualities" (Whitehead, pp. xiii–xiv). It is this fact of relatedness, that master and slave "dissolved into each other," that makes it impossible for Moses Green to execute Mingo for the murders of Jensen and Bridgewater. Clearly unprepared for suicide as well as the destruction of a highly prized and expensive project, Green confesses his own culpablity in the murders: "I'm guilty. It was me set the gears in motion. Me" (p. 22).

A story marked by what Whitehead terms "transition" or the movement from "particular existent to particular existent," "The Education of Mingo" closes with yet one more shift and adjustment in Johnson's fluent fictional world. In yet one more repetition of process, both master and slave have become fugitives en route to Missouri, thereby actualizing a vision of mutual guilt and destruction, alienation and a blurring of identities, that is revealed to Green shortly after the murder of Jensen and shortly before the murder of Bridgewater: "They'd been running forever, across all space, all time—so he imagined—like fugitives with no fingers, no toes, like two thieves or yokefellows, each with some God-awful secret that could annihilate the other" (p. 19). In the shifting world of "The Education of Mingo," this strange possibility has become an even stranger actuality.

Equally strange actualities abound in the world of "Exchange Value." First published in *Choice* in 1981, "Exchange Value" is a tale of theft and crime set in present day Chicago. In contrast to "The Education of Mingo," in "Exchange Value" Johnson elects to explore further Whitehead's theory of organism in the first person, that is, through the voice and consciousness of Cooter, an eighteen-year-old black male who finds himself involved in a burglary with his older brother, Loftis, that has unsettling and surreal consequences for both of them.

The victim of this bungled burglary is Elnora Bailey, a maid who inherited the entire estate of Henry Conners, an industrialist without a scion and her employer for two decades. Interestingly, the peculiar turn in this burglary is that Bailey, the apparent victim, is deceased, a corpse decaying in her deathbed at the crucial moment when Cooter and Loftis unlawfully enter her apartment:

> See, 4B's so small if you ring Miss Bailey's doorbell, the toilet'd flush.
> But her living room, webbed in dust, be filled to the max with dollars of

all denominations, stacks of stock in General Motors, Gulf Oil, and 3M Company in old White Owl cigar boxes, battered purses, or bound in pink rubber bands. It be like the kind of cubbyhole kids play in, but filled with . . . *things*: everything, like a world inside the world, you take it from me, so like picturebook scenes of plentifulness you could seal yourself off in here and settle forever. (P. 30)

Having completed their cursory inspection of the living room, Cooter and Loftis enter Miss Bailey's bedroom:

> The room had a funny, museumlike smell. Real sour. It was full of dirty laundry. And I be sure the old lady's stuff had a terrible string attached when Loftis, looking away, lifted her bedsheets and a knot of black flies rose. I stepped back and held my breath. Miss Bailey be in her long-sleeved flannel nightgown, bloated, like she'd been blown up by a bicycle pump, her old face caved in with rot, flyblown, her fingers big and colored like spoiled bananas. Her wristwatch be ticking softly beside a half-eaten hamburger. Above the bed, her wall had roaches squashed in little swirls of bloodstain. Maggots clustered in her eyes, her ears, and one fist-sized rat hissed inside her flesh. My eyes snapped shut. My knees failed; then I did a Hollywood faint. (P. 32)

Leaving the body of Miss Bailey to decay in her apartment, Loftis and Cooter haul all of her "queer old stuff to [their] crib" (p. 34). After completing their inventory, Cooter, in his inimitable voice, observes that "that cranky old ninnyhammers's hoard came to $879,543 in cash money" (p. 34). Once poor, they are now, by their standards, rich. The bleak world of Chicago has become, at last, a place of possibility.

"Be like Miss Bailey's stuff is raw energy, and Loftis and me," remarks an ebullient Cooter, "like wizards, could transform her stuff into anything else at will. All we had to do, it seemed to me, was decide exactly what to exchange it for" (pp. 34–35). This is the critical passage in this dense, expertly paced short story. From this moment forward, Cooter and Loftis undergo a series of subtle processes that in their totality yield a macabre and grotesque reversal of their naive fantasies of wealth. After their decision to rob Miss Bailey's apartment, Cooter and Loftis are robbed of the ability to decide, to make choices, to exert their will. This ironic and unexpected shift from agency to passivity is, it seems, a function of the operations of the "raw energy" of Miss Bailey's "stuff." At one point Cooter speculates about the possibility that Miss Bailey and her possessions are cursed, but Loftis, a positivist to the core, dismisses this speculation as "weak-minded." In characteristic fashion, Cooter, however, has raised a vital point. Here and in other stories in *The Sorcerer's Apprentice*, Johnson summons the rich tradition of conjuration in African American folklore. In "Exchange Value" conjuration and philosophy of science are seamlessly intertwined as Cooter and Loftis function as examples of two discrete processes: one concerns the stages in what appears to be a powerful and malevolent conjuration;

the other concerns the stages in Whitehead's theory of organism. What these two brothers in crime exchange, as we discover, are their lives for the occult former life of Miss Bailey. To recast this metamorphosis in the language of Whitehead, Cooter and Loftis body forth the manner in which a "living immediacy becomes a real component in other living immediacies of becoming" (Whitehead, p. xiii). Although deceased, the "raw energy" of Miss Bailey's possessions is, within the framework of the story, a "living immediacy" which become a "real component" in the lives of Cooter and Loftis—one which alters their lives completely. To recast the metamorphosis in the language of black folklore, two confident, streetwise hustlers become, in a very short period of time, two paranoid, niggardly recluses. In other words, the thieves, as if prey to the operations of a malediction, assume the personality of their victim.

Cooter dutifully notes the onset of these subtle processes in his brother and in himself. After inventorying Miss Bailey's possessions, Cooter observes that Loftis "looked funny, like a potato trying to say something . . . and sat, real quiet, in the kitchen." After a shopping spree, Cooter returns to the apartment and is conscious that "a funny, Pandora-like feeling hit me. I took off the jacket, boxed it—it looked trifling in the hallway's weak light—and, tired, turned my key in the door" (p. 35). Initially unable to enter the apartment because a paranoid Loftis has changed the locks, once admitted he notes that his older brother is "looking vaguer, crabby, like something out of the Book of Revelations." Cooter also observes that Loftis has constructed an "elaborate, boobytrapped tunnel of cardboard and razor blades behind him, with a two-foot space just big enough for him or me to crawl through. That wasn't all. Two bags of trash from the furnace room downstairs be sitting inside the door. Loftis, he give my leather jacket this evil look, hauled me inside, and hit me upside my head" (pp. 35–36). Enraged by what he regards as his younger brother's excesses, Loftis lets out a tirade punctuated with the following pronouncement: "As soon as you buy something, you *lose* the power to buy something" (p. 36). This statement is at odds with what we know of Loftis, the spendthrift and materialist. Further, it is additional proof of not only the ways in which he has become more like Miss Bailey in temperament and outlook, but it is also an instance in which she articulates her penurious point of view from the realm of the dead.

Before leaving for work, Loftis issues the following command to Cooter: "Don't touch Miss Bailey's money, or drink her splo, or do *any*thing until I get back" (p. 36). What is significant about this imperative is that Loftis, the thief, has returned, after a fashion, what he has stolen. Strangely, he speaks of "Miss Bailey's money," he curiously invokes her as a living presence, a "living immediacy" to conjure Whitehead, even though she is deceased and he and Cooter have stolen her belongings. Loftis has exchanged the role of thief for that of caretaker who zealously guards the inheritance of another. He has, in effect, exchanged one role, one value, for another. There are other stages in this double metamorphosis worth noting. After the fashion of Miss Bailey, Loftis hoards everything and discovers a use for seemingly obsolete objects. Although surrounded by large amounts of money and food, Cooter neither spends nor eats anything belonging to Miss Bailey. Feigning indigence, he begs for his meals. Strangely but predictably, both men continue to exhibit the eccentric behavior of Miss Bailey. They function as custodians of the inheritance that, in a psychic and spiritual sense, immobilized her and which will soon immobilize them.

Departing for work on Wednesday, Loftis returns to the apartment on Sunday in a catatonic state. In this calculated inversion of the resurrection, Loftis returns a somnambulist. Crawling into bed, he resembles more the dead than the living. As Cooter tells us, Loftis is "sleeping with mouth open. His legs be drawn up, both fists clenched between his knees. . . . In his sleep, Loftis laughed, or moaned, it be hard to tell. His eyelids, not quite shut, show slits of white" (p. 39). Examining his brother's possessions, Cooter discovers "a carefully wrapped piece of newspaper" in which he discovers a penny. In the final moment of this tale, the brothers together move toward what Whitehead terms the satisfaction or the final stage in their double metamorphosis.

> The sunlight swelled to a bright shimmer, focusing the bedroom slowly like solution do a photographic image in the developer. And then something so freakish went down I ain't sure it took place. Fumble-fingered, I unfold the paper, and inside be a blemished penny. It be like suddenly somebody slapped my head from behind. Taped on the penny be a slip of paper, and on the paper be the note "Found while walking down Devon Avenue." I hear Loftis mumble like he trapped in a nightmare. . . . Me, I wanted to tell Loftis how Miss Bailey looked four days ago, that maybe it didn't have to be like that for us—did it?—because we could change. Couldn't we? Me, I pull his packed sheets over him, wrap up the penny, and, when I locate Miss Bailey's glass jar in the living room, put it away carefully, for now, with the rest of our things. (Pp. 39–40)

The brothers are "trapped in a nightmare" they now share with Miss Bailey. The state or satisfaction they have achieved, to return to that crucial stage in Whitehead's theory of organism, is, ironically, absent the rich satisfactions they had naively imagined. Change for Loftis and Cooter is of the darkest kind. Cursed, they have degenerated to the existence of somnambulists, or worse, zombies, trapped in a nightmare whose physical corollary is a gloomy apartment "filled with. . . . *things*," which more and more resembles a tomb crammed with the clutter of wasted lives.

In contrast to "Exchange Value," the processes which propel "China" forward are neither malevolent nor exploitative but rather benevolent and hopeful. First published in *MSS* in 1983, a year after the publication of the deeply metaphysical *Oxherding Tale*, "China" is an excellently rendered story that bears the imprint of Johnson's pronounced interest in Asian philosophy and marital arts. In theme and situation it antici-pates and complements the later "Kwoon," a story in which Asian phi-losophy and martial arts are the intellectual apparatus for a deeply thoughtful exploration of individual potential and possibility. In "China" Johnson explores the spiritual evolution of a student engaged in learning a martial arts form; in "Kwoon" he explores the spiritual evolution of a teacher engaged in teaching a marital arts form. As in "The Education of Mingo" and "Exchange Value," in "China" Johnson treats again the vital concept of change and transformation, more particularly the con-cept of process as set forth by Whitehead in his theory of organism.

Set in present day Seattle, "China" has as its protagonist Rudolph Lee Jackson. Originally from Hodges, South Carolina, Rudolph is a postal worker married to Evelyn Montgomery, also a native of Hodges (the principal setting for *Oxherding Tale*). Childless, Evelyn and Rudolph have a stable marriage and a life defined by routine banalities, as well as endured disappointments. Rudolph seems resigned to the security of his marriage, his hypochondria, and the tame pursuits of retirement until he witnesses a trailer for a grade B marital arts film of the kind that immortalized (and killed, as some believe) Bruce Lee. Amazed by the gravity-defying acrobatics of the actors, Rudolph asks an unim-pressed Evelyn: " 'Can people really do that?' He did not take his eyes off the screen, but talked at her from the right side of his mouth. 'Leap that high?' " (p. 65). Evelyn's cynicism and her delight in revealing the ruses designed to achieve such pyrotechnics does not spoil the beauty of the spectacle for a much-entranced Rudolph. This is the pivotal, decisive moment in the story. This fateful encounter with unknown possibilities will determine Rudolph's future choices, thus setting in motion a series of processes which, over time, will endow him with the confidence and skills that will enable him to leap and float in the same manner as the actors in the trailer.

Soon after this evening at the movies, Rudolph begins in earnest a process of self-education and self-development. He begins reading such martial arts magazines as *Inside Kung Fu*. He attends the Seattle pre-miere of such films as *Deep Thrust* and *The Five Fingers of Death*, at which he meets members of a kwoon, which he informs a disbelieving Evelyn is "a place to study fighting, a meditation hall" (p. 72). Recalling the demonstrations of "kata and kumite" he witnessed at the premiere, Rudolph remarks, "I've never seen anything so beautiful" (p. 72). He then informs Evelyn, who by now has become suspicious and appre-hensive, that he has "signed up for lessons." Predictably and dramati-cally, Evelyn informs Rudolph that he is "fifty-*four* years old" and that he is neither "Muhammad Ali nor Bruce Lee." Rudolph is not dissuaded by the sarcasm. While the postman is not a trained fighter of any kind, he is keenly aware that he is engaged in a fight, a metaphysical struggle, in which what is at stake is the meaning and vitality of his own existence. Days later, in yet another dispiriting exchange with Evelyn, who, while loving her husband, has placed limitations upon his potentiality, Rudolph defines the nature of this metaphysical contest and in the process explains the applications and meanings of *"Gung-fu"* for his own life:

> That's what it means. *Gung-fu* means "hard work" in Chinese. . . . I don't think I've ever really done hard work in my life. Not like this, something that asks me to give *every*thing, body and soul, spirit and flesh. . . . I've never been able to give *every*thing to *any*thing. The world never let me. It won't let me put all of myself into play. . . . Every job I've ever had, everything I've ever done, it only demanded part of me. It was like there was so much *more* of me that went unused after the job was over. . . . But sometimes I get the feeling that the unused part—the unlived life— *spoils*, that you get cancer because it sits like fruit on the ground and rots. . . . Don't ask me to stop training. . . . If I stop, I'll die. (Pp. 76–77)

Undaunted, Rudolph continues to advance in his life struggle, and in the fashion of a true fighter he successfully overcomes each symbolic and actual opponent. He changes his diet, develops his body, practices meditation, eschews conflict, abstains from sex, and ignores the uncharitable comments of Evelyn.

Very predictably, this ritual of self-purification has profound consequences for Rudolph's psychology and temperament: "He was humbler now, more patient, but he'd lost touch with everything she [Evelyn] knew was normal in people: weakness, fear, guilt, self-doubt, the very things that gave the world thickness and made people do things" (p. 89). At moments a "Bodhisattva in the middle of houseplants," Rudolph's process of self-purification recalls the regimen of Buddhism and Taoism. Again, it is important to recall that "China" was written during the rich period of the composition of *Oxherding Tale*, a novel whose situations and trajectory are based in large measure upon major texts in Taoism and Zen Buddhism. In his now very disciplined approach to existence, Rudolph possesses many of the traits and values of Reb, a fugitive slave and by turns a Taoist monk in Johnson's metaphysical slave narrative.

As Evelyn is unalterably opposed to Rudolph's new commitment to *Gung-fu* and its attendant, by her estimation, bewilderments, he receives support and encouragement from members of his kwoon. Diverse in terms of age, race, and temperament, the men of Rudolph's kwoon share the same commitment to the process of self-development. This shared commitment produces a kinship by which Evelyn is predictably threatened: "Her husband liked them, Evelyn realized in horror. And they liked him. They were separated by money, background, and religion, but something she could not identify made them seem . . . like a single body" (p. 82). The kinship Rudolph enjoys with members of his kwoon recalls the "concrete unity" of Whitehead's theory of organism.

Whitehead rejects fragmentation as a permanent condition, for, as he postulates, "to be something is to have the potentiality for acquiring real unity with other entities" (p. 212). The sense of unity and purpose Rudolph enjoys with such men as Truck, a Vietnamese, and Tuco, a Puerto Rican, sustains him and provides him with confidence and courage in his life struggle. Through their shared commitment to the discipline of *Gung-fu*, Rudolph has achieved a heightened degree of self-awareness that enables him to imagine his particular life struggle in relationship to other such struggles, that is, in relationship to what Whitehead terms other "living immediacies of becoming." To a stubborn and bewildered Evelyn he asserts: "I only want to be what I *can* be, which isn't the greatest fighter in the world, only the fighter *I* can be" (p. 91).

Johnson's fine story closes with a splendid image of a fully self-actualized Rudolph, the man who has become the fighter he "can be." Attending his first martial arts tournament, an apprehensive and skeptical Evelyn witnesses the metamorphosis about which she had the greatest doubts and which she has resisted, out of fear and love, at every turn.

> And then Evelyn was on her feet, unsure why, but the crowd had stood suddenly to clap, and Evelyn clapped too, though for an instant she pounded her gloved hands together instinctively until her vision cleared, the momentary flash of retinal blindness giving way to a frame of her husband, the postman, twenty feet off the ground in a perfect flying kick that floored his opponent and made a Japanese judge who looked like Oddjob shout "ippon"—one point—and the fighting in the farthest ring, in herself, perhaps in all the world, was over. (P. 95)

In this carefully orchestrated sentence whose well-placed clauses recall the breaks, hesitancy, and stages of Rudolph's metamorphosis, Johnson returns to the decisive moment in this carefully orchestrated story. Having come full circle in this manner, we feel more deeply the impact of Rudolph's wholly visible, fully articulated sense of unity, but mercifully not as deeply as his prostrate opponent. Having surmounted each barrier, having achieved the final unity or what Whitehead terms the satisfaction, in other words having become the fighter he "can be," the strife, the struggle in himself, in Evelyn and "perhaps in all the world," Johnson writes in this transcendent moment, dissipates. While the central metaphor of "China" is fighting, at the story's conclusion there is a peace which enters a deeply divided world, a peace not born of violence but rather harmony as well as a disciplined commitment to self-development and the organic processes which advance this human, and humane, activity.

Just as the "flux of things is one of the ultimate generalizations around which" Whitehead weaves his theory of organism, so too Johnson, in the daring, characteristically independent and suggestive manner of the artist, also weaves this fine collection of short stories around "this ulti-mate generalization." In selecting three of the eight stories of this col-lection for analysis, my wish is to be suggestive not exhaustive, to re-veal the richness and coherence of this collection, not to posit that such richness and coherence exist only in "The Education of Mingo," "Exchange Value," and "China." To be sure, Whitehead's "ultimate gen-eralization" and its specific refinement, his theory of organism, is reg-istered with depth and variety in each of these eight discrete but the-matically related stories. In "Menagerie, A Child's Fable," Whitehead's concept of the fluid world is expressed in the violent and unexpected collapse of the animal universe of Tilford's Pet Shoppe so prized by Berkeley, a "pious German shepherd" and the story's protagonist. In "Alethia," a stodgy professor who believes his authority is absolute, his knowledge of the world comprehensive, discovers himself at the mercy of a manipulative coed operating worlds above him. Ordered by com-pression and the accelerated flow of images that is the distinguishing feature of film, "Moving Pictures" breathlessly tracks the shifting, col-lapsing, interlocking worlds of an anonymous writer of film scripts. In conversation with an alien who has lost control of his "edible, fifty-four-thousand-ton Hershey bar" space ship, Dr. Henry Popper in "Popper's Disease" is challenged, as a physician, to confront the psychic maladies in his world and elsewhere in the universe and, in the process, chal-lenged to heal himself. In "The Sorcerer's Apprentice," the final story of this collection, Allan Jackson, the young apprentice to the sorcerer Rubin Bailey, discovers, in this allegory for a young artist, that his ini-tiation into the privileged mysteries of the chthonic realm depends upon the affirmation of the authority of his own experience and the rejection of sycophancy which lead, ultimately, to amateurism.

The richness of the shifting realities of *The Sorcerer's Apprentice,* and the force and intelligence with which these realities are rendered, have earned Johnson a central place in the tradition of American short fiction while also advancing the almost century-old tradition of black philo-sophical fiction—to date his central artistic project. In these stories which address, again and again, the fluid, organic, interlocking pro-cesses of the world, Johnson, like Whitehead and Johnson's literary ancestor Ralph Ellison, insists that the world is possibility. It is this insistence, this affirmation of humankind, posited in prose as vital as the stories themselves, that summons the reader back, again and again, to this unbroken dream, this dynamic organism which has assumed the reality of fiction.

Notes

1. Charles Johnson published "Kwoon" in *Playboy* (1991). This allegory of pedagogy that recalls themes and situations explored in "China" was sub-

sequently reprinted in *Prize Stories 1993: The O. Henry Awards* (New York: Doubleday, 1993), a collection edited by William Abrahams.

2. Richard Wright, "Blueprint for Negro Writing," in *Black Aesthetic*, ed. Addison Gayle, Jr. (New York: Doubleday, 1971).

3. Alfred North Whitehead, *Process and Reality: An Essay in Cosmology* (1929; reprint, New York: Free Press, 1978), p. 208. Further references to this edition appear in parentheses in the text.

4. S. E. Frost, Jr., *Basic Teachings of the Great Philosophers* (New York: Anchor, 1962), p. 267.

5. Charles H. Kahn, ed., *The Art and Thought of Heraclitus* (New York: Cambridge University Press, 1979), p. 53.

6. Charles Johnson, *The Sorcerer's Apprentice: Tales and Conjurations* (New York: Atheneum, 1986), p. 6. Further references to this book appear in parentheses in the text.

Interrogating Identity

Appropriation and Transformation
in *Middle Passage*

Daniel M. Scott III

My final prayer: O my body, make of me always a man who questions!
—Frantz Fanon[1]

Staging an inquiry into the nature of origin, experience, and meaning, Charles Johnson's *Middle Passage* scrutinizes the structures of identity and the role writing plays in the reconfiguration of the self. *Middle Passage* confronts fundamental assumptions about human and literary identity and problematizes these assumptions by means of allusion and appropriation, which subvert—and, through subversion, revitalize—textual authority. Examining "how race . . . figures into how we give form, in literature and life, to our experience,"[2] the novel is what Johnson calls "art that interrogates experience."[3] Referencing Melville's sea adventures, Homeric peregrinations, Platonic parable, and Cartesian dualism, *Middle Passage* simultaneously and contradictorily acknowledges its debt to preceding Western writing and defines itself against it. As it narrates Rutherford Calhoun's evolution from unreflective lassitude to an awareness that enables him to cross the "countless seas of suffering" forgetful of himself, the novel maintains a primary focus on its own status *as text*, its own textuality.[4] It exposes the roots of human "being," complications of African-American experience, and the position that writing occupies in relating experience, enacting consciousness, and performing its own self-consciousness. Standing at the crossroads of these questions of identity and the difficulties such questions present, Johnson's phenomenological reconfiguration of writing—formulated in *Being and Race* and other essays—supplies the theoretical framework for his fiction and provides the critic valuable insight into the methods and meanings at work in *Middle Passage*.

As the title *Being and Race* suggests and as Johnson makes explicit, the intersection of consciousness and experience is identity. For Johnson and for *Middle Passage*'s protagonist, Rutherford Calhoun, identity is the precarious "middle" experience of the African American: offspring of the middle passage, refugee from an uncertain origin, subject to the marginalization of his experience, searcher of meaning. Situating his work within the tradition of Edmund Husserl and Maurice Merleau-Ponty, Johnson notes that "each new story teaches us what a story can *be*, which underscores for a serious artist the necessity of approaching racial and social phenomena in a humble, patient spirit of listening and letting be whatever the world wishes to say to us."[5] Johnson writes in order to approximate what Husserl calls the "question of what cognition can accomplish, the meaning of its claims to validity and correctness, the meaning of the distinction between valid real and merely apparent cognition."[6] Such a project depends upon the analysis of the tensions between structures of being, a delving into the status of subjectivity (and objectivity); such a project demands an active, dynamic, fluid re-interpretation of that which seems to be stable and established (that which is "real"). Johnson questions the structures of human and literary identity by testing the capabilities of binary opposition, dualism, and abstraction to contain meaning and experience. "Our faith in fiction comes from an ancient belief that language and literary art—all speaking and showing—clarify our experience."[7] By situating this questioning within the sphere of African American experience, he radicalizes this faith and makes innovative demands on writing to show and speak the complexities of experience, consciousness, and change. As Jonathan Little has noted, Johnson's "phenomenological and metafictional techniques work to deform and defamiliarize experience (spiritual and literary) to achieve revelation and transcendence."[8] Taken in this light, Johnson seems to take the novel's expansive and yet tentative epigraph (attributed to Saint Thomas Aquinas) literally: *Homo est quo dammodo omnia*—"*in a way*, man is everything." In a way, Rutherford Calhoun is Everyman. In a way, *Middle Passage* is every text. It echoes Homer's *Odyssey* and Melville's *Moby Dick*. It pays homage to the picaresque, the confession narrative, and the adventure story. It owes much to Daniel Defoe and Frederick Douglass. And yet it grows out of the soil of a particular African American experience.

Johnson's examination of identity (human and textual) depends on appropriation for its literal and philosophical method. At once embracing and rejecting, appropriation stands in for the writer's anxiety and sincerity when faced with the weight of written tradition, the protagonist's equivocation when faced with the conundrum of America (Americanness and the slave trade), and for the text's problematic stance vis-à-vis its own narrative pretensions and aspirations. The contradictory position of celebration and confrontation, embrace and rejection, motivates the action of the novel (Rutherford's rejection and embrace of Reverend Chandler, his brother Jackson, his father) and in the procedure by way of which the narrative inscribes itself between the cracks: across the middle of tradition and innovation. By alluding to preceding narratives, Johnson locates his text both within and outside of the tradition of Western fiction. The contradictory space of allusion and appropriation, in turn, opens up the space of transition (neither/nor) into which Calhoun's transformation and Johnson's fiction appear and disappear. The "middle" passage is the ontological and epistemological material that gets locked out of binary oppositions and dualisms or the matter of experience and consciousness that exists not in pure allegiance with one or another extreme but rather in those Heraclitean regions in between, where an abstraction fades and blurs into its exact opposite.

"What I am outlining here," Johnson writes in *Being and Race*, "is the enduring truth that if we go deeply enough into a relative perspective, black or white, male or female, we encounter the transcendence of relativism; in Merleau-Ponty's terms, 'to retire into oneself is to leave oneself.' "[9] The novel certainly does not reject the tradition of the West or of Western dualism out of hand but *needs* to keep it in play in order to erect a set of alternative responses and possibilities. To open the tradition up to the infinitely vast material caught in between any set of binary oppositions, any structure of dualistic thought: the novel not so much asserts the middle as it opens it upon itself, expands it—by indicating the limits of absolute existence—to include abstraction and extreme. By charting the journey of Rutherford Calhoun through his blackness, through his maleness, through his status as an American, Charles Johnson—"an archaeologist probing the Real for veiled sense"—crosses boundaries of textual containment; the rules of fiction (This Is Not True; This Has No Claim on the Real; Just Kidding! This "Lie" Speaks to the Highest Truths) are exposed and examined.[10]

One can situate *Middle Passage*'s examination of human and literary identity by focusing on a few "arenas" of identity: the body, culture, and text. These fundamental fields of discourse operate throughout the novel, variously constructing explanations of origin, motive, and meaning as the text frequently confronts its own contradictory claims to accuracy, inaccuracy, mimesis, and imagination. By way of allusion, appropriation, and narrative self-consciousness, these arenas stage and foreground the text's contingent, constructed status: the text's essential and enduring allegiance to the author's interrogation of self. "Philosophical Black fiction—art that interrogates experience—is, first and foremost, a mode of thought."[11] *Middle Passage* situates this textual self-awareness and struggle around the interrogation of the status of body, cultural and textual positions. These three arenas focus and order sets of identity factors (man versus woman, Europe versus Africa, truth versus falsity) that are problematized by Johnson's textual process. All are embedded in the contexts of appropriation and transformation that frame and contain the transitional, "middle" space of Johnson's ontic search, his writing.

The body occupies an especially pivotal position in the novel, from small moments such as Rutherford's hiccupping whenever he is caught in a philosophical dilemma (pp. 125–26) to the momentous but casual enfolding of death and unconsciousness that marks the moment of Rutherford's most profound transformation: "Then I fainted. Or died. Whatever" (p. 171). The boundaries between body and that which is not the body, between individual experience and universal process, break down in the novel's attempt to loose the self's reliance on the body for its identification. This slippage of identity anchors Rutherford's shifting perspective on gender relations, the novel's documentation of the encounter with the Allmuseri, and motivates the text's self-conscious, self-disruptive lurches toward ontological depths. "It all had to do with an old Allmuseri belief (hardly understood by one Westerner in a hundred) that each man outpictured his world from deep within his own heart. . . . As within, so it was without. More specifically: What came *out* of us, not what went in, made us clean or unclean. Their notion of 'experience' . . . held each man utterly responsible for his own happiness or sorrow, even for his dreams and his entire way of seeing" (p. 164). Reality is relative. Perception defines the real. And most important, each man is ultimately responsible for that reality.

Middle Passage traces over the length of the text the line of race and gender in a similar breakdown and restructuring of what it means to be a man, what it means to be black, what it means to be human. Like the body's involuntary response to untruth or the loosening of Rutherford's grasp on the boundaries of life and death, gender undergoes a shift from the more automatic and involuntary (uncritical) assertion of social givens—"Of all the things that drive men to sea, the most common disaster, I've come to learn, is women" (p. 1)—to confounding those regulated borders by gaining access to the validity of particular experience and awareness: "my memories of the Middle Passage kept coming back, reducing the velocity of my desire, its violence, and in place of my longing for feverish love-making left only a vast stillness that felt remarkably full, a feeling that, just now, I wanted our futures blended, not our limbs, our histories perfectly twined for all time, not our flesh" (p. 208). These transformations leave Rutherford outside of the system of sexual battle and conquest and with the strangely fraternal identification with woman at the novel's close: "she lowered her head to my shoulder, as a sister might" (p. 209). They mark his and the novel's movement away from the empirical physical limitation of the body as essential and oppositional object and toward an idea of the body that is just as expressive, infinite, and flexible as spiritual reality. The accident of his genitals, the color of his skin, the desperate clinging to life at any cost, are set aside one by one and replaced by an investment in the contradiction of a body wedded as much to what one *is* as to what one *does*. A body that acts, responds, and loves not by reflex but out of consideration, with care and awareness. Certainly Rutherford's sex and race and life are not inconsequential in the end, but they have been reconfigured according to more complex, less oppositional strategies of identification and—once identity has been well considered—living.

Thieving and lying (one might write "appropriation and writing") both belie and betray Rutherford's "middle" position—neither European nor African, neither man nor woman, neither American nor anything else. The crew perceives him as neither/nor (or both/and), a trickster, a shyster, fluid: "Calhoun'll go his own way, like he's always done, believin' in nothin', belongin' to nobody, driftin' here and there and dyin', probably, in a ditch without so much as leavin' a mark on the world—or as much of a mark as you get from writin' on water" (p. 88). Johnson consciously links Rutherford's thieving with the status of the African American—"Theft, if the truth be told, was the closest thing I knew to transcendence" (p. 46)—and resolves this criminality once Rutherford's existence has undergone the tests of confrontation, reflection, and transformation. Johnson fashions these transitions and transformation into a text that, like its thief-liar narrator, appropriates and wanders through the storehouse of culture, looking for (it)self. "I felt culturally dizzy, so displaced by this decentered interior and the Africans' takeover, that when I lifted a whale-oil lamp at my heels it might as well have been a Phoenician artifact for all the sense it made to me. Yet in the smoking debris there was movement, a feeble stirring of Icarian man, the creator of cogs and cotton gins, beneath contraptions that pinched him to the splintery floor" (pp. 142–43). All the while, though, this process of allusion, imitation, and appropriation (whether metaphorical or referential) never claims completion or absolute values; it is always particular, tentative, dynamic as it shifts noiselessly from ancient Phoenicia to Eli Whitney, from the storehouse of cultural plunder to an encounter with the Allmuseri god. Appropriation signals cultural critique, historical transgression and an aggression toward the sanctities of mimetic poetics.

Appropriating Western "civilization" from Thales to Johannes Kepler to Albert Einstein into its apparently linear and referential narrative, *Middle Passage* mixes and matches and frames the history of Western thought within and against the backdrop of a black man's encounter with the European values around, within, and beside him and the Africa that he encounters. The novel structures much of this allusion into a critique of the West, identifying Falcon as a *Übermensch*, the logical product of binary thinking. His ship is the *Republic* ("from stem to stern, a process"), both microcosm of the ship of the American state and the test case for Plato's hierarchical society ruled by philosopher-kings (p. 36); Falcon—"the nation was but a few hours old when Ebenezer Falcon was born" (p. 49)—is Icarian man who flies too far and too high outside

of himself without regard for others' warnings. Determined "to Ameri-
canize the entire planet" (p. 30), this brilliant, vicious dwarf, his body
as stunted as his imagination, sees only strict opposition and separation
of the self and the other: "For a self to act, it must have somethin' to
act *on*. A nonself—some call this Nature—that resists, thwarts the will,
and *vetoes* the actor" (p. 97). He is the spirit of opposition, dualism,
repression, and conflict. " 'Conflict,' says [Falcon], '*is* what it means to
be conscious. Dualism is a bloody structure of the mind. Subject and
object, perceiver and perceived, self and other' " (pp. 97–98).

If indeed the "mind was *made* for murder" and "slavery is a social
correlate of a deeper, ontic wound" (p. 98), then *Middle Passage* clearly
sets Falcon's (the West's) dualism against the unifying vision of the
"captured" Allmuseri who "saw [them] as savages. In their mythology
Europeans had once been members of their tribe—rulers, even, for a
time—but fell into what was for these people the blackest of sins. The
failure to experience the unity of Being everywhere was the Allmuseri
vision of Hell" (p. 65). The "madness of multiplicity" is set against the
dualism of the West (p. 65). Rutherford negotiates the space between
the one that has no history ("A people so incapable of abstraction no
two instances of 'hot' or 'cold' were the same for them") and those who
have too much (p. 61). Caught between the two, Rutherford and the
American experience (and by extrapolation any human endeavor that
searches for identity, experience, and new beginnings) is a fantastic
exercise in neither/nor. America carving its way out of the two in between the two. America is not only the result of European invasion and
immigration; it has flourished in the light of African, Asian, and Native
American presences. This contradictory America, so invisible to Rutherford at the novel's opening, is clear at the end. The narrative itself is
intimately bound up with this process of cultural appropriation. And
the evasion of capture—if the narrative slips, slides, withholds itself,
postpones itself, relies on a known liar for its provenance, and loves it,
it alters narrative expectations and expands narrative possibility. The
greatest truth we can obtain depends upon acknowledging, even celebrating, our lies. When fiction asserts its own fictionality, it gains a
veracity as document (of the imagination) that is more "real" than mimetic illusion.

The narrative establishes a chaos of contradictory justifications, motivations, explanations, revelations, and denials against which the story
struggles (and by which it is propelled), but which reflects the interrogation of identity in its interrogation of mimetic reality and narrative
"truth." The narrative oscillates between naturalistic representation and
a super-real representation of a self-conscious (antimimetic) telling.
The novel uses parenthetical intrusions which promise, withhold, delay,
betray, falsify, and verify the narrative and finally reveal it as performance: "that Jackson stayed, more deeply bound to our master than any
of us dreamed. But I am not ready just yet to talk of Jackson Calhoun"

(p. 8); "living parasitically on its body. Do I exaggerate? Not at all" (p. 168). By making outright appeals to be believed, the narrative fore-grounds its own status as fiction: "failed at bourgeois life in one way or another—we were, to tell the truth, all refugees from responsibility" (p. 40). Rutherford's (and the reader's) implosive experience is reflected, redeemed, and redoubled by Johnson's textual prestidigitation. The novel leaves its provenance uncertain; is it the diary Rutherford started keeping after Falcon's death? It foregrounds the discrepancies between narrative time and story time and retains self-reflexive moments of nar-rative collapse when the telling intersects with the told, when the "char-acters" "hear" the narration—as well as the dialogue—and respond to it:

> No question that since my manumission I'd brought a world of grief on myself but, hang it, I wished like hell I had someone to blame—my parents, the Jackson administration, white people in general—for this new tangle of predicaments.
> "Blame for what?" Squibb stared at me.
> "Nothing. I was just thinking out loud."
> "Oh." (Pp. 92–93)

These dislocations of mimesis denaturalize the mimetic role of fic-tion and serve to both invalidate the novel as story and revalidate it as ontic document (invalidate the referentiality of the novel in favor of its status as performance and artifice). It is dearer to us as an artifact of the imaginative exploration of the investing principles of identity than it is as naturalistic tale. It is, in fact, another cleansing of experience through the word, another emptying of material into spirit, experience into document. Johnson writes that writing is a mode of thought, that writing works out problems of self, just as Rutherford needed "to tran-scribe and thereby transfigure all we had experienced, and somehow through all this I found a way to make my peace with the recent past by turning it into Word" (pp. 189–90). Certainly the work collects so much about itself as to be parodic, emptying, a pastiche of names and ideas. Like Rutherford, the novel pilfers this and that. All writing is this appropriation, this reiteration of writing that has come before it, this reproduction and recirculation of the written and the play of new writing in reference, response, and reaction to the Tradition. The man's rein-tegration of his individual past, present, and future with that of the collective. They mark the textual aporia by way of which *Middle Passage* opens up Rutherford's experience beyond the limits of fiction, beyond the specificity of African American writing, without taking these factors (fiction and race) out of play. Self-conscious narration, parenthetical intrusions, disjointed chronology—Rutherford gets the log book during the chapter entitled "Entry, the seventh (July 3, 1830)" and writes from memory?—undermines the novel's semblance of chronological action and reliable narration. Clearly Rutherford Calhoun (ex-slave, liar and thief) constructs the story not as it happens (though it is written in logbook fashion, in the first person and the present tense) but retrospectively, as it will lead to a preexisting, known end.

Rutherford's "quirky, rhetorical asides" (p. 104) are, in fact, deadly serious markers of the text's breaking with mimetic tradition and experimenting with the bounds of textual reference and self-reference. They litter the narrative and serve to undermine the text's apparent accuracy, referentiality, mimesis, which is—interestingly enough—already thrown into question when it receives Falcon's exhortation to "include everything you can remember, and what *I* told you, from the time you came on board" (p. 146). In essence, Rutherford stands in the same position vis-à-vis authority as Johnson; granted the leave to write, charged to "tell the truth," he does: "But I promised myself that even though I'd tell the story (I knew he wanted to be remembered), it would be, first and foremost, as I saw it since my escape from New Orleans" (p. 146). Truth is a slippery thing that depends entirely on who claims it and from what perspective. While Falcon expects balance, proportion, and objectivity, Rutherford recognizes that such a project is impossible as long as one pretends that one does not have eyes of one's own; that one does not see as one sees. One must acknowledge the particular, the partial, the subject who speaks. Not the seamless, naturalized narrative of beginning, middle, and end but a chaotic telling machine that crisscrosses versions of truth and illusion to expose not only its mechanisms but also its manufactured contingency.

Instances of radical revelation expose the text's simultaneous claim to utter falsity and the naked truth. Problematizing the conundrum of fiction, they also wed the fluidity of textual identity in *Middle Passage* to the difficulties of human identity. "As a general principle and mode of operation during my days as a slave, I always lied," our guardian of truth admits, "and sometimes just to see the comic results when a listener based his beliefs and behavior on things that were Not" (p. 90). That which is material (body), that which is spiritual (culture), and that which combines the two to document or construct "truth" (the text) are all subject to the complications of racial experience, expectation, and the transcendence of these: "the Reverend's prophecy that I would grow up to be a picklock was wiser than he knew, for was I not, as a Negro in the New World, *born* to be a thief? Or, put less harshly, inheritor of two millennia of things I had not myself made? But enough of this" (p. 47).

While certainly a matter of body, race has implications in *Middle Passage* for the whole realm of human and literary identity. In the construction of identity, it is deeply involved with the cultural values dualistic thought has attached to racial difference. Its potential to provide the space for new perceptions is Johnson's point of departure: "because all conception—philosophy—is grounded in perception, there is no reason, in principle, that we cannot work through the particulars of Black life from *within* and discover there not only phenomenon worthy of philosophical treatment in fiction, but also—and here I'll make my wildest claim today—significant new perceptions."[12] In accordance with Charles Johnson's own position to address and disrupt what he calls "the Cartesian bifurcation of *res cogitantes* and *res extensae*, and of course to the more primordial Platonic dualism, indicating how Western onto-logical divisions between higher (spirit) and lower (body) coupled with Christian symbologies for light and dark develop the black body as being in a state of 'stain.' "[13] Race spans the entire novel as corporal reality, cultural source, and textual foundation. To this end, Rutherford—"a fatherless child," (p. 126) abandoned by a black father, rejecting a white one (Chandler)—confronts his past outside of Falcon's "devilish idea that social conflict and war were, in the Kantian sense, a *structure* of the human mind," Jackson's decision to stay with Reverend Chandler be-comes linked with the self-emptying, unifying wisdom of the Allmuseri, and Rutherford himself identifies with the boy he throws overboard (p. 50). In general the Allmuseri come to represent an (African/non-Western/antidualistic) philosophy that pertains more to Rutherford's search for origins and meanings than it does to the genetic details of color: "In a way, I have no past. . . . When I look behind me, for my father, there is only emptiness" (p. 160). More than any other event, it is Rutherford's encounter with the Allmuseri god, who adopts the ap-pearance of his father, that problematizes Rutherford's relationship to his father and to his forefathers. The particular encounter plays on the larger cosmic proportions of body, origin, self, culture, humanity, divinity:

> I came within a hair's-breadth of collapsing, for this god, or devil, had dressed itself in the flesh of my father. . . . for the life of me I could no more separate the two, deserting father and divine monster, than I could sort wave from sea. Nor something more phantasmal that forever con-fused my lineage as a marginalized American colored man. To wit, his gradual unfoldment before me, a seriality of images I could not stare at straight on but only take in furtive glimpses, because the god, like a griot asked one item of tribal history, which he could only recite by reeling forth the entire story of his people, could not bring forth this one man's life without delivering as well the *complete* content of the antecedent universe to which my father, as a single thread, belonged. (Pp. 168–69)

Quite literally, the Allmuseri are flesh of his flesh. Despite Cringle's early assertion that they are "not like us at all. No, not like you either, though you are black," they are the key to Rutherford's transformation into a self-defined and defining human being, experiencing and exam-ining the world for himself" (p. 43).

Race, that meeting point of body, culture, and text for the African American writer, is the crucial moment of the identity search. And the key to this questioning in *Middle Passage* is the history of Rutherford's encounter with the Allmuseri. Ashraf Rushdy asserts that the Allmuseri are the "theory and . . . symbol for the postmortem condition."[14] But, taking the growth of the Allmuseri into account, they are and are not. In the course of the novel they go from being exotic, romanticized avatars of a perfect, timeless age—"About them was the smell of old temples. Cities lost when Europe was embryonic" (p. 61)—to being "like any other men" or at least like Rutherford:

> They were leagues from home—indeed, without a home—and in Ngon-yama's eyes I saw a displacement, an emptiness like maybe all of his brethren as he once knew them were dead. To wit, I saw myself. A man remade by virtue of his contact with the crew. My reflection in his eyes, when I looked up, gave back my flat image as phantasmic, the flapping sails and sea behind me drained of their density like figures in a dream. Stupidly, I had seen their lives and culture as timeless product, as a finished thing, pure essence or Parmenidean meaning I envied and wanted to embrace, when the truth was that they were process and Heraclitean change, like any men, not fixed but evolving and as vulnerable to metamorphosis as the body of the boy we'd thrown overboard. (P. 124)

Inasmuch as Rutherford—in time—distances himself from the constricting first theoretical, symbolic speculations on the Allmuseri (most of which comes from Cringle, who denies identity between Rutherford and the tribe), it is more important to consider them as the representatives of the process from encounter to discovery to identification that dispossesses them and Rutherford of constricting dualistic structures. It is linked with Rutherford's original assessment of the Allmuseri and with his final identification not with the ideal vision of them—"they might have been the Ur-tribe of humanity itself" (p. 61)—but with the ultimate identifications he makes between them and his brother—"There was something in this, and the way he canted his head, that reminded me so of how my brother sometimes stood alone on the road leading to Chandler's farm after our father left, looking. Just looking" (pp. 118–19)—his father, and himself. "He was close to my own age, perhaps had been torn from a lass as lovely, lately, I now saw Isadora to be, and from a brother as troublesome as my own. His open eyes were unalive, mere kernels of muscle, though I still found myself poised vertiginously on their edge, falling through these dead holes deeper into the empty hulk he had become, as if his spirit had flown and mine was being sucked there in its place" (pp. 122–23). Neither wholly on one side of the cultural opposition nor entirely on the other, *Middle Passage* settles down into cultural multiplicity and versatility: being "sucked there in its place" does not compromise Rutherford's identity but peppers it with experience, breadth, complexity, and—in this case—with the first whiff of its origins. And as an African American, he is such a complexity.

Middle Passage asserts racial identity as a hybrid, active process of being that reads and interprets itself and the culture that surrounds it.

It is this identity that Johnson holds as a means to a larger, humanistic "end": the liberation of perception, the opening up of epistemological perspective and of ontological meaning, not just for African Americans but for all people. Caught in the moment of this revelation, Rutherford cries "for all the sewage I carried in my spirit, my failures and crimes, foolish hopes and vanities, the very faults and structural flaws in the blueprint of my brain (as Falcon put it) in a cleansing nigh as good as prayer itself, for it washed away not only my hurt after hurling the dead boy overboard but yes, the hunger for mercy as well" (p. 127). It is at this point of utter self-consciousness, this moment of ultimate responsibility devoid of the desire for the mercy that relies on justification or excuse, that the body not so much loses its grip on Rutherford's soul as it merges within it. He is black, but he is not bound to sit on one or the other side of an artificially imposed and enforced racial, social dichotomy.

Washed by the moments of tears, prayers, and acceptance of responsibility, Rutherford—thief and liar caught in the loop of appropriation and definition—becomes himself, far more responsive to the injustice of slavery now than when he joined the crew of the *Republic* without hesitation, far more certain of how his life and those of every other man overlap, join, and depend on each other. Rutherford the wily survivor of before, ironically ensures his greater survival from this point on by relinquishing his death grip on his interests, himself: "and, searching myself, I discovered I no longer cared if I lived or died" (pp. 126–27). At one and the same time, *Middle Passage* celebrates the particular (Rutherford as individual, his text as unique and uniquely wedded to the process it documents) and addresses itself to general, universal "truths." Johnson questions the validity of construction of the universal. "Universals are not static," he writes, "but changing, historical, *evolving* and enriched by particularization; the lived Black world has always promised a fresh slant on structures and themes centuries old."[15] It is from the particular transitions and transgressions African American experience contains that Rutherford's struggles arise, but ultimately they go far beyond specifics, feeding the universal questions of origin and destiny.

While the problem of identity is central to the novel, it is left—to a large extent—unresolved. The novel rests on a question mark, a struggle, resolves itself around a black center, a void and a fullness that holds the text in thrall. Gayatri Spivak asserts that "the only way to argue for origins is to look for institutions, inscriptions and then to surmise the mechanics by which such institutions and inscriptions can stage such a particular style of performance."[16] *Middle Passage* interrogates the mechanics of identity and meaning. The middle passage is writing. The novel is inscribing the crossroads in response to, against, and across the parameters of identity, gender, race, history, social rank, and provenance that define, limit, and/or deny access to being and becom-

ing. Within the interzone of contradiction, chiasmus, overlap, indeterminacy, liberation, removal, retrieval, disinscription, reinscription, the
middle passage—never ending, always shifting—is writing itself: the
word sculpted, shaped, held for a moment in reflection and in radical
difference to experience.

In the end, Rutherford is left alone; the text itself (the writing that
Rutherford is charged to complete, which is this novel) begins here on
the threshold between being and nothingness, the heretofore sparsely
documented space of black America. When objectivity and subjectivity
have vanquished each other, they leave behind them an aftermath of
contradiction (objective subjectivity, subjective objectivity) and question, the fertile valley of questions without easy, clear, stable resolution
in which, according to Johnson, writing flourishes:

> Such egoless listening is the precondition for the species of black Ameri-
> can fiction I see taking form on the horizon of contemporary practice, a
> fiction of increasing artistic and intellectual generosity, one that enables
> us as a people—as a culture—to move from narrow complaint to broad
> celebration. . . . we will see a fiction by Americans who happen to be
> black, feel at ease both in their ethnicity and in their Yankeeness, and
> find it the most natural thing, as Merleau-Ponty was fond of saying, to
> go about "singing the world."[17]

Balancing of the contradictory demands of subject and object, meeting in the middle of opposition, writing (for Johnson, for the transformed Rutherford) is what Johnson terms the "individual consciousness grappling with meaning."[18] This is the contradictory middle space
(a concatenation of ambivalent, convergent, suspended, contradictory,
indeterminate "middles") in which he stages *Middle Passage*'s search for
meaning.

While one may write about the body, culture, and textual situations
in *Middle Passage* separately, they are in fact links each to the other,
feeding into a network of interrogation of the structures of identity,
belief, and value that underlie the unexamined, unquestioned life. If
the unexamined life is to become pointed, fulfilling, and fulfilled, these
assumptions of self must undergo and withstand such scrutiny. Interrogating identity and identity's modes of expression, *Middle Passage* confronts such factors and asserts Rutherford Calhoun's "middle" condition
(black in America, suspended between cultures, at odds with his past
and future) as symptomatic of not just one "man," nor one race, but of
us all. The "middle" space and "middle" energy is ever evolving, never
"there," and always "here"—always both partial and complete, contradictory and changing. Between embracing tradition and revolutionizing
it there is the transitional (and contradictory) space of embrace-and-
rejection, the "middle" space of problematic identities and problematic
documents of those identities. By emphasizing Rutherford's choices of
gender relations, the cultural dialogue between Europe, Africa, and the

tertium quid that is America, and the text's contradictory stance toward mimetic illusion, *Middle Passage* re-presents Calhoun's and the reader's odyssey into the middle. A middle of ambivalence and in-betweenness and contradiction and indeterminacy that Calhoun (and, one can assume, Johnson) identifies as particularly American:

> If this weird, upside-down caricature of a country called America, if this land of refugees and former indentured servants, religious heretics and half-breeds, whoresons and fugitives . . . was all I could rightly call *home*, then aye: I was of it. . . . Do I sound like a patriot? Brother, I put it to you: What Negro, in his heart (if he's not a hypocrite), is not? (P. 179)

Crossing body boundaries, cultural boundaries, and textual borders, *Middle Passage* belies stasis in favor of dynamic; it evacuates structures of self (whether physical or metaphysical, whether corporal, cultural, or textual) and fills them with all that dichotomy denies. This crossing of boundaries simultaneously erases them and collapses the structures of Being in upon themselves. These transgressions, this insistence on transition, this collapse of "reality," is the site of meaning; it is a leap of consciousness that attempts, as Foucault writes, to "rediscover the point of rupture, to establish, with the greatest possible precision, the division between the implicit density of the already-said, a perhaps involuntary fidelity to acquired opinion, the law of discursive fatalities, and the vivacity of creation, the leap into irreducible difference."[19] The outcome of this leap, the outcome of these interrogations of experience is a fluidity of meaning and value that revivify all regions of meaning and consciousness. Identity founded on this is the identity not of opposition but of contradiction, of liberated perception.

In the end, *Middle Passage* reconfigures, transforms the structures of reality, for one man and for us all. Consciousness and writing surround dualism and either/or definition with the space of transition.[20] Identity is history, race, and gender and is not these things. It is revealed, rewarded in the unpredictable but inevitable improvisation of the living self (male or female) that marries himself to himself. The text is written and read in the space of contradiction, which is not negation but a radical form of problematizing and destabilizing fixed manners of belief and being, the juxtaposition of one fixity impossibly next to another: what it means to be a man impossibly close to and dependent upon what it means to be a woman, without the destruction or belittling of either; with the expansion of meaning and possibility, the open-ended dynamic of writing at the crossroads that Spivak characterizes as a "notion . . . as broad and robust and full of affect as it is imprecise. . . . It belongs to that group of grounding mistakes that enable us to make sense of our lives."[21]

As Johnson sings the world he searches experience and perception for the roots of reality and the doorways to transformation. Writing, understood as a mode of thought, *is* the middle passage, between what has been and what will be, between the word and the world. "To put it bluntly, language is transcendence. And so is fiction."[22] Johnson writes the collapsing, melic, ontic language of the self "forgetful of ourselves, gently cross[ing] the Flood, and countless seas of suffering" (p. 209). As a text, *Middle Passage* crosses borders of containment and identity, eluding the false gods of fixity and resolution. This contradictory balance, this transitional space, is the key to *Middle Passage* and to Johnson's argument in favor of "philosophical hermeneutics and the exploration of meaning [as] native to all literary production; that universality is embodied in the particulars of the Black world; and that the final concern of serious fiction is the liberation of perception."[23] Indeed, *Middle Passage* is the realization of this liberation of perception.

Notes

1. Frantz Fanon, *Black Skin, White Masks*, trans. Charles Lam Markmann (New York: Grove Press, 1967), p. 232.
2. Charles Johnson, "Philosophy and Black Fiction," *Obsidian* 6 (1980), p. 55.
3. Ibid., p. 56.
4. Charles Johnson, *Middle Passage* (New York: Plume Books, 1990), p. 209. Subsequent references to *Middle Passage* will be cited parenthetically in the text.
5. Charles Johnson, *Being and Race: Black Writing since 1970* (Bloomington: Indiana University Press, 1988), p. 122.
6. Edmund Husserl, *The Idea of Phenomenology*, trans. William P. Alston and George Nakhnikian (The Hague: Martinus Nijhoff, 1964), p. 20.
7. Johnson, *Being and Race*, p. 3.
8. Jonathan Little, "Charles Johnson's Revolutionary *Oxherding Tale*," *Studies in American Fiction* 19 (1991), pp. 148–49.
9. Johnson, *Being and Race*, p. 44.
10 .Johnson, "Philosophy," p. 58.
11. Ibid., p. 56.
12. Ibid., p. 57.
13. Johnson, *Being and Race*, p. 27.
14. See Ashraf H. A. Rushdy, "The Phenomenology of the Allmuseri: Charles Johnson and the Subject of the Narrative of Slavery," in this volume.
15. Johnson, "Philosophy," p. 57.
16. Gayatri Chakravorty Spivak, "Acting Bits/Identity Talk," *Critical Inquiry* 18 (1992), p. 781.
17. Johnson, *Being and Race*, p. 123.
18. Johnson, "Philosophy," p. 60.
19. Michel Foucault. *The Archaeology of Knowledge and The Discourse on Language*, trans. A. M. Sheridan Smith (New York: Pantheon, 1972), p. 142.
20. See the discussion of "either/or" "and/but" dichotomies in Johnson's *Faith and the Good Thing* in Norman Harris, "The Black Universe in Contem-

porary Afro-American Fiction," *College Language Association Journal* 30 (1986), pp. 1–13.

21. Spivak, "Acting Bits," p. 781.
22. Johnson, *Being and Race*, p. 39.
23. Johnson, "Philosophy," p. 60.

The Phenomenology of the Allmuseri
Charles Johnson and the
Subject of the Narrative of Slavery

Ashraf H. A. Rushdy

The Allmuseri are a tribe on the West Coast of Africa. They are, in the words of the one who first discovered them, "a remarkably *old* people." Physically, they are tall (taller even than the Watusi); they are dark, with skin as soft as black leather, and their palms are blank because they have no fingerprints. Also, the Allmuseri are reported to have a second brain at the base of their spines. They impress the anthropologist with what can only be called their *accumulatedness*: They seem "a synthesis of several tribes, as if longevity in this land had made them a biological repository of Egyptian and sub-Saharan eccentricities—or in the Hegelian equation—a clan distilled from the essence of everything that came earlier." Part of this can be explained by their history. They began as a seafaring people who had deposited their mariners in a part of India which historians would later call Harappa. There they blended with the pre-Aryan Dravidian inhabitants, afterwards sailing to Central America (between 1000 and 500 B.C.) where they brought their skills in metallurgy and agriculture to the Olmec. By the time they eventually returned to Africa, they had made themselves a part of the Old World and the New. Because of this history, including their diverse minglings with tribes from other lands, they seem indeed, as the anthropologist notes, to be "the Ur-tribe of humanity itself." But there is another reason for their accumulatedness—their philosophy, evolved through millenia. The Allmuseri believe in a form of intersubjectivity so basic that their ideas of failure and hell are represented by division, individuality, or autonomy. "The failure to experience the unity of Being everywhere was the Allmuseri vision of Hell." It is reported of one Allmuseri tribesman who had encountered a vile American influence that "he had fallen; he was now part of the world of multiplicity, of *me* versus *thee.*" It is because they project and embody this strong belief in the "unity of Being" that the Allmuseri impress anyone who meets them with the sense of being in the presence of antiquity, and the feeling that one is encountering "the presence of countless others *in* them."

The Allmuseri, unfortunately, do not exist in this world. They might well exist in a parallel universe—one that their god is rumored to be able to create and sustain—but, for our purposes and according to our best lights, they exist only as a fictional product of Charles Johnson's fertile imagination.[1] They are also a continuing presence in his fictional universe that, I will argue, represents a philosophical solution Johnson has developed for an aesthetic problem he encountered when he first began his career as a writer. The aesthetic problem is analogous to the one which James Baldwin intimated is part of the dilemma of being a black writer (3) and similar to the one Houston Baker has analyzed as being part of the problem with an academy unwilling to acknowledge anything beyond a crude dualism (381–95). It is an aesthetic problem to which Johnson, following both Baldwin and Baker, has given the name *Caliban's dilemma* (*Being* 40). His solution to that dilemma, I am arguing, is what can be called the "phenomenology of the Allmuseri." To appreciate the protocols of the dilemma and to begin tracing the contours of the solution, we need to see how Johnson represents his origins as a writer.

Charles Johnson began his career by writing what he calls "six bad, apprentice novels" (*Being* 5). According to his own assessment, three of the novels were bad because they were servilely imitative of the styles of James Baldwin, Richard Wright, and John A. Williams; and the other three novels were too heavily influenced by the rigid conventions of the "Black Aesthetic." What Johnson found himself writing was fiction belonging to what Zora Neale Hurston has called "the sobbing School of Negrohood" ("How It Feels" 153).[2] By his own account, the narratives were "misery-filled protest stories about the sorry condition of being black in America and might be called 'naturalistic' " (5).

Johnson's career genuinely began only when he started to rethink the relationship between literature and life, between sign systems and referents, when he realized that the problem of "recording" the "black experience" was a problem about the nature of "experience" at the same time that it was a problem about the nature of "recording." That realization came in two forms. First, he came to the same conclusion shared by early American pragmatists and some contemporary French poststructuralists, that "writing doesn't so much record an experience—or even imitate or represent it—as it *creates* that experience" (6). Second, he concluded that all aspects of communicative life were transcendental. "To put this bluntly," he writes in *Being and Race*, "language is transcendence. And so is fiction" (39).[3] Regarding language, he concluded that "in words we find the living presence of others, that language is not—nor has it ever been—a neutral medium for expressing things, but rather that intersubjectivity and cross-cultural experience are already embodied in the most microscopic datum of speech" (38). Regarding fiction, he concluded, with Maurice Merleau-Ponty (133), that writing is "the trespass of oneself upon the other and of the other upon me . . . " (*Being* 39).

Given the state of language and fiction, then, Johnson offers us a poetics in which the art of reading becomes the act of inhabiting the role and place of others, and the art of writing requires an authorial "act of self-surrender" of such magnitude that the writer finds her or his "perceptions and experiences" coinciding with ones that preceded her or him. Johnson recognizes that this state of affairs is prohibitive for both "contemporary black and feminist writers" because language "is the experience, the sight (broad or blind) of others formed into word," and not only are these "others" most often "white" and "male," but they have also "despoiled words" (*Being* 39). The art of writing for those who discover that the history of language and fiction is "*not* sympathetic with their sense of things" becomes an art of writing against a tradition— indeed, of contesting the "antithetical vision and perspectives of our predecessors." While recognizing that this is the situation of all writers in a minority tradition (including women of all cultures), Johnson employs the name *Caliban's dilemma* to describe it. This dilemma, writes Johnson, and he is iterating the conclusions of both a contemporary generation of African-American critics and an earlier generation of African critics of African literature, is that of the "solitary black writer" who discovers that every attempt to express an "experience" is couched in a "compromise between the one and the many, African and European, the present and the past" (40).

The answer to Caliban's dilemma, in Johnson's career as a writer of fiction, has been to write a theory of intersubjectivity into his four "narratives of slavery" published between 1977 and 1990. That theory of intersubjectivity is what I am calling the "phenomenology of the Allmuseri." By *narrative of slavery* I mean to designate that form of writing which has emerged as the most amenable and most effective way of bringing to life the subject of the hidden history of the black experience in contemporary African-American writing (cf. Rushdy, "Daughters"). There are four basic types of the narrative of slavery.

The first type includes narratives which either set their action in the slave communities of the antebellum South or represent in third-person narration the memory of a former slave reliving the time of slavery. This type numbers such novels as Toni Morrison's *Beloved* (1987), Barbara Chase-Riboud's *Sally Hemings* (1979), and Johnson's two short stories

"The Education of Mingo" (1977) and "The Sorcerer's Apprentice" (1983). The second type includes narratives which set their action in contemporary, late-twentieth-century America, but which deal, implicitly or explicitly, with the lives and psychological makeup of modern men and women whose ancestors were enslaved. One could probably make the case that perhaps half the novels written in the African-American tradition deal with this scenario in some way or other. From an earlier generation, *Native Son* and *Invisible Man*, for instance, would have to be included in this form of writing, the former because it is implictly about the effects of a historical determinism in which a Chicago community of the 1930s is comparable to the situation of an antebellum Southern plantation, the latter because the invisible man's most profound revelation of history comes when he discovers the freedom papers of an evicted couple and finds himself remembering the slave stories told him by his ancestors: "of remembered words, of linked verbal echoes, images, heard even when not listening at home" (*Invisible Man* 266). More recent examples of this type include David Bradley's *The Chaneysville Incident* (1981), Carlene Hatcher Polite's *The Flagellants* (1967), Octavia Butler's *Kindred* (1979), Paule Marshall's *The Chosen Place, The Timeless People* (1969) and *Praisesong for the Widow* (1983), Gayl Jones's *Corregidora* (1975), and Gloria Naylor's *Linden Hills* (1985).

Third, there are narratives of genealogy which represent the slave experience in the process of tracing the history of a family through the broad outlines of the Black experience. We can include among this type such texts as Margaret Walker's *Jubilee* (1966), John Edgar Wideman's *Damballah* (1981), and Alex Haley's *Roots* (1976). The fourth type of the narrative of slavery is that text which imitates the forms and conventions of the slave narrative, that form of writing which Johnson calls the "ancestral roots of black fiction" (*Being* 7; cf. Bell 28–29).[4] Under this rubric we can list such novels as Ishmael Reed's *Flight to Canada* (1976), Ernest J. Gaines's *The Autobiography of Miss Jane Pittman* (1971), Sherley Anne Williams's *Dessa Rose* (1986), and Johnson's novels *Oxherding Tale* (1982) and *Middle Passage* (1990).

Johnson, then, writes in both the first and fourth forms of the narrative of slavery. What is more worth noting, though, is that in all four of Johnson's narratives of slavery there is at least one character who has descended from the Allmuseri. It is only in his most recent novel, *Middle Passage*, that the Allmuseri actually take center stage—thirty individuals from the Allmuseri tribe and an Allmuseri god form the cargo of the *Republic*—but their presence in each of the three previous narratives of slavery is highly significant. In all four narratives, the Allmuseri embody Johnson's theory of intersubjectivity. Moreover, throughout the narratives of slavery Johnson's American characters discover in the Allmuseri an ideal of intersubjective relations—that condition of resolving Caliban's dilemma by inhabiting what Johnson calls the "transcendence of relativism" (*Being* 44). Before we examine the unique phenomenology of the Allmuseri, we might first discuss a European counterpart which Johnson has used as his own "first philosophy."

The phenomenology of the Allmuseri, like Edmund Husserl's project of pure phenomenology, is concerned with a philosophy of a subject's "experience." It is also, like Husserl's project, concerned with the constitution of intersubjective relations, with interrogating the connections between a subject's experience and a community within which experience is made possible and then validated. For Husserl, the "experiencing subject" must become part of an "intersubjective community," which is a transcendent community of the spirit, so that what is critically called "subjective experience" gives way to what Husserl calls "objectivities of higher order" (*Ideas* 389; cf. *Crisis* 182–83, 254–55). As Husserl writes, part of the transition from a "pure phenomenology" to a "phenomenology of reason" involves seeing the relation between "an essentially possible individual consciousness" and "a possible community-consciousness." This "community-consciousness" is composed of a "plurality of personal centres of consciousness and streams of consciousness enjoying mutual intercourse." It is only within such a community that any "experience" can be "given and identified intersubjectively" (*Ideas* 346). Once an experience is so identified, we have a significant alteration in the relations between the individual subject and the community, and within the individual subject itself.

Johnson's interesting phrase *transcendence of relativism*, then, carries with it a plurality of meanings. Not only does it articulate a form of transcendence in which intersubjective relations are made possible, in which "relativism" is a condition of being open to others and others' ideas; but it also suggests that this transcendence is part of an overall project in which "relativism" will be transcended, in which "intersubjective experience" will supercede what, since Kant, has been criticized as being merely "subjective experience." This plurality of meanings of intersubjectivity is what the Allmuseri phenomenology is all about.

We have the fullest exploration of Allmuseri history and philosophy in Johnson's most recent novel *Middle Passage*. Although I am interested here in offering a reading of the prehistory of Allmuseri phenomenology—that is, in Johnson's fiction prior to *Middle Passage*—we might begin by noting briefly what this novel offers us in terms of understanding what is called this "four-dimensional culture" (*Middle Passage* 180).

Rutherford Calhoun, the narrator of *Middle Passage*, begins his career as a thief. Stealing, for Rutherford, is more than just an occupation; it is a philosophy, indeed a phenomenology. He treats the world as a mine of property from which to hoard "experiences"—as "if *life* was a commodity, a *thing* we could cram into ourselves" (38; cf. 162). Rutherford then meets the Allmuseri, who are themselves being stolen from Africa in the summer of 1830, and finds that his life and his philosophy are indigent. As he learns about their philosophy, their history, their lan-

guage, he finds himself, for the first time in his life, in a position of want-
ing to possess something that, by definition, could only be *had* if it is
not possessed. "As I live, they so shamed me I wanted their ageless
culture to be my own . . . " (78). During the course of the middle passage, Rutherford discovers several things. First, he learns that a culture
cannot be possessed because it is an unstable entity. The Allmuseri, he
learns, "were process and Heraclitean change . . . not fixed but evolving"
(124). He also learns, though, that bonds and connections are a matter
of surrendering to another order of being, and are not simply determined
by racial or biological destiny. The Allmuseri, he notices, "seemed less
a biological tribe than a clan held together by values" (109).

Eventually, and after a course of adventures rivaling the plots of *Moby
Dick* and *Benito Cereno*, Rutherford surrenders to that order and discovers that "experience" is not a property belonging to a "subject" but
rather an intersubjective process by which subjects are formed and
transformed. As Rutherford puts it,

> . . . In myself I found nothing I could rightly call Rutherford Calhoun,
> only pieces and fragments of all the people who had touched me, all the
> places I had seen, all the homes I had broken into. The "I" that I was, was
> a mosaic of many countries, a patchwork of others and objects stretching
> back to perhaps the beginning of time. . . . I was but a conduit or window
> through which my pillage and booty of "experience" passed. (162–63)

In the end, the exposure to the Allmuseri, whose concept of experience
Rutherford is articulating here, leaves him and his world altered. "The
voyage had irreversibly changed my seeing, made of me a cultural mon-
grel, and transformed the world into a fleeting shadow play I felt no
need to possess or dominate, only appreciate in the ever extended present" (187). This is, essentially, the phenomenology of the Allmuseri.

According to Allmuseri phenomenology, the individual subject's ideal
condition involves the renunciation of being situated in the material
world. In other words, the ideal of intersubjectivity includes the condition of the individual's being "unpositioned" in the world, of each person's having a relationship with the tribal community that is so integral
that the individual is rendered "invisible" in the "presence of others."
Like "writing," as Johnson theorizes, this is a form of intersubjectivity—
the sharing of the "same cultural Lifeworld," a "common situation, a
common history"—which is premised on the "transcendence of relativism." Even though it theorizes such a radically postindividualistic mode
of being, Allmuseri phenomenology nonetheless holds that there are
certain individual functions. Echoing Johnson's own theory of the transformative power of writing, the Allmuseri hold that each person creates
experience by "outpicturing" the world from deep within her or his own
heart. The soul, we are told, is "an alchemical cauldron where material
events were fashioned from the raw stuff of feelings and ideas." Experience, therefore, is considered not as an entity which goes into a per-

son, but rather as that quality which comes "out" of a person (*Middle Passage* 164). The Allmuseri, it soon becomes clear, are a tribe who have developed their own concepts of history, identity, the performance of doubles, nonlinear and nonbinary modes of mentation, and their own theory of subjective and intersubjective being.

Ꮼ Ꮼ Ꮼ

As I have suggested, my interest is in discerning the prehistory of Allmuseri phenomenology in the three narratives of slavery before *Middle Passage*. A large part of Allmuseri phenomenology, like Husserl's phenomenology, is concerned with what role language plays in intersubjective relations. Clearly, writes Husserl in *The Origin of Geometry*, "it is only through language and its far-reaching documentations, as possible communications, that the horizon of civilization can be an open and endless one" (*Crisis* 358). The Allmuseri language is a very important phenomenon in their phenomenology: "not really a language at all, by my guess," notes Rutherford, so much "as a melic way of breathing deep from the diaphragm that dovetailed articles into nouns, nouns into verbs. . . . the predication 'is' . . . had over the ages eroded into merely an article of faith for them. Nouns or static substances hardly existed in their vocabulary at all." Their spoken language, then, is an ideal construction for intersubjective relations. Their written language consists of pictograms. Reading it requires the lector to gaze at the characters as if they were old friends; the meaning can be grasped only in a "single intuitive snap" (*Middle Passage* 77). Their written language, too, like the form of "writing" Johnson describes in *Being and Race*, is transcendent and embodies in every instance the preconditions of "intersubjectivity and cross-cultural experience."

Johnson's first three narratives of slavery (and also *Middle Passage*) are all concerned with how language mediates what Stanley Crouch calls Johnson's "sense of play among history, cultural convention, and the assertion of identity in personal and ethnic terms" (138–39). In the two short stories, Johnson organizes this "play" around the concept of *listening* and in each of his novels around the concept of *writing*.

In a short story titled "The Education of Mingo" (1977), Johnson begins his exploration of the theme of slavery as a way of exploring what he calls the "deadly upas of race and relatedness" (*Sorcerer's* 21).[5] In this story, the slaveowner Moses Green buys a slave named Mingo and then educates him so thoroughly that Mingo becomes the incarnation of Moses's own deepest desires. That education involves taking the African acculturation out of Mingo, who speaks no English, in order to replace it with an American outlook. "Mingo's education, to put it plainly, involved the evaporation of one coherent, consistent, complete universe and the embracing of another one alien, contradictory, strange" (6). After a year of educating Mingo in this form of cultural displacement, Moses discovers that he has created a being just like himself: "exactly the product of his own way of seeing . . . a homunculus, or a distorted shadow" (7). Moses looks at Mingo, educated as both property and son, "now like a father, now like an artist" (5). Mingo not only loses a world view, but he also loses his desiring function. Because he has no desires of his own, he acts on the half-understood desires of his master: " 'What Mingo know, Massa Green know. Bees like *what* Mingo sees or don't see is only what Massa Green taught him to see or don't see' " (15).

The result of this education (which enforces the atrophy of the desiring function) is fatal. Mingo kills a man his master had wished dead in an idle moment of fancy, and he murders the woman his master is reluctantly considering marrying. At first, Moses considers that Mingo is simply not responsible because his education and his status as chattel make him what he is:

> You couldn't rightly call a man responsible if, in some utterly alien place, he was without power, without privilege, without property—was, in fact, property—if he had no position, had nothing, or virtually next to nothing, and nothing was his product or judgment. "Be damned!" Moses spit. It was a bitter thing to siphon your being from someone else. (18)

Towards the end of the story, Moses resolves to kill Mingo because Mingo represents, in some indefinable way, Moses's worst desires:

> "Mingo, you more me than I am myself. Me planed away to the bone! Ya understand?" He coughed and went on miserably: "All the wrong, all the good you do, now or tomorrow—it's me indirectly doing it, but without the lies and excuses, without the feeling what's its foundation, with all the polite makeup and apologies removed. It's an empty gesture, like the swing of a shadow's arm. You can't never see things exactly the way I do. I'm guilty. It was me set the gears in motion. Me. . . . " (22)

Although Mingo is without responsibility, according to Moses's own theory, it is Mingo who would suffer the punishment of the person who claims responsibility. The story concludes with Moses's having a change of heart. Instead of sacrificing Mingo, Moses decides that they should both set out for Missouri.

In effect, then, we have in Moses's ruminations on the psychically destructive effects of slavery an inchoate form of the sort of historical determinism associated with the early Richard Wright. Moses notes that it was the form of education—the school of slavery—that is responsible for Mingo, and that the corrective is simply to kill the student. Moses, though, we are told, is not "the most reliable lens for looking at things." In fact, the narrator steps in to develop Moses's theory in ways that destroy the social-deterministic aspect of it and construct in that place a theory of the intersubjective relations of all human interactions: "How strange that owner and owned magically dissolved into each other like two crossing shafts of light (or, if [Moses had] known this, which he did not, particles, subatomic, interconnected in a complex skein of relatedness)" (19).

Instead of rehearsing the conventional themes of what Johnson himself has called the "misery-filled protest stories about the sorry condition of being black in America" associated with the school of "naturalistic" fiction in the African-American tradition, Johnson develops his narrative into what he terms a "Fable." It is fabular not only in its brevity and its tone, but also in positing a subterranean spirtuality which undermines the "naturalistic" surface of the story and eludes the mental abilities of its actors. As Johnson notes in *Being and Race*, underpinning the world of the fable are "esoteric and moral laws often unknown to the protagonist, who must act nevertheless and, in ignorance of the ways things work beneath the level of mere appearances, finds his actions turn out wrong or prove themselves too ambiguous for reason, so limited, to fully grasp" (49). In this fable, an early product of Johnson's career, we find many themes Johnson would develop in his later fiction. He here asks questions about the effects on a young boy of being considered by his owner both "son" and "slave." He considers the question of how property ownership destroys all relationships. He meditates on how the relations of capitalism are comparable to the relations of slavery, a theme he will develop more fully in his wonderful short story "Exchange Value" (*Sorcerer's* 27–40).

Finally, Johnson begins here to articulate a concern—we might say the concern of his later career—with the problematics of intersubjective relations. It is worth noting that he begins to articulate his concern with a general theory of intersubjectivity in his first exploration of the relationship between slaves and slaveowners—in what is also his first narrative of slavery. The "relation between slave and master," wrote James Pennington, an escaped slave, "is even as delicate as a skein of silk: it is liable to be entangled at any moment" (v). Johnson develops that insight by examining in his first narrative of slavery the relationship— what Johnson himself calls "a complex skein of relatedness"—between an American slaveowner and the slave Mingo who, we learn, is rumored to be the "youngest son of the reigning king of the Allmuseri, a tribe of wizards" (4).

☙ ☙ ☙

In his other short story on slavery "The Sorcerer's Apprentice" (1983), Johnson turns from examining the relationship between a slaveowner who pretends to treat his slave as a son (while at the same time treating him as a vassal) to the relationship between an actual father and his son.[6] This narrative is set in Abbeville, South Carolina, in a time "not long from slavery" (149). In fact, the sorcerer of this tale, Rubin Bailey, is one who gains the appreciation of former slaves because he is able to blight "the enemies of newly freed slaves with locusts and bad health"

(149). Finding himself aging, Rubin seeks out an apprentice in order to pass on his magical knowledge. He chooses Allan Jackson, son of Richard Jackson. The story putatively revolves around Allan's apprenticeship, about how he learns from Rubin what he can learn about becoming a sorcerer. The relationship between Rubin and Allan, though, is only supplementary to the key relationship between Allan and his father. What makes this an interesting story is that it organizes itself around an examination of the conditions of familial love for that crucial transitional generation in African-American history in which parents were born and raised in slavery and children were born and raised in freedom (actually, I prefer, with Patricia Williams, to refer to emancipation as simply a time when "slaves were unowned" [21]). This story is like *Beloved* in that it explores the problematics of love in the emergence of a first generation of "unowned" citizens.

In *Beloved*, we are presented with a series of ex-slaves who have muted their capacity for loving in order to avoid the pain that loving without empowerment necessarily brings. Paul D, for instance, maintains that it is best for a slave or ex-slave to " 'love just a little bit' " because anything loved by someone without power could be taken away (45). Even more extreme is Ella, another ex-slave, who simply believes in her own philosophy: " 'Don't love nothing' " (92). It is only with the maturation of Denver, who is born on the symbolic (and real) Ohio River during her mother's escape from her Kentucky slave plantation, that we have a renewal of the possibilities of love for the family living in 124 and the community living in Cincinnati (cf. Rushdy, " 'Rememory' " 316–21; "Daughters" passim). This theme is also part of the subject of the novel Johnson had published the year before he published "The Sorcerer's Apprentice." As Andrew Hawkins reflects, the "view from the [slave] quarters changes the character of everything, even love—especially love—and in ways not commonly admitted" (*Oxherding Tale* 101).

In "The Sorcerer's Apprentice," the father Richard is, like Paul D and Ella in Morrison's narrative, a victim insofar as he demonstrates a strength consisting of denying feelings of pain or caring. "He was the sort of man," we are told, "who held his feelings in, and people took this for strength" (*Sorcerer's* 152). His son recognizes that this so-called "strength" is an inheritance of the days of slavery:

> Allan supposed it was risky to feel if you had grown up, like Richard, in a world of nightriders. There was too much to lose. Any attachment ended in separation, grief. If once you let yourself care, the crying might never stop. (153)

In the interim, Allan continues his apprenticeship under the tutelage of Rubin. Allan has one moment of sublime success when he exorcises a pain from Esther Peters. The work of exorcising the pain came from a source Allan did not respect because it did not belong to "knowledge" and it was, according to his education, "wholly unreliable." That source is "his native talent." After the exorcism, Rubin praises Allan not for being an agent of healing, but a vessel for a power greater than their own: " 'God took *holt* of you back there—I don't see how you can do it that good again' " (155). Eventually, after five years' apprenticeship, Allan begins his career as sorcerer. He is reluctant to commence because he believes that he is not yet fully educated. " 'There must be *one* more strategy,' " he begs Rubin. " 'One more maybe,' " replies the wizard. " 'But what you need to know, you'll learn' " (157).

His first professional attempt at magic seems to be a failure. He sits in a bar with his seventh tequila in front of him. He searches through his mind for the incantation that transmogrifies liquids into vapors. Uttering it, he opens his eyes to discover a full glass of liquor and his father sitting in front of him: "Maybe he'd said the phrase for telekinesis" (159). Maybe. His father is there to call him to his first real challenge as a professional sorcerer—to cure Lizzie Harris's baby daughter Pearl of her inability to keep down her food. Before Allan undertakes his task, he sets for himself a condition that exhibits his infidelity in the art he is performing:

> The Sorcerer's apprentice, stepping inside, decided quietly, definitely, without hope that if this solo flight failed, he would work upon himself the one spell Rubin had described but dared not demonstrate. If he could not help this girl Lizzie—and he feared he could not—he would go back to the river and bring forth demons—horrors that broke a man in half, ate his soul, then dragged him below the ground, where, Allan decided, those who could not do well the work of a magician belonged. (161)

Allan does not perform the miracle. He gathers his things to go and prepare himself for damnation. Saying farewell to his father, he kisses him on his "rough cheek." His father is startled and pulls back sharply. " 'I'm sorry,' said Allan. It was not an easy thing to touch a man who so guarded, and for good reason, his emotions" (164). Not listening to his father's attempts to keep him at home, he sets out in order to perform "one last spell." As he leaves, he asks his father not to follow him.

As Allan walks down to the river to summon the evil forces who will destroy him, he meditates on his failed career. After all his training, he would not be able to perform a genuine spell. "For that God or Creation, or the universe—it had several names—had to seize you, *use* you, as the Sorcerer said, because it needed a womb, shake you down, speak through you until the pain pearled into a beautiful spell that snapped the world back together." He was privileged to feel this possession only once. After that, he felt nothing but an absence, an emptiness, and a sterility at his center. This absence translates itself in a feeling of indebtedness. "Beyond all doubt, he owed the universe far more than it owed him. To give was right; to ask wrong. From birth he was indebted to so many, like his father, and for so much" (165). As he summons the evil spirits to destroy him, he hears a voice calling him in the distance:

"His father. The one he had truly harmed." Turning away from the voice calling him, Allan addresses the evil spirit from the West, and tells the sorry tale of " 'one who studies beauty, who wishes to give it back, but who cannot serve what he loves.' " (166). Allan thinks that what he loves and cannot serve is magic. It is, we will learn, not magic but his father.

In a scene reminiscent of the crucial moment in Hawthorne's "Young Goodman Brown," Allan comes to a half-understood realization of

> the real criminality of his deeds. How dreadful that love could disfigure the thing loved. Allan's eyes bent up toward Richard. It was too late for apologies. Too late for promises to improve. He had failed everyone, particularly his father, whose face now collapsed into tears, then hoarse weeping like some great animal with a broken spine. (167–68)

Having decided to perish, Allan comes to the realization that his death will cause his father extreme anguish. His life, he discovers, "trivial as it was in his own eyes," is "his father's last treasure." "Don't want me, thought Allan. Don't love me as I am" (168). But his father does want and love him; and Richard has, for the first time in his emancipated life, let himself care. As Allan sits on the cusp of life and death, he begins to feel within his chest "the first spring of resignation, a giving way of both the hunger to heal and the anxiety to avoid evil. Was this surrender the one thing the Sorcerer could not teach? His pupil did not know" (168). Allan does surrender himself to whatever it is directing his actions now. While he had performed his spells with his left hand in servile imitation of Rubin (who was himself left-handed), he now surrenders to his "native talent":

> Awkwardly, Allan lifted Richard's wrist with his right hand, for he was right-handed, then squeezed, tightly, the old man's thick ruined fingers. For a second his father twitched back in an old slave reflex, the safety catch still on, then fell heavily toward his son. (168–69)

The evil spirits depart.

Allan becomes a full-fledged sorcerer once he learns to value himself as "his father's treasure" and at the same time to devalue himself as an agential being for otherworldly acts. He must "surrender" himself to creation. He must renounce a certain residual individuality, an unwillingness to act out what does not belong to the realm of binary reasoning, in the performance of sorcery. When he had exorcised Esther, he had felt like a reed-pipe which the wind had whipped through, or like a "tool in which the spell sang itself" (156). What he has to learn in order to move beyond his apprenticeship is that miracles belong to "a web of history and culture," that they are not owned by, but only performed through, individuals (154). In other words, what Allan learns is what Milkman Dead learns in Morrison's *Song of Solomon*: "If you surrendered to the air, you could *ride* it" (341). To free one's being from an imprisoning selfhood, to soften the intractability of individual resolve, so that one can enter and be sustained in another order of being—this is the path to serving what one loves. It is the path to genuine strength.

Richard, on the other hand, must learn to serve love by regaining some selfhood, some concern for his being, and, thereby, regaining some of his ability to love and to care. It is especially apt that Allan touches Richard's hand at the end of the story, for Richard's show of what people took to be "strength" was first exhibited when Richard did not respond with any visible pain upon having his hand crushed by a wagon wheel. Rather, " . . . he stared [at it] like it might be a stranger's hand" (152). Insofar as Allan must learn to surrender, Richard must learn to desire and to care. He must recognize his body as his and learn to love its tissues, its sinews, and its productions as his. In other words, Richard must learn what Paul D struggles to learn in *Beloved*: "To get to a place where you could love anything you chose—not to need permission for desire—well now, *that* was freedom" (162). At the end of the story, then, Allan surrenders himself to a power to which he is indeed right to think himself indebted, and Richard surrenders himself to the emotions he had been wrong to deny. The first and final miracle Allan performs is to love and to serve whom he loves—to face up to the ancient demons and exorcise his father's "old slave reflex."

In this narrative of slavery, Johnson again writes in an Allmuseri char-acter. Rubin, it turns out, has been "born among the Allmuseri Tribe in Africa" (159). Because he belongs to that culture of wizards who have developed a psychology of intersubjectivity, the sorcerer is able to me-diate the relationship between the father and the son. He had initially healed Richard's hand, physically. He has educated Allan in the arts of sorcery, literally. What he has done, then, is set up the preconditions for Allan to heal Richard psychically and for Richard to cause Allan to perform miracles spiritually. It is up to Allan to learn to devalue his own agency, to unposition himself in a material world in order to have access to a spiritual, and to surrender to an African form of intersubjectivity in order to learn what in this world is most worth loving. (Milkman, remember, learns the lesson of surrendering to the wind from Shalimar, the African forebear of the Dead family). Richard must learn not to deny his own repressed feelings, to be willing to return to and belong to a tribal condition (of familial love) in which he too can surrender to an African form of intersubjectivity in order to learn that in this world it is worth loving. As long as either father or son refuses to surrender the divisiveness of thinking of self as an autonomous entity—Allan by desiring to own the magic, Richard by not desiring to own up to his love—they both inhabit the Allmuseri Hell which, we recall, consists of the "failure to experience the unity of Being everywhere." What both learn, at the end of this story, is the way to inhabit the Allmuseri realm of intersubjectivity which is Heaven.

Before turning to Johnson's contribution to the narrative of slavery in the form of his novel, it is worth noting that his short stories implicitly deal with the concept of listening. In "The Education of Mingo," Mingo learns everything from his master's mouth. Although the story is mostly about how world views get formed, transformed, and deformed, it is also about how Mingo learns to express his new world view in exactly the same accents as his master. As Moses notes, " ' . . . Mingo says just what I says' " (10). In fact, Mingo sounds so exactly like Moses that he even develops the same "reedy twang" on his *ts* as Moses (7). In "The Sorcerer's Apprentice," Allan devotes himself to learning to *listen* to Rubin: " 'I will study everything—the words and timbre and tone of your voice as you conjure, and listen to those you have heard' " (151). He too is educated by listening. The difference is that Mingo is an Allmuseri; what he hears in Moses's voice is the undercurrent of desire (an outpicturing of experience) as well as the superficial tone. He knows the hidden desires expressed by Moses. Allan, on the other hand, is not an Allmuseri and he listens without hearing the subtle magic of Rubin's voice. Just as he servilely imitates Rubin's left-handedness, believing that precision in imitation will compensate for selflessness, so does he hear the timbre and tone of the speaker without attending to the message of the speaking voice. In neither short story does Johnson make much of writing, which, remember, is where he had begun his meditations on intersubjectivity.

As might be expected in a tradition of writing that began with what Henry Louis Gates has called the "talking book" and the "speakerly text," African-American fiction deals extensively with the topos of listening (*The Signifying Monkey* 127–69). I have written elsewhere on John Edgar Wideman's representation of listening as the art of blues communion ("Fraternal"). As an instance of the significance of hearing to fraternal relations, Wideman writes about learning to attend to his brother: "I had to depend on my brother's instincts, his generosity. I had to listen, to listen" (80). "Such egoless listening," writes Johnson in another context, "is the precondition for the species of black American fiction I see taking form on the horizon of contemporary practice, a fiction of increasing artistic and intellectual generosity, one that enables us as a people—as a culture—to move from narrow complaint to broad celebration" (*Being* 123). Johnson's concern is still with a revision of the literary tradition of African-American naturalistic writing, and his concept of "egoless listening" forms part of the Allmuseri phenomenology. As we turn to his novel *Oxherding Tale*, we will find that part of Johnson's strategy of inhabiting the place of "celebration" involves the rewriting of history.

ᛟ   ᛟ   ᛟ

The eighth chapter of *Oxherding Tale*, a novel cast into the form of an antebellum slave narrative, is titled "On the Nature of Slave Narratives." According to the narrator Andrew Hawkins, there are three forms of slave narratives: the interviews conducted with former slaves in the 1930s by the Works Project Administration, the fraudulent slave narratives commissioned by Northern Abolitionists as propaganda, and the authentic narratives written by escaped slaves.[7] Andrew compares the authentic slave narrative to the early American Puritan Narrative. Both forms, he comments, are the offspring of the original narrative confessions of "the first philosophical black writer: Saint Augustine." The movement of the slave narrative, then, like the movement in Augustine's *Confessions*, is from a state of "ignorance to wisdom, nonbeing to being" (119).

Andrew's metafictional commentary on the form of the slave narrative is significant not only because it directs our attention to Andrew's own movement in his narrative—from ignorance to wisdom, from nonbeing to being—but also because it suggests something of the aesthetic imperative involved in Johnson's use of the slave narrative as a form. No form, notes Andrew, loses its ancestry; rather, as the form evolves, it accumulates layers of significance. The modern writer, he continues, can delve into the hidden secrets beneath the form of this narrative, and understand better the relationship between the history of form *and* the form of history, if that modern writer is willing to "dig, dig, dig—call it spadework" (119).

It is history most of all that interests Andrew (and Johnson), but history is of interest here only as it is played out in terms of theories of what constitutes a "subject." In the other metafictional digression in the novel, the eleventh chapter titled "The Manumission of First-Person Viewpoint," Andrew, if that is who is speaking in this chapter, notes that the narrator ("the Subject of the Slave Narrative") is not someone who "interprets the world" but rather someone "who is that world" (153). The subject of the slave narrative, in other words, is writing. And Johnson, as we have seen, has already noted that "writing doesn't so much record an experience—or even intimate or represent it—as it *creates* that experience" (*Being* 5–6). In *Middle Passage*, for instance, the dying Captain Falcon asks Rutherford to continue writing the ship's log. Rutherford agrees but, to himself, stipulates that he will tell the story as he, Rutherford, sees it (146). When it comes time to write the history of the *Republic*, he finds himself writing in two modes. First, he writes feverishly in order to "free [him]self from the voices in [his] head" (189). Having spent his pain, he then takes to writing in order to "transcribe and therefore transfigure all we had experienced" (190). Or, as Johnson's liberated narrator points out in the eleventh chapter of *Oxherding Tale*, "The Self, this perceiving Subject who puffs on and on, is, for all purposes, a palimpsest, interwoven with everything—literally everything— that can be thought or felt." This "subject," then, is "forever *outside* itself in others," drawing its life from everything it is not (generally called "others") at precisely the instant that it makes possible the appearance of those others (152). The absence at the crux of Andrew's life and the one that most forcefully directs his meditations on subjectivity is history.

Consider the scene in which Andrew has "passed" for white as William Harris. In order to pass without suspicion, Andrew has had to construct a false history of his forebears. Foremost amongst these is his fictional grandfather who fought in the Revolutionary War, Edwin Harris. As Andrew sits to dinner with the white family into which he will presently marry, his future father-in-law remarks that he expects a civil war in the near future and " 'all on account of the Negro.' " Asked about his inclinations to fight, given his historical background, Andrew lapses into meditation on what history means for identity. This thought inspires Andrew to think of the difference between being white and being black. The point of their similarity, he begins, is the

> feeling in both that the past is threatening; in the Black World a threat because there *is* no history worth mentioning, only family scenarios of deprivation and a bitter struggle—and failure—against slavery, which leads to despair, the dread in later generations that they are the first truly historical members of their clan; and in the White World the past is also a threat, but here because, in many cases, the triumphs of predecessors are suffocating, a legend to live up to, or to reject (with a good deal of guilt), the anxiety that these ghosts watch you at all times, tsk-tsking because you have let them down: a feeling that everything significant has been done, the world is finished. An especially painful form of despair, I thought, and I admit to suddenly despising Edwin Harris for placing this burden upon me, although I had spun him from my imagination. No matter; I felt uneasy. (132–33)

In the person of Andrew Hawkins, the black son of George Hawkins, slave and prototypical "Race champion," he feels an absence of history. In the persona of William Harris, the white grandson of Edwin Harris, slaveowner and Revolutionary War hero, he feels a surplus of history. Neither theory of how history forms, informs, and transforms racial subjectivity is tenable for Andrew's liberation. Each is untenable not simply because the distinction between the two attitudes toward history is facile, which Johnson clearly intimates by having Andrew listen to Reb's accounts of the wondrous history and civilization of the Allmuseri, but also because Andrew does not account for his own genuine racial makeup. Andrew has more than a fictional white grandfather; he has an actual white mother. It is only when he comes closer to terms with both his paternal and maternal heritages that he may begin to move toward wisdom and being.

That movement in Johnson's novel is also strongly integrationist—although, we ought to say, it is integrationist in a postmodernist way. For in the end, Johnson's concern is with developing a theory of subjectivity that dissolves what he suggests is the spurious concept not only of "race" but also of "personal identity." Here, above all else, we find the articulation of Allmuseri phenomenology. It will take Andrew several key encounters before he is able to understand, as does Allan in "The Sorcerer's Apprentice," what constitutes the difference between "passing" in the world of society and surrendering to the world of phenomena, between loving as a slave and loving as a free citizen, and between having a history in which to deplore one's ancestors and having a history in which to glorify them.

Again, the ex-slave James Pennington helps us set out on the path to understanding the nature of slavery in relation to history. The condition of the slave as chattel, writes Pennington, destroys the slave's sense of existing as a historical being.

> Suppose insult, reproach, or slander, should render it necessary for him to appeal to the history of his family in vindication of his character, where will he find that history? He goes to his native state, to his native county, to his native town; but nowhere does he find any record of himself *as a man*. On looking at the family record of his old, kind, Christian master, there he finds his name on a catalogue with the horses, cows, hogs and dogs. (xii)

Pennington sets out to write himself into existence, to recreate the history of his family and to set the record straight of his life as a man. As a friend of his wrote in a poem appended to the narrative: "The chain of the oppressor breaks . . . / The language of liberty speaks" (87). The relationship between freedom and speaking (or writing a narrative of a slave's escape) is one worth pondering as we return to Andrew's slave narrative.

Like *Tristram Shandy*, the narrator Andrew begins his autobiography by recounting the night of his conception. The slaveowner Jonathan Polkinghorne and his slave/butler George Hawkins are sitting on the porch drinking Madeira and home-brewed beer. Fearing the consequences of returning home besotted to their respective spouses, the two decide (at Jonathan's suggestion) to exchange homes and spouses for the night. The result is that the slave George Hawkins and the slaveowner's wife Anna Polkinghorne conceive the hero of this narrative, Andrew. As Stanley Crouch notes, Johnson effects a reversal of the situation between slave and slaveowner in much the same way as Melville had done in *Benito Cereno*. In this reversal, Anna Polkinghorne is turned from "master's wife into the position of slave woman by proxy" and is, therefore, "forever changed by experiencing the other side of slavery" (Crouch 138–39).

While Crouch is correct about Anna's change, it also has to be noted that this novel pretty well excludes Anna from its purview. In fact, at the end of his recitation of the scene of his conception, Andrew notes, "This, I have been told, was my origin. It is, at least, my father's version of the story; I would tell you Anna Polkinghorne's, but I was never privileged to hear it" (7). Andrew maintains that distinction—"my father" . . . "Anna Polkinghorne"—throughout his narrative. Only once does he refer to Anna as his mother—although he refers to Mattie Hawkins throughout as his "stepmother"—and that one pronounce-ment of his mother's name is made only with his eye on passing for white (68). What the silence about and by Anna Polkinghorne suggests is the difficulty of rehearsing the story of a mixed racial background.

Probably the finest contemporary meditation on this difficulty is to be found in Patricia Williams's ruminations on how to come to terms with the "hidden subjectivities" of one's heritage (11). Williams's great-grandmother Mary was born to a twelve-year-old slave named Sophie and a thirty-six-year-old master named Austin Miller (17–19, 155), a Tennessee lawyer who eventually became a judge. When Williams was preparing to set out for Harvard law school, her mother sent her off with the assurance that " 'the Millers were lawyers, so you have it in your blood' " (154, 216). Reflecting on what it means to come to terms with "this bitter ancestral mix," of recognizing that one's great-great-grandfather was a "self-centered child molester" (155), Williams reached much the same conclusion as does Andrew in *Oxherding Tale*. "Reclaiming that from which one has been disinherited is a good thing," she notes, because self-possession is the companion to self-knowledge. "Yet claiming for myself a heritage the weft of whose genesis is my own disinheritance," she continues, "is a profoundly troubling paradox" (217). Like Williams, who finds plenty of recorded documentation about her white ancestors but only oral family lore about her great-great-grandmother, Andrew tells the story he can tell, which is primarily, al-though not exclusively, his father's version, in order to construct the sort of subjectivity he desires to inhabit.

Like Mingo, Andrew learns his first lesson from his slaveowner, Jonathan Polkinghorne. Jonathan, according to Andrew, loved him "like a son" (14). From Jonathan, however, Andrew learns the lesson that in their relationship the terms for filiality are polluted by the terms of property. Andrew recalls the day that a candidate for the job of his teacher looked at him and asked Jonathan, " 'Is he yours?' " Jonathan responds by glancing at Andrew, wagging his head, and saying, " 'No. . . . What I mean to say is that Andrew is my property and that his value will increase with proper training' " (12). Here, for the first time, Andrew learns how ownership destroys the potential of any relationship. Upon discovering how corrupt the term *yours* becomes once it signifies own-ership, Andrew begins to think anew about his status:

> And what was I thinking? What did I feel? Try as I might, I could not have told you what my body rested on, or what was under my feet—the hallway had the feel of pasteboard and papier-maché. A new train of thoughts were made to live in my mind. (12)

These new thoughts center on how to escape "the sausage-tight skin of slavery" and to become what the age called a "self-made man."

My argument was: Whatever my origin, I would be wholly responsible for the shape I gave myself in the future, for shirting myself handsomely with a new life that called me like a siren to possibilities that were real but forever out of reach. (17)

Wielding a philosophy of pulling oneself up by the bootstraps, Andrew sets off in search of an inhabitable subject position.

As part of that search, Andrew encounters five people who educate him in what it means to be what he is. Three of these five give Andrew partial lessons on partial themes. The other two teachers give Andrew full lessons in which they involve their own histories and their own lives. The struggle between them at the end is what helps Andrew reach a state of wisdom and fullness of being.

Andrew's first teacher is also his only official teacher. Ezekiel William Sykes-Withers is hired by Polkinghorne to teach Andrew how to read and write. What Andrew receives instead is an educational program modeled by Ezekiel on James Mills's curriculum for John Stuart. Andrew is taught Greek (especially Xenophon and Plato) and Latin; lectured to on monadology, classical philology, and Oriental thought as a preparation for reading Schopenhauer; and given a full lesson on the "165 Considerations, Four Noble Truths, the Eight-Fold Paths, the 3,000 Good Manners, and 80,000 Graceful Conducts" (13). He also takes lessons on Voice, Elocution, and Piano. The most important lesson Ezekiel teaches Andrew, however, has to do with the theme of manhood as an existential state. In answering his pupil's question about the story of Ezekiel's father (who murdered his wife and all his children save Ezekiel, who was not home at the time), the teacher responds:

"It is not easy to be a full-grown man, Andrew. We are not like women." He swung his eyes toward me. "We are weaker."

"Weaker?" It made no sense. "How are we *weaker*?"

Spiritually, I think. Perhaps all philosophy boils down to the simple fear that the universe has no need for us—men, I mean, because women are, in a strange sense, more essential to Being than we are. . . . We build machines, Andrew, create tribal languages in philosophy—like little boys with secret codes in their clubhouse—to get back at the universe because she has failed to give us a function. All our works, *male* works, will perish in history—history, a male concept of time, will vanish, too, but the culture of women goes on, the rhythms of birth and destruction, the Way of absorption, passivity, cycle and epicycle." (30–31)

This is one of the partial lessons Andrew acquires in order to work through. At first he tends to believe what Ezekiel has taught him. For instance, he muses on how ". . . *men* were unessential" and "Being" was a "vast feminine body." He also echoes Ezekiel in believing that men "fell back on thought in the absence of feeling, created history because [they] could not live Being's timeless cycles" (55). In time,

Andrew learns the degree to which such polarized gender roles are unacceptable in a truer philosophy of intersubjective relations.

The first step to learning that lesson comes in the form of his next teacher, Flo Hatfield. After receiving an education about as steeped in mysticism and transcendental philosophy as is possible from Ezekiel, Andrew sets off for an "education of the senses." From Flo he learns that men don't enjoy sex because they haven't the capacity for relaxing or imaginatively using pain as a stimulant (45). Flo's thoughts on manhood in general are somewhat contradictory. She is a protofeminist insofar as she complains about a society which stipulates that " ' . . . a woman is *nothing* without a man' " (59). She is cannibalistic, though, insofar as each of her reflections on black men is couched in terms of appetite. She "feeds" on her slave/lover's anxieties (39) and looks at her slaves "like a woman comparing chunks of pork at Public Market" (41) or as if one of them were "a six-foot chicken quiche" (42). She also equates making love with eating: " 'Eating a good piece of meat is like making love' " (42). At another time, she ponders aloud in the presence of Andrew, " 'I wonder what you'd taste like' " (45), and she gets her answer when she licks Andrew and discovers he tastes " 'milky' " (53).

This image of ingestion is crucial to understanding Flo. For what Andrew learns from Flo is that making love can be used as a way of incorporating others within oneself. As the two lay in bed spent, Andrew asks Flo, " 'What do you feel when you touch me?' " She responds, " 'Me. . . . I feel my own pulse. My own sensations.' " " 'That's all you feel?' " " 'Yes' " (53). The "education of the senses," it turns out, is an education in a form of appropriation, of denying the other (in this case, the sexual partner) any existence save as a part of the self. What Flo does in this appropriative act is to deny the very being of "experience." For one to understand the "very concept of experience," writes Derrida, "one must begin to identify with the other" (115).

Flo's is one more lesson Andrew must work through. Initially, he falls prey to Flo's philosophy. When Andrew meets another man who has slept with Flo, he finds himself immediately drawn to this man as a friend. As Luce Irigaray has pointed out, the bonding of men often takes this form of sexual commerce in women (170–91). As Andrew notes of his new friendship, it was based on the kind of relationship "only shared by men who have slept in the same places" (96). In other words, what Andrew learns from Flo is to discount the being of others (to make people into "places") in the service of selfish love.

But there is another side to this lesson. Although their lovemaking is based on a practice in which Flo denies Andrew's status as a being, as another presence in the act of bodily pleasure, she nonetheless offers a theory of a more authentic relationship. She teaches Andrew that, of all the skills required for becoming adept at making love, by far the "greatest of these skills was listening. Note well, a lover *listens*" (60). By listening, the individual self learns how to share subjectivity with another, rather than incorporating the other into the self. It is what the characters in Wideman's novels learn; it is what Johnson himself calls "egoless listening" (*Being* 123). In order to learn how to listen to the other, and thereby how to relate to the other in a noncoercive and nondominating way, Andrew must first learn one side of his history—and that is the side represented by his father.

There are several things George teaches Andrew, but what is especially important is that Andrew learns to be true to himself—or, as George puts it, " 'Be y'self.' " But selfhood, in George's lesson, is only another way of saying be true to your race. As George expands on the theme of being one's self, " 'Whatever you do, Hawk—it pushes the Race forward, or pulls us back. You know what I've always told you: If you fail, everything we been fightin' for fails with you' " (21). This sort of obligation is the obverse side of what Edward Bland calls "pre-individualistic thinking." As Ralph Ellison interprets Bland's idea, this form of thinking is effected socially through an elaborate scheme of taboos: "To wander from the paths of behavior laid down for the group is to become the agent of communal disaster" (*Shadow* 84). The way to safety—which is what Baldwin was repudiating when he sought "the end of safety"—is to conform personally to what is expected of the community from the dominant powers. In less abstract terms, individual blacks were not to upset the equilibrium expected of the black community by the white community.

The presupposition of pre-individualistic thinking is that individual accomplishments endanger the larger cultural community. When Joe Louis knocked out Max Baer, for instance, Richard Wright notes the tension involved as what he calls "a sweet fear," a "mingling of fear and fulfillment" (34). On the one hand, the community felt fulfilled because one of its own had established black superiority ("Joe was the concentrated essence of black triumph over white"), while, on the other, the community feared the reactionary backlash of racial beatings and lynchings which historically followed each of Louis's victories. As Wright continues, the black crowd of twenty-five thousand eventually left the streets for safer havens because "they were afraid now" (35). "It wouldn't do for a Black man and his family," writes Maya Angelou, recalling Joe Louis's knockout of Primo Carnera, "to be caught on a lonely country road on a night when Joe Louis had proved that we were the strongest people in the world" (115). The other side of this "sweet fear" is the presupposition George articulates for Andrew: " 'If you fail, everything we been fightin' for fails with you.' " Or, as Angelou puts it, "If Joe lost we were back in slavery and beyond help" (113).

Johnson has argued that these social constraints wrought from pre-individualistic thinking, imposed by the community on its own members, are destructive and prohibit genuine creativity (*Being* 29). In *Oxherding Tale*, he shows how George's lesson carries with it a necessary corollary. Because he sees everything the individual does as either raising or lowering the race's ideals (" '*If* you succeed. . . . *If* you fail' "), George himself lives what Andrew refers to as "a life that could only be called conditional" (102). Moreover, in order to determine the world in these conditional terms, George had to delimit his view of the world to radically divided terms. Andrew remembers how George sometimes prayed: " 'Oh Lord, kill all the whitefolks and leave all the nigguhs.' " When his wife Mattie, hearing this, would slap him on the back of his head, George would yelp, " 'Lord! Don't you know a white man from a nigguh?' " (142). Humorous as it is, this incident also demonstrates the way that George views the world in alienating, binary terms. In the end, George finds himself wholly alienated from everything: "this warped and twisted profile of the black (male) spirit, where every other bondsman—everything not oneself—was perceived as an enemy" (50).

For Andrew, the lesson of George's life and teachings requires a complex response. First, Andrew has to reject the marked division between whites and blacks and between oneself and "everything not oneself." He finds George's reduction of existence—his simplifying a "world so overrich in sense it outstripped him"—untenable. The solution Andrew reaches after he comes to terms with his father's lesson is one that leads him towards Allmuseri phenomenology. He now realizes that his earlier philosophy of assuming "responsib[ility] for the shape I gave myself in the future" is unacceptable because to believe that the determination of one's life "depended on himself and no one else" is the same thing as believing in a "self-inflicted segregation from the Whole" (142). After passing through the school of the mystics, of the senses, and of the races, Andrew is finally ready to enter the school of the Allmuseri.

The Allmuseri phenomenologist in *Oxherding Tale* is Reb the Coffin-maker. Not only does Reb tell stories about Allmuseri civilization that give Andrew some idea of what his father had been trying to tell him about the glory of African history and culture, but he also teaches Andrew about true interdependence, about an authentic form of inter-subjectivity that does not rely on George's racial divisiveness or Flo's appropriative attitude towards others. The lesson Reb teaches Andrew is to place in suspicion all pronouns of selfishness and to distrust all designations of racial distinction. Upon first meeting Andrew, he asks, " 'You *folks* . . . or white people?' " To Andrew's reply, " 'Oh, folks. . . . Definitely folks,' " Reb snorts, " 'You ain't folks or white. . . . You fresh meat, boy' " (36). Andrew also learns that Reb "hated personal pronouns." In fact, " . . . the Allmuseri had no words for *I, you, mine, yours*. They had, consequently, no experience of these things, either, only proper names that were variations on the Absolute" (97).

The story which signifies the lesson Andrew is supposed to learn to be free is the narrative of Rakhal, the Allmuseri *osuo* and Reb's great-grandfather, and Akbar, the Allmuseri king who adopted Islam late in life. Rakhal, angered at Akbar's rejection of the tribal religion, swore revenge on the king by telling him that he would bring the rains of madness on the tribe within a week. Akbar starts storing away jugs and jugs of fresh water, but the rains come and all fall mad, including Rakhal, who eventually drinks the waters of madness along with the rest. Initially, Akbar walks through the streets telling everyone that he is still sane and they are all mad, but they all laugh at him because *they* share a coherent world. No longer willing to remain alienated in his sanity, Akbar drinks the waters of madness. The lesson, we learn, is that " . . . the Real, if it was anything at all to the Allmuseri, was a matter of consent, a shared hallucination" (49).

This lesson takes its practical form for Andrew in his conversation with Reb about Flo. " 'If you got no power,' " muses Reb, " 'you have to think like people who *do* so you kin make y'self over into what they want' " (62). This, let me hasten to add, is not another aspect of pre-individualistic thinking. To make oneself over into what the powerful want is, as Reb makes clear in his further comments, but a subversive way of unpositioning oneself in the world. It is part of a strategy of joining the shared hallucination as an equal, as a subject. Andrew learns this lesson and then transfers it from the Allmuseri to the African-American community generally. "The Negro," he comments, " . . . is, as Reb told me, the finest student of the White World, the one pupil in the classroom who watches himself watching the others, absorbing the habits and body language of his teachers, his fellow students" (128). This is the education of Allmuseri phenomenology—the empowering of the individual who surrenders to Being, who outpictures experience by absorbing the world and becoming absorbed in its diverse unity.

We have seen that Allmuseri phenomenology has a dangerous side—the side represented by Mingo's education, for instance. In *Oxherding Tale*, this dangerous side is represented by Bannon the Soulcatcher. Turning the phenomenology of the Allmuseri on its head, Bannon, like Mingo, but without the benefit of a disruptive education as an excuse, conflates desire with murder. Like Reb, Bannon lives by the idea of empowering himself by absorbing the habits and existential traits of others. As he explains to Andrew, " 'You *become* a Negro by lettin' yoself see what he sees, feel what he feels, want what he wants' " (115). After absorbing into himself his prey's modalities of experiencing the world, Bannon easily manages to capture his victims, who are then absorbed into his features, his body. In other words, Bannon represents the corruption of Allmuseri phenomenology, the form of surrender not to the Absolute but to a facsimile of the Absolute. He represents what happens when one understands only half of Reb's philosophy—making oneself over into what the powerful want without unpositioning oneself. As Bannon notes, the thing he looks for to mark the "Negro" he tries to catch is the investment of spirit in positioning a self in the world. " 'You look for the man who's policin' hisself, tryin' his level best to be *average*. That's yo Negro' " (115).

The conditions for the final battle are set, then. Bannon, who has made a lifelong promise to give up slavecatching when he meets the slave who eludes him, sets off after Reb.

At the end of the novel, we discover that Bannon has come to terms with both Andrew's biological father and with his surrogate (philosophical) father. As a slavecatcher, Bannon murdered George; but because he has been unable to capture Reb, he has given up slavecatching. As he explains to Andrew, the reason he is unable to catch the Allmuseri tribesman is because Reb desires nothing. " 'That's hit right there—what threw me off, why hit took so long to run him down: yo friend didn't want *nothin'*. How the hell you gonna catch a Negro like that? He can't be caught, he's *already* free' " (173). Existentially free, Reb the Coffinmaker finds himself in the end politically and socially emancipated also; his most famous coffin would, in time, bear Lincoln's body. Reb, continues Bannon, " 'didn't have no place inside him for me to settle. He wasn't *positioned* nowhere.' " Reb escaped from the Soulcatcher because he possessed nothing inside of him—nothing "dead or static," like a negative image of the self—which the slavecatcher could latch on to. George Hawkins, on the other hand, was bound to the world by " 'fifty-'leven pockets of death in him.' " He possessed " 'li'l pools of corruption that kept him so miserable' " that he simply desired death (174). Reb was unpositioned and outpictured the experience of freedom, whereas George was unable to surrender to Being and outpictured nothing but the experience of misery.

In the last scene of the novel, we find Andrew acceding to the lesson of Allmuseri phenomenology. As Bannon takes off his shirt in order to show Andrew how George had become a part of the topography of his body (as did everything Bannon murdered), Andrew finds answered "in this field of energy . . . the profound mystery of the One and the Many." He learns that his father is part of the Absolute now—his love ranging "in every being from grubworm to giant sumacs." He learns, with a Wordsworthian flair, that the relation between them is reversible in the terms of Western chronology and history: "I was my father's father, he my child." He learns that he can, given the intersubjective relations accruing to his way of viewing the world, still have his father's love: " . . . the profound mystery of the One and the Many gave me back my father again and again." And he learns, in the end, that "all is conserved; all" (176). That "all," of course, includes history. The same Andrew who had believed that blacks despised history because they had none learns anew that the history of African-Americans is a thing to inhabit (and not to deny or to abuse). The same Andrew who had rehearsed his father's version of his story, because he did not have access to his mother's, learns that "all is conserved" when he names his daughter Anna.

The lessons on which Andrew concludes are numerous—although they can be summed up by saying that, like Allan in "The Sorcerer's

Apprentice," he learns to love and to surrender to Being. But he learns to do this only after he finally works his way through his earliest lesson, Ezekiel's philosophy of the alienation of male beings in a female universe. "I cried," he notes towards the end of his story, because

> the woman I had sought in so many before . . . was, as Ezekiel hinted, Being, and she, bountiful without end, was so extravagantly plentiful the everyday mind closed to this explosion, this efflorescence of sense, sight frosted over, and we—I speak of myself; you will not make my mistake—became unworthy of her, having squandered to a thousand forms of bondage the only station, that of man, from which she might truly be served. (172)

This way of seeing Being, though, is as much a heritage from George as it is from Ezekiel. As he notes, " . . . I was returned to slavery; I have never escaped it—it was a way of seeing, my inheritance from George Hawkins: *seeing distinctions*" (172). Andrew will escape that bondage to a way of seeing the world in terms of division, as he is doing here (male person . . . female Being), when and only when he learns to quit "seeing distinctions." Like Allan in "The Sorcerer's Apprentice," he too asks the forces that can destroy him how it comes to be that a "man may love the Good, pledge his life to it and, in spite of his best efforts, still be the steward of suffering and evil?" (172). The answer for Andrew, as it is for Allan, is to surrender to the world of Being, to be unpositioned in the way that only Reb is unpositioned. Andrew must cease to see distinctions of gender, of race, and, ultimately, of self and other. The intersubjective identity that becomes possible after such a complete surrender to the Whole is as complex as it is rewarding.

ॐ ॐ ॐ

In his meditations on artistic creativity, Charles Johnson has noted that there is a "curious, social, intersubjective side of art [which] is, as the best estheticians report, central to the artistic personality and the creative process" (*Being* 52). Part of Johnson's achievement is to promote this intersubjective aspect of art and describe the immense benefits obtaining for us if we act on this desire to inhabit fictional worlds which challenge our parochialism. But the greater part of Johnson's achievement is to enact intersubjective relations in the making and to discover in the phenomenology of the Allmuseri a theory and a symbol for the postmodern condition discernible in much of the fiction written by those Johnson calls "Americans who happen to be black" (*Being* 123). The discovery of the Allmuseri has been, one suspects, at least one of the reasons that his most recent novels have not only enjoyed a fate different from his first six, but have broken new and very fertile ground in the field of African-American letters.

Notes

1. My researches have led me to conclude, reluctantly, that the Allmuseri are fictional. Being no anthropologist, I initially believed that Johnson was representing a real tribe, and a tribe well worth learning about. But a trip to the library and a more than cursory search through the *Encyclopedia Brittanica* and George Peter Murdock's helpful *Outline of World Cultures* have led me to believe that the tribe does not exist outside of Johnson's representations of them. The descriptions I have used in the first paragraph are all from *Middle Passage* (61, 76, 61, 65, 140, 61). For the description of the power of their god to create parallel worlds, see *Middle Passage* 100.

2. Cf. Hurston, "What White Publishers Won't Print" 169–73, and "Art and Such" 21–26.

3. Part of Johnson's project has been anticipated by Kenneth Burke—indeed, we might say, part of all postmodern and poststructuralist projects that have anything to do with communicative norms have been so anticipated. Regarding the transcendence of language and fiction, Burke writes that the two realms of "language" and "story" form the "double provenience" of "all human attitudes," and that both realms are "transcendent" (*Attitudes* 382–83). As for the relationship between "experience" and the nature of "recording," Burke writes: "A specifically symbol-using animal will necessarily introduce a symbolic ingredient into every experience" (*Language* 469). Thus, as he notes, " 'Reality' could not exist for us, were it not for our profound and inveterate involvement in symbol systems" (48).

4. For more thorough studies of the significance of the slave narrative to modern African-American fiction, see the essays in Davis and Gates, McDowell and Rampersad, and Starling 295–310. On the slave narrative generally, see Starling passim and Andrews, *To Tell a Free Story* 1–31.

5. This story was first published in *Mother Jones* (August 1977).

6. "The Sorcerer's Apprentice" was first published in *Callaloo* (February 1983).

7. It is important that *Oxherding Tale* is written as an antebellum, and not postbellum, slave narrative. The antebellum slave narrative, as William L. Andrews has shown, is concerned with demonstrating "the evolution of a liberating subjectivity in the slave's life, up to and including the act of writing autobiography itself" ("Representation" 64), while the postbellum slave narrative tends to treat slavery as if it were an "economic proving ground" rather than an "existential battleground" (69).

Works Cited

Andrews, William L. "The Representation of Slavery and the Rise of Afro-American Literary Realism." McDowell and Rampersad 62–80.

———. *To Tell a Free Story: The First Century of Afro-American Autobiography, 1760–1865*. Urbana: U of Illinois P, 1986.

Angelou, Maya. *I Know Why the Caged Bird Sings*. 1970. New York: Bantam, 1971.

Baker, Houston, A. "Caliban's Triple Play." *"Race," Writing, and Difference.* Ed. Henry Louis Gates, Jr. Chicago: U of Chicago P, 1986. 381–95.

Baldwin, James. *Notes of a Native Son.* 1955. London: Corgi, 1965.

Bell, Bernard W. *The Afro-American Novel and Its Tradition.* Amherst: U of Massachusetts P, 1987.

Burke, Kenneth. *Attitudes toward History.* 1937. Berkeley: U of California P, 1984.

———. *Language as Symbolic Action: Essays on Life, Literature, and Method.* Berkeley: U of California P, 1966.

Crouch, Stanley. "Charles Johnson: Free at Last!" *Notes of a Hanging Judge: Essays and Reviews, 1979–1989.* New York: Oxford UP, 1990. 136–43.

Davis, Charles, and Henry Louis Gates, Jr., eds. *The Slave's Narrative.* New York: Oxford UP, 1985.

Derrida, Jacques, and Jean-Luc Nancy. " 'Eating Well,' or the Calculation of the Subject: An Interview with Jacques Derrida." *Who Comes After the Subject?* Ed. Eduardo Cadava, Peter Connor, and Jean-Luc Nancy. New York: Routledge, 1991. 96–119.

Ellison, Ralph. *Invisible Man.* New York: Random, 1952.

———. *Shadow and Act.* New York: Random, 1964.

Gates, Henry Louis, Jr. *The Signifying Monkey: A Theory of African-American Literary Criticism.* New York: Oxford UP, 1988.

Hurston, Zora Neale. "Art and Such." *Reading Black, Reading Feminist: A Critical Anthology.* Ed. Henry Louis Gates, Jr. New York: Meridian, 1990. 21–26.

———. "How It Feels to Be Colored Me." Walker 152–55.

———. "What White Publishers Won't Print." Walker 169–72.

Husserl, Edmund. *The Crisis of European Sciences and Transcendental Phenomenology: An Introduction to Phenomenological Philosophy.* Trans. David Carr. Evanston: Northwestern UP, 1970.

———. *Ideas: General Introduction to Pure Phenomenology.* Trans. W. R. Boyce Gibson. 1931. London: Macmillan, 1962.

Irigaray, Luce. "Women on the Market." *This Sex Which Is Not One.* Trans. Catherine Porter. Ithaca: Cornell UP, 1985. 170–91.

Johnson, Charles. *Being and Race: Black Writing since 1970.* Bloomington: Indiana UP, 1988.

———. *Middle Passage.* New York: Atheneum, 1990.

———. *Oxherding Tale.* Bloomington: Indiana UP, 1982.

———. *The Sorcerer's Apprentice: Tales and Conjurations.* New York: Atheneum, 1986.

McDowell, Deborah E., and Arnold Rampersad, eds. *Slavery and the Literary Imagination.* Baltimore: Johns Hopkins UP, 1989.

Merleau-Ponty, Maurice. *The Prose of the World.* Ed. Claude Lefort. Trans. John O'Neill. Evanston: Northwestern UP, 1973.

Morrison, Toni. *Beloved.* New York: Knopf, 1987.

———. *Song of Solomon.* 1977. New York: NAL, 1978.

Pennington, James W. C. *The Fugitive Blacksmith: Or, Events in the History of James W. C. Pennington, Pastor of a Presbyterian Church, New York, Formerly a Slave in the State of Maryland, United States.* 2nd ed. London, 1849.

Rushdy, Ashraf H. A. "Daughters Signifyin(g) History: The Example of Toni Morrison's Beloved." *American Literature* 64 (1992): 567–97.

——. "Fraternal Blues: John Edgar Wideman's Homewood Trilogy." *Contemporary Literature* 32.3 (1991): 312–45.

——. " 'Rememory': Primal Scenes and Constructions in Toni Morrison's Novels." *Contemporary Literature* 31.3 (1990): 300–23.

Starling, Marion Wilson. *The Slave Narrative: Its Place in American History.* 1981. Washington: Howard UP, 1988.

Walker, Alice, ed. *I Love Myself When I Am Laughing . . . And Then Again When I Am Looking Mean and Impressive: A Zora Neale Hurston Reader.* New York: Feminist, 1979.

Wideman, John Edgar. *Brothers and Keepers.* 1984. New York: Viking, 1985.

Williams, Patricia J. *The Alchemy of Race and Rights: Diary of a Law Professor.* Cambridge: Harvard UP, 1991.

Wright, Richard. *Richard Wright Reader.* Ed. Ellen Wright and Michel Fabre. New York: Harper, 1978.

Selected Bibliography

Books by Charles Johnson

Cartoons

Black Humor (1970)
Half-Past Nation Time (1972)

Fiction

Faith and the Good Thing (1974)
Oxherding Tale (1982)
Sorcerer's Apprentice (1986)
Middle Passage (1990)
Dreamer (1998)

Nonfiction Prose

Callaloo 7.3 (1984). A special issue on fiction edited by Charles Johnson.
Being and Race: Black Writing since 1970 (1988)
Black Men Speaking (1997), edited by Charles Johnson and John McCluskey,
    Jr., with art by Jacob Lawrence.
Africans in America: America's Journey through Slavery by Charles Johnson and
    Patricia Smith (1998).

Scholarship on Charles Johnson

African American Review, volume 30, Number 4, Winter 1996. A special issue
  edited by Herman Beavers and Michael Boccia on Charles Johnson.
Charles Johnson's Spiritual Imagination (1997) by Jonathan Little.